School, Soccer, Social!

Miller

EXCELLENCE & HONOR

Copyright © 2015 by The Pingry School
All rights reserved
For information about permission to reproduce
selections from this book, please write:

The Pingry School
Office of Communications
131 Martinsville Road
Basking Ridge, N.J. 07920
908-647-5555
www.pingry.org

Published by
Roessner & Co. Strategic Design
2 Coventry Road
Hardyston, N.J. 07419
908-963-0983
gil@roessner.net

ISBN #: 978-1-4951-2009-1

E. Thomas Behr, Ph.D.
Eight Decades at The Pingry School:
The Life & Times of Miller A. Bugliari

Foreword

"It's not about all the victories and championships; it's about a life of love."
                                                       Bronson Van Wyck '63

Author's Preface

The best way to tell the story of someone so profoundly complex as Miller is to tell it as simply as possible, which Bronson Van Wyck does in the foreword to this book. Ultimately, Miller's story really is about a life of love. He learned that love as a child from his father Joseph Bugliari, his mother Margaret Dorothy Miller, and their intensely loyal housekeeper and companion Margaret Archibald. He has lived that love with everyone he's met and befriended. That same love has been the steady center for his wife Elizabeth and sons Boyce, Anthony, and David.

To have done it for so long and so well, Miller has had to love coaching and teaching. But, and the distinction is telling, it's not so much what he teaches – although he has done that with creative brilliance for decades – it's always about his students and players. His lifelong friend Martin O'Connor '77 captures the heart of that love when he says, "Most people require that you come to them for acceptance and affection. With Miller it's just the opposite. He's always reaching out to you, from a place that's so strongly, unshakably authentic that responding to him is the most natural thing you could imagine yourself doing."

Miller also loves the potential grace and spontaneous creativity of soccer as a sport – when it is combined with a ferocious defense that reveals Miller's Italian roots in the unrelenting pressure of *catenaccio*. He's always taught his players to not just play the game with skill, but to understand it, to feel it as teammates working and sacrificing and succeeding – together.

And of course, Miller loves life, with an infectious, irrepressible comic spirit and competitive drive. In his presence one is almost compelled to treasure the time we are given to live fully and enthusiastically, to laugh at misfortune and meet challenges and setbacks with courage and resolve. These are the gifts he's given all of us, including me, as a young, confused, fumbling new teacher at Pingry in 1962. This book is just a way of saying an extended "thank you," not just from me, Gil Roessner, and George Ellis, but from everyone whose life Miller has touched.

— TOM BEHR '58

Acknowledgments

First, our thanks to Nat Conard, Warren Kimber '52, Steve Newhouse '65, Olaf Weckesser, Melanie Hoffmann, Breanne Matloff, Stacy Schuessler, and Greg Waxberg '96 for the support they have given to this entire project in celebrating the "Excellence and Honor" of Miller's Pingry career.

Without David Fahey '99's tireless efforts and deep loyalty to Pingry soccer and to Miller, the soccer sections of this book could not have been written. Peter Behr '58 and Mary Behr were early readers who gave wise counsel and unflagging encouragement. JoAnn Behr lived through the three years it took to write this book with great patience and support.

Thanks to the following Pingry alumni and friends for their memories of the irrepressible "Bugs" as a Pingry student: Jubb Corbet '50, Warren Kimber '52, Gordon Lenci '52, Jere Ross '52, Bob Thurston '52, Phil Scrudato '53, Jack Bryan '54, Phil Burrows '55, Gene Shea '57, Owen Shea '58, and Joe Irenas '58. Miller's Springfield College teammate and NSCAA Board Member Bob Nye was a wonderful resource in bringing to light that chapter of Miller's life.

Recreating the astounding 55-year history of Pingry soccer under Miller was made both possible and thoroughly enjoyable through the contributions of Peter Wiley '60, Gordy Sulcer '61, John Geddes '62, Les Buck, Bob Ziegenhagen, and Ken Wachter '64, Bob Dwyer '65, Gene Mancini '66, Joe Cornwall '67, Alan Berger '68, Claus Hamann and John Mindnich '69, Peter Mindnich, Tim Gufstafson, and Ian Shrank '71, Paul Ciszak and Ian Alexander '72, Rob Kurz and Robbie Kurtz '72, Mike Mindnich '74, Chris Merrill '75, Frank DeLaney and Leo Stillitano '76, Chuck Allan '77, Rob Curtis, Phil Lovett, Leighton Welch, Chris Bartlett, and Tom Trynin '79, Jim Gensch and Sander Friedman '83, Dave Freedman '84, Mike Canavan '85, Todd Gibby and Steve Johnson '87, Brian Crosby and Rob Range '89, Crico Krantz '91, Chris Pearlman '92, Jamie Newhouse '93, Dave Margolis '95, Chris Marzoli and Nick Ross '97, Mike Roberts '99, Gianfranco Tripicchio '00, Anthony Tripicchio and Kevin Locke '01, Matt Wilkinson and John Rhodes '02, John Porges '03, Seth Flowerman and Liam Griff '04, John Stamatis '05, Tom Strackhouse and Lenny Coleman '06, Will Stamatis and Matt Fechter '09, Scott Keogh '10, Randy Falk and Freddy Elliot '11, Mael Corboz '12, Brian Costa, Cameron Kirdzik, and Christian Fechter '13, Matt Mangini '14, Jamie Cooke and Max Lurie '15, Jack DeLaney '16, and Ibo Ikoro '17.

Special thanks to Miller's sons, Boyce '86, Anthony '90, and David '97, to former Pingry assistant coaches Manny Tramontana, Dan Phillips '59, Don Burt '69, Warren Kimber '76, Adam Rohdie, Bob Jenkins '80, Brian O'Donnell '81, Rob Macrae '82, Mike Coughlin '90, Jake Ross '96, and Kris Bertsch '99, and to Gary Baum '63, Dick Manley '63, Bronson Van Wyck '63, Alan Gibby '66, Bill Maas '69, Nate Zinsser '73, Guy Cipriano '74, Sean O'Donnell '75, Martin O'Connor '77, Charlie Stillitano '77, Jon Pascale '93, Mike Chernoff '99, and of course David Fahey '99, for their deep insights into Miller's unchanging character and continuous evolution as a coach.

We are grateful to be able to use previously published testimonials from Miller's 50th Anniversary Celebration from Nils Adlerbert '59, John Rush '60, Dave Rogers '61, Ted Manning '62, Stu Lavey '63, Todd Williams '63, Rik Alexanderson '64, Glenn Erickson '64, Don Keel '64, Pete Borden '65, Bob Dwyer '65, Bill Duncan '66, Kip McKay '67, Vic Pfeiffer '67, Ray Robinson '67, Jim Stearns '67, George Ways '67, Bruce Conway '69, Mark Biedron '70, Charlie Cox '70, Richard Engel '70, Ward Tomlinson '71, Gary Giorgi '72, Charlie Homer '72, Chuck Cuttic '73, Jim Page '73, Mark Zashin '75, Scott Alenick '76, Doug Macrae '77, Chris Meyer '77, Bruce Jacobsen '78, Debbie Richman '78, Cope Eschenlauer '80, Andy Ehrlich '81, Marc Feldstein '82, Michael White '86, Michael DiChiara '88, Christian Breheney '89, Jeremy Goldstein '91, Frank Puleo '91, Woody Weldon '91, Chris Pearlman '92, Sara Ike '95, Genie Makhlin '95, and Nicholas Sarro-Waite '99.

Former students Gordy Sulcer '61, John Geddes '62, Burr Hazen, Bill LaCorte, and Ernie Moody '66, and colleagues Tom Johnson '59, Dan Phillips '59, Don Burt '69, Dave Allan, Fred Fayen, and Manny Tramontana provided both hilarious and touching glimpses into Miller as a teacher.

Insights, memories, and "Miller Moments" for the Waganaki chapter were provided by Annette, Bruno, and Greg Tomaino, Gene Shea '57, Bob Popper '61, Bill Hanger '64, Woody Hanger '67, Jim Hodge, Bruce Smith, and Don Burt '69, Mark Biedron '70, Ian Alexander '71, John Boffa and Paul Ciszak '72, Guy Cipriano '74, and Rick Raabe '75.

Miller's forays into Europe are the stuff of legend. Thanks to Bob Thurston '52, Aldo Tripicchio, John McLaughlin, and Richard Schonberg for adding both facts and more fantasy to the legend.

The Production **Team**

We gratefully acknowledge the testimonials from present and former Headmasters Nat Conard, John Neiswender, John Hanly, and David Wilson '59, from Assistant Headmaster Ed Cissel '39, and from Trustees Kim Kimber '52, Steve Newhouse '65, and Stu Lederman '78 in illuminating Miller's contributions to the life of the school as a whole.

Pingry parents Tom Boova, Alison Casey, Conor Mullett '84, and Jerry Pascale generously shared their appreciation for the impact Miller has had on their children's lives.

Thanks to Lesley McManus for her skilled, creative layout work. In addition to his painstaking text editing, George Ellis '66 has enlivened the book with dozens of cartoons that are as funny as the stories they illustrate.

We thankfully acknowledge permission to quote from Christopher Merrill's *The Grass of Another Country: A Journey Through the World of Soccer*. He also has recently published *The Tree of the Doves: Ceremony, Expedition, War*. He directs the International Writing Program at the University of Iowa (www.christophermerrillbooks.com).

Brief quotations from newspaper articles used in the soccer history section are taken from the Pingry Soccer Scrapbooks for the various years. Citations from Troupe Noonan's *The Greatest Respect: Pingry at 150 Years* are used with permission of The Pingry School. The picture of Farcher's Grove (page 111) is used with permission of the Union Township, N.J., Historical Society.

Thanks to Patrick Reid O'Brien for permission to use his painting of Miller on the front cover, and to Bruce Morrison '64 for the use of his superb sports photographs throughout this book.

One of the delights of writing this book has been the conversations with so many people who have shared their appreciation for Miller. If we have inadvertently omitted mentioning someone who contributed, we apologize deeply. While we may have unfortunately overlooked your gratitude to Miller, you know that Miller hasn't.

Elizabeth Bugliari has been the guiding spirit for this book, as she has been for Miller, her family, and countless Pingry students. Her love, unswerving commitment, and wise judgment have been essential in enabling us to tell Miller's story with the passion, humor, and truth it deserves.

Finally, the most profound acknowledgment must be to Miller, himself, for what he has given all of us.

Tom Behr '58 *Author*
Tom graduated from Pingry in 1958 and from Colgate University in 1962; he earned an M.A. at the Middlebury College Bread Loaf School of English in 1968 and a Ph.D. from Princeton in 1976. Tom taught English and coached football and lacrosse at Pingry for nine years following his graduation from Colgate. He then taught at Newark Academy before embarking on a career in corporate consulting in 1981, starting his own consulting firm in 1985. Tom has written *The Tao of Sales: The Easy Way to Sell in Tough Times* (1979), and *Blood Brothers, A Novel of Courage and Treachery on the Shores of Tripoli* (2011), and is currently working on the sequel to that novel (www.tombehrbooks.com). Tom and his wife JoAnn live in Millington, N.J., and have two daughters, Mary and Jenny, and two grandchildren, Maggie and Finn.

Gil Roessner '66 *Design, layout, and production supervision*
Gil graduated from Pingry in 1966 and Alfred University in 1970 (B.A. in Fine Arts and Business Administration), and earned an M.F.A. from Pratt Institute in 1976 (Graphic Design/Communications). Gil worked for an international corporate communications design firm in Manhattan for several years before founding his own firm, Roessner & Co. Strategic Design, in 1976. Since then, Roessner & Co. has been creating award-winning publications, video, and online communication projects for a broad range of major corporations, non-profits, and academic institutions throughout America. The firm's projects can be viewed at www.roessner.net. Gil and his wife Susan reside in Sussex County, N.J., and have one daughter, Jenny, who graduated from Lehigh University.

George Ellis '66 *Cartoons, editing, and proofreading*
George graduated from Pingry in 1966 and Dickinson College in 1970 (B.A. in Fine Arts). George was accepted into the copy editing training program at McGraw-Hill Inc., which prepared him for nearly 40 years of editorial and production work at publications serving a wide variety of industries, from computers and the Internet to solar energy and the automotive industry. George's father, the late Ray Ellis, was a distinguished artist who taught George how to draw at an early age. George continues his art interests, and his gallery of automotive art can be viewed at www.georgeellis.com. George has two sons, Shaun and Mark, and two grandsons, Dylan and Wyatt. George and his partner, Barbara Brottman, live in St. Augustine, Fla.

Table of Contents

1. The Early Years 6
   - Miller Stories #1-5 14
2. Miller at Springfield College 18
   - Miller Stories #6-9 26
3. Miller in the Army: 1957–1962 28
   - Miller Stories #10-15 32
4. Camp Waganaki 36
   - Miller Stories #16-20 46
5. Miller the Teacher 50
   - Miller Stories #21-27 70
6. The Cadillac Limousine 74
7. Adventures in Europe 77
8. Bugliari Soccer – The Beginning 84
   - The 1959 Season 86
9. The 1960s: The Championship Quest ... 88
   - The 1960 Season 90
   - The 1961 Season 92
   - The 1962 Season 94
   - The 1963 Season 96
   - The 1964 Season 98
   - The 1965 Season 100
   - The 1966 Season 102
   - The 1967 Season 104
   - The 1968 Season 106
   - The 1969 Season 108
10. The 1970s: Union County Dominance .. 110
    - The 1970 Season 114
    - The 1971 Season 116
    - The 1972 Season 118
    - The 1973 Season 120
    - The 1974 Season 122
    - The 1975 Season 124
    - The 1976 Season 126
    - The 1977 Season 128
    - The 1978 Season 130
    - The 1979 Season 132
11. The 1980s: Challenge and Change 134
    - The 1980 Season 138
    - The 1981 Season 140
    - The 1982 Season 142
    - The 1983 Season 144
    - The 1984 Season 146
    - The 1985 Season 148
    - The 1986 Season 150
    - The 1987 Season 152
    - The 1988 Season 154
    - The 1989 Season 156
12. The 1990s: National Prominence 158
    - The 1990 Season 164
    - The 1991 Season 166
    - The 1992 Season 168
    - The 1993 Season 170
    - The 1994 Season 172
    - The 1995 Season 174
    - The 1996 Season 176
    - The 1997 Season 178
    - The 1998 Season 180
    - The 1999 Season 182
13. The 2000s: New Opponents 184
    - The 2000 Season 188
    - The 2001 Season 190
    - The 2002 Season 192
    - The 2003 Season 194
    - The 2004 Season 196
    - The 2005 Season 198
    - The 2006 Season 200
    - The 2007 Season 202
    - The 2008 Season 204
    - The 2009 Season 206
14. The 2010s: A Different World 208
    - The 2010 Season 212
    - The 2011 Season 214
    - The 2012 Season 216
    - The 2013 Season 218
    - The 2014 Season 220
15. Miller the Coach 222
16. Miller's Records 238
17. Miller's Office 240
18. Miller Miscellany 246
19. The Bugliari Family 252
20. Index 264

The Early Years

Miller at age 6.

When present and former players, students, and colleagues share their memories of Miller, the conversations typically begin with laughter – at Miller's spontaneous, bizarrely inimitable sense of humor and his unquenchable, joyful enthusiasm for life. Most people, however, soon start talking about love – their lifelong gratitude for the impact of Miller's deep, steadfast concern and support on their lives. The seeds of that laughter and love were planted in Miller's family life and his 12 years as a Pingry student.

Growing Up in the War Years

Margaret Dorothy Miller and Joseph Vincent Bugliari's second son, Miller, was born on May 7, 1935. His Pingry saga began in 1942, the year he entered the second grade, just nine months after the attack on Pearl Harbor propelled the nation into World War II.

The first Pingry School building Miller attended was the old Lower School, a converted residence at 586 Westminster Avenue, just a few blocks from where Miller lived with his parents and older brother Joe.

Joseph Vincent Bugliari was the founder and owner of a large trucking company. With America's impending entry into hostilities, his company became vital to the war effort. By 1942, American industry was on a 100 percent war footing, and automobile manufacturers were feverishly churning out jeeps, trucks, and Sherman tanks – not family cars. And the Bugliaris needed a car at a time when people weren't selling them. So his father arranged through his company for a tiny Fiat, about the size of today's

Miller in his early days as a Pingry student.

Smart Car, to be shipped from Mexico to Hillside, N.J. It arrived without tires: Given the wartime economy, new tires for civilian cars weren't simply rationed, they were unavailable. To this day, Miller doesn't know what arguments his dad used with New Jersey Governor Charles Edison, but sure enough, courtesy of the governor, a set of new tires for the little Fiat eventually arrived, and the Bugliaris happily crammed themselves into a car about the size of the kind used by circus clowns. In retrospect, how fitting that Miller spent his earliest years driving around in a clown car.

Miller's father with the mini-Fiat.

A few years later, when his parents discovered they couldn't add on to their house in Hillside, the family moved to an enormous Dutch Colonial home in Plainfield known as the Stender House. Miller remembers hours of fun playing basketball on the third floor with his brother Joe and their friends. Jere Ross '52 recalls: "Miller's mom always provided a warm welcome and a timely snack." Perhaps the best feature of the house was the front hall elevator, which Miller would use to crash his parents' dinner parties – clearly a premonition of things to come.

The Stender House in Plainfield.

Once the Bugliaris moved to Plainfield, Miller became one of many Pingry students over the years whose trip to school often involved sprinting madly after a departing Jersey Central train, grabbing the handrail with their right hand on the dead run, flinging their book bag onto the train with their left, and hauling themselves aboard the moving train Jesse James style.

THE LIFE & TIMES of MILLER A. BUGLIARI

Early Family Tragedy

One morning when Miller was 10, their father dropped them off at the train station for the commute to Pingry. Both boys jumped out of the car to run for the train when their father called them back. "Don't ever leave without giving me a hug and a kiss," he reminded them. They never saw him again. That evening, at work and at the age of 44, he had a massive stroke and died a few days later. Miller adored his father; it was a devastating loss.

His father had just opened his new shipping business with offices across the United States and Mexico when he died. He *was* the business. The strength of his personality was the driving force behind his success, and with him gone, the business faltered. Miller remembers that to her great credit, his mother went through an intense period of mourning but emerged stronger than ever, picking up the pieces and "getting on with it."

Like so many of her contemporaries in the war years, she took on the responsibility of working at two jobs, while raising two extraordinarily active boys. Her burden was eased somewhat because the boys' nanny, Margaret Archibald, a stalwart little Scottish lady, absolutely refused to leave, even when there wasn't money to pay her. Between them, they worked out a schedule so that someone was always home when the boys got home from school. Their life lessons were simple: "Be honest with and respectful toward everyone you meet." Generations of Pingry students, soccer players, and faculty members can attest to how deeply those lessons sank in.

Miller's father, Joseph Bugliari.

Miller's mother, Dot Bugliari.

Miller, left, and his brother, Joe, with their nanny, Margaret Archibald.

Advised by everyone in the family to take the boys "out of that expensive school," their mother instead went to see E. Laurence Springer, Pingry's renowned but intimidating headmaster, to figure out a way to keep the boys at Pingry. She knew that they needed the influence of the all-boys school and the guidance and support of men like Mr. Les and Reese Williams more than ever. Larry Springer made it possible for them to stay at Pingry; perhaps that commitment is the key to Miller's extraordinary loyalty to Pingry and his amazing ability to connect with those students who have most needed his friendship and guidance. Looking back on those years, what Miller remembers is realizing that he had to take responsibility for handling things himself: when you encounter a problem, solve it. When you experience a setback, laugh at it – and move on.

Miller, left, with his mother, Dot, and older brother, Joe.

Miller and Joe after a fishing expedition at Moosehead Lake, Maine.

Joseph Bugliari and Joe.

The Parker Road Campus

The Pingry Middle School Miller entered in sixth grade was the old Parker Road campus, which by then was in its sixth decade and showed the effects of hard, if exuberant, use. Miller still has fond memories of that venerable building. "We had a furnace," he recalls, "that would regularly stop working in winter, so we had to wear our overcoats in class to stay warm." He remembers the hallways and stairs shaking ominously every time classes changed.

Then there was the swimming pool. "The pool would be so cold in winter that for swim meets, kids wore their overcoats there, too, before shedding them to race. The pool had a low ceiling, so to protect the divers, they hung a mattress on the ceiling above the diving board." Because of the moisture in the pool, the floor of the gym above it was warped in places. "We would try to make the opposing basketball teams have to dribble on the dead spots," he remembers, "and then laugh as the ball caromed sideways out of bounds."

The pool at the Parker Road campus.

The same lovable quirks characterized the outdoor athletic fields on which Miller excelled. The baseball field in the old "Pingry Oval" had a very short left field, so if you pulled the ball over the fence in left, it was ruled a double, not a home run. "I'll never forget the high jump during track meets," Miller says. "In those days we used an old bamboo pole for a crossbar, which obviously warped over time. When Pingry kids jumped, the concave side would be put up, giving the Pingry jumpers an extra few inches of room over the bar. When the other team jumped, Mr. Les placed the bowed convex side facing up."

Entering the Big Leagues

Of course, life at Pingry was not all giggles and hijinks. Then, as now, living legends walked among the faculty: David Buffum and his "Nine-Year-Old Club," Abel "Sapristi!" DeGryse, and the irrepressibly humorous Andy Kirk. His remedy for students chewing gum in class was to require the offender to come to the front of the room, place his gum on the lip of the physics lab table, remove someone else's rock-hard piece of gum, and chew *that*.

Mr. Buffum

Mr. DeGryse

But the teacher who really caught Miller's attention was, of course, Albie Booth. "Mr. Booth, with his fiery red hair and equally flamboyant enthusiasm for his beloved Latin, was a creature of enormous magnitude for all of us," says Miller. "I remember coming up the back stairs at Parker Road as an eighth grader. As I reached the top floor, I saw a door burst open and an Upper School student come flying through it, land on the floor, and careen into the water fountain. The door slammed shut and then it reopened. This time a very big, very formidable red-headed figure appeared and threw a handful of books at the student, who was just getting to his feet. As the classroom door slammed shut again and the student dusted himself off and went on his way, I suddenly grasped reality: In the near future I would be entering the Upper School – the big leagues – and had better pick up the quality of my game."

Miller, left foreground, in Latin class with Mr. Booth in the Parker Road building.

Miller: A Uniquely Organized Student

Classmates' recollections of Miller as a student usually start with his personal style – which, even on his best days, appeared impossibly chaotic. Miller's fondness as a coach for wearing an old, rumpled sports coat as a good luck charm started when he was a student. Phil Scrudato '53 remembers: "He always looked half-dressed, his tie loosely knotted, his shoes untied, and his shirt hanging out – until I reminded him to tuck it in. Miller's eating habits were equally haphazard. He would leave half his food on his shirt and face."

It would be easy, meeting him for the first time, to think this was a hopelessly scatterbrained, clueless kid. Once you got to know him, though, you recognized Miller was one of the smartest, most deeply centered people you'd ever know in your life.

Warren "Kim" Kimber Jr. '52 noted the same qualities in Miller as a student. "Lots of kids were very meticulous in studying, preparing, and taking notes. Miller's 'notes' were almost illegible scrawls on scraps of paper he dug out of his pocket, pulled out of a notebook, or picked up from the floor or out of a wastepaper basket. God knows how he kept them straight in studying for quizzes and tests. You'd think, 'This guy is totally disorganized and dysfunctional' – until you got into class and realized that somehow this 'system,' which wasn't a system at all, worked for him."

Jubb Corbet '50 recalls, "In the 1950s, students weren't allowed to wear jerseys with their favorite player's name and number as kids do today. Miller idolized Sugar Ray Robinson, the fighter. Miller saw a photo of Robinson with a white dress shirt, so he bought one just like it. Miller was paying tribute to his idol." The picture on this page captures that moment. Robinson was also a natty dresser. Miller clearly didn't care to emulate that aspect of his hero.

"When you're a young student," Miller recalls, "you look to upperclassmen as role models and are grateful when they notice and care about you. Some of the older students who made a real impact on me that way were Norm Tomlinson and Buddy Kreh '44; Mahlon Scott, Harry Hoyt, and John McLain '45; Dave Baldwin and Woody Phares '47; Gerry McGinley, Bill Burks, "Red" Alley, John Thomas, and Jim Toffey '48; Bill Ginden and Joe Carragher '49; Jubb Corbet, Park Smith, and Duane St. John '50; and Ron Dressen, Peter Jasper, and Judge Landis '51.

Learning to Learn

"My senior year at Pingry, I was still only 16 years old, and Dr. Springer and my mom arranged for me to spend a PG year after my class graduated. It made a huge difference. I went academically from around the middle of my class to being a top 10 student. That final year, I'd 'learned the ropes.' I worked hard, and I hung on my teachers' every word, not just to pass a test, but to understand what they were saying and how they saw things. It was about listening, respecting what they had to offer, and accepting different points of view.

"I realized there is obviously a time to buckle down, but along the way, having fun in life was important, too.

"People have asked me why I didn't get in trouble as a Pingry student with all the stunts I pulled. Part of it was just being aware of the situation; when they told me to stop, I stopped. For a while. But I think the faculty accepted me for who I was. What I was doing was harmless. More than that, I was then and still am the kind of person who talks to everyone, doesn't have a hidden agenda, reaches out to people as a friend, and gets them laughing, sometimes in spite of themselves. I guess my teachers appreciated that."

Impresario Bugliari

"One of my highlights as a student," Miller says, "was writing the humor column for *The Pingry Record*, which gave me the opportunity, in a good-natured way, to pick on an unsuspecting faculty member or student. When you think about it, funny things happen all the time; we often just don't notice them. Besides creating a lot of laughs, my humor articles were a way to remind people of that."

At Pingry in Miller's years, serious drama was the purview of the Drama Club. But the Drama Club wasn't the only show in town. Impresario Bugliari had a different kind of theater in mind. He was quite willing to yield the field of serious academic theater to the Drama Club; his sights were set gleefully lower.

Among many choices, Miller's production of "Dr. Frankenstein's Monster" may represent the pinnacle of his artistry as producer, director, scenic designer, and, of course, lead actor, playing the title role, with Jay Harbeck '52 as his faithful servant Igor and Bob Thurston '52 as the foreboding monster "Zarkoff."

Try to imagine it as it might have been, all those years ago. The students file into the Pingry Chapel, already anticipating a production that will be hilarious – and short. No long, tedious development of plot and characters through four acts for Miller. Cut right to Act V when the bodies start dropping on stage like shot sparrows.

The curtain opens on Dr. Frankenstein at the very moment his dreams reach fruition and his creature, Zarkoff, is brought to life. Strange vials bubble with mysterious liquids; stranger equipment hums ominously. Zarkoff lies on a table, covered completely with a sheet.

Dr. Frankenstein presses a switch. And waits. (By this time, everyone in the audience may have forgotten to breathe.) The sheet moves! Almost imperceptibly, a leg starts twitching, then an arm. A hand gropes out from under the sheet and… "Do you see it? Look there! Look there!"… the body starts to rise from the table.

Dr. Frankenstein is elated, until the moment when Zarkoff, the sheet now completely fallen away, stands and starts lumbering toward his creator, evil malice in his eyes. "Stop him, Igor!" Dr. Frankenstein yells in panic, his joy now turned to terror. Igor is swatted to the floor like a fly. "I can't control him!" cries Dr. Frankenstein. "He's too strong! Even his eyes have muscles!"

Blackout. Curtain. And from behind the closed curtain comes one last terrified scream: Dr. Frankenstein meeting the tragic fulfillment of his hubris? His monster realizing what Frankenstein has done to him? We will never know.

And the students file out in delighted laughter, wondering, "How, after this, can I pay attention to quadratic equations, the Smoot-Hawley Tariff Act, or the absolute ablative?"

Athletic Adversity and Courage

As a sixth and seventh grader at Pingry, Miller excelled at football, where his speed, strength, and competitive desire made him an outstanding running back.

Then, in eighth grade, disaster struck. Miller was diagnosed with a degenerative hip condition that as it progressed made even taking a few steps excruciatingly painful; the only possible treatment was to put the leg in a full cast for months. When the doctor finally removed the cast, Miller's leg was pretzel-thin, and his leg muscles had basically disappeared.

"The full leg cast was successful," the doctor told Miller, "but you'll never play football or competitive sports again." That wasn't a message or a future that Miller was willing to accept.

Anyone who has suffered a serious injury – in sports or as an unfortunate byproduct of advancing age – knows the pain and tedious rigor required for rehabilitation, especially if the goal is to regain the strength and flexibility required for competitive athletics. And in those days, as with surgery, the extraordinary expertise and resources now available to recovering athletes simply didn't exist. So Miller created and followed his own rehab program, month after lonely month of stretching and weight training through his freshman year, watching the other students compete on the athletic fields and wanting desperately to join them.

Miller had fully recovered by the start of his sophomore year, but his doctor had ruled out competitive football, so Miller's only outlet was touch football with the handful of Pingry students who chose not to "go out for a team." One day at the start of the school year, Pingry's soccer coach, Frank West, noticed this kid flying around on the touch football field next to the soccer practice field. He approached Miller at the end of the day and told him, "You've got great speed. Have you ever considered playing soccer?"

"What's soccer?" asked Miller.

"Come out for the team," said Mr. West, "and I'll teach you."

Mr. West

By the end of his sophomore year, Miller was a starter. In his junior and senior years he was a star. Having skipped a grade in primary school, Miller was a year younger than most of the boys in his grade, so he took a postgraduate year at Pingry and began helping Mr. West coach the team. He was only allowed to play against other private schools that had postgraduates.

The Player-Coach

"I think Miller was born to coach," says Kim Kimber. "I played on the basketball team with him, and during the long holiday break, when most teams basically fell apart in terms of conditioning and play, Miller kept us working. He'd drive up to Summit, where I had an outdoor basketball backboard on a large driveway, and the starters would play 3 on 3 in the freezing cold. We might have chosen just to play for fun; Miller had a different agenda. He had us practicing drills and running pick plays and back cuts. When we were scrimmaging, after a basket or a miss he'd stop play and, in a gentle, non-pushy way, point out how we might have moved better, where there was a better opportunity for a pass, and how to set each other up by movement into open space.

"You have to remember what Pingry sports were like in the 'English country day school' model of those years. At the end of the academic school day we all played sports – and our teachers coached us, whether they knew anything about the sport or not. All very 'gentlemanly,' and completely unprofessional. A 'good game' was one in which we competed hard, even if we lost. I've often wondered if Miller's passion for coaching didn't stem from that experience of wanting to play better and win and realizing the only way for that to happen was through practice and discipline. If our coaches couldn't provide that for us, he would."

"When I think back on my Pingry years," Miller recalls, "what stands out are the people who made a difference in my life. They include headmaster Springer and teachers Charlie Atwater, Dick Baldwin, Albie Booth, Ed Cissel, Abel DeGryse, George Dimock, Caz France, Dave Koth, Herb Hahn, Vince Lesneski, Mabel Prevost, Otho Vars, Frank West, and Reese Williams.

"I was blessed as well with great friendships: from the class of '52, Peter Ackerman, Bruce Baekey, Peter Buchanan, Bob Clark, Dick Corbett, Dick Dzina, Jerry Graham, Bill Gusmer, Jay Harbeck, Tom Hartley, Ted Hewson, Kim Kimber, Bill Ledder, Gordon Lenci, Craig McClelland, Hugh Morrell, Jack Noe, Jack Orr, Jere Ross, Fred Schroeder, Bill Tatlock, Tommy Thomas, Bob Thurston, and Ned Ward; the class of '53, Buck Bryan, Dick Feleppa, Bob O'Brien, Bob Pierson, Fred Mueller, Bernie Peckman, Jim Porter, Phil Scrudato, and Clark Warren; the class of '54, Bob Arace, Jack Bryan, Amos Hostetter, Rob and Wimp Hall, Guy Leedom, Helmut Weymar, and Bill Williams; the class of '55, Herb Busch, Phil Burrows, John Holman, Jack O'Brien, Frank Randall, and Chuck Wynn; and the class of '56, Bob Meyer, Charley Orr, Bob Shippee, and Rick Richardson."

"I remember that Miller was basically everywhere during my six years at Pingry. My introduction to Miller came in 9th grade, when I and my classmates entered the Upper School – the sacrosanct space inhabited only by the reverent and holy, and forbidden territory for any Lower Schooler daring enough to climb the rickety stairs.

"One day in my freshman year, I was in the Upper School study hall with other Pingry 'hackers,' trying to look busy, when a very strange person appeared in the doorway to the left, at the front of the study hall. He held aloft a large beaker containing some type of biology detritus, probably stolen from Mr. Kirk's lab in the rear of the building, while singing part of a very popular Joni James song, 'Here is a heart that is lonely.' Then he disappeared as mysteriously as he had arrived. Such was my introduction to a Pingry legend. I laugh every time I think of that scene!"

Jack Bryan '54

"I remember meeting Miller as a young boy, years before I graduated from Pingry and went on to Princeton and a career as an attorney and later a federal judge.

"I lived on DeWitt Road in the Westminster section of Elizabeth, in those years the heart of 'Pingry Country.' Mr. Les lived at the end of the block, and my other neighbors were families with names like Urner, Eichorn, Pinneo, Kellogg, Hopkins, Schweitzer, Gelber, and Stein. Across the street were the Jaspers, whose claim to fame was a basketball net in their spotlighted driveway. In his high school years at Pingry, Miller was a constant participant in the evening pickup games hosted by Peter Jasper.

"For older teenagers, 10- and 11-year-old kids like my buddies and me who hung around trying to get court time – we were inevitable targets for verbal abuse, if we were noticed at all. But Miller was different. To this day I remember Miller's generous attitude toward us kids. He treated us with respect and let us play, even though we were just pains in the butt to the older boys."

Joe Irenas '58

Pingry's Gifts

In summarizing his Pingry years as a student, Miller says, "What I got from Pingry was what any student can get: a thoroughly solid education and strong academic skills. That competence translated into the confidence in college to take on tough challenges and overcome them. My teachers empowered me to believe I could succeed.

"There was another important lesson I learned from my Pingry experience: the importance of patience. I was pretty scattered at times as a young student – not so different from many of the hundreds of students I've worked with over the years. It was really important to me that faculty members stayed with me until I woke up. They gave me time and space to figure things out for myself. That's a lesson I've never let myself forget when I became a teacher and coach.

"But the best thing I received from Pingry was the realization that I wanted to be an excellent teacher and a coach – to pay back the gift that had been given to me – and the place where I wanted to do that was Pingry."

THE LIFE & TIMES of MILLER A. BUGLIARI

MILLER BUGLIARI
May 7, 1935
Inman Avenue, Plainfield, N. J.

Bugs, Mill   Undecided

Eleven years at Pingry

One of the liveliest, one of the youngest, and one of the funniest Sixth Formers, Bugs is always to be found in the midst of some fun-making group. Besides his humor, Mill made quite a name for himself athletically, too, starring in soccer, basketball, and baseball. On the **Record** Bugs devoted much of his time to the humor articles or to humoring the other editors on Wednesday nights. Wherever he may go, we are sure that his ready wit and radiating personality will win Miller Bugliari many lasting friendships.

Spanish Club, V; Record, IV, V, VI,
Associate Editor, VI; Soccer, V, VI;
Baseball, V, VI; Basketball, V, VI.

Where's Miller? Look for the one person whose tie is hanging loose.

Miller Stories

"Miller, why in the world did you climb the Rockefeller Christmas tree?"

"I thought it would be fun."

One of Miller's former headmasters described him as an "eccentric genius." As far as it goes, that's an accurate characterization, but it still falls short of capturing Miller's essence.

The "genius" part is obvious enough to grasp – just measure the devotion and loyalty he has inspired in countless soccer players, students, classmates, and colleagues over eight decades.

The "eccentric" part seems equally apt. Some people march to the beat of a different drummer; Miller hires the entire band.

"Normal" behavior for Miller in his younger years was to travel around with a gorilla mask and other assorted props close at hand, looking for opportunities to startle strangers. Who *does* that?

Many of us, perhaps, might look at the Rockefeller Christmas tree and think, "Wouldn't it be fun to climb that?" And in the time it would take us to consider the idea and discard it as inappropriate or too risky, Miller would be halfway up the tree. Some of us might look at a party attended by famous people in politics and entertainment and think, "Wouldn't it be cool to get into that party?" Fewer of us would have the courage and skill to crash a Kennedy wedding successfully.

But at the same time, rather than being "eccentric," Miller is an extraordinarily centered, completely authentic person. So there's more going on here.

Thinking about his legendary antics, one might recall the fearless, mischievous characters from ancient myth – think Loki, Hermes, or Kokopelli – or the animals from folklore like the monkey, fox, coyote, and raven, who help people and outwit opponents with their cleverness. One might even be reminded of the jester and "wise fool" throughout European literature – zany entertainers/advisors to kings who, in the guise of humor, communicated truth.

From the moment he put on the gorilla mask for the first time, Miller has slid easily into different identities: The Red Baron, The Ray, The Phantom of the Opera, a *maître d'*, a Secret Service agent, a Wall Street investment analyst, or a limousine driver. And like the ancient oracles and Zen masters or their more modern representations like Yoda from *Star Wars*, Miller often speaks in riddles, apparently nonsensical analogies and impenetrable utterances that simultaneously capture and confound us.

Miller is all of these things: wily trickster with a lightning-fast mind; magnetic, hilarious showman and storyteller; shape shifter; irrepressible risk taker; perpetually innocent naïf – and wise sage. And at the center is Miller's unshakable love of people and an almost childlike, spontaneous sense of joyful delight in being fully alive.

Reading or reliving the impossibly audacious accounts of his escapades, we are invited to awaken that same joyful delight within ourselves. Much as our ancestors might have shared the earliest myths and legends in the gleam of a fire, we tell and retell the stories, with laughter – and wonder.

> "One day, while I was leading the team for the usual campus jog as a warm-up for practice, we got back to the field quicker than Miller expected. He didn't see us come up over the hill. We surprised him running and jumping up in the air, yelling at a bee that was flying around him, trying to kick it. It had to be one of the funniest things I have seen him do. But even funnier was the fact that he acted like nothing had happened and lectured us for coming back too early. It was fantastic."
>
> **Frank Puleo '91**

Miller Stories #1

The Rockefeller Christmas Tree

Summers when Miller was a student at Pingry and Springfield usually included trips to the Jersey Shore, often as guests aboard the Chuck Wynn '55 family boat berthed in Mantoloking. It was a comfortably sized cabin cruiser that could sleep six. Since there were usually 12 or more passengers, however, things were a bit crowded. But with all the laughing and carrying on, nobody cared.

Escapades were certainly the order of the day. Phil Burrows '55 also had a boat, a 30' Chris Craft, that was frequently the "boat of choice" for the gang. Phil vividly remembers being sound asleep on his boat at midnight when he woke up suddenly to find himself being drenched with water. Miller, Herbie Busch '55, and Tim McCarthy had run a hose from the marina in through the window of the cabin where Phil was sleeping.

Miller's acrobatic stunts began one of those summers on the Jersey Shore. They finished a trip on Phil's boat, and were back at the dock cleaning up and hosing the seawater off the polished teak decks when they noticed Miller wasn't around. It wasn't that he'd escaped the work detail – that might have been predicted – but he had completely vanished from the dock area. Then, way above their heads, they heard a distant "Hellooooo!" There was Miller, 40 feet up a huge construction crane overlooking the marina.

The crane escapade gave Miller an appropriate sense of scale for his exploits, so his next acrobatic caper was climbing the Christmas tree in Rockefeller Center.

Decades ago, the Rockefeller Christmas tree wasn't so big a deal – and was accordingly less well guarded. That made it easy for Miller to get over halfway up the tree before he was spotted. What may have tipped people off was that he was taking the decorations, which in those days were dinner-plate-sized discs, and scaling them like Frisbees down West 50th Street. From that height, with a good wrist snap, you could send the decorations quite a distance.

"Looking back," says Miller, "I liked the physical challenge of doing something like that – and the risk involved was exciting." Miller emphasizes that these were different times. You could do pranks that really harmed no one, and they weren't treated as federal crimes or a violation of someone's civil rights punishable by jail time. "We were just kids having fun. If you were clever enough, you could usually talk your way out of trouble," Miller remembers. "It's a pity you can't do that now."

Miller Stories #2

The Attack of the Grave Robbers

The Eisenhower years from 1952-1960 are remembered as a time of technological change: the nationwide arrival of TV, paperback books, LP records and Super 8 home movies. Those years have also been characterized by some as a time of almost boring, conservative dullness. Miller picked up immediately on the potential for home movies; the "boring, conservative dullness" aspect, however, clearly didn't take.

Among the earliest of Miller's movie creations was "The Attack of the Grave Robbers." Miller talked some Pingry buddies, classmate Peter Van Leight '52 and juniors Bob O'Brien '53, Dick Feleppa '53, and Clark Warren, into helping him film the exhumation and revival of a "corpse." The setting they chose was an ancient cemetery on White Oak Ridge Road in Short Hills, near the current Pingry Lower School. The shoot went really well until the moment that the grave robbers, dressed in white lab coats and pulling a body wrapped in burlap from the newly dug-up earth, were spotted by the passersby on White Oak Ridge Road on their way to church. Within minutes the road was clogged with gawking spectators, and the resulting traffic jam snarled traffic all the way to Parsonage Hill Road. As the sound of sirens announced the arrival of the cops picking their way through the snarled traffic to the crime scene, Miller and his accomplices made their escape. It's a pity that in the confusion Miller didn't film the madly sprinting burlap-wrapped corpse, now miraculously brought back to life.

Miller Stories #3

The Gas Station Caper

"Let's go make a movie!" Miller said one day to a group of buddies that included Gene Shea '57, Owen Shea '58, Phil Scrudato '53, Phil Lobo, and Dick Roder. "About what?" they asked. "How about a gas station robbery?" said Miller.

They arranged with a gas station owner in Scotch Plains to let them use his station for a set, and showed up on the day of shooting with Owen dressed in coveralls, playing the attendant, and everyone else in appropriate thug costumes, armed with fake pistols and submachine guns. They had reached the point where the robbers were shaking down the attendant when a local resident pulled up to fill his tank, saw the holdup in progress, and took off to call the police.

That accelerated the end of the movie. They made their escape, Miller in his convertible and the others in a sports car, driving home along Springfield Avenue in New Providence, blazing away at each other from the open cars with their make-believe arsenal. None of the startled pedestrians they passed on the street had cell phones in those days, so the hoodlums made it home safely.

Miller Stories #4

Fun on the Water with Herbie Busch

In Miller's summer adventures on the Jersey Shore, one of the regulars was Herb Busch '55, Pingry's star basketball player from the early 1950s. Like Chuck Wynn '55 and Phil Burrows '55, Herbie had a boat. Herbie's was a bit smaller, however. And since Herbie stood 6'8" and weighed well over 320 lbs., the net effect was that of a giant riding in a rowboat. But when Herbie invited Miller and Tim McCarthy to go out for a dusk cruise, Miller of course said "yes" – and decided it might be fun to bring an air horn with them.

The Mantoloking drawbridge always opens for large vessels upon a signal. So as Herbie's tiny boat approached the bridge, Miller blew the horn – loudly – several times. It's not clear whether the bridge operator actually saw them; he might not have spotted the boat, although he shouldn't have been able to miss Herbie towering over the gunwales. But on went the warning lights, stopping traffic, and to the whirring grind of machinery, the massive drawbridge slowly creaked up. The intrepid sailors passed under the raised span in fine style. Judging by the obscenities hurled at them by the bridge operator when he discovered the tiny boat he had opened the bridge for, and the honking horns from the motorists stuck on the bridge, not everyone appreciated their style.

Miller Stories #5

The Creature from the Black Lagoon

The trip on the little boat had been so much fun that Miller convinced Herbie to try something even more daring: navigating the Passaic River from New Providence to Newark Bay. After an adventurous trip downriver, Herbie, Miller, and their pal Tim McCarthy showed up, somewhat later than expected, at a bridge over the Passaic near Kearny right next to a popular bar, where 20-plus friends and Pingry classmates led by Chuck Wynn, Greg Pierson, and Frank Randolph '55 were waiting to cheer their arrival – dressed in outlandish costumes.

Herbie and his crew might have made another triumphant passage under this bridge to tumultuous applause. They might at least have pulled smoothly into the wharf outside the bar. Instead, they ran aground. In an attempt to free the boat, Herbie stepped out and promptly disappeared in the mud of the river bottom. By now, drawn by the unruly, bizarrely dressed crowd on the bridge who had fortified themselves at the bar for the evening's excitement, the police were on hand. The cruiser's searchlight picked out the boat in the growing darkness. "Who's in charge of that boat!" yelled one of the cops. "I'm the captain," announced Herbie, rising enormously out of the river's muck like the Creature from the Black Lagoon. The cop yelled "Captain? Of that piece of junk? I don't know what planet you guys are from" (he might have used stronger words than "junk" and "guys"), "but get the hell back to where you came from!" A good idea, in principle, but the planet Miller came from hasn't yet been discovered.

Miller at Springfield College

The college Miller attended, Springfield College in Springfield, Mass., has long been one of the premier learning centers for men and women interested in coaching and sports medicine. James Naismith invented basketball there in 1861, and another alumnus, William G. Morgan, invented the sport of volleyball in 1895. Today, Springfield alumni serve many college and professional teams, including the NFL's Buffalo Bills, Chicago Bears, and Indianapolis Colts, as trainers and strength and conditioning coaches. NFL coach Steve Spagnuolo is among the thousands of Springfield graduates who have achieved outstanding success as coaches in high school, college, and professional sports. Within its Group 3 NCAA Division, Springfield has won many conference and national championships in wrestling, field hockey, and both men's and women's basketball, lacrosse, swimming and diving, and soccer.

Academic Excellence: Miller's Style

It's hard to imagine a better college experience for someone who wanted to devote his life to coaching than Springfield was for Miller, and he took advantage of everything the school had to offer, graduating cum laude and winning the graduation prize in Journalism. Miller being Miller, however, it's no surprise that academic excellence wasn't just a matter of acing tests and papers.

Miller tells the story of how he and some friends handled their final assignment for the First Aid course required of all Springfield students. To pass the course, they had to present a demonstration of some aspect of their study, such as treating a severe head injury involving concussion, or reducing a compound fracture. Miller and his friends decided their "skit" (Miller's appropriate term for "academic practical demonstration") would focus on helping someone recover from frostbite and hypothermia. For their "patient" they selected a friend and told him he needed to prepare for the skit by spending time dressed in shorts and a T-shirt in the Springfield College Ice House, which in those days served as a deep-freeze meat locker. So in he went and they closed the door. Then Miller got busy with something else and completely forgot about him.

Their buddy was reportedly a wonderful guy and a really tough football player, but not, perhaps, the brightest bulb on the Christmas tree. Lots of people would have said "the hell with it" and given up once ice crystals had started to form on their hands and feet – but not this guy. He stuck it out, so when they finally rescued him to start the demonstration, he didn't need to simulate hypothermia; his fingers and toes were blue – he was shivering uncontrollably and exhibiting all the classic symptoms of lethargy and "foggy brain." After they succeeded in reviving him, Miller and his friends, naturally, passed the course with distinction. "Extraordinarily realistic demonstration!" was the instructor's comment.

Besides offering opportunities to excel academically – if at times unconventionally – Springfield also gave Miller the grounding in soccer at a very high level that would shape his career as a coach.

Cafe-Woods Hall

Marsh Memorial Hall

The Player-Coach

Springfield College soccer teammate and National Soccer Coaches Association of America (NSCAA) colleague Bob Nye remembers Miller's profound impact on the team and its success. "We used the traditional 'W' formation of those years. Miller played in what would now be a halfback position behind the two strikers. His job was to get and distribute the ball on offense, and to break up opposing attacks before they could start. He wasn't the fastest guy on the team, although he certainly was the toughest.

"What set Miller apart was his understanding of the game. He had an uncanny awareness of the players around him, and where to go with the ball to get it out of traffic and to an open man. Defensively it was like he knew what the other team wanted to do before they did and was always in position to cut off a pass or strip an opponent of the ball."

Today's soccer commentators would also say that Miller had an extraordinarily high "work rate." He ran and competed all game long – the idea of giving in to fatigue or adversity just wasn't in his nature. And by his personal example, he defined how everyone on the team needed to lift their level of play. His teammates didn't want to let him down by not rising to his standards.

Nye also describes Miller as the glue that held the team together, much as Miller had done with his Pingry basketball teammates. "It was like he turned us into a big Italian family. He was friends with everybody on the team, listening, supporting, and encouraging each of us. Looking back now, it's fair to say he was actually coaching us behind the scenes with subtle, quiet leadership to help us work better as a team. He seemed to be a step ahead of what teammates thought they could or should do, and had a real gift for explaining the game and players' roles in ways that made his teammates understand. I've seen the same thing dozens of times in NSCAA executive meetings. We'll all be seated around a table, debating and arguing about an issue as people do in meetings, and Miller would just walk around the table, rubbing his hands together, listening deeply but saying nothing until it all became clear to him. Then he'd speak – and we'd all listen."

Irv Schmid, Miller's Mentor

Springfield's soccer coach during Miller's college years was the legendary Irv Schmid, who, like Miller, is a member of the Springfield College Athletic Hall of Fame and the NSCAA Hall of Fame, and served as president of the NSCAA. Schmid's coaching style was distinctive. The *Soccer Coaching Bible*, published by the NSCAA, describes Schmid's style: During a game, Irv sometimes looked disinterested in what was going on. He would sit impassively on the bench, not raising his voice or yelling instructions to his players. He rarely questioned a referee's call. His teams were always completely under control and well schooled in the fundamentals. They were never out of any game.

Anyone who has watched Miller chew nervously on a used roll of athletic tape or yell in exasperation in a tense moment of a game to "GET THE BALL OUT OF THE MIDDLE!" might question what Miller learned from Irv Schmid's demeanor. But then you wouldn't expect a fiery, emotional Italian to be anything other than what he is.

Irv Schmid, Springfield College soccer coach.

Miller as a soccer player at Springfield College in Springfield, Massachusetts.

Miller Mayhem

Besides his academic and athletic accomplishments, the other notable aspect about Miller at Springfield College was his irrepressible humor. Bob Nye recalls the team's bus trips as extended Marx Brothers comedy routines, with Miller playing all five brothers. "When we boarded the team bus with our bags of gear for the game, Miller's would be three times bigger than anyone else's. In addition to his cleats, jersey, shorts, socks, jock, and warm-up jacket, it carried his other equipment for the trip: several really ugly masks, gloves that looked like large monster hands, a WW I aviator helmet and goggles, and whatever else he'd dreamed up for the next prank. We called our trips 'Miller Mayhem.' When we got off the bus, the rest of the players would walk on the other side of the street from Miller as he worked his way, in costume, down the sidewalk, terrifying or convulsing innocent bystanders."

As Miller recalls, "I thought it was important to help the guys stay loose before games. I'd started using the gorilla mask in skits as a counselor at Camp Waganaki and figured it might be useful with the soccer team, too." Inevitably, some of the players dared him to use it in a game, so at the player introductions before a pre-season game there were the 10 Springfield starters – and one gorilla.

Bob Nye still thinks Miller's best madcap moment came in New Haven on their way to play Yale. "We got stopped in traffic in the center of the city at a congested six-way intersection.

"The cop at the intersection was carefully, calmly directing traffic to move it through the mess. Miller jumped out of the bus and took a position behind the traffic cop, facing the cars coming in the other direction, and started mirroring the cop's directions – the opposite way. The cop was too busy directing the cars in front of him to bawl Miller out or get him to stop.

"What resulted was unimaginable chaos. Miller tied traffic up in a knot. The only reason there wasn't a string of head-on and rear-end collisions was that cars were creeping forward a foot at a time, drivers honking their horns and yelling angrily. Of course, by then Miller had managed to clear space in front of our bus, so he hopped back on and we went on our way. It may have taken that poor cop an hour to unravel the jam Miller had created.

"Oh yeah," Nye concludes, "we did beat Yale." Miller scored the winning goal, breaking a 0-0 tie – and his nose in the process.

Irv Schmid (top) attempting to impose discipline on the Springfield College soccer team bus.

Miller (left), in mask, staging a mock holdup in downtown Providence, R.I.

> "I was a freshman in Coach's biology class when one day he invited me into his office. He asked me, 'Is your dad Peter Bartlett, and did he play soccer at Yale?' I responded yes, and he then promptly showed me the article describing how he headed the ball 'like a bullet' past All-Ivy League goal tender Pete Bartlett. Dad went on to hold the career shutout record for Yale for over 50 years. Coach always reminds me that he slipped one by him! My son Nicholas played soccer at The Brunswick School in Greenwich, Connecticut, and played against Pingry the past few years. So three generations of Bartletts have experienced Bugliari soccer firsthand."
>
> **Chris Bartlett '79**

The Death Ray

One of Miller's crowning pranks at Springfield College was his "Death Ray" – a large mirror he removed from his room and took to the roof of the dormitory. As the sun moved into the west, Miller would catch its rays in the mirror and angle them into adjacent buildings.

One of his favorite targets was the library. He could direct the reflected beam of light right through the large windows at the backs of the kids studying in the library. Not knowing what was happening, they would start to squirm as the focused heat of the sun's rays played across their backs and necks.

But the capper was when he lit up the Dean of Admissions' office in the Administration building. The dean was in the midst of interviewing prospective parents when Miller blasted them with the Death Ray. The family started blinking and shielding their eyes. The dean, by now embarrassed, first tried drawing the blinds to block the light. Miller just tightened the angle to concentrate the beam even more intensely.

The dean came running out of the Ad building on fire, heading straight toward the dorm. He sprinted up the dorm steps and burst through the door. That was his first mistake. Miller wasn't the only one playing tricks that day, and two buckets of water some students had placed above the door toppled over, drenching the dean. So now the dean wasn't just hot. He was boiling.

Meanwhile, up on the roof, Miller was spotted by a buddy, a senior football player who had come up to get some sun.

"Hey, Bugs. What are you doing?"

"Check this out. It's a Death Ray. Look. You can shine the beam on kids and teachers in the quad."

Then he handed the mirror to the football player and made a fast escape that would have done Tom Sawyer proud. The other student was caught red-handed by the dean and given a tongue-lashing that could have peeled paint off a wall. The next day Miller went to the dean's office and owned up to the prank to get his friend off the hook.

Why Miller wasn't expelled for that, or any of his other antics at Springfield, remains a mystery. But as a former president of the NSCAA and – along with Bob Nye – a member of the select group of NSCAA leaders called the "Red Aprons," charged with organizing the huge association conventions for several thousand coaches, Miller is a frequent speaker at awards ceremonies. And every time he mounts the podium, the massed audience chants: "Time for the Ray!" "The Ray!" "The Ray!"

As a member of the Varsity Club (first row, far right).

With the NSCAA Red Aprons.

Star of Stage and Radio

Miller showed up at Springfield already an accomplished humor writer, movie producer/director, and master of improvisational theater performances. Springfield gave him the opportunity to polish those talents.

His theatrical debut was in a production of *Stalag 17*, the 1953 film and play about American airmen in a German prisoner of war camp in World War II. The cast of Springfield's 1955 production followed the list of characters in Donald Bevan and Edmund Trzcinski's Broadway show with one notable – if completely predictable – exception. The character Bugs, an addition for Springfield's performance, was played by the "character" Bugs.

Miller's most ambitious dramatic effort, however, was his short-lived mystery serial show on the Springfield campus radio station. Miller wrote the scripts and directed the production. He also cast the show, and in retrospect he might have done a better job with that. The stars of "Mystery Theater," which aired live across the campus on Monday evenings from 9:00-9:30, included classmates Lou Racca, Charlton Schwayze, and Windy Windylass. "They were terrible," Miller laughs, remembering how his buddies absolutely fell apart on air.

Miller (hatless) and the "Mystery Theater" cast.

The Springfield College Dramatic Club

Presents

"STALAG 17"

By Donald Bevan and Edmund Trzcinski

Directed By
Emile O. Schmidt

THE ATTIC PLAYHOUSE
Room 100 — Memorial Field House
November 17-18, 1955

CAST OF CHARACTERS
(In Order of Appearance)

S. S. Guard .... Dan Simonds
Stosh .... John Zaccaro
Harry Shapiro .... Arthur Corbett
Price .... Wesley Snapp
Herb Gordon .... Alan "Jocko" Hanscom
Hoffman .... Tyrrell Belville
Sefton .... Dave Martens
Duke .... Don McCullough
McCarthy .... Will Chassey
Horney .... Dewey McGowen
Marko .... Roger Gates
Cpl. Schultz .... Bill MacNeill
Dunbar .... Douglas Snow
Reed .... John Hanley
Witherspoon .... Fred Mould
Bugs .... Miller Bugliari
Red Dog .... George Benedict
German Captain .... George Jessup
Geneva Man .... Wally Foster

DAN SIMONDS (S. S. Guard) — "Mikado," "Iolanthe," "Sweethearts," "The Only Girl."

FRED MOULD (Witherspoon) — First play.

GEORGE BENEDICT (Red Dog) and MILLER BUGLIARI (Bugs) make their theatrical debut tonight.

"They couldn't learn lines or even read them properly. It instantly turned into an unscripted comedy routine of dropped lines and giggles that quickly degenerated into uncontrollable laughter. So the entire first show consisted of bloopers and outtakes; they never actually finished the script. We were an instant hit," remembers Miller. "By our second show, it seemed as if the entire college was tuning in to 'Mystery Theater,' but the only mystery was how outrageously bad we'd be. After a few more disasters, they took us off the air. There's only so much fun you can get from 30 minutes of bedlam by college kids acting like eight-year-olds. And that ended my script writing and producing career."

Today, Miller is justifiably proud of his son Boyce's success as a writer/producer in Hollywood, and even happier to know that when Boyce writes a show, the actors can actually perform it.

Miller's Roommates

Miller developed lifelong friends among his teammates and fellow students at Springfield, but he was especially fond of his roommates during those years. "All four of us are now in the Springfield College Athletic Hall of Fame," Miller notes, "my roommates for their athletic achievements and I for my coaching success."

Springfield College's *History of Football, 1890-2010* suggests why Miller and George Benedict would have become close friends: "On the bus and in the locker room Benedict was a jokester, but on the field, he became a veritable monster." Benedict was selected as a second team All American at the end of his senior year. He was also the New England wrestling champ in the 285 pound weight class. After graduating, Benedict was drafted by the Washington Redskins, but he chose to bypass pro football to join the Army, where he starred on the Fort Dix team with NFL players.

Bob Litchard played tackle alongside Benedict on the 1957 Springfield team that outscored opponents 282 to 67 in an 8-0-1 season that culminated with winning the Lambert Cup as the outstanding NCAA College Division team. Like Benedict, Litchard is a member of Springfield College's All-Time Football Team. Litchard also starred in baseball, being named to the All American Team as a first baseman. Drafted by the New York football Giants, he played on their taxi squad before entering college coaching at Cornell.

Dave Martens was a standout teammate of Litchard's as a pitcher for Springfield; he was named to the 1955 All–New England All Star Team and pitched in the College World Series that same year. He went on to play with the Milwaukee Braves before beginning an illustrious career as a high school coach and athletic director in New York State until his passing in 2010. In honoring Dave's induction into the National Interscholastic Athletic Administrators Association Hall of Fame, the New York Senate noted his extraordinary commitment to the development of girls' sports programs and his founding of Operation Offense to lead in the fight for education and prevention of substance abuse among high school athletes.

"One reason we all got along so well," remembers Miller, "is that we were all fierce competitors who loved to win. The other reason was I could always crack them up. George, in addition to his athletic skill and sometimes fiery temper, was somewhat forgetful, especially with his room key. So his usual way of getting into our locked suite was to smash through the lock and force the door open. After a while, the college got tired of replacing the door and lock, so our room was always open. It became the gathering spot for the other guys in the dorm.

"Bob was just an upbeat, funny guy who was quick to see the humor in anything we did – the perfect straight man. Dave was more quiet and withdrawn, a really neat, organized guy. I think the rest of us drove him crazy at times. But he, too, had the gift of being able to laugh at life. We gave him a lot of life to laugh at."

If part of the college experience is discovering the kind of person you want to become, Miller's roommates couldn't have been better friends and role models.

(Left): Miller with Springfield College alums Bill Nedde and Dave Martens. (Above): with Bob Litchard and George Benedict.

EIGHT DECADES *at* THE PINGRY SCHOOL

Springfield's Impact

Springfield College was where Miller learned how to be an inspiring coach and a hilarious teacher. The greatest similarity between Schmid and his protégé has been their gift for teaching the fundamentals of soccer, so that players have the confidence and skills to handle whatever happens in the unpredictable, constantly changing flow of a game – and, more than that, to understand the game. And each is notable for their deep awareness of and concern for each player as a person, not just an athlete. The real lessons they have taught their players are about life, not soccer.

Irv Schmid's Springfield Athletic Hall of Fame commendation reads:

Schmid's impact goes well beyond the College. His influence, be it direct or indirect, is still very much felt today. His contact with so many young people over the years has obviously had a ripple effect on coaching and teaching. His professional integrity and dedication to Springfield College are beacons for others to emulate, and his true impact on the game, in the coaching ranks and in teaching, may never really be accurately measured.

The same words could be used to sum up Miller's career at Pingry.

> "My son Peter '06 played soccer at Bowdoin College, and on the first day of practice his freshman year, the volunteer assistant squash coach – a Bowdoin legend named Charlie Butt, age 83 – approached Peter and said, 'I see you went to the Pingry School. Do you know Miller Bugliari?' And of course Peter said, 'Why, yes, I played for him, as did my dad, and he's the greatest guy in the world.' Charlie Butt then said, 'Well, young man, I agree. I coached Miller as a freshman at Springfield College. Toughest player, with the greatest hustle and desire of anybody I ever coached. You and your father are lucky to have played for a man like that.' Truer words were never spoken."
>
> **Guy Cipriano '74**

Left: The Springfield varsity soccer team in 1956 with Miller in the second row, second from right; and (above) the 1957 team with Miller fourth row, fourth from left.

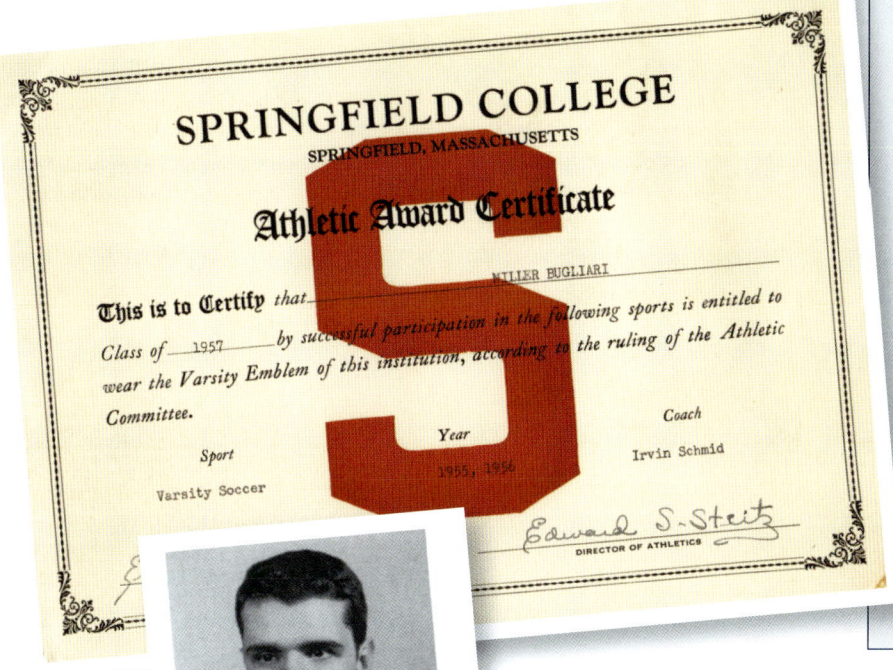

You Can't Fill Miller's Shoes

Bob Nye starred with Miller as a junior on the 1957 Springfield College team that lost to West Chester in the NCAA Championship Finals.

During Bob's college career, Springfield College soccer was a low-budget program, so soccer shoes would be reconditioned at the end of each season and reissued to players. His senior year, Bob got Miller's shoes.

"We've all seen how Miller runs," recalls Bob, "somewhere between the fast scurry of a road runner and the shuffle of an orangutan. His shoes, as a result, were bizarrely misshapen and worn – actually they were bent into a rigid 'U' shape like a banana. They were the right size, but I couldn't even get them on. I had to get a new pair. The next year, Miller's shoes went to another star player for Springfield, Terry Jackson. He wore them for one day before begging for real shoes that a normal foot could fit into.

"Given the astounding success Miller has achieved as a coach, teacher, and leader of young men and women, anyone would be challenged to fill Miller's shoes. What I discovered is that you can't even wear them."

Bob Nye

MILLER ALBERT BUGLIARI
Plainfield, New Jersey
MAJOR: School of Physical Education
ACTIVITIES: Maroon Key 2,3,4; "Student" 1,2,3,4; Varsity 'S' Club 3,4 (Treas. 4); Men's Physical Education Club 2,3,4; Junior Prom Committee.
SPORTS: Soccer 1,2,3,4; Wrestling 1; Baseball (Manager).
INTRAMURALS: Basketball 3; Softball 2,3

Miller lettered in soccer for three years: 1955, 1956, and 1957.

His college yearbook from 1957.

Miller (left in front row) on the 1956 basketball team.

Miller Stories #6

The Red Baron

Especially early in his career, Miller liked to take on the identity of famous heroes and villains like The Phantom of the Opera, King Kong, The Ray, Al Capone, and Karl Wallenda. One of his favorite characters was Baron von Richthofen, the celebrated German Ace from World War I. Or maybe Miller, driving his beat-up convertible wearing a WW I aviator's helmet, goggles, flight jacket, and the long scarf to match, was just channeling Snoopy playing the Red Baron.

One day he was stopped by a cop for speeding. Miller pulled over and the cop got out of his cruiser and approached the driver's side of the car. We all know the drill: you rummage through the glove compartment trying to find the registration, hoping you didn't leave the insurance card in an envelope back home, pull out your license, and try desperately to think of a way to talk the officer into just giving you a warning. But Miller stayed motionless, his hands gripping the wheel, staring straight ahead with intense concentration. The cop waited for Miller to notice him standing by the driver's door. And waited. And waited.

Finally the cop rapped impatiently on the door with his nightstick. Miller turned, rolled down the window, looked at the cop with startled amazement, and said: "Wow, officer! What are you doing up here?" According to Miller, the cop was laughing so hard he let Miller go without a ticket. Crime doesn't (or shouldn't) pay. Laughter usually does.

Miller Stories #7

Winning the Jersey Shore Grand Prix

Miller's most exciting car trip came when he was a passenger in a car driven by the late Mark Donahue '55, member of the International Motorsports and the Sports Car Club of America Halls of Fame and winner of the 1972 Indy 500 before his death in an accident at the 1975 Austrian Grand Prix.

They were at the Jersey Shore, coming back from a bachelor party late at night in Mark's souped-up Porsche, around the time Mark was blowing away Trans Am competition in Roger Penske's Chevy Camaro. It was the off season, and the streets were deserted – a perfect opportunity for Mark to test his theories and technique in rapid acceleration, high-speed turns and power braking: "If you can make black marks on a straightaway from the time you turn out of a corner until the braking point of the next turn, then you have enough horsepower."

Early in his career, Donahue had been nicknamed "Captain Nice" for his irresistible smile. After he began carving up competitors, his name changed to "Dark Monohue," and that's who drove Miller in a hair-raising, breath-stopping, high-speed attack on the side streets of Mantoloking, Bay Head, Point Pleasant, and Brielle en route to their motel. Like the sonic boom that follows a jet breaking the sound barrier, the roar of Mark's engine and the squealing of tires must have trailed behind, waking up sleeping residents: "What was that?" This was one adventure in which Miller never had to worry about getting caught by the police. If the best race car drivers in the world couldn't catch Mark, the cops would never have had a chance. You may never get Miller to say an adventure was "too exciting." This one came close.

Miller Stories #8

Dining with Miller

For Miller, one of the high points of going to New York with friends was dining out and taking in the night life. But Miller never liked waiting in a line to be seated at a restaurant. So he polished the art of studying the seating chart at the *maître d*'s stand at the front of the restaurant, figuring out where an empty table was. When the *maître d'* left the stand to seat someone, Miller would just mark the table he wanted as "occupied," and take his party in to be seated. In the bustle of a crowded restaurant, no one ever noticed.

A *maître d'* would leave his stand at his own peril when Miller was around. Miller loved to grab the mike and "announce" nonexistent celebrities entering the restaurant: "Good evening, ladies and gentlemen. Tonight we have the pleasure of welcoming New York Yankee star Joe DiMaggio and his lovely wife Marilyn Monroe. Let's give them a big round of applause!" Then they'd watch the restaurant patrons start applauding and craning their necks to see the famous people who never would appear.

Phil Burrows remembers one time they went into New York to catch Charley Drew's show at the Tap Room of the Hotel Taft. The line to get in was huge, and they were at the back of it. Miller disappeared into the kitchen and came out a few minutes later, having traded his blazer for a waiter's jacket, and seated the party.

Miller Stories #9

The Peppermint Lounge

On one of the many highlight-reel moments in New York, Miller and his buddies, dressed like Mafia newly arrived from Palermo, pulled up in front of the Peppermint Lounge, the hot spot of the 1960s. The line to get in stretched around the block, and the bouncers at the door were harder to get past than the Secret Service guarding the president. The gangsters, driving Dick Shyers '62's 1928 Rolls Royce, pulled up by the front door and got out. "We have some people coming later," Miller barked at the guy at the curb. "They sent us to check the place out." And in they went, leaving the car in the street.

Another time at the Peppermint Lounge, during a break by the house band, in those years Joey Dee and the Starliters, Miller and a couple of friends took the stage and grabbed the instruments. "What do you know?" somebody asked Miller. It turned out that the only song Miller knew was "Silent Night" – so that's what they performed. They got kicked off the stage pretty quickly. Miller's rendition of "Silent Night" didn't challenge the Starliters' #1 hit "Peppermint Twist" on the charts.

Miller in the Army: 1957–1962

You have to be a certain age now to remember when compulsory military service was the expected next step in a man's life after graduation from high school or college. For college graduates like Miller, that meant six months of active duty followed by two years in the Army Reserves, as part of what was officially called the RFA – Reserve Force Army – but more scornfully labeled by the regular Army as "Russia's Friendly Ally."

Active duty began with basic training. For the out-of-shape civilians thrust into the rigors of military service, it could be a harrowing experience. Miller was in superb condition and never backed away from a competitive challenge, so before long he was leading his training battalion in the continuous physical competitions against other units.

Miller's never been the kind of person to seek a fight unless someone he cares about was threatened – just as well for anyone foolish enough to take him on, since one of the sports he excelled at was boxing. After basic training, he continued to serve as a physical training instructor. Two of his most notable trainees were Sandy Koufax and Don Drysdale.

Following basic training, Miller went through the obligatory testing and was assigned to a signal battalion, where he quickly mastered the requirements of Morse code and radio transmission, and then began his Reserve commitment.

Battling Boredom and "The Brass"

Military service has always represented a dramatic contrast between the fear, courage, and often extraordinary sacrifice of combat – and the long tedium of routine duties and training. But unless you served in a Reserve unit in those years between the Korean and Vietnam Wars, it's hard to appreciate the unimaginable boredom, punctuated by brief periods of frenzied, often purposeless activity, that characterized the service of America's "civilian soldiers."

Recruits reporting for basic training at Fort Dix, N.J., in 1957. Miller is top row, far left.

To kill time during the long hours in the radio truck at Fort Drum, N.Y., doing absolutely nothing, Miller would break radio silence with quick "Tokyo Rose" announcements: "American fighting man – you die," and then sign off before the location of the broadcast could be traced. His officers weren't pleased, but the troops certainly enjoyed the "enemy propaganda."

Miller has always been particularly irritated by pompous, arrogant incompetents in leadership roles – which perfectly describes his commanding officer on one of his Camp Drum tours of duty. This particular reservist colonel was insufferable. Everything about him was starched: his jacket, his pants, his blouse, his underwear, and his mind. Each day he would show up at the unit's headquarters and carefully hang up his jacket before proceeding to make everyone's lives miserable for eight hours. And each day Miller would flip the colonel's eagles on his epaulets so they were backwards. The colonel never noticed. Clearly, sterner measures were called for.

So one rainy night Miller tied a rope from the colonel's tent to the battalion's Jeep, and then called in an emergency. Sure enough, the response crew jumped in the Jeep and floored it – with the desired result of turning the tent and the colonel's meticulous uniforms into uncontrolled flying objects, before dragging them 20 yards through the mud. Trapper John and Hawkeye Pierce from M.A.S.H. would have applauded.

A Close Brush with Combat

Miller's one potential brush with actual combat occurred near the end of his service in 1961. He and his signal battalion were going through their obligatory summer service at Fort Drum when an officer came in, assembled the men, and one at a time asked them: "Do you have a will?"

"A will?" Miller responded. "What do I need a will for? The only thing I own is a beat-up car."

The next day the entire battalion was assembled and given a series of shots against tropical diseases. When Miller asked, "Why are we being inoculated against tropical diseases?" the predictable answer was "I'm sorry. That's only on a 'need to know' basis. And you don't need to know."

The third day, the same officer came back and this time asked the men: "What's your experience parachuting?"

Miller answered, "I went off the parachute jump at Coney Island twice."

"That's fine," the officer said. "You'll do."

"Do for what?" Miller asked.

"I'm sorry," was the now predictable answer. "That's only on a 'need to know' basis. And you don't need to know."

It was only many months later that Miller learned how close he had come to being called on to rescue the collapsing Bay of Pigs invasion of Cuba.

Left: Miller was assigned to the Signal Corps stationed at Fort Drum in upstate New York.

Right: Miller's unit was almost called upon to rescue the failed Bay of Pigs invasion of Cuba in 1961.

The Best Marksman in the Division

Miller's crowning service achievement came, interestingly, on the rifle range – interesting because while Miller loves competition and excels at meeting challenges he cares about, shooting an M-1 Garand rifle wasn't one of those challenges he cared about. But as a reservist, he had to qualify on the M-1 every summer or repeat the practice sessions for re-qualification.

When Miller's turn came on the range, his first shot hit the sand in front of the target, 100 yards away. He expected to see a "Maggie's Drawers" flag, indicating a complete miss, hoisted from the bunker where a scorer would grade each shot. To Miller's surprise, his score came back as a perfect bull's-eye with a hole in the center of the target.

So did the next complete miss, and each successive shot after it. Joe Poli, the soldier in the bunker downrange responsible for scoring him, was one of Miller's many buddies in his unit.

Joe just kept jabbing a pencil through the center of each untouched target. As Miller continued to rack up a spectacularly perfect score, a crowd gathered to watch this stunning display of Annie Oakley-style marksmanship. At the end of Miller's qualifying round, the commanding general at Fort Drum, who had watched the performance, pulled him aside.

"That was the most amazing display of accuracy I've ever seen in my time in the service," the general exclaimed. "I've just had the pleasure of watching the best rifleman in the division demonstrate his talent. I want you to join our rifle team. You also should consider applying for advanced sniper training. We need men like you!"

It took every bit of Miller's persuasive skills to convince the general that his commitment to teaching and coaching at Pingry was a greater priority for him. At the end of summer camp, Miller was called to the stage to receive the medal and award for best marksmanship in the division. His buddies roared with laughter and applause: "Bugs! Bugs! Bugs!"

The Army Reserves didn't offer Miller the specific opportunities he sought to meet the challenges of achieving honor and real excellence. That would change, forever, as he prepared to take on his life's work: teaching, coaching, and inspiring young people.

Miller and the Sweet Science

There was a time when boxing – "the gentleman's sport," as opposed to professional prize fighting – was a sport like tennis and golf that young men learned to master. Miller enjoyed the physical challenge and skill of "the sweet science" and competed in amateur boxing tournaments in the Army. The one time his judgment overruled his competitive spirit occurred in a tournament at Fort Dix. Miller and another soldier were scheduled to fight for their unit. The opponent who stepped into the ring against them looked really fast. "You take this fight," said Miller, "and I'll be your corner man." Given the pummeling his buddy took, it was a smart decision on Miller's part.

But Miller certainly wasn't averse to squaring off against opponents. In fact, Phil Burrows '55 remembers several times during their time in the service when, coming back from leave with Miller, he had to intervene to keep Miller from taking on argumentative MPs.

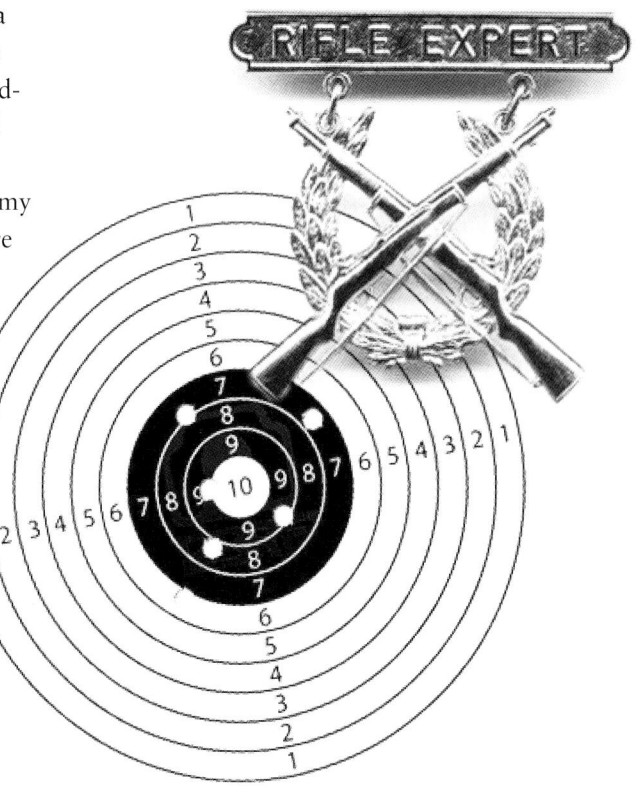

THE LIFE & TIMES of MILLER A. BUGLIARI

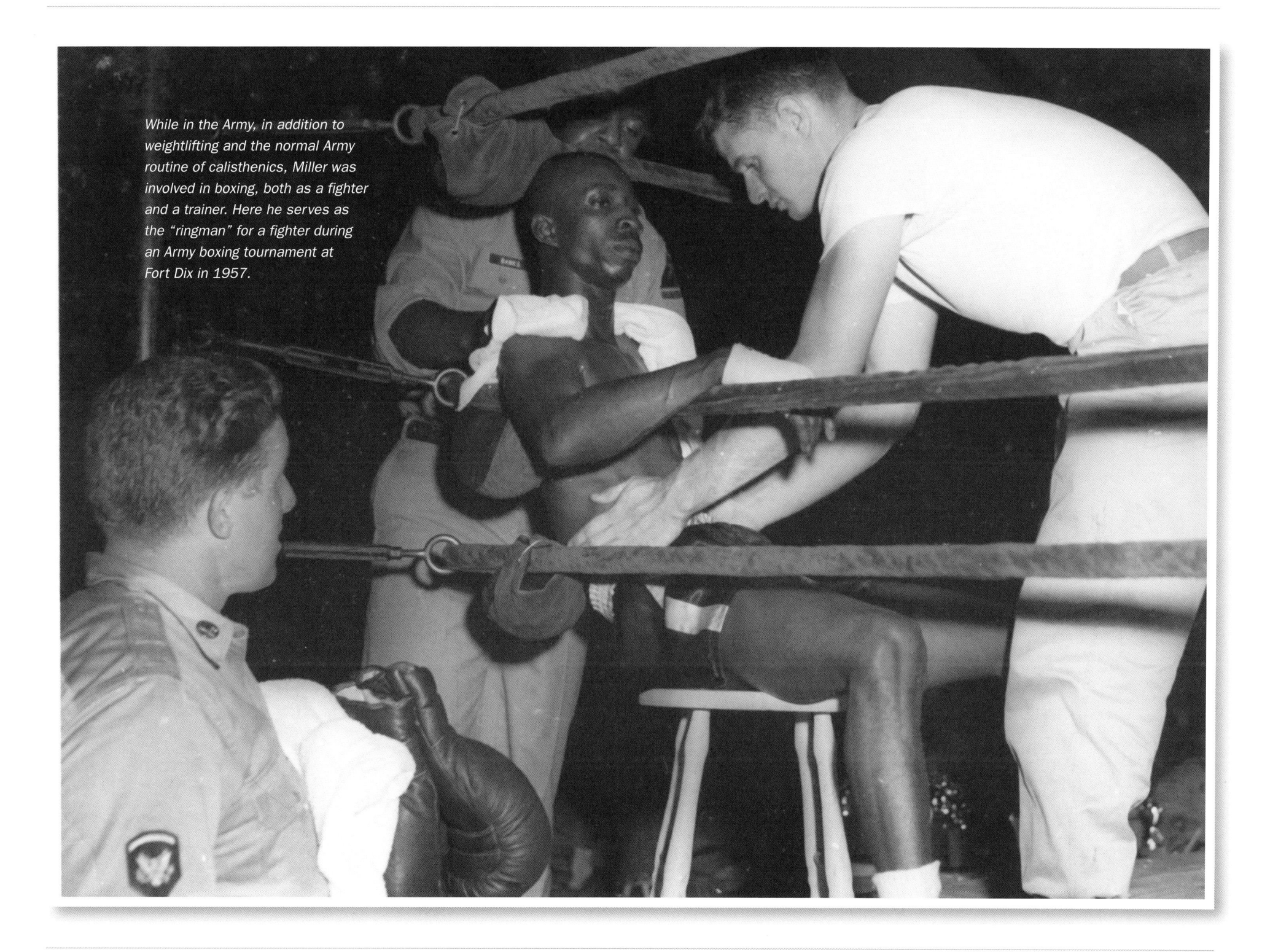

While in the Army, in addition to weightlifting and the normal Army routine of calisthenics, Miller was involved in boxing, both as a fighter and a trainer. Here he serves as the "ringman" for a fighter during an Army boxing tournament at Fort Dix in 1957.

Miller Stories #10

The Colonel's Golf Course

On one of Miller's summer "vacations" in the Army Reserves, he was stationed with his signals unit at the New York Thruway rest area that troops used for a break on their way up to Fort Drum near the Canadian border in the Adirondacks. Since, as usual, the signals unit had nothing to do, Miller had a lot of time on his hands.

Miller's constant nemesis, the colonel, had a tent set up for his personal use but was never there; Miller saw an opportunity to put the beautiful grassy lawn in front of the colonel's tent to good use. Like Trapper John from M.A.S.H., Miller always carried golf clubs with him on military duty – he just needed a golf course. So Miller and one of his buddies laid out a three-hole pitch-and-putt golf course in front of the colonel's tent, complete with poles and flags, and started playing.

It all would have gone wonderfully, except for the fact that Miller's buddy had a totally bald head that shone in the bright sunlight like a reflecting mirror, catching the attention of the Army helicopter crew flying over the rest stop. They looked at the guy, saw the golf course, an obvious infraction of military order and discipline, and called it in.

That managed to get the colonel's attention. When he pulled up from wherever he'd been summoned by the irate higher brass, he wasn't pleased – even when Miller offered to spot him five strokes.

Miller Stories #11

Military Disaster at Fort Drum

Miller's Army Reserve summers at Fort Drum typically concluded with "war games," simulated combat between the Reserve units and regular Army units. Miller was attached to his Reserve battalion's Headquarters Company, in charge of the signals unit responsible for radio transmission.

The night before the start of the simulated combat, the colonel retired for the night. Miller decided that the colonel was setting a good example to follow, so he went to bed, too, after turning off the lights – and the electricity powering the unit's radios.

When the aggressors launched their attack after midnight, there must have been frantic calls from the front line platoons engaged with the enemy. With nobody awake at headquarters, those calls went unanswered. And when the colonel awoke the next morning, his entire battalion had been wiped out. The procedure in a war game when units were captured or overrun was for the aggressors to put a big white "X" on the equipment or tents of the units they were attacking. There were "X's" on the headquarters company's vehicles and equipment, on Miller's signal tent, and on the colonel's tent, too There might even have been an "X" on the colonel's forehead. It was the most devastating destruction of a military unit since Little Big Horn.

Miller Stories #12

The Phantom of The Opera

"Back in the day," Miller says, "I used to always carry my monster mask with me in my pocket wherever I went. I never knew when it might come in handy. Wearing the mask, I was a lot less likely to get identified when I was pulling off stunts."

One evening, during a trip to Philadelphia, Miller took a stroll around the downtown. He was on Broad Street by the Academy of Music when he noticed they were putting on a production, Gilbert and Sullivan's *Pirates of Penzance* perhaps, and it occurred to Miller that here was an opportunity for "innocent enjoyment." Why walk around with a monster mask in your pocket if you're not going to use it?

So Miller snuck backstage, put on his mask, and started strolling casually across the stage in the midst of a big production number. The audience gasped. The orchestra and singers faltered for a moment, and then gamely went on, in spite of the fact that they were no longer the show the audience was watching. By the time Miller was halfway across the stage, the fact that he was the center of attention for over 2,000 people, including the Academy's security guards, caused him to pick up his pace. He was at a full sprint as he cleared the stage, dodged the guards, and lit out through an exit.

The next day's *Philadelphia Inquirer* headline read: "Phantom Strikes the Opera." Fortunately, this time the chandelier didn't plummet into the audience.

Miller Stories #13

Miller in the Fight Game

For someone like Miller in his twenties who loved boxing, the old Madison Square Garden on Eighth Avenue between 49th and 50th streets was the place to be: the squeak of fighters' shoes on canvas, the pop and thud of blows blocked and landed, the roar of the crowd, and the smell of sweat, beer, and perfume mixing with the tobacco smoke that gradually settled over the ring like a cloud. It was the best ticket in town, but Miller couldn't afford it. So he found another way in.

Miller and a friend equipped themselves with a canvas and wood stretcher, drove to the Garden and went in by the side entrance for fighters, carrying the open stretcher on the run. The cigar stub-chewing geezer at the desk guarding the door to the arena looked up from his racing form. "Hurry!" Miller said. "We gotta get the guy inside." Without a word, he buzzed them in. Once inside, Miller and his pal ditched the stretcher and looked for empty seats near the ring to enjoy the fights.

It was such a good scam, they decided to try it again. But this time, when they got to the door, the guard said "It's about time you got here. He's right inside!" Inside the door was a guy passed out on the floor. Miller gave him CPR until the real emergency squad arrived, then both he and his buddy got out of there before people started asking questions. And that ended the Madison Square Garden scam.

Miller Stories #14

Field of Dreams

Throughout the years, trips to the West Coast to link up with his classmate Bob Thurston '52 have been a constant in Miller's routine. One of the trips Bob remembers most fondly is their visit to Catalina Island off Los Angeles.

Few people will remember now that during the decades it was owned by the Wrigley family, Catalina Island served as the spring training headquarters for the Wrigleys' team, the Chicago Cubs. In 1951 the Cubs switched their training site to Mesa, Arizona, but the ball field they practiced on in Avalon Canyon still remained when Miller and Bob visited the island.

Bob can still see Miller, looking at the field for a few minutes to get everything in place. Then Miller strides up to the plate, takes a few practice swings and waits for the first pitch. The imaginary pitcher delivers. Crack! The crowd roars. "Sharp double to left," Miller cries out. "Now I'm on second base." He steps into the batter's box again, and after fouling off a couple of pitches he makes solid contact with the ball, driving it into right field. "I'm on first and third!" he yells to Bob. His next at bat results in a screaming baseline triple just past the lunging third baseman's glove. "Two runs in!" Miller cries, then he points excitedly at third base as the relay comes in from the outfield. "He dropped the ball! I'm coming home!" Miller safely slides under the catcher's tag, scoring an inside the park home run.

With his team now up by three runs, Miller takes the field. Again the explosive sound of bat meeting ball and Miller, in center field, is racing to his left. At the last possible moment before the high-arcing ball drops in for a base hit, Miller leaves his feet, dives, stretches his left hand, and scoops up the ball, tumbling over and into a standing position with the ball raised triumphantly in his imaginary glove. Once more, the crowd roars.

Miller closes out the ninth inning on the mound with three straight strikeouts that even Mariano Rivera would have admired. Bob can't remember a more exciting game. Naturally, Miller's team won handily.

They built the ball field, and Miller came. And he didn't even need Ray Kinsella's cornfield in order to create a team.

Miller Stories #15

Miller's New Ride

Miller and his pal Phil Burrows '55 completed their Army basic training at the same time, and now, free to enter civilian life, they turned their attention to serious things – like getting a new car. Phil had his heart set on buying the ultimate "chick magnet." Miller's needs were a little simpler – he just needed a car that would run. Phil found exactly what he wanted: a brand new, glistening black 1959 Chevy Impala convertible with red leather seats. He arranged with the dealer to hold the car for him until he came back in a couple of days to buy it. Knowing that the car was his, he didn't bother to put down a deposit. That was his first mistake. His second was boasting to Miller about his triumph.

The next day, Miller showed up at the dealership. "I'm buying a car today. That car," Miller said to the owner, pointing to Phil's black Impala, being prepped for delivery. "I'm sorry," the owner replied. "That car's been promised to someone else. Can I show you another model?" "Not really," answered Miller. "That's the one I want. I have cash and need the car now." Faced with an offer he couldn't refuse, the owner caved in, and Miller drove out of the lot in Phil's car.

That night, Miller showed up at a party at Chuck Wynn's, knowing Phil and the rest of the usual crowd would be there. He walked in after the party had started and invited everyone to step outside to see his new car. His buddies, knowing Miller's eccentricities with cars, laughed and responded with comments like, "What's wrong with the junk heap you already have?" But they went out to look anyway. Phil is still a close friend of Miller's, and they've had their share of adventures together, but he's never forgiven Miller for one-upping him on his dream car.

As it turns out, however, maybe there is justice in the world after all. Miller's joy in his new ride was short-lived. On his way back from a day at the shore with Tim McCarthy, Miller fell asleep at the wheel and smashed into a telephone pole, severing it from its base and knocking out all the power in Wall Township. Fortunately, even if blind justice was against him, luck was still on his side – the pole fell right between Miller and Tim. But the car couldn't be salvaged.

Camp **Waganaki**

Camp Waganaki was founded in 1919 by Carl O. Warren of Plainfield, N.J. Its purpose, sustained by Waganaki's subsequent owners – starting in 1928 with Walter Gardell and Charles Hamilton, followed by Vincent "Mr. Les" Lesneski from Pingry in 1945 – was succinctly expressed in Carl Warren's camp brochure:

"Waganaki is not just another camp for boys. It is too intimate for that, too much like a big family."

Miller's career at Waganaki started in 1953. "Dick Corbett '52, my longtime friend, told me I might like being a counselor," Miller recalls, "so Dick and I rode up to Maine in his late 1930s Packard convertible. We had a lot of laughs. The car was like a tank, and we never put the top up. It had a rumble seat, where we packed the luggage (and at other times smuggled friends into drive-in movies). Dick amazed me one time when the water pump broke and he spent five hours in a junkyard until he found and replaced the part.

The Grove showing campers' cabins.

"I really enjoyed being a counselor. I taught baseball and boxing and led overnight trips. On days off, I played for the Norway-South Paris baseball team. I was in left field once when a black bear decided to join the game and came over the outfield fence. You never saw players run so fast to get off the field."

Bob Popper '61 remembers Miller as a counselor: "I was one of many Pingry boys who attended Mr. Les's summer camp in Maine. Many of its counselors were Pingry boys too, and one of them was Miller Bugliari. He was the same vigorous, athletically involved, amusing, and engaging person we knew at Pingry, but at camp the showman within emerged.

"During amateur nights, and sometimes between reels of the weekly movie, he would produce props from his pillowcase 'bag of tricks' and ad lib to everyone's amusement. For example, he might don a pair of glasses with a rubber nose and mustache and do Groucho Marx. Or he would imitate a well-known TV pitchman – 'Dave Clark, For Better Living' – and try to sell us combination storm and screen windows."

Along with Pingry colleagues and former Waganaki counselors Dave Koth and George Christow, Miller bought the camp from Mr. Les in 1964. Miller and Elizabeth became sole owners a year later.

"When I bought the camp from Mr. Les," Miller says, "I had a clear idea of what I wanted Waganaki to be as a camp. I remembered from my Army days that a lot of new recruits had no idea how to take care of themselves or get along with a group of people. I was surprised how many of the guys I served with were lost, even homesick, at the start of basic training. I thought Waganaki could offer kids of all ages a well-rounded summer: living and cooperating with others, having fun and developing skills in team and individual sports, and experiencing the outdoors on camping and canoe trips. It was an opportunity to quietly teach values – dealing with sometimes difficult situations where they might not always get their own way, and learning to become leaders."

A Different Kind of Camp

A camp like Waganaki in Miller's years as owner and director couldn't exist today. It was a simpler, more primitive, more physically demanding, and certainly more innocent world, one without cell phones, e-mail, Twitter, and helicopter parents. Kids were less pampered and protected than they are now.

Actually, a camp like Waganaki should not have existed even in its own day. In order to attract the children of affluent suburban families, most sleep-away camps offered modern, air conditioned cabins with comfortable beds, toilets, and often showers. Waganaki's cabins may have been built by the Civilian Conservation Corps in the 1930s – and they looked it. In addition to "the Bink" – the bathhouse and lavatories in the Grove – the "toilets" the kids used upon getting up in the morning were the nearby woods. When Miller took over as director, recognizing the environmental harm it represented, he ended the long-standing Waganaki tradition of getting everyone clean for Sunday services by bathing in the lake – with soap.

When Miller invited Bruno Tomaino to come to Waganaki as Assistant Director, Annette Tomaino, with three small boys to take care of, asked Miller, "Will Waganaki be able to accommodate me and my children?" "Of course," Miller answered. "It's a camp. We'll provide housing for you." When Annette arrived at Waganaki and saw what Miller meant by "housing," she almost put the kids back in the car and headed home to Chatham. The rickety cabin she would have to spend the summer in had one small bedroom, an even smaller sitting room, a screened-in porch for the kids to sleep in, a toilet with a cold-water sink, and no bath or shower. As for recreation, she and the boys were only allowed to hike down to the lake for a swim when the campers were tucked away in their cabins for their rest period, and then their arrival would be announced with the same warning shouted out anytime a woman came down the hill: "Snakes in the Grove!"

But Annette and her family did wind up falling in love with Waganaki's natural beauty and quirky nature. Her three sons, Chris, Greg, and Mark, thrived as campers, and she and Bruno bought a cabin on Lake McWain, where they still vacation many decades later.

From the *Waganaki Log*, 1955

First Mount Washington Trip

The campers were transported by camp truck to Dolly Copp campsite outside of Gorham, New Hampshire, where they spent the night. After dinner, we went to the dance at Dolly Copp. Miller Bugliari, while going through his antics, was joined by a lady who felt sorry for him, so she danced with him.

The Bendito Dance

On Friday, twenty boys from the older cabins and six counselors and junior counselors went to Camp Bendito for a dance…. Miller was a big hit when he danced two numbers with his partner. He was such a big hit, in fact, that no one else danced; instead we all watched his performance. Miller also did a hilarious imitation of Fats Domino's *"I'm in Love Again."* One of the highlights of the camp when Mr. Les ran it and Miller was a counselor were Miller's (silent) 8 mm and 16 mm productions filmed during the summer and then shown to the boys the following summer and during camp reunions in winter. We called him Cecil B. DeMiller.

The Camp Movie

On Saturday night after the banquet, our camp had a double feature. The second film was Miller "Bugs Bunny's" production *"Robin Hood,"* starring Bert Lesneski as Robin Hood, Mr. Mente as King John, Mr. Speidel as Little John, Wix Borden as the Sheriff, and a cast of thousands. All the counselors were in the movie.

Memories of Waganaki

"At 7:00, we awaken to the sound of the 'Acme Thunderer.' Then, it's off to the wash house to brush our teeth. Up the hill to breakfast at 7:45. A bowl of Rice Krispies followed by French toast. After breakfast, we race back down the hill. The first campers to the sign-up board get their first choice of activities. Water skiing, riflery, archery, and woodshop are usually the first to get filled up.

"Cabin clean-up for 15 minutes, then off to morning activities. At 11:00, the Acme Thunderer signals time for instructional swim. Back up the hill at noon for lunch. Ravioli today washed down with grape bug juice. Red Jell-O for dessert. Then, time for the second big race down the hill for afternoon sign-ups.

"What's on the board for this afternoon? A baseball game against Wig-Wam? How does the wind look on the lake, a good day for sailing? Are the fish biting today? This is also the time to sign up for trips. A two-night trip leaving tomorrow for Mt. Washington. I could be back just in time to head right back out for a canoe trip on Flagstaff.

"Back to the cabin for 'rest' hour. Nobody (except the counselors) sleeps now. Time for letters home or reading comic books. At 2:00, time for afternoon activities followed by free swim. After swim, back up the hill (are you sensing a pattern here?) for dinner. Chicken and mashed potatoes are the fare tonight.

"After dinner, time for evening activities. Wednesday is movie night and woodcraft on Sundays. Some cabins walk to Springer's for ice cream. In the rec room, a few games of pool and ping-pong. In the lower Grove, tetherball, horseshoes, and basketball. On the level spot, always a softball game. If it is still warm at 8:00, time for a dip (not to be confused with an official 'swim'). At 8:30, milk and crackers for the younger campers, a trip to the wash house, and taps at 9:00. For the older campers an extra hour to read, joke, and play their transistor radios (680 AM WRKO from Boston) until sleep overtakes us."

Greg Tomaino

The Waganaki Experience

While parents may not have sent their kids to Waganaki for a luxurious summer experience, it's fair to say that most put their children in Miller's care expecting that they would return home stronger, more resilient, and better disciplined.

Regardless of whatever rules may or may not have applied at home, even the youngest campers in Cabins One and Two were expected to keep their personal space orderly, the cabin swept and clean, and their beds neatly made each day. Depending on the cabin counselor, that could include square "hospital" corners and a blanket "tight enough to bounce a quarter." It was easy to get into better physical shape at Waganaki, since getting to meals meant climbing to the dining hall at the top of a steep hill rising from the waterfront three times a day.

Kids learned to shoot at the rifle range following the NRA program. Range safety at Waganaki had a unique twist: Bruce Smith '69 remembers constantly having to be ready to yell "cease fire" when Geordie, the Bugliaris' basset hound, would come romping down the hill behind the rifle range.

Everyone learned how to swim. As Bill Hanger '64 recalls, "Miller couldn't swim, or at least we never saw him swim, and yet he taught the Red Cross Junior and Senior Lifesaving classes. He used to be rowed out to the float wearing black rubbers over his shoes. Imagine. He never got in the lake, and yet he was a superior instructor."

For many campers, Waganaki offered the first opportunity to experience the thrill of waterskiing, on Lake McWain. The more adventurous took the thrill to extreme levels. Guy Cipriano '74 remembers driving the camp boat past the dock at the girls' camp Wazayatah across the lake, with Timmy Heekin skiing behind with his swim trunks around his ankles, giving the girls a full Monty. He also remembers getting strongly disciplined by Miller for that prank, even as Miller worked hard to keep a straight face. One reason Miller might have had a hard time criticizing forays on Wazayatah was his own track record. When he was a counselor, a standard evening entertainment was "Throwing noise at Camp Wazayatah" – sneaking out in one of the canoes, paddling over to Waz', yelling at the top of their lungs, then quickly hiding their canoe in the trees along the shoreline to avoid the searchlight beam from Wazayatah's outraged owner. Invariably, the next morning Mr. Les would get yet another complaining phone call from Wazayatah; invariably he also knew how to find the perpetrator: "Bugs! What have you been up to this time!"

Among the most powerful learning experiences were the backpacking and canoe trips in the nearby White Mountains and on lakes and rivers in northern Maine that all campers, even the youngest, participated in. For many campers, experiences like sliding down the sand dunes of the Saco River, looking for the drowned village beneath Flagstaff Lake, ascending the headwall over Mt. Washington's Tuckerman's Ravine, or traversing the wind-buffeted, desolate alpine beauty of the Presidential Range above the timberline remain indelible images of their childhood.

Developing Leaders

Possibly reflecting on his own experience as a counselor, Miller challenged teenage boys to take on increasingly more difficult and demanding leadership roles – at an earlier age than in most other camps. It became a practice at Waganaki for a group of 20 of the older kids to break into smaller groups of five, led by a teenage counselor-in-training. Each group would start up the mountain range on a different trail, following its own route and checking in with White Mountain National Forest rangers to ensure they were keeping pace with the other groups.

Over the next days, groups would meet at a designated camping ground or Appalachian Mountain Club high-peak hut. Each kid in a group was responsible for himself, and the counselor-in-training was responsible for all of their safety. Map reading and compass navigation skills became second nature.

The six- to seven-day canoe trips on the Allagash and Penobscot rivers for the older campers were even more demanding. Once the truck, usually driven by Bill Hanger '64, dropped a group off at the put-in place, the kids and counselors were on their own, with a deadline to meet Bill a week later and a hundred miles to the north. Look at a map of Maine: North of Millinocket to the east and Greenville Junction at the foot of Moosehead Lake, there's no civilization until you reach the little town of Allagash on the Canadian border.

> "Miller gave me tremendous responsibility when he asked me as a first-year college student to take over running the entire tripping program, following Tom Behr. It taught me a lot about organization and taking on responsibility. I think I may have worked as hard that summer as almost any time in my life (and that includes 120-hour work weeks as a surgical resident). The only good thing about that job compared to being a resident is that I usually got to sleep at night. I think Miller's giving me the position as director of the tripping program was probably the greatest gift he ever gave me, as he taught me to take responsibility and lead. It also forced me to be extremely organized and to work well with others, which served me well in later life.
>
> "Miller was also very good about moving on when things didn't go perfectly, without placing blame. At camp I remember forgetting the food on a trip, and Eddie had to drive four hours back to get it; again, he let it go – I am sure he knew I felt bad. I think that has had an influence on how I handle mistakes in our business, although the stakes can be quite a bit higher in my job as a surgeon."
>
> **Ian Alexander '72**

If it rained, you either took care of your equipment and tent, or you would sleep in a wet sleeping bag and dress in soggy clothing. If you ran into strong headwinds on one of the lakes, you'd keep paddling – losing a day of progress was not an option. To make the trips for the older campers appropriately challenging, it was critical to develop leaders like Peter Sheldon, Wayne Curtis '75, and Fred Silhanek, who, regardless of

"For the 1971 camp season, Miller had bought eight gorgeous Old Town fiberglass canoes to replace the ancient, battered and dented 16-foot Grumman 'aluminum cans' he'd inherited when he bought the camp. Miller liked to walk up to the ball field, where they were stored. I suspect he would have preferred that the canoes could just stay there on the canoe trailer all summer, glistening in their pristine, shiny red beauty. So I immediately took them out for a day of whitewater training on the nearby Swift River. Unfortunately, the water level in the river was lower than I had anticipated, so instead of a swift river, we spent several hours picking our way through a 'New England rock garden,' leaving streaks of red paint on every rock we hit or scraped our way past. When we got back to camp and Miller saw what had happened to his once-perfect canoes, I think he wanted to cry. I figured it was just a process of seasoning: getting both the campers and the canoes ready for the challenge of the Allagash.

"And a challenge it was. Rapids can flip the best team in a heartbeat, regardless of their training, teamwork, and skill. So we dumped a canoe in the heavy water of the Chase rapids. It was submerged, open-end into the current, wedged against the rocks, with thousands of pounds of water pressure straining the fiberglass. Ian Alexander, my tremendously competent assistant, and I – helped by the strongest campers in the group – worked feverishly and hopelessly to free the canoe, and then we heard the fiberglass start to give way. We scattered to safety as the canoe simply exploded into pieces. We finished the trip with the two campers in that canoe riding in other canoes as passengers.

"On the eight-hour ride back to Waganaki from Fort Kent on the Canadian border, I thought of how I could explain to Miller that I'd lost one of his beloved new, and previously beautiful, canoes: A trick of the current had pulled the canoe free from the shore during the third-of-a-mile portage around the Allagash Falls and the canoe was swept over the 40-foot-high thundering cauldron; it was stolen off the trailer by a group of larcenous loggers; two kids were kidnapped by Quebec Separatists and I had to give them a canoe to gain their safe return. I thought about creating a story about alien abduction, but figured Miller would have preferred that I had been taken into the spaceship, not the canoe. In the end, Miller was happy that everyone made it back safely, although he still mourns the loss of his eighth canoe and never fails to remind me of it, now more than 30 years later."

Tom Behr '58

how tired and often soaked they might be after a day's paddling in the rain, would see that there was dry firewood and an organized kitchen at each campground stop.

The greatest challenge on those trips, however, was the real physical danger provided by the Class 2 and, in high water, Class 3 rapids the group was likely to encounter on the Allagash and other Maine rivers. White water can spill a loaded canoe in a second, dumping gear and paddlers into fast-moving water surging past potentially lethal rocks. A paddler's life could depend on developing the awareness and discipline, in the frenzied chaos of an overturning canoe, not to get trapped between a submerged canoe and a rock – and remembering, once you were in the water, to face downstream, feet up for protection, following where the water wanted to take you. It was up to kids like Tim Heekin, Scott Townley '75, and Scott Biedron '74 to go on point for the other canoes, finding the best way through hundreds of yards of fast-moving water and treacherous rocks for the others to follow.

Above: Miller with Bert Lesneski '54 after filming one of their pirate movies at Camp Waganaki.

The Sunday Night Council Fire

There was one element of a sleep-away summer camp that was noticeably not part of the Waganaki experience: the widespread ritual of "color wars," in which campers would be divided into rival teams for heated competition and awards for the winning team. These traditional internal clashes between campers were, in their own way, a team-building experience, but the desire to win often brought with it the less desirable consequences of hostility toward one's opponents and bullying by the older campers within one's team. That kind of disrespect for others was not Miller's vision for Waganaki.

What took the place of weekly color war awards was the Waganaki Sunday night council fire. Miller would use the end of the week to summarize what he thought had been the important lessons he wanted kids to think about. Then the show started. It was a bizarre, wholly unhistorical mix of different Native American cultures, presided over by a chief, or "Sachem," dressed in Plains Indian attire (in the historic homeland of the woodlands Abenaki) and wearing Walter Gardell's magnificent Sioux eagle feather war bonnet, with the floor of the council ring decorated by a feeble attempt at reproducing a Navajo sand painting.

The weekly council fire started with the lighting of the fire itself – as impressively as possible. One standard ploy was to place a camper some 20 feet up in one of the trees surrounding the council ring, holding a kerosene-soaked roll of toilet paper leading down a wire to the three-foot-high stack of wood, itself well drenched in kerosene. At the appropriate moment, the drums would reach a crescendo, the kid in the tree would light the roll, the fireball would plummet downward to ignite the council fire in an explosion of flame, and the chief would cry the name of the Great Spirit: "Wakanda!"

Pyrotechnics Engineered by the Sachem

Bob Hale '64 was Waganaki's Sachem for several years. He had an arsonist's love for impressive council fire lighting. Perhaps his greatest masterpiece was the time he laid a line of gunpowder along the dirt path leading through the woods to the campfire. At the right moment, the gunpowder would be lit, sending a fiery trail snaking through the woods toward the bonfire platform. That was the plan, anyway. Unfortunately, one of the "Indian" trail guides, Billy Miller '69, was a little careless with the flaming torch he was holding and prematurely set off the gunpowder underneath him – in the process igniting his breechcloth, the only garment he was wearing. Happily, Billy escaped without harm, but as people recall the story, his high-pitched cries and frantic gyrations would have made the most war-crazed Abenaki envious. "Wakanda!" indeed.

> "After being elected captain of the upcoming 1971 soccer team, I spent the summer of 1971 as head of the kitchen crew at Camp Waganaki. Every Sunday it was 'expected' that soccer players – counselors and kitchen crew – would participate in a full scrimmage or game against another team. But I enjoyed playing Indian at our Sunday night 'Woodcraft' campfires! Whenever Tom Behr needed someone to perform Indian dances, I would volunteer. One particular Sunday, Coach got really angry with me after I told him that I was performing that evening and couldn't play. After completing the 'Devil Dance' at the beginning of Woodcraft, which included loud rattles and an elaborate black-hooded, masked headdress, I made my way through the woods, up the hill, over the ledge, around the tennis courts and into the tall grass that framed the soccer pitch, all in my high-fashion Indian garb. I was hidden, watching the run of play, when the ball came down the sideline. In full war paint, whooping at the top of my lungs, and rattles shaking noisily, I sprinted onto the field, stole the ball from the other team, dribbled right by Coach Bugliari and shouted, 'are you happy now?' I passed the ball and continued sprinting off the field, down the path to the shower. I got Coach even better than I thought I would!"
>
> **Paul Ciszak '72**

Ghost Stories Around the Council Fire

Besides having a gift for incendiary drama, the other requirement for a Waganaki Sachem was to be a good teller of ghost stories, the final event of the Sunday council fire.

Bob Hale was a gifted storyteller, but to make sure the kids were sufficiently scared – that's the point of ghost stories, after all – he'd often hide an accomplice in the dark woods behind the last row of wooden benches, charged with leaping out with wild cries at the exact moment of the story's climax.

Miller recalls, "When Tom Behr was running the Sunday night council fires, I always got a little nervous, because he liked to make things dramatic and surprise me – and everybody else. And he loved the stage. If it started to rain in the midst of his final ghost story, he just kept going. The campers went home scared…and wet. His best, or worst, stunt – depending on whom you talk to – was when he buried Tim Heekin beneath a thin layer of dirt under the sand painting, where Tim stayed motionless through the entire ceremony, breathing through a plastic tube! At the climax of the ghost story, first Tim's hands and then his grotesquely made-up face emerged from the ground. It was spectacular. The entire first two rows of the youngest campers erupted in panicked flight through the woods back to the safety of their cabins. The next morning, the counselors in Cabins One and Two had a lot of sheets to wash."

But that was Waganaki. As befits a camp run by Miller, who once dashed across an opera stage in a monster mask, the Waganaki experience was intended to be both exciting and fun.

The Kitchen Crew

In addition to campers, counselors, and the senior staff and their families, the other members of the Waganaki community were the kitchen help, almost all of whom were members of Miller's soccer team. Even though the Pingry soccer players called Waganaki "Miller's illegal soccer camp," Miller was careful to follow the state athletic association's rules and restrictions on formally coaching his players in the summer. That doesn't mean they didn't spend eight weeks working hard on developing new skills and getting in shape – often until 9 o'clock in the evening. What they didn't get, however, was rich from the experience. Miller's unvarying response to the kitchen crew's pleas for a raise was "It costs me money to keep you here!"

Rick Raabe '75, co-captain of the state and prep school championship 1974 Hall of Fame soccer team, remembers:

"I accepted a job (an offer from Miller I couldn't refuse) to work at Waganaki in the kitchen. As head of the kitchen crew, in addition to my $150 salary for the entire eight weeks, I had a rare camp privilege – use of Miller's 15-year-old station wagon for an occasional trip into civilization. On one occasion, due to no fault of my own, a slight fender-bender occurred. Fellow teammate Mark Zashin '75 remains my witness. Upon our return to camp Miller immediately noticed the minor left-side and undercarriage damage. Although the car still worked fine, despite a few unusual noises, Miller insisted on a full, detailed accounting of the mishap. Upon counsel from then attorney-to-be Martin O'Connor '77, I told the truth: A red Mustang convertible with Arizona plates ran me off the road and I was fortunate to swerve out of harm's way and then brake hard, barely grazing a large pine tree. Miller, although suspicious of this tale but trusting his upcoming season's co-captain, alerted the Maine state troopers to 'Find that red Mustang.' The state troopers are still looking for the Mustang. At the end of that camp season when I went to get my $150 summer salary from Miller, I was instead presented with his estimate of damage repairs (surprise: $150!) for the old station wagon and given a firm handshake and a reminder that pre-season would start in two weeks and that I should get a haircut."

The Pingry students who served as counselors had a similar hard time prying money out of Miller's wallet. John Boffa '72 wrote: "Chris Colford and I were campers at Waganaki starting at age 10, and then we became counselors. We probably spent more time at Waganaki than Miller ever imagined or wanted. One year we decided to start a counselors' union. We felt that working conditions could be improved and counselors' salaries were much too low. So we formed Local 289, Counselors International. We even got a signed photograph from labor leader George Meaney mailed to Miller. I don't recall how we pulled that off, but Miller was impressed. The union became a forum for many counselor-centered activities – lobster feasts with large quantities of beer late at night, among other enjoyable events.

"To Miller's credit, he was amazingly tolerant of these activities, which no doubt caused him some trepidation from time to time. He had a great perspective on people, and he allowed us to do things which were great fun, and perhaps reminded him of outrageous things he did at the ages we were then."

The Presence of Miller

For Miller, every camper was important and deserved attention and respect. Jim Hodge '69 remembers: "The only time I saw Miller truly upset was when he learned that a group of Pingry boys at camp were picking on a quiet and shy boy who had the temerity not to come from Pingry. He was upset with the boys, but more upset with the counselors, me included. Why had we not stopped the teasing? Why had we not educated the Pingry boys about the meanness of what they were doing? Why were we not doing more to work with the quiet boy to ensure he had a good and happy summer?"

"It's fair to say the overwhelming percentage of Waganaki campers loved the experience, which is why we had so many returning kids year after year. But occasionally a new camper would get homesick. I remember one new boy who was just miserably unhappy his first week and told Miller at lunch, 'I want to go home.'

"Miller told him to come by the camp office after dinner and he'd put the call through to the boy's parents. In those days Waganaki was on a party line: three rings for the camp, two rings for the farm up the hill, and one ring, I think, for Springer's Store down the road. So when the teary-eyed boy sat down in Miller's office, Miller first dialed the party line and got a dial tone, which did no good, of course, and then flashed the off-on button of the phone twice. The phone rang a long time at the empty farm before Miller said, 'They must not be home. Let's try again tomorrow morning.' Meanwhile, Miller had gone to the boy's counselor to alert him to give the boy more attention and try to find something at camp the boy really enjoyed doing.

"The next morning the boy showed up again after breakfast. This time Miller rang for Springer's Store, suspecting that Wilma Springer would be on the line, which she was. He handed the phone to the boy so he could hear the conversation, then said. 'We're on a party line, and it's being used now. Why don't we try again at lunch?' This went on for a few more days, always with a different excuse; Miller is very creative. Perhaps four days after the boy came to him, Miller sat down next to him at breakfast; the boy was happily chatting and laughing with his newfound friends. 'Would you like to call your parents today?' Miller asked. 'Oh, no,' said the boy. 'I'm having too much fun. You call them and tell them I'm fine.'"

Bruno Tomaino

Through all the challenges, excitement, and at times chaotic bustle of a Waganaki summer, Miller's concern for each camper was the pervasive, unifying spirit that made Waganaki so memorable. He reached out to every single camper in caring, personal, and often hilarious ways, going from table to table at mealtimes to see how kids were doing, amazing campers by lifting impossibly heavy weights in the weightlifting shed – with two fingers – or calling on Chris Colford '72 at breakfast in Miller's characteristic bellow for the ritual of the previous day's sports news: "T-Bone! Time for ball scores!"

More than anything else, Waganaki in Miller's years as owner was an expression of what he believed in as a person. As Bill Hanger comments, "Miller took each of us where we were, sought out our strengths, recognized our weaknesses, and strived to make us more confident and stronger. I love Miller Bugliari for all the nice things he did for me. At a difficult moment in my young teenage life he told me that I was okay, and that made all the difference."

Miller Stories #16

Miller Breaks into Broadcasting

In the 1950s, TV broadcasting was still in its infancy and busy expanding into new markets. The first live broadcast in Maine took place in 1954, when White Mountain TV was licensed as an ABC affiliate operating out of Poland Spring, with a new 105,000-watt transmission facility high atop New Hampshire's Mount Washington. For its studio, WMTW chose the dining room of the historic Riccar Inn, built in 1913 to house the servants of the nearby Poland Spring Hotel. Broadcast TV in the 1950s was primitive by today's standards: The "set" consisted of a desk and microphone for the newscaster and a paper enlargement of a world map for a backdrop. WMTW's initial live broadcast with a studio audience was a big deal, and when they learned that the first-ever live TV broadcast from Maine would take place in Poland Spring, Miller and another counselor, perhaps Bert Lesneski or Phil Lobo, decided they'd catch the show. Not surprisingly, they showed up a bit late and ran through the portico entrance only to find the dining room doors closed and locked, with a sign saying "No Entrance. Broadcasting in Progress. Quiet." Having come this far, they figured they could still get in through a side door, so they sprinted around the side of the dining room to a set of tall glass doors. They could hear the newscaster's voice in the room.

They first tried gently turning the handle to quietly open the door. The door wouldn't budge. So they put their shoulders to it. At this point, it's worth mentioning that Miller was a serious athlete who put in regular time at the Waganaki weightlifting shed, and perhaps in the excitement they applied more force than was necessary. Or maybe the door was just stuck a bit. But when they hit it together, the door burst open, catapulting them through the paper map of the world that served as the backdrop of the broadcast set, ripping it in half. They tumbled on top of the newscaster, tipping over his desk, chair, and microphone and knocking him to the floor – as the cameras kept rolling.

In 1963, late-night talk show pioneer Jack Paar bought the station and began broadcasting a weekly show, but his were definitely not the first comedy skits on WMTW. Miller gets that award.

Miller Stories #17

Crashing the Carling Open

When one of Miller's buddies, Dave Skillman, invited him in August 1965 to attend the Carling Open in Sutton, Mass., Miller jumped all over the opportunity to hang out with golf's legends like Jack Nicklaus, Arnold Palmer, and, in his final PGA tournament appearance, Ben Hogan.

Miller flew to the tournament with John Nebel '65 in Nebel's Piper Cub. They took off from a farmer's field in Maine, but had barely gotten airborne when Nebel announced "We're experiencing equipment difficulties." With that, he threw the compass out the window and announced, "I have a road map. We'll get there by dead reckoning." Nebel completed the flight flying just above the treetops and *under* every set of high tension wires they passed. When they finally arrived safely at the airport in Massachusetts, Miller thanked John and said, "Thanks for the ride, John. No need to fly me back. I'll take a bus."

They were met at the airport by Dave Skillman, but when Miller asked about his tickets and passes, Dave announced "I don't have tickets for you. We're sneaking you in." Then he pointed to the pink Cadillac belonging to his friend, the club president, and told Miller, "Get in the trunk."

When they arrived at the Pleasant Valley parking lot, Dave popped the trunk and Miller hopped out, right into a crowd of curious kids. Miller gave them a serious look. "Be quiet about this, OK? I'm a special investigator operating under cover." Of course the kids spread the story like wildfire, so that by the second day, Miller was surrounded by all the famous players he had come there to observe, interested in learning what he was "investigating." Miller had a great time talking with them but never blew his "cover." He did take a bus back to Maine, however.

Miller Stories #18

Luck at Scarborough Downs

One summer before camp opened, Harold, the farmer up the road from Camp Waganaki, invited Miller to go to the races with him. "I got a horse running at Scarborough Downs; should do pretty good," was Harold's assessment. Harness racing, in those days at least, was a dicey business: trainers juicing up horses with gout medicine, baking soda or sheep dip; drivers fixing races or conspiring to block the favorite to let one of their pals win. Miller thought it would be a fun afternoon. So Harold and Miller made the hour-and-a-half trip to the racetrack, with Harold getting his betting courage up by taking repeated pulls from his flask.

Harold's horse, Candy Royal, performed as promised, taking second and winning $300. By the end of the day, Miller was still pretty flush, and he and Harold were talking about their bet when a driver Harold knew approached him with a hot tip. "We got a sure thing in the last race," he promised. So Miller gave his winnings to Harold to bet for him. They were at the rail, cheering like crazy, as their driver forged into the lead only to lose by a nose in the final seconds.

The next day, Harold showed up at camp with a big wad of money for Miller. "I thought our driver lost that race," Miller said, surprised. "Oh, I know," said Harold. "The guy threw the race. But we didn't bet on him."

Miller Stories #19

Paul Ciszak's Girlfriends

Paul Ciszak '72, captain of the 1971 soccer team, was one of countless players who dedicated themselves to emulating Miller. In Paul's case, however, the aspect of Miller's personality he decided to master was Miller's crazy antics – more specifically, he studied ways to drive Miller nuts, usually with great success. In the early days before political correctness imposed its calming hand, Miller was famed for being tough on players. His angry bellows would carry across the field and over the Pingry campus, probably disturbing residents on nearby Westminster Avenue. Paul's shenanigans actually drove Miller speechless at times, so that Miller's only recourse was to yank on Paul's hair in frustration. Why Paul isn't completely bald now is a tonsorial mystery.

Among Miller's pet peeves was the fact that Paul, a committed ladies' man, would often be accompanied by girlfriends at home games, like Debbie DeRosh and Patty Sullivan, who would stand on the sidelines and cheer Paul on: "Paulie, Paulie, he's our man…." To this day Paul still hears Miller's voice: "PAUL! GET IN THE GAME! LEAVE THE GIRLS ALONE!"

It would be unimaginable for Miller, therefore, not to look for revenge at being so misused. He got it when Paul, like so many other soccer players in the 1960s and '70s, got shanghaied to work on the Waganaki kitchen crew. Like most of the kitchen crew, Paul took advantage of the relaxed rules in the summer to let his hair grow fashionably long – which in those days meant shoulder-length hippie style. Paul still remembers getting all spruced up for a day off with a girl and coming into Miller's office to try to squeeze some advance pay out of Miller. When Paul walked in, freshly showered and with his hair neatly pulled into a ponytail, Miller looked at him without recognition, then stood up, walked around his desk, and offered to shake Paul's hand. "Hi. I'm Miller Bugliari, Camp Director. How can I help you?"

Miller's best stroke, however, occurred whenever Paul used the camp's phone to set up dates, especially with a serious girlfriend, Mary Ann Sideris, who came to Maine in the summers. Miller would wait until Paul had started the phone call with Mary Ann and then break in on the party line: "Paul? This is Mr. Bugliari. There are a couple of calls on the other line for you, one's from Debbie, I think the other girl's name is Patty. Both girls want to know if you're going to be seeing them tonight." Then he'd hang up and laugh while Paul tried to talk himself out of the mess Miller had put him into.

Miller the Wall Street Guru

Taking risks never bothered Miller personally. As Waganaki's director, however, being responsible for the safety and well-being of close to a hundred campers and counselors was an entirely different matter. Elizabeth remembers the anxiety that would weigh on Miller all summer long. So her mission each summer was to occasionally get Miller out of camp for a day just to relax, with Don Burt '69, a former soccer player and now a senior counselor, as her ally. But it wasn't easy. Miller could find a dozen ways to put off leaving camp for longer than a few hours.

Elizabeth was sure she had the perfect idea for a getaway in 1976, when one of Miller's friends, Ben Appruseze, came up with complimentary four-day tickets to the Montreal Olympics for Miller and Don. But even then, with their bags in the back of Miller's 1964 Chevy and Don in the driver's seat with the motor running, Miller was still procrastinating: "I can't leave yet. There's too much to do." Elizabeth solved the impasse. "Miller," she said, "You're going! GET IN THE CAR!" Then she told Don, "Don't come back with him until the four days are over!" Since Don was far more intimidated by Elizabeth than he ever had been by Miller, Don had no intention of bucking her instructions.

The Olympics were a wonderful experience. They had a great time catching Bruce Jenner's run to the decathlon title, the near sweep of gold medals for the USA swimming team, and Nadia Comanici's incredible performance in gymnastics. In the process, they discovered that along with their complimentary hotel room, they had passes to a VIP suite hosted by a Wall Street firm. The first time they walked in, Miller checked out the crowd and said to Don, "This is great! Let's pretend we're stockbrokers!"

The first evening after the games, Miller just mingled with the high rollers and listened, while Don, feeling utterly out of his element, stayed out of trouble with his mouth glued shut. The second night, Miller started mixing into conversations and sharing stock tips to an increasingly attentive audience. The U.S. market was still creeping back from the 1973-74 crash, so perhaps these guys thought some new ideas might help. As Don remembers, "By the third night, we were out on the veranda after dinner – cigars, premium single malt scotch, the whole deal – and there was Miller, in the center of a big crowd, with all these heavy hitters scribbling notes on what he was telling them. It was like they were listening to Warren Buffett. If I hadn't seen it, I wouldn't have believed it. Too bad I didn't have money to invest in his picks."

Miller Stories #20

Miller the Teacher

A Different Kind of Colleague

As a student, Miller, along with generations of other young boys, had passed each day beneath the wooden sign carrying Dr. Pingry's stern motto, a reminder that the excellence Pingry expected of students was not intended to be a carefree walk in the woods. Miller brought a refreshing, liberating sense of laughter and fun into that foreboding world in his years as a student, irresistibly engaging his many friends in his zany exploits and madcap humor. When he began teaching at Pingry in 1959, Miller naturally looked for allies among the faculty who shared his joyfully irreverent love of life. He found one in another new teacher, "Count" Tony duBourg.

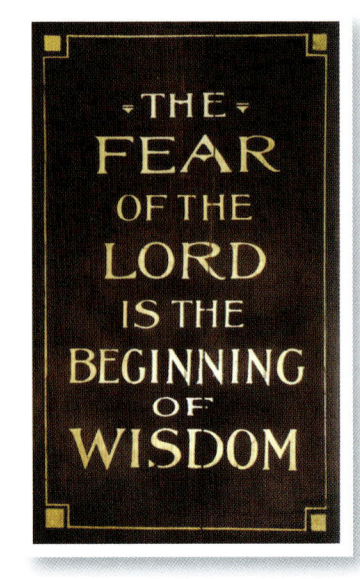

As Miller remembers, "We were both young teachers – Tony was obviously really smart and seemed somewhat normal when I first met him. That first impression of 'normality' changed very quickly. Early in my first year, Tony and I decided to go out for dinner, so he stopped by soccer practice after school. His glasses were broken and his nose was a little out of position. When I asked him what had happened, he said he had been scrimmaging with the 4th team football squad – in his Harris tweed sport coat and khakis. I knew we would get along.

"Of the many escapades that enlivened our friendship, one stands out. We were on a trip to Bermuda, and I wanted to explore the fossils in Bermuda's fabulous limestone caverns, so I invited Tony to come with me. We descended by a rope into the Crystal Cave with a group of scientists and professors, and after a short while found ourselves alone in a cave filled with stalactites and stalagmites; the rest of the party had gone on ahead. The temptation was too much for Tony. He began playing music on the stalactites as if they were gigantic chimes. It was an eerie, beautiful sound – and very loud.

"Back came the scientists and professors on a dead run, in angry disbelief at the noisy desecration Tony was committing. They demanded to know who we were and why we were there. Tony and I exited quickly."

The Far-Reaching Effects of Laughter

Anyone who has ever taught knows that teaching, done well, is hard, often frustrating work, with more than its fair share of drudgery. In department and faculty meetings, social gatherings, on sports fields and in gyms, or just in the hallways, Miller has always had the ability to remind colleagues that teaching – and life – becomes not just bearable, but meaningful when richly seasoned with humor.

And actually, his gift turns out to be even more profound. It was 20 years after Miller began teaching at Pingry that Norman Cousins first published the results of his experience with laughter in mitigating heart disease, and 40 years before the movie "Patch Adams" popularized the healing effects of humor. So there's no way Miller could have scientifically realized then what medical researchers are just now learning about the physiological and spiritual effects of laughter in successfully combating respiratory, cardiovascular, and cancer disease. Somehow, it wasn't surprising to see Miller intuit some things it would take scientists years to discover.

The Herb Hahn Breakfast Club

The laughter that emanated from Miller as a Pingry teacher gradually echoed throughout the school, and Miller found sometimes unexpected allies, like Herb Hahn. Herb was a teacher whom Miller, both as a student and later as a colleague, deeply respected and admired. Herb was, arguably, the wisest man to teach at Pingry in his generation, and even among the many brilliant teachers who have followed him, he would still stand out. He was also one of the quietest. Students learned to listen in Herb's classes because his whispered deep bass monotone compelled you to listen closely. Students made the effort because they sensed that what he was saying, however hard to hear, was wonderful stuff. But who would have guessed Herb's finely balanced sense of humor was as deep as his voice – and mind?

Bill LaCorte and Ernie Moody in the class of 1966 were not your "typical Pingry students." They were irreverently independent in a time when those qualities weren't appreciated – or even tolerated. So on the first day of discussion of *Catcher in the Rye*, when Herb asked Ernie what he thought of the book, Ernie's response was to toss the book into the wastebasket – a high lofting shot that dropped into the wastebasket perfectly. Nothing but net.

Lots of teachers would have thrown Ernie out of class. Herb just chuckled and said, "It's clear you don't think much of the book, Ernie. Could you tell us why?" It's not surprising, therefore, that when Ernie and Bill sat down in class one day and finished off the bagels they'd brought for breakfast, Herb simply commented that it wasn't considerate of them to be eating without sharing the food. Bill and Ernie reflected on that, decided Herb had a fair point, and showed up for the next class with coffee, bagels, pastries, cereal – the works. And Herb and the whole class had a breakfast that couldn't be beat.

For Bill and Ernie, looking back now on their Pingry years from the perspective of their very different, but similarly brilliant and creatively iconoclastic professional careers, the connection between Miller and Herb Hahn is clear. Without pushing the point too far, it's fair to say Miller opened the door for other teachers to treat students as individuals, valuing their differences and encouraging their creativity. A few teachers, like Herb Hahn, were already standing quietly on the other side. Many others followed Miller's lead and walked through that door themselves – along with their students.

The Italian Wing

When Pingry's new science wing was added in 1958, unlike the adjacent Hyde Athletic Building, it lacked a name. That changed in 1960 when Miller arrived to teach biology, followed shortly afterwards by the new head of the math department, Frank Romano, and new math teacher Manny Tramontana.

"Bugliari, Romano and Tramontana" gave the floor its new name: "The Italian Wing." When students walked past the old chemistry lab and Jack Dufford's office into the new math and biology classrooms, they entered not just a different part of the building; they entered what at times might have been a different planet.

Its epicenter was Miller's domain: the biology growing room. Doubtless the architects who laid out the plans envisioned something sedately academic – perhaps little plants blossoming innocently. With Miller running things, it quickly morphed into something much closer to the primordial ooze out of which life emerged. It became a menagerie. Students would drop off pets and stray animals to keep company with the animals Miller collected, including a stuffed cobra in striking position that terrified visitors and a large boa constrictor – a gift of George Ellis '66.

The boa constrictor, unfortunately, developed a talent for escaping from its cage. The first time it got loose over spring vacation, the janitors who stumbled on it when they came to clean the biology classroom were so terrified they refused to clean the room until Miller assured them the boa constrictor was more securely locked up. The boa constrictor didn't get the message. The next time it escaped, it slithered up onto the lab table, wrapped itself around the gas jet, and turned on the gas. Why the science wing wasn't blown up in an explosion is a miracle. Told he had to get rid of the boa, Miller went to look for him, and couldn't find him. The boa constrictor had escaped into Pingry's network of heating ducts to disappear forever into Pingry legend.

The strangest animal to take up quarters in the growing room was a student's pet monkey, newly arrived from Africa. Miller was naturally concerned about the health implications of contact between students and the monkey, and called the school's physician, Dr. Gonczy, who confirmed Miller's fears. The monkey had to go. So Miller arrived the next day to find that the monkey had suddenly died, and its owner had stretched it out on the biology lab table and was happily performing an autopsy, including removing the top of the monkey's skull.

> "When Pingry hired me in 1964 to teach math, I was really nervous coming to such a fancy prep school. I hadn't experienced anything like Pingry before, and like most new teachers (who in those days just got thrown into the job without any training or support), I worried about being able to succeed. I was well aware that I was joining a faculty where everybody knew everybody and I was a newcomer – I felt in those early days at times like an outsider. So I will always be grateful to Miller for being the first person to befriend me. He sat down at lunch with me, and made me feel welcome and part of the school. He also made me feel part of 'The Italian Wing,' with another terrific teacher, Frank Romano, even though Miller's way of 'welcoming' me was to torment me mercilessly."
>
> **Manny Tramontana**

It's hard to startle Miller – but the dead monkey with its brains sprawling over the lab table was too much. "Get that monkey out of here NOW!" he roared. The student gathered up the remains and headed for the door. Several minutes later, Miller looked out of the window, and there was the student, driving home in his convertible with the top down, and the grisly remains of the monkey buckled into the right front seat.

Not everything in the growing room was alive, however. Another of Miller's prize possessions was a sheep's heart, well on its way to decomposition. One of Miller's favorite ploys was to use it to illustrate to biology students the diffusion of particles in the air – in this case the particles that carried the nauseous smell of the rotting heart all the way to the back of the room. Miller must have thought that Manny Tramontana would benefit from the same science lesson, so from time to time, the sheep's heart would show up on the desk in Manny's classroom.

Somewhere, Miller also picked up a really loathsome, 14-inch-long stuffed rat. Miller thought Manny might enjoy that, too, so he hid it in the knee well under Manny's desk while Manny was at lunch. Manny got about 10 minutes into his next class before he pulled back his chair and saw the rat. Miller popped into the room from where he'd been hiding just outside the door to see Manny standing on top of his desk, screaming.

Don Burt '69, who returned to Pingry to teach biology, remembers the time an alumnus with a passion for ornithology donated his collection of hundreds of stuffed birds to Pingry, all of which were deposited, carefully boxed and labeled, in the growing room. Don and fellow teacher John Hutchinson liked to liberate a few small birds at a time and stuff them into the pockets of Miller's sports jacket to keep him company on his way home after school. Miller put a stop to that quickly, but he and Don thought Manny might appreciate the bird collection. So Don and Hutch took a huge bird, probably an Andean condor with a seven-foot wingspan, rigged it up with fishing line, and dropped it out of the window of Don's classroom right above Manny's, so it would appear to fly right outside Manny's window.

Manny, with his back to the window, couldn't see the bird; his students certainly could. As the class erupted in yells and laughter, Don and Hutch jerked the bird up out of sight. Once Manny had restored order, down went the bird again, to an even more riotous explosion from the kids. This went on several times until the class was in an uncontrollable uproar. Then Miller burst through the door into Manny's room yelling, "Hey Trem! Can't you control your class! I'm trying to teach next door!"

Then, as icing on the cake, he went to Frank Romano, Manny's department chairman, and told him, with a classic Miller straight face, "Frank, you've got to talk to Manny. I'm trying to run my lab and the noise from his classroom is deafening. My kids can't concentrate. Can't you keep your department quiet?"

It wasn't exactly "the Fear of the Lord," but when you worked in the Italian Wing, you had to keep your wits about you.

> "After graduating from Pingry in 1959, like Miller, I went to college at Springfield and returned to Pingry to teach biology and coach from 1966 to 2001. I consider Miller a great friend. We shared many wonderful times together. He still takes the time to call me often to tell me about Pingry and to ask how Joan and I are enjoying retirement in North Carolina.
>
> "I have many fond memories of Miller, but one in particular I find rather amusing: Each year we had a Back-to-School Day for parents to learn about courses and to meet the teachers. Since one of our sons had a Parents' Weekend at his college on that day, I wasn't able to be at Pingry. I taped a presentation to play for the parents and left the tape on a cart in the Bio room for another teacher who was going to cover my class.
>
> "Miller still claims he thought the tape was his and took it, leaving a soccer tape in its place. You can imagine how surprised the parents were when they were shown a soccer tape in a biology class rather than my presentation. Leave it to Miller!"
>
> **Tom Johnson '59**

More Fun with Miller

Miller's fun with faculty members wasn't just limited to school. For many years, Miller and Elizabeth had a standing bridge game with faculty colleagues Fred Fayen and Manny Tramontana. In spite of the fact that Miller, like his father, is an accomplished, passionate bridge player, according to Fred, he and Manny never lost (and a Harvard graduate like Fred would certainly not distort the truth).

Miller's idea of "fun" extended, as well, to offering to chauffer alumni to weddings and other events in his classic 1949 Cadillac. Sometimes they actually arrived at their destination on time.

Besides many escapades in New York restaurants and clubs, Miller also participated with faculty friends and students as a member of the Metropolitan Opera in the 1960s.

Alumni Quiz: How many faculty members can you correctly identify?

Alumni Quiz: Can you spot Miller in this photo? (See page 72 for the answer)

"I first met Miller when I joined the Pingry faculty in the Fall of 1960. As two of the younger and more athletic members of a predominantly male faculty, Miller and I quickly became friends as well as colleagues. During those first few years, Miller was a truly supportive advisor for me, easing my path into Pingry and New Jersey, and leading to an event in our home which ultimately became Miller's 'first date' with his wife-to-be, Elizabeth Budd, whom I helped hire as a member of the Pingry faculty.

"Miller makes you part of his 'family,' which in Connie's and my case included our sons, all of whom played for Miller and continued soccer in college – Dave at Wesleyan, Chuck at College of Wooster in Ohio, and Chris at Connecticut Wesleyan, where he was captain his senior year.

"Over the years, Miller and I spent many evenings in New York – largely at jazz clubs – which generated multiple humorous (and occasionally embarrassing) experiences. We still go into New York City frequently to visit art museums and enjoy our shared interest in World War II history. We often have lunch with our joint friend and ex-boss, John Hanly, reminiscing on old times and keeping our mutual and ongoing friendship alive.

"I know from firsthand experience that Miller is one of the main pillars that make Pingry the giant in the educational world it has become."

Dave Allan

Miller as a Competitor

At Pingry, the best ticket in town for years was courtside in the old gym to watch the three-on-three half court battles after school among the faculty.

At any point in time, the game might include Frank Romano, George Christow, Dave Allan, Tom Johnson '59, Toni Bristol '41, Manny Tramontana, Dan Phillips '59 and, naturally, Miller. The competition was fierce. They were all close friends – until they stepped on the court – then the gloves came off.

"Nobody really wanted to guard Miller," Dan Phillips recalls, "or contest him for a rebound." The games were also side-splittingly funny. At any point in the game, Miller could throw in a Harlem Globetrotters move that would have delighted Sweetwater Clifton or Goose Tatum. Miller loved basketball like a gym rat and would play it anywhere – as he did in his early years in the summer industrial league for Futter Brothers Shoes on a "Pingry All Star Team" that included Herbie Busch '55, Frank Romano, Dave Allan, and students Tony Borden '62, Rick Ill '61, Walt Long '63 and Howie Zatkowsky '63. They led the league in fouls and physical play. As the newspaper write-up of one game reported, "…tempers flared and several players squared off, but order was restored." Just another night on the court for Miller.

"In the spring of 1963 I was in the Buttondowns under the direction of 'Count' Tony duBourg. One evening after rehearsal we wound up at a nearby golf driving range. Miller was there, too. I had been playing golf for a couple of years and thought I was an OK player. Imagine our astonishment when Miller got up and hit ball after ball, straight and true, with only one hand! We expressed our admiration, and the biology teacher said to the physics teacher, 'It's only physics!'"

Todd Williams '63

Miller as a Mentor

But Miller's gift to his colleagues hasn't just been laughter. Generations of new Pingry teachers, struggling to understand the difficult, challenging role they have taken on, have found in Miller a wise and supportive mentor. And teachers and administrators are no more immune to the pain and tragedies of life than anyone else. His friends on the faculty have always appreciated what his students have learned: when you're in trouble, see Miller. When one is going through a hard time, one's friends, with the best of intentions, usually tell us what they think we should do – based on their own experience. Miller asks a different question: "What do you think you should do?" No matter what he's doing at the time, when you need him, he's there – and he stays with you.

In thinking about how he has related to colleagues over the years, Miller says, "Most people don't see their own faults easily, including me. A lot of faculty members get too serious. But when you take your work too seriously, you can make big mistakes or wind up burning yourself out; when you take yourself too seriously, you can hurt others.

"Humor and laughter open the window for us to see ourselves more clearly, in ways that let us change where we need to change. It doesn't work to keep harping on what people did wrong. Over the years I've learned, probably slower than I should have, that what works best for me is constructively asking what others think might be a better approach – not laying down the law, but clarifying choices and consequences. You never want to discourage people. When things go wrong, sometimes you have to wait to give feedback, and share in the responsibility yourself. 'When we did this, what were we thinking? How did that work out? How might we do it better?' But you have to confront problems and mistakes. If you don't, people just fail later on. That's bad for them and bad for the people they work with and the students they teach."

From Teacher to Advisor

In 1978, Miller began transitioning from the role of a teacher to that of advisor to the school's headmasters when he was appointed Director of Alumni Affairs and his teaching responsibilities were reduced. It was an obvious appointment: in many ways, Miller was a touchstone for everything that alumni valued about their Pingry experience. As former Pingry teaching colleague and headmaster (1980-1987) David Wilson '59 acknowledged, "Miller was Pingry's director of alumni affairs long before he was given that title. He has always had an impressive following of former students who have stayed loyal to him and, through him, to the school. It just came naturally. As an individual who has been instrumental in keeping so many alums connected to Pingry, he has contributed to the school's success way beyond his efforts in the classroom and on the soccer field. I'm not sure how often Miller actually asked alums for their support. I am sure he was a major reason they gave it."

By 2000, Miller had reached the age when many men start thinking about golf courses and grandchildren. But Pingry wasn't done with Miller yet, and anyway, it's impossible to imagine putting the words "Miller" and "retirement" into the same sentence. That year, one of new headmaster John Neiswender's first steps was to appoint Miller Assistant to the Headmaster for Alumni Affairs.

Neiswender was deeply committed to making Pingry a more student-centered school. In that effort, he couldn't have found a better ally than Miller. In fact, Miller has always been a champion for the needs of students since his earliest days at Pingry. Miller's Pingry teacher, mentor, and friend Ed Cissel '39, who left Pingry in 1967 to become a revered headmaster at the John Burroughs School in St. Louis, noticed this quality in Miller early on: "What stood out most about Miller was his extraordinary ability to relate to and gain the trust and confidence of students while still holding them to the highest standards of expectation and achievement."

He still upholds that commitment to students now with John Neiswender's successor, current headmaster Nat Conard, who observes: "As headmaster, I have to pay attention to the many stakeholder groups that make up the school community. Among all those different viewpoints, it might be easy for voices of students to get drowned out. Miller makes sure that doesn't happen. He cares about students as the lifeblood of the institution."

A headmaster, like any other person in a leadership role, has to balance at times significantly differing agendas while recognizing that each stakeholder group he deals with, faculty, students, parents, trustees and alumni, sees the complex whole of a school largely from their own often partial perspective. A major part of Miller's value to headmasters is the same quality of fairness that has made him so trusted and beloved by so many students and alumni. He understands and relates to people as they are, without judgment – while invariably focusing others on the question: "What's best for the school?" Miller sees the forest and each separate tree at the same time.

Generations of trustees have felt that same confidence in Miller's wisdom. As Miller's classmate, Kim Kimber Jr., reflects on Miller's influence with him as Chairman of the Board of Trustees from 1988 to 1995: "I knew I could always count on Miller's insight, his integrity, and his tactful respect for people to help me clarify issues and provide guidance to the administration as a trustee."

That trust has also allowed Miller to be an unofficial "advisor" to headmasters in his latest role as Special Assistant to the Headmaster. When Nat Conard joined Pingry as headmaster, Miller remembers, "I would tell him to make sure he goes once a day on a little trip around the school and goes in the classrooms, or goes to see the last guy on the ladder in tennis or the 25th guy on the team." From a coaching perspective, it's not all that different from telling a talented soccer player: "Get rid of the ball faster to an open teammate instead of dribbling into a crowd."

Kim Kimber Jr.

As it has with so many students, trust between Miller and the Pingry headmasters he's worked with turns into friendship. Conard notes, "Over my nine years as headmaster, Miller's role has evolved into 'Ambassador at Large' for the school. We've made countless trips across the country together meeting with alumni groups; he's a wonderful, enjoyable traveling companion. But when our formal duties are over and we're no longer 'on stage' in the different roles we need to play in representing the school, what I treasure most are the personal moments afterwards with Miller. We'll go to a famous restaurant in whatever city we're in – Miller seems to know them all – and spend a quiet time in reflection and conversation about the deeper questions and issues that can so easily get submerged under the constant pressure of official responsibilities." Generations of Pingry students have enjoyed that same experience.

Mr. Pingry

But arguably, with all that he does, Miller's greatest contribution to the seven headmasters he's served and the many trustees he's supported goes to the foundation of their joint mission: ensuring that Pingry survives and grows as a vibrant institution while still reflecting its deep roots, traditions, and heritage. Miller's Pingry classmate and Pingry colleague, Gordon Lenci '52, who became headmaster of The Barstow School in Kansas City, observes: "What Miller offers is what every headmaster would kill for: someone who captures the school's traditions and history and turns them into a living presence for current students and a powerful motivation for alumni to stay connected with the school." Nat Conard agrees: "The truth is, first and foremost he cares profoundly about the school as an institution with great history and character. It's remarkable how closely he identifies with Pingry and for so many people is synonymous with the school."

"When people ask Nat Conard what 'Special Assistant to the Headmaster' means, Nat usually tells them: 'It means I work for Miller.' Nat may chuckle when he makes that comment, but it is clear that there is something powerful behind the humor: Miller's vast network of very close relationships across generations of Pingry students, parents, and trustees. I have never seen Miller abuse his unique position and influence, but he has never been reluctant to give respectful, candid, and constructive advice when he thought it appropriate.

"In general, Miller has been uniquely positioned to provide perspective and continuity to headmasters and trustees as they assumed and exercised their roles over the years. Eight decades of Pingry experience give him that perspective. New leaders often have new ideas and different approaches about how the school should be run. This is generally a good thing. It allows the school to stay on the cutting edge of secondary education and to remain contemporary in its methods and curriculum. A great school needs to adapt to stay great. But it is equally essential to maintain a certain continuity with the best of the school's defining traditions and to preserve the core values that made the institution great in the first place. That is the role that Miller has assumed. Honor and excellence are watchwords at today's Pingry. But qualities such as personal integrity, fair play, teamwork, mutual respect, and civility are values Miller also makes sure continue to be an essential part of what makes Pingry a great school.

"Miller believes that Pingry has from its earliest beginnings sought to produce multi-dimensional individuals. 'Well rounded' is a hackneyed phrase these days, but behind it is the idea that adolescents should test the waters of different areas of endeavor rather than being specialists in one thing at the expense of trying others. It goes without saying that he feels athletics and team sports are one obvious way to foster this broader concept of education, and he is tireless in efforts to convince administrations and school leaders that athletics are not extra-curricular, they are core-curricular.

"But Miller is not just the Ghost of Pingry Past, haunting recalcitrant school leaders at midnight. He is a counselor, a friend, a resource, and the source of a wealth of knowledge that can help headmasters and trustees fulfill their duties. If he is occasionally a bit of a burr under the saddle for some, most suffer that gladly, given the value he adds. And when someday he is no longer around to provide the benefits of his wisdom and perspective, future headmasters – and the school – will be the worse for it."

Stephan F. Newhouse '65
Pingry Trustee

A Different Kind of Teacher

Miller wasn't just a startlingly different colleague, he was a different kind of teacher. His guiding principle was then, and has always been, Dr. Pingry's other motto: *Maxima Reverentia Pueris (et Puellis) Debetur.* Miller's teaching style, however, was far more reminiscent of "Miller Mayhem."

Bill Thiele '65 remembers: "I took biology with Miller that first year, and his class was unlike any other I had ever taken before (or since). He breathed life into biology and brought the same enthusiasm to class that he used so effectively as a legendary soccer coach."

Marc S. Feldstein '82, M.D., remembers Miller's infectious sense of humor and creativity. "Mr. Bugliari was my 10th grade biology teacher. Because of him, I STILL remember the mnemonic COFGSV for class/order/family/genus/species/variety. He would walk around the school, and when he saw you he'd yell 'It is because of the bio!' – everything was bio! When he was teaching, in the middle of a sentence he'd walk out the door of the classroom and keep talking from the hallway. We students loved it. Classic!"

But Miller's humor was always in the service of learning. Cope Eschenlauer '80 speaks for many Pingry students in acknowledging Miller's influence: "I pursued a doctorate in biochemistry because of my love of biology that began as I studied under Mr. Bugliari's and Mr. Whittemore's instruction." Ray Robinson '67, M.D., started on the 1966 soccer team. For him, the lessons Miller taught as a teacher and coach were inseparable. "The work ethic [I learned from Miller] has been critical to my own successes, and I can only hope that I have been able to instill the same spirit in my own orthopedic resident teaching responsibilities here at the University of Washington. My best memories of Miller are actually in his biology class. His sense of humor was infectious. It made learning fun."

Bruce Jacobsen '78 remarks, "I will always remember biology with Miller because he constantly sang 'Urea' to the tune of 'Maria' from *West Side Story*. You could hear him bellowing it out halfway across the school. I'm not sure Miller knew any of the words from 'Maria' besides the word Maria, so his Urea song was blessedly brief.

"One of Miller's great virtues is his self-deprecating sense of humor. At times we got sick of biology, of course, as we tried to memorize all the parts of a flower, or stages of cellular mitosis. Our class decided to starting chanting 'Boo Bio.' Of course, Miller picked that up as his theme, so he too would start chanting 'Boo Bio' as he would hand out tests and the like. Instead of taking it as an insult, he could just commiserate with us, and we knew he was the type of teacher who would not take too much offense. It was amazing how that made him one of us, and helped us trust him."

"In the spring of 1965 Miller coached the freshman baseball team, of which I was a member. Besides the fact that we were always the only team still on the field practicing while it was pouring rain, he also used to drive a number of us to the away games in his convertible. In his car, for some unknown reason, Miller had a sign, kind of a small placard that read 'CLERGY.' After one game and another loss, Miller was racing to get us back to school, and himself off to some other escapade, when he cut off another driver on busy Rt. 24. Astutely, the team's catcher, Pete Davenport, flashed the 'CLERGY' sign to the other driver as the small contingent of the freshman baseball team and their coach sped away. Just another of the expected antics of this intense yet fun-loving Pingry personality. Time with Miller was often unusual!

"Years later I did manage to somewhat return the hair-raising favor – sans the 'CLERGY' sign – in attempting to get him to an Amtrak train following a Baltimore alumni event."

Vic Pfeiffer '67

The Method in the Madness

Miller's madcap sense of humor is the most obvious aspect, perhaps, of his teaching. It's far from the only aspect of how he has helped generations of students learn, however. Miller is also a coach, and a coach's effectiveness, unlike that of a teacher's, gets measured every time the team steps out on the field against an opponent. A coach who cares about success can't afford to put a team on the field whose skill level and competitiveness are measured on a curve. Opposing coaches and teams will find the "C" and "D" players and exploit their weaknesses. As a coach, therefore, Miller had to do everything in his power to ensure that every single player improved continuously, as measured against the highest possible standards of excellence. That challenge meant understanding deeply how players improve physically and mentally, recognizing and capitalizing on their unique individual strengths. It also meant simplifying what players needed to learn so they could master it step by step, gaining confidence in their ability with each new skill they developed.

The same approach has characterized Miller as a classroom teacher. And beneath all the combination of pressure and humor, Miller has always communicated a deeper message to his students – the same message his soccer players have always understood: "I believe in you. You *can* do this."

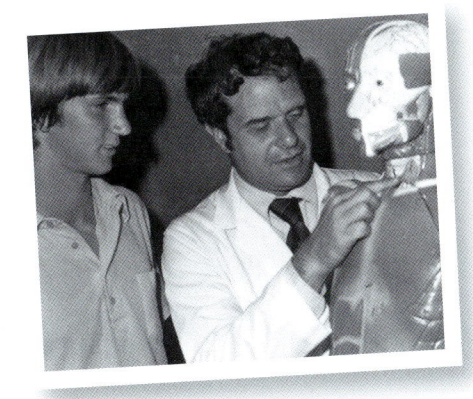

Since the beginning of time, teenage kids have tested, challenged, and often tormented teachers as part of figuring out what it means to become adults themselves. Miller has always welcomed that competition – while making sure that, as with any competition, he doesn't lose. What most biology students didn't know was that Miller angled the windowed door to his office next to the biology classroom so that he could secretly observe what kids were doing in the room when he wasn't present. In retrospect, it was probably even harder for students to get "one up" on Miller than it was for opposing coaches to walk away from a Pingry game with a victory.

"After my father, Miller Bugliari is one of the best men I've ever known. He never coached me – I played football, not soccer – but he truly influenced my life.

"At the end of many of my biology classes, wearing his white lab coat and holding a yardstick, Miller would move from student to student and gently tap them with the yardstick on the arm, chest, or shoulder while asking phylum questions. When he got to me, he didn't tap or whack, because I stuttered and he was sensitive to that.

"I stole Miller's technique five years later and applied it as an Army Airborne Ranger lieutenant in Vietnam. Before every mission, my teams and I spent hours planning, map reading, reconnoitering, and rehearsing. Before we loaded the Hueys for the infiltration, there was a last inspection. I had my guys jump up and down to ensure there were no rattles or giveaway noises. Then Miller's technique took over. I didn't use a yardstick, I used an M-16 cleaning rod. I'd tap my Rangers on the arm, chest, or shoulder while asking them questions about the mission. 'What's the alternate radio frequency?' 'Where's the rally point if we make contact at map reference X-Ray Papa?' Miller used the technique to help kids learn; I used it to help my men stay alive. I think that my troops respected me for my cleaning rod as much as I know Miller's students loved and respected him for his yardstick."

Burr Hazen '66

"I took Miller's Biology class in the fall of '59 – my first year at Pingry – along with a mixture of sophomores, juniors, and two seniors. Our first test was tough, and one of the seniors asked Miller if he would add a 'bonus' question, so Miller obliged: 'How many penguins are in the picture on page xx of the textbook?' (Remember that these were closed-book tests in those days.) The correct answer, for which you received the full bonus credit, was sixteen and a half...."

Rik Alexanderson '64

Antoine the Skeleton

George Ways '67 told the following story at the 50th Anniversary Celebration for Miller: "In 1963 I was a freshman taking Miller's biology class on the old Hillside campus. And all of the apocryphal stories of how he used to rant and rave and punish the class or individual 'hacking' offenders with writing multiple copies of the Okapi (forest giraffe) phylum are absolutely true. Our problem was, of course, how to get back at him for this monotonous practice – in an appropriately respectful way, of course. The one true prize of Miller's classroom was 'Antoine' (named after Tony duBourg). Antoine was Miller's complete, wired-together skeleton that was always hanging in the front of the class. As with all things Miller, it came replete with the obligatory side story as to how he found the body in the streets of Calcutta, and had it cleaned up and shipped back to Pingry.

Miller in Biology class with "Antoine" the Skeleton.

"Looking back on it now, I'm not even sure Antoine was real or plastic, but we all believed. So following either a lab or mandatory Okapi session, three of us set out to rewire Antoine. Basically, we loosened the connections to the legs just enough for them to continue to hang, but then release at the slightest touch. In the ensuing class we expected Miller would, as always, use Antoine in some manner of explanation and set off the leg release on his own – thus none of us would be directly linked to the deed. But as with all ill-conceived acts of vandalism, it wasn't going according to plan. Miller lectured for 75 percent of the class without ever once referring to Antoine. Those of us who were in on the plan grew more and more frustrated with each minute.

"Finally, I could stand it no more, and in a split second of potential career-ending angst, I acted. While Miller was discussing the disease rickets, I asked him where it manifested. He naturally verbally replied. Persisting, I asked him to show us on Antoine. He complied, the bones scattered, the class roared, I was awarded seeming millions of Okapis to write, and a Pingry tradition was born. After he later convinced us that Antoine could suffer damage if we took him apart, we wired Antoine for thread-assisted puppet-like obscene hand/finger gestures. More Okapi! I knew some stuff about 'forest giraffes.'"

Ward Tomlinson remembers the yearly assemblies in which Miller recounted some of the incredible pranks that he and his pals had pulled off, a few of which were even on film. Ward's favorite was the time Miller and his crew "borrowed" some ConEd barriers and signs, dressed up in coveralls and hard hats, closed off a street in Manhattan, pretending to be digging up the road – and then fled the scene. "We thought these were the absolute funniest stories ever, recounted in Miller's own uniquely entertaining style. They, along with Mr. duBourg's annual physics show, were the highlights of the assembly year."

Ward Tomlinson '71

"When I saw Mr. Bugliari at our class's 25th reunion, the experience he remembered immediately was one Jim Mullen and I gave him in a biology experiment. Let's just say it involved trains and was an admittedly lame-brained effort at creativity (mostly on my part). He laughed in 1981 at Jim and me and he is still laughing today.... Miller Bugliari helped me understand the concepts of competitiveness, team leadership, and respect for others. He truly is a man who cannot be replaced, in my mind."

Andy Ehrlich '81

Rufus Gunther Day

Rufus Gunther Day was begun by Joel Rogers '70 as a way to bring some fun into the life of the school by having students dress in costumes on Halloween and put on humorous skits about school life. In 1972, Dan Phillips '59, now a Pingry teacher, turned it into a Pingry tradition. As Dan recalls, "If you give kids a reason to celebrate Halloween and make it cool with costumes and prizes, they do it and love it. I wanted to juice up student life a little."

Today, Rufus Gunther Day is also a time for students in grades 6-12 and faculty volunteers to perform community service projects that center on helping the less fortunate or participating in environmental and historical restoration initiatives. But the fun of the day is still inspired by Miller as Master of Ceremonies. Dressed in a top hat and wearing the by now famous bellman's jacket from the Willard Hotel in Washington, which Miller appropriated from Charlie Cox '70, Miller's introductions and involvement in the student skits and performances have become a treasured memory for generations of students – and one more illustration of the wisdom in Miller's understanding that "Excellence" and "Honor" need self-deprecating humor to keep these ideals from turning into arrogance and hypocrisy.

> "Some of my fondest memories of Mr. Bugliari stem from his announcing on the Rufus Gunther Day parade and performances. He was able to make an already festive occasion that much more fun. I particularly recall one year, possibly my senior year, where four of us were dressed as the band 'Kiss.' As we crossed the stage, in full 'heavy metal regalia' trying to do our best impression of hardened rockers, Mr. Bugliari announced us as 'The Calico Cats.' It took the wind out of our sails a bit, but gave us a good laugh too."
>
> **Christian Breheney, '89**

The Greatest Respect is Due to Girls

In 1974, the arrival of female students ushered in co-education at Pingry. For many teachers and students, it was a difficult change to adapt to – but not for Miller. To him, all students, regardless of gender, were uniquely important people, each with his or her own value, personality, and untapped potential to be discovered and developed.

Debby Richman '78 was among the first girls who entered Pingry. She recalls, "In freshman biology class it didn't matter that we were girls or boys. Other teachers took time adjusting, but Miller never communicated that it was a big change. Things seemed normal – at least 'Miller normal.' He would bellow at least once per class. I believe there were several reasons for this teaching tactic, but all can be disputed. First, to emphasize something (probably not). Second, to wake us up (plausible). Third, to amuse himself as we jumped (most likely)."

For the 50th Anniversary Celebration, Eugenia "Genie" Makhlin '95 wrote: "Favorite memories: Mr. Bio throwing a frog at me – hiding on Mr. Bio during biology class – going through Mr. Bio's desk and making fun of all of the random jarred snakes, valve oil, dead pens, etc. Years of abuse from Mr. Bio – Kitty and I thinking of ways to drive you crazy all day, every day – me sitting in the back row talking the entire class and then yelling 'You favor the boys!' whenever you would get mad at me. 'Mr. Bio – why did you show up to class with 57 textbooks and 370 pens every day? Ha!'

"You influenced me, Mr. Bio, like no other teacher during my time at Pingry! You have filled my life with hours and hours of laughs, and more than anything, have taught me how to be a loyal friend. Genie, your favorite student of all time."

Coaching Girls

In the mid-1980s, the girls' Middle School lacrosse coach broke her leg, so Miller was asked to take over the team. On the first day of the season he was there at 3:00 for the start of practice. The girls started to stroll onto the field around 3:15. Miller believed in treating girls with the same tough fairness he used with boys, so he pointed out to them that they couldn't expect to win games if they didn't show up on time to maximize their practice opportunities. His voice may have been a bit more assertive than they were used to.

Many of the girls immediately burst into tears. It was not a good start.

Miller went for help to the school psychologist, who told him "You can't yell at girls." Miller protested that he wasn't yelling, just explaining. "Then you need to explain more gently," the school psychologist replied.

As the season progressed, Miller was gentler with the girls – but not with referees. That would have been asking too much. In the first game, the referee missed a call. Miller yelled out "What do you mean! That's our possession!" The referee, an experienced lady official of a certain age, stopped play and just stared at Miller as if he were a creature from a different planet. "No coach has EVER questioned my judgment in 30 years of officiating," she snapped. Miller took that – correctly, as it turned out – to mean "Shut your pie hole, Mister, or I'll throw you out of the game."

There were more surprises. In one early game, the girls were playing miserably and were down by three goals at the half. As Miller gathered them for the critical halftime talk and adjustments, one of the girls started passing out cookies. "What are you doing?" asked a dumbfounded Miller. "These are inspirational cookies to help us play better in the second half," she replied. The team then scored four goals in the second half and won the game.

Coaching Boys

Although Miller's first love was soccer, for years he was also a highly successful coach of JV basketball and baseball. He could be just as tough on these teams as he was with his soccer players, but he was just as caring and supportive of his baseball and basketball players, too.

As a Pingry sophomore, Don Keel '64 was 6'5" and weighed perhaps 160 pounds. In his words, "I had grown so fast that I was TOTALLY uncoordinated. In my first junior varsity basketball game, I held up the rest of the team going out onto the court because I was fumbling with the laces of my Converse All-Stars. When we got out onto the court and were into the lay-up drills, Miller noticed that the other team was looking at us because I was taller than any of their players. So he took me aside and said to me: 'Take the ball in your two hands close to the basket, jump up and jam it two-handed down into the basket.' 'OK, Coach,' I said. So when it was my turn to receive the ball in the drill, I ran up to the basket, received the pass, took it in my two hands, and jumped up above the rim. The only problem was I came up directly under the basket and went up through the net. But he believed in me more than I did in myself. That season, Miller said to varsity coach Frank Romano, 'He will be playing for you next year.' Sure enough, I did make the varsity team and played first string in my senior year."

More than a 9-to-5 Commitment

Today's teachers might have a hard time adjusting to what was required of Pingry teachers in the 1960s and '70s as part of a country day school program. After a full day of teaching you were expected to coach a sport until school dismissed at 4:50 p.m. But for Miller the commitment often didn't end after the last bus had left and the last carful of students had roared out of the parking lot.

Bronson Van Wyck '63 relates an experience that was one of the earliest examples of Miller's commitment, but far from the last. "In early March 1962, my father died in an American Airlines plane crash in Jamaica Bay. Miller came to live on the third floor of our home in Montclair, New Jersey. I was in 11th grade at Pingry, and my brother was in college; my mother asked Miller to come live with us as we were adjusting to the loss of my father.

"The story we all recall the most during this period was when my mom went to Florida for a week and it was Miller and Bronson – one on one. Up until this week, we'd had a daily routine: school during the day; after sports practice Miller would drive us home; then homework, dinner, practice the piano, and off to bed. And of course before my mom left for Florida, she had fully prepared meals, labeled for each day, and put them in the refrigerator for our evening dinners. So off she went, and Miller and I had our routine and instructions in writing.

"The first night we were home alone, with Miller suggesting it was time to study, I went straight to the piano. I played – Miller listened – his favorite song at the time I recall was 'Personality,' sung by Lloyd Price! Of course, it was not long before we were starving and in the car for the five-minute ride to Pal's Cabin Restaurant for cheeseburgers and fries. This restaurant is still in business at the southwest corner of Mt. Prospect Ave. and Eagle Way. I can hear myself saying 'Miller, as soon as we get home, I will hit the books!'

"Of course, after a few minutes of studying I was too sleepy, and we were off to bed. For one week we had a 'new' routine! When my mom came home she could not believe we had not eaten any of the meals that she had prepared!

"Miller was, in his natural way, nurturing. He is like a magnet. He latches on and before either of you knows it, you are buddies – a team getting stuff done. Some would say this is an approach – it's more. It is his love for others. At that moment someone was hurting more than they realized, and he was there helping – it is one of his greatest strengths."

"In my freshman and sophomore years I had played football, but decided that my interests lay more on the artistic side of the curve. It was a very difficult decision to abandon a sport for which I had all the physical and mental zeal, and I always questioned whether or not I had done the right thing. I asked Miller later on that year if he thought I was making the right decision in my pursuits, and he was so supportive and encouraging. 'Just give it 100 percent, and you'll not have any regrets in whatever you do.'

"During the autumn days of senior year, in the fall of 1972, I was doing photography for the Blue Book and was snapping away during and after a game which we had won convincingly. As dusk was approaching, I was still out at the far soccer fields at the Hillside campus, and while the team was running in after its victory, there was Miller, quietly walking back toward the school in his Adidas sweatpants. The light of the day was waning and was just perfect for the photo I was able to capture. I always treasure that photo, because it showed the essence of the man – tireless effort, strong-willed, yet never neglecting a student when they approached him about a problem or difficulty they were having. I take that thought into the operating room with me on every case that I do, and I've tried to pass the same message on to both of my boys as they move on in life. Thanks, Miller, for your caring and kindness."

Charlie Cuttic '73

Elizabeth's Perspective

Elizabeth Bugliari remembers another example from early in their marriage. "Shortly after our marriage in 1965 (nearly the entire school crammed themselves into the Episcopal Church in Morristown where my parents had been married), we lived in a small garage apartment in Short Hills. Frequently, my fifth- and sixth-grade students would stop by after school to make chocolate chip cookies, and the entire soccer team would often come over for a lasagna dinner. It was a modest apartment, with a living room, kitchen, one bedroom, and an office downstairs. When the telephone rang in the middle of the night, I could hear every word of Miller's side of the conversation.

"One night the phone rang. Apparently, a Pingry student was so upset with his parents that he had decided to run away from home. Because he was a soccer player, and because Miller was Miller, he had called to let his coach know. Miller listened quietly to the boy, then I heard him say, 'I don't think it's a good idea to leave home in the middle of the night. Why don't you try to get some sleep and come and see me in my office in the morning when you get to school…but if you can't stay there, come over here, and we'll figure out another plan.' 'Come over here?' I thought. 'There's only one bed, and I'm in it.' But – he had not told him what he could not do, but what he *could* do. He was, and still is, a master at dealing with all ages, including an extremely upset adolescent."

Mark Biedron '70 recalls a similar incident when he and classmates Craig Badami and John Spagnolo were determined to run away from home and told Miller. "That's OK," said Miller, "but we have Lawrenceville tomorrow. Why don't you wait until after the game?" "We did," recalls Biedron, "and by then we'd cooled down and decided to stay in school."

Fear and Love

In the entrance foyer to the Pingry library, a place that has become a favorite area for students to relax and socialize, stands the old table that used to serve as the altar for the Pingry Chapel in Hillside. On the side facing the students are written the words of Dr. Pingry's admonition about the Fear of the Lord.

THE FEAR OF THE LORD IS THE BEGINNING OF WISDOM

On the other side, facing the outside world, is another quotation, from John 13:34, inscribed when the table was moved to the new campus: "This is my commandment, that you love one another."

THIS IS MY COMMANDMENT THAT YOU LOVE ONE ANOTHER

"Love" and "fear": the twin gravitational poles on which Miller's teaching and coaching are balanced, the Yin and Yang of his approach – and his ethical center.

The "love" part is easy to understand: Just talk to the many hundreds of students and alumni Miller has gone out of his way to help in moments of crisis, sometimes decades after they have graduated.

Spend time with him in his office "museum." The meeting will be constantly interrupted by students popping in to get help with an academic or social problem or by players checking with Miller, in and out of season, on their development. Several times in an hour-long interview, Miller will pause the conversation to make a phone call: to a college coach or admissions director in support of a student seeking admission, to a soccer camp to place a younger player in a program that will help him improve, or to any of hundreds of alumni. Miller being Miller, his conversations with alumni typically include a clearly remembered, usually hilarious personal memory or good-natured gibe.

David Gernert '74 remembers one such moment. He had sustained a serious injury to his foot when he was 20, and in the process of negotiating with the insurance company, his father asked Miller, as Dave's coach, to attest to David's athletic potential as a former soccer player. "Which foot?" Miller asked. "His right foot," was the reply. "Then I'll be happy to," Miller said. "Had it been his left foot, I couldn't have done it because he never used his left foot when he played." Miller and David still laugh about it.

At the party to celebrate Miller's 600th soccer victory, the late Stu Lavey '63 shared this memory of Miller as a coach and friend:

"Miller was my JV baseball coach along with Frank Romano. I had a strong arm but struggled with control as a relief pitcher. One particular afternoon early in the season on a cloudy and misty day, I went in to pitch batting practice. Suddenly, all of the mechanics worked, and I threw fastballs past everyone on the team, including (to his amazement) Frank Romano. Miller was nonplussed and simply said 'OK, Lavey, when it rains, you pitch.' This event repeated itself several times during the course of that baseball season, and it became accepted that when it rained, I pitched!

"To this day, like clockwork, my phone in the office will ring early on some rainy spring morning and I will hear Miller's voice on the other end saying 'Stu, it's raining. Are you warmed up and ready to pitch?'

"Miller demanded as a coach, and he expected us to be dedicated and to put out 100% at all times and to be the best that we could be. We learned how to win and to lose gracefully."

Stu Lavey '63

A Fear of the Lord

The "fear" part may seem harder to understand, especially in today's politically correct, gentler (although not necessarily kinder) world. Certainly, a biblical scholar like Dr. Pingry would have understood the rich, complex meanings of the Hebrew phrase *yirath jehova*, which includes, in addition to "fear," the qualities of "reverence, love, and obedience."

Did Miller want students to be mindful of not misbehaving in class? Certainly. Even more important was making them aware of the importance of not being inconsiderate or mean to others. Does Miller still want players to take their responsibilities to themselves and the team seriously and to self-govern themselves accordingly? Certainly. Does "fear" play a role in a player's decision to start getting in shape during the summer so that pre-season practice will be less painful? Does fear of the penalty for disobedience help motivate a 17-year-old to leave a great party early to make sure he's home by training curfew? Certainly – especially because he knows Miller may call him at home at 10:00 p.m. Have generations of players made extraordinary sacrifices in games because they were unwilling to let Miller down as a person? Certainly.

"I co-captained the soccer team in 1998 with Kris Bertsch and Mike Roberts. The night before our county semi-final game against Watchung Hills, Gianfranco Tripicchio '00, Dave Alchus '00, and I went to a movie and then to Starbucks. Because they were a year younger, and because we all lived nearby in Plainfield, Clark, and Fanwood, I was the driver for our little trio. Franco got picked up in Westfield, and made curfew, but when I dropped Alchus off, his father was standing in the doorway with a look of anger on his face. I knew immediately it was because we had missed curfew (it was probably 10:10 when I dropped him off). When I got home five minutes later – literally 10:15 – my mom was sitting there with the cordless phone in her hand. 'Miller called, he asked you to call Coach Rohdie the minute you get home,' she said. I did. 'Be in Coach's office at 9:00 a.m.,' he said. It was a 2:00 p.m. game. That wasn't a good sign. You can't imagine the guilt and anxiety I felt. Miller and Coach Rohdie were two men I knew cared greatly about me and expected me to be a leader. And I had failed to live up to their expectations.

"I thought Miller would yell at me. Instead he was quiet, serious, and genuinely sad in explaining how I had let down the coaches, my teammates as captain, and myself. 'This isn't just about soccer,' he said. 'What would your brothers think if they were relying on you and you showed up late?' My older brothers were successful attorneys; I worshipped them. I got his point.

"Then I had to live with the consequences of what I had done. A lot of coaches, facing a critical championship game, might have let it go with just a lecture or even rationalized the breach in rules: 'Fifteen minutes late isn't all that bad, and you had to get the other players home first.' Miller's standards are higher than that. I had to sit out the first fifteen minutes of the game. We eventually lost 1-0, knocking us out of a tournament which, as the top seed and four times defending champions, we should have won.

"Since that day, I make sure I'm always early for appointments so I'll never be late. And now as Miller's assistant varsity coach, I remind players of this story each year to help them understand their responsibility to Pingry soccer and, most importantly, to themselves."

David Fahey '99

Love One Another

In essence, Miller has always understood teenage kids in profound ways that elude many other teachers – and parents. One can argue that the obedience that arises from deciding to avoid unwanted consequences is a critical element in the maturing of young people whose mental capabilities for self-restraint are largely still behaviorally undeveloped. A big part of Miller's magic with people is founded in the recognition that when "fear" is seamlessly combined with "love," then "obedience" changes into self-discipline.

And the essential element that allows Miller to be so successful in simultaneously challenging and supporting kids is his fairness: Miller simply doesn't play favorites or pre-judge people – and his students and players know it. In an academic world in which teachers, coaches, and administrators can all too often jump to conclusions about young kids, labeling them as "failures," "unmotivated," or "dumb," Miller invariably speaks up for the importance of seeing the untapped potential in every child and doing everything possible to bring that potential to fruition.

Sean O'Donnell's family had sacrificed to enable him to attend Pingry as a sophomore, so Miller offered to help by driving Sean to and from school each day, making the trip down the mountain from Short Hills to pick up Sean outside the Farcher's Grove soccer field. They didn't talk much on those trips, Sean remembers. Miller was, after all, his coach, and Sean was a teenage kid with a lot of things on his mind – including trying to figure out how he was going to pass that morning's first-period test. On their ride home, Sean was often thinking back to that afternoon's grueling practice: "Can I ever please this guy?"

What does stand out for Sean, however, was how they entered school each morning. Miller would lead the way up the steps, with Sean a few steps behind, then open one of the huge blue doors in the Pingry portico, stand aside, and let Sean enter first. Invariably.

"I don't think it was a conscious decision on Miller's part at all," Sean says. "He was just instinctively being who he is. But the message he sent me couldn't have been clearer: 'I care about you; I respect you.' I can't tell you how much that meant to a kid trying to figure out how to become a man."

Sean O'Donnell '75

Looking Back

"I have had the pleasure of working with seven headmasters," Miller reflects: Larry Springer, Charlie Atwater, Scotty Cunningham, Dave Wilson, John Hanly, John Neiswender and now Nat Conard.

"In the early years, I deeply enjoyed my friendships with colleagues like Dave Allan, Tom Behr, Brett Boocock, Albie Booth, Toni Bristol, Frank Carter, George Christow, Ed Cissel, Abel DeGryse, Tony duBourg, Jack Dufford, Fred Fayen, John Hesketh, Tommy Johnson, Dave Koth, Ted Mayhew, Jack Morgan, Dan Phillips, Frank Romano, Bill Russell, Ed Scott, Ernie Shawcross, Rick Weiler, John Whittemore, Dave Wilson, and, of course, Coach Williams and Mr. Les.

"In the middle years, encompassing the move to Basking Ridge, those friendships included faculty members Sue Alford, Frank Antonelli, Judy Baker, Tom Boyer, Sara Boisvert, Tony Garcia, Gail Cascaldo, Lucas Dee, Joann Demartino, Miles Boyd, Sherman English, Mark Fishani, Clare Gesualdo, Andrew Lacey, Mike Lalley, Joe Lavalley, Jack Lewis, Pat Lionetti, Ed Macauley, Ginny McGrath, Mike Richardson, Bob Rodgers, Kevin Rooney, Barbara Stockhoff, Jackie Sullivan, Dean Sluyter, Brad Touma, Annette Tomaino, and Pat Vergalito.

"I never played soccer for Miller and I never had him for biology, but I will always remember him for one reason: his heart.

"My senior year, a couple weeks before graduation, one of my classmates found out Pingry wasn't going to let her graduate. She had taken a few months off to go to Florida to compete in her sport. It was pre-approved by Pingry, but apparently she hadn't fulfilled all of her requirements by the time graduation came around. Certain faculty weren't going to budge. I remember feeling so helpless as a friend. My sister, Beth '92, said I should go talk to Mr. Bugliari about the situation.

"Just days before graduation, we found out that she would receive her diploma. She didn't attend graduation, but a bunch of us cheered when they called her name. I don't know what he said. I don't know what strings he pulled. But he stuck his neck out for a student when he didn't have to. He went above and beyond the call of duty. It wasn't the first time, and it wasn't the last. His heart is huge. What lessons we can learn from him!"

Sara Ike '95

> "As a 13-year-old camper at Camp Waganaki in Maine, I heard our cabin counselor saying, 'Get your act together! Mr. Bugliari is coming round.' I knew him first as the person in charge in the Grove, the person with all the skills who was always willing to show us how to do something right.
>
> "At a camp picnic, the boys in the front of the line took most of the food, leaving little for us in the back of the line. I felt furious. But Mr. Bugliari cheered me up: 'Don't let a little unfairness get in the way of having fun.'
>
> "I was trying to help a couple of younger campers at some project. 'Wachter,' he said, 'don't explain and explain. Just show them: here's how we do it.' I had occasion to repeat Miller's words last week to one of my graduate students, who was lost in too many explanations of one of her genetic calculations. I told her, 'This is advice (which I don't always manage to follow) which I learned at camp.'
>
> "At Pingry in my time, from 1958 to 1964, Miller's enthusiasm was felt, of course, in science and in sport, but also in the religious life which we shared at school. What I remember from the Pingry religious conference in April 1963 are words to me from Miller during the break about faith coming into ordinary moments of each day.
>
> "On a Tuesday in September, 1963, after the alumni soccer game, Miller told me 'I'm going to keep you on the squad.' He gave me a chance at doing what I wasn't best at, and what I learned from Miller as a coach has shaped my life.
>
> "In 2007, thirty years after graduation, the instincts of teamwork and stamina that Miller taught me proved crucial in a courtroom witness box, when I served as an expert for the Department of Justice in a case about the U.S. Census decided 9-0 by the Supreme Court. In my life as a teacher, I have learned from Miller when to say 'Hustle! Be nervous!' and when to lighten up and say 'You've done your best.'
>
> "Before the 2007 Pingry Commencement, where I was the guest speaker, Miller and Elizabeth welcomed me back for luncheon at their home. Looking out at their donkeys and reuniting with classmates, like so many of the extended Pingry family which he holds together with such warmth and energy, I felt astonishment at how many moments from my own life Miller can remember and bring back vividly.
>
> "I often hear in my mind Miller's voice saying, 'I'll tell you when you're tired.'"
>
> **Ken Wachter '64**

"Among current faculty members and staff, I continue to value my relationships with Apu, Bill Bourne, Denise Brown-Allen, Allie Brunhouse, John Crowley-Delman, Ananya Chatterji, Phil Cox, Ted Corvino, Sr., Charley Coe, Peter Delman, Susan Dineen, Joe Forte, Lydia Geacintov, Tim Grant, Vicky Grant, Eileen Hymas, Evelyn Kastl, Tom Keating, Norm LaValette, Tim Lear, Judy Lee, Jon Leef, Ted Li, John Magadini, Dave Maxwell, Andrew Moore, Jason Murdock, Jim Murray, Victor Nazario, Ronalee Newman, Deirdre O'Mara, Susan Ortner, Joan Pearlman, Al Romano, Chris Schultz, Peter Thomson, Gerry Vanasse, Gerardo Vazquez, Mike Virzi, Mike Webster, and my longest-standing colleague, Manny Tramontana."

Summing It All Up

If you add up the years from 1861 to now, you realize Miller's been part of Pingry for close to half of its existence – his close friendships begin with members of the class of 1944. He's helped guide the school through times of challenge and change and has been an instrumental part of its remarkable success.

Pingry today is a far more richly diverse school than the all white, all boys, Christian-oriented school Miller attended in the 1940s and '50s. Through these years, as the character of society has changed, so too has the school changed, reflecting the world from which its families, students and faculty have come.

In spite of all this change, Miller has kept faith with the simple, essential truths that lie at the center of what it means to "gladly learn and gladly teach." Treat each student – and colleague – with respect for his or her unique value and potential. Be truthful with others, and especially with yourself. Don't be so serious that you miss out on the joy and purpose of life in the first place. And in whatever you undertake, aim high.

At today's Pingry, the official motto has changed from the governing process Dr. Pingry espoused, Fear of the Lord, to the intended outcomes of that process: Excellence and Honor. Miller has not only lived up to those goals; he has defined them in ways few other administrators, teachers, or coaches can ever equal. But if one is to summarize Miller's career – and legacy – at Pingry, three more words need to be added to Excellence and Honor: "Love one another."

"I really enjoy the camaraderie with the kids. When you're not going out to practice with a lot of excitement, it's time to leave."

Miller Bugliari

The Bimini Sailing Adventure

In 1962, Tony duBourg decided to sail his boat, the *Unda Maris,* to Bimini with Miller and colleague Dave Koth as crew. If Tony was concerned that both of them lacked any experience whatsoever in blue-water ocean sailing, he never let on.

They set out in the early evening, "Captain Tony" giving commands as if he were in a regatta. Since neither Dave nor Miller had any idea what he was telling them to do, once they cleared the marina they promptly ran aground.

It took a while to free the boat and head out to sea again. As night approached, the sky darkened ominously and the churn of the Gulf Stream grew steadily rougher. Soon they were pitching and corkscrewing in 10-foot swells under reefed sail. Tony's boat had no ship-to-shore radio, so even if they had wanted to call the Coast Guard for help, they couldn't have.

As Miller remembers the adventure, "After a few hours of constant battering, Tony got deathly seasick. He showed me how to read the radio directional signal coming from Bimini, then went below to suffer. It wasn't long before Dave joined him in the same miserable condition. So for the next eight hours I fought the sea all by myself, lashed to the binnacle with my belt so I didn't get washed overboard. I knew we were in a major shipping channel, so each time the boat crested a swell I kept looking for merchant ships on a collision course with us. It was a long night."

By morning the sea had calmed, and Miller's sharp eyes spotted the grey blur on the horizon that miraculously turned out to be Bimini.

They headed back to Miami the next day in calmer seas. Dave Koth remembers that "it was both beautiful and exciting being in the trough of waves, surrounded entirely by blue-green color visible because of the brilliant sky above." As evening was approaching, Tony, at the helm, squinted at the horizon and confidently declared he could see the Miami skyline ahead. Miller asked, "Since when does the Miami skyline move?" They were headed toward an approaching cruise ship.

Miller continues, "Tony cried 'come about!' (I was still wondering, 'come about what?') and we changed course. I assured Tony that Columbus was right: If you keep sailing west, sooner or later you'll hit land – perhaps Miami…or Mexico…or Canada. Tony didn't think that was funny. As night fell, we were unsuccessfully trying to locate the navigational signal for Biscayne Bay harbor in the darkness. Tony announced finally that he could see the entrance light for the harbor. I asked him why the light we were looking at kept changing from green to yellow to red. Tony was steering us right toward a traffic light on shore! We frantically 'came about' before we ran aground.

"After a few more hours, we finally found a place to land, not in Biscayne Bay but in Fort Lauderdale, 37 miles to the north, in the midst of a violent thunderstorm. Tony advised us to stay far away from the aluminum mast – hard to do in a small boat. We were all very happy to set foot on dry land again."

Miller Stories #22

Miller's Best Round of Golf

In 1962 Miller had started teaching at Pingry, and during the summer decided to take a trip to Mexico with a stop on the way back in San Francisco to visit an old friend, Bob Thurston '52. Bob graciously invited Miller for a round of golf with two friends at Bob's club, the prestigious Olympic Club of San Francisco (host to the 2012 U.S. Open).

The golf match turned out to be more challenging than Miller had anticipated. He had to borrow a pair of Bob's shoes, two sizes too large, and play with an old set of clubs from the Pro Shop. Miller recalls the clubs had wooden shafts.

The bigger challenge was the game: a $200 Nassau. Those stakes were a reasonable wager for club members; Miller, as a new teacher at Pingry, was making a salary of less than $400 a month. He had $180 left in his pocket for his return trip to New Jersey, so a bad round of golf would have left him penniless, stranded in San Francisco.

Under huge pressure (which he couldn't show), and playing with borrowed equipment on a demanding, unfamiliar course, Miller shot an 81, and wound up winning $400 for the game. Bob's buddies, both weekend duffers, were less than amused that Bob had set them up in a game with a hustler as a partner, so Miller did the honorable thing: he actually picked up the tab for dinner – with his golf partners' money, of course – and went home with extra cash.

Miller Stories #23

A Trunk Full of Saltines

Miller's replacement for his wrecked '59 Impala was another convertible, a grey 1964 Impala, the same car in which he courted Elizabeth. Doubtless because of her calming influence, that car survived longer – but not unscathed. At one point early in their relationship, when Miller was still trying to impress Elizabeth, he opened the trunk and found it stuffed with packages of Saltine crackers.

To get the full measure of this prank, you need to remember the size of a 1960s car trunk – you could fit a VW Bug inside. Then consider the size of a single package of Saltines. It was as heroic an effort as any victory his early teams ever accomplished. It took Miller months to get rid of the last of the Saltine packages – at which point the perpetrators completed the meal by refilling the trunk with soup cans. To this day, Miller still is friends with Jim Whitlock '60 and John Geddes '62, the possible culprits, but their alibis have proven to be unshakable (what are friends for?).

Miller continues to wish, now that the statute of limitations on the crime has run out, that the evil-doers' guilty consciences will finally compel them to fess up.

Miller Stories #24

Miller the Opera Star

Stu Lavey '63 and Dick Manley '63 were serious singers who had worked their way into the chorus at the Metropolitan Opera as extras. Figuring the company could always use some extra spear carriers for production numbers like *Aida*, they got Miller and George Christow into the show. Miller already had experience on an opera stage, having run across the stage of the Philadelphia Academy of Music wearing his ubiquitous monster mask; Stu and Dick figured he would be a natural.

"I had a wonderful time at the old Met on Broadway before they closed it in 1966," says Miller. "I loved hearing the famous artists like Leontyne Price, Birgit Nilsson, Robert Merrill, and Franco Corelli. I didn't have a great voice, but I was so excited I usually sang along with the chorus anyway – even though as an extra I wasn't supposed to."

Since the only lyrics Miller really knew were to "Silent Night" and "Urea," it must have been an interesting performance. Miller's moment of fame came near the end of his operatic career, when he had bulked up to 180 lbs., and James Levine tapped him for the role of the High Priest in the Triumphal March in Act II of *Aida*. "It was thrilling to be sitting high on the throne on stage with so many great singers around me. This time I didn't sing along with them."

Miller Stories #25

Miller Playing Cupid

After graduating from college in 1973, before deciding on a career in medicine, Don Burt '69 joined the Pingry faculty to coach soccer and teach science under Miller as his department head. Miller naturally took Don under his wing, and that included playing Cupid as Don was thinking about marrying and settling down. Miller had met Judy Bolan, Don's future wife, at soccer practice and instantly liked her. "She seems like a good catch," Miller told Don. "The thing is, you've got to impress her. I know she likes basketball, here are some tickets to a Knicks game."

The tickets came with a complimentary dinner, so Don and Judy were treated to a wonderful meal at the Captain's Table restaurant, which Don could never have afforded on his Pingry salary. When he and Judy pulled into the Madison Square Garden parking area, a valet parked the car for them and pointed to the elevator they should take. There was just one button on the elevator, so Don pressed it. When the doors opened, they emerged into a VIP lounge: leather seats, big TVs, free drinks, the whole treatment. At game time, the waiter took them to their seats – at courtside! Don and Judy watched the NBA Champion Knicks with legends like Clyde Frazier, Dave Debusschere, Bill Bradley, and Willis Reed beat Wilt Chamberlain's Lakers. At halftime, the waiter even came down to usher them back to the lounge for refreshments. Needless to say, Judy was impressed.

Miller Stories #26

Out-driving Miller

Miller takes a lot of pride in his golf game; you might even say he's competitive when he plays.

Gene Shea '57 remembers a golf match in which Miller, as usual, was out-driving and out-scoring him until, on one of the last holes, Miller uncharacteristically hit a weak dribbler off the tee. "That was terrible," Gene said to Miller. "I bet I can throw the golf ball farther than that!" He picked up his ball and winged it for all his might. It landed a few feet in front of Miller's ball. "Miller wouldn't talk to me for a month," Gene remembers, laughing at having gotten "one up" on his old friend. Miller did win the round of golf, of course.

The highlight of Pingry's Annual Alumni Weekend for many is the Alumni, Faculty and Guest golf outing, a best-ball scramble for mixed foursomes. Miller rides around the course in a golf cart with the Headmaster, stopping with each foursome to play the hole, playing his own ball either at the tee or on the green, and of course trying to out-drive or out-putt everyone else – and almost always succeeding. Gordy Sulcer '61 remembers an exception. "One year I actually managed to out-drive him by a couple of yards. Miller looked at his ball, then at mine, then with a deep scowl masking his inner laughter, he growled at me, 'Nice shot. Don't do that again.' Classic Miller!"

Miller Stories #27

Miller's Golf Triumph at the LACC

Miller's longtime friend Jerry Pascale, father of Jon '93, recalls a memorable golf match with Miller at the prestigious Los Angeles Country Club in Beverly Hills. The stakes couldn't have been higher: Jerry and Miller were playing Jerry's brother-in-law and best friend. "We got to the final hole with Miller needing to sink a tricky fifteen-foot putt for the victory. Losing would have meant being tormented by my brother-in-law and best friend for years afterwards." A lot of professional golfers, let alone amateurs, might tighten up under that kind of pressure: Arnold Palmer in the 1966 U.S. Open, Greg Norman in the 1996 Masters, and Phil Mickelson in the 2006 U.S. Open come to mind. Not Miller. Miller approached the ball, slapped a goofy, "Watch this!" look on his face, and like Spanky from the *Our Gang* movies, turned his cap sideways (in utter disregard for club rules which require that "Caps are to be worn with the bill forward"). As Jerry relates, "He held his putter by the tip of the handle, like a pendulum, as if he were measuring the lay of the green – without even looking at it. Then he nonchalantly drained the putt."

The **Cadillac** Limousine

Finding the Cadillac

Perhaps Miller fell in love with strange old cars as a child, crammed into his family's mini-Fiat. But whatever the cause, it turned out to be an insatiable love. At Pingry, Miller and friends would take trips to New York City in the 1928 Rolls Royce belonging to Dick Shyers '62. It was a splendid car, an heirloom, in fact. But while they knew how to drive it, slowing down at the Lincoln Tunnel toll plaza was a challenge. They solved the problem by having one of the group ride outside on the running board and sprint ahead with the toll so they could slide through the toll plaza without stopping. The alternative plan for the Garden State Parkway was to time their passage through the booth so they could roll by and hand the toll collector a quarter – attached to a fake rubber hand.

Dick Corbet '52's rumble-seat-equipped 1930s Packard convertible was another gem, but the hands-down winner for both style and longevity has been Miller's 1949 Cadillac limousine.

Don Burt '69 was there when Miller found the Cadillac in 1978. "I was working at Camp Waganaki, and Miller and I were on our way back to camp from a day off. We were driving along the highway when Miller yelled 'STOP THE CAR!' I slammed on the brakes and steered the car onto the right shoulder. 'BACK UP! BACK UP!' Miller cried. I flipped on the hazard lights and slowly backed up until Miller called out again, 'STOP! LOOK AT THAT! I WANT IT!' He was pointing into the field next to us. I didn't get it. 'You want to buy a field?' I asked. 'No' said, Miller. 'That car! Look at that car.'

"I did. Abandoned forlornly in the farmer's field next to us was an ancient limousine whose good days were long behind it. We got out, hopped the fence and went to examine the car. There wasn't much to look at. All four tires were flat and the car was sitting on its metal rims. Its paint had all faded, there were rust spots in places, and the windows were cracked and broken. Grass was growing underneath the engine and poking through the front grille. The inside looked like an animal shelter. Birds and mice had made nests in the now torn upholstery, and there was litter on the floors I didn't want to investigate. Miller has the gift of looking at a gangling, still uncoordinated 13-year-old, like me, for example, and seeing the star player that kid could become. It was the same with that old Cadillac."

Miller had found the car of his dreams. Now he had to acquire it. So on one of their rare days off together, Miller and Elizabeth, accompanied by their youngest son David, set out on the road to Portland, traversing back roads in the sweltering August heat, not exactly how Elizabeth might have chosen to spend "their" day together. Then, just as a cloudburst ended, Miller spotted the black hulk in the farmer's field. Miller found the owner, and negotiated the sale.

The Cadillac Goes into Service

Miller has a lot of good friends, some of whom had the skills back then required to bring a long-dead car back to life. After two years of work, the Cadillac was now beautifully restored and in good running condition (most of the time). It went into service immediately, serving as the vehicle of choice as Miller chauffeured dozens of friends to or from their weddings, like Sean O'Donnell '75 and Rob Curtis '79. Miller's style on arrival at a location was impeccable. He would stop the car in a no parking zone in front of the church (or on the sidewalk if things were crowded), get out looking like an FBI agent in a trench coat and dark glasses, and say to the cop managing arriving traffic, "Watch the car, will you?"

Miller's trust in his beloved Cadillac, however, was not universally shared. When Don Burt '69 and his bride Judy Bolan were getting married, Miller of course volunteered to take them to the church. Judy and Elizabeth had become good friends, and they both decided a backup plan was in order. That turned out to be a smart decision when the limo broke down on Fairmount Avenue in Chatham on the way to the service. So Miller rolled into the closest driveway, gave the surprised homeowner $10 to watch the car until a tow truck arrived, and had Elizabeth, driving the chase car, complete the trip.

For the wedding of his school friend Phil Burrows' daughter, the trip was even shorter. Miller drove the car to the service, intending to take the couple to the reception. During the service, Miller surprised everyone by sitting in the very back pew near the open church door. When Phil asked him, "Miller, why are you sitting back here?" Miller answered, "I left the Caddy running. If I turn the engine off I'm afraid it won't start again." So the Cadillac ran, in the hot sun, for about an hour. And when the happy new husband and wife left the church to the applause of family and friends to go to the reception, the Cadillac promptly sputtered, coughed a few times, and gave up the ghost.

Over the years, the black limousine has had as many lives as a black cat. On one trip back from New York, Miller and Greg Pierson, who was riding shotgun, were driving back on the Turnpike when the car's hood became unlatched and flew up, smashing into the windshield. Miller managed to get to the shoulder of the road, steering by craning his head out of the driver's window while Greg, with his head out the other side window, watched the right side of the car. They found a coat hanger and used that to secure the hood so they could make it safely back to New Jersey.

That mishap sidelined the limousine for a while, but a couple of years later, Miller found a replacement for the hopelessly mangled hood. "Elizabeth," he said. "I found a hood for the Cadillac in a junkyard. It's from a 1949 Cadillac ambulance. I'm going to pick it up!" "Fine!" said Elizabeth, "but if that ambulance comes back here, I'm leaving." Somehow, Miller managed the ensuing negotiations, and the Cadillac is now back up and running – with a new hood.

Crashing the Kennedy Wedding

The Cadillac's finest moment might have been as part of perhaps Miller's greatest exploit: crashing a Kennedy wedding. Next to Miller, Owen Wilson and Vince Vaughan in the 2005 movie "Wedding Crashers" would be amateurs.

Elizabeth's brother Boyce Budd had married Karen Naess; Karen's sister had married Frank Gifford, and their daughter was getting married to one of Bobby Kennedy's sons. If the wedding connection seems a little convoluted, remember that this was a Kennedy wedding: a host of dignitaries were invited. One of them, however, was not Miller.

Of course Miller chauffeured Boyce, Karen, and other guests to the wedding at St. Patrick's Cathedral in New York. He pulled right up in front of the cathedral, in a restricted zone, and opened doors to let his passengers out. This was in 1980; Teddy, who also was attending the wedding, was running for president, and security was tight. When the Secret Service agent approached Miller, Miller instantly challenged him: "How's the security here? Where did you post snipers?" The agent promptly pointed out the places where they had people stationed, and Miller responded: "Good job." Then he drove the 1949 Cadillac to the area reserved for VIP limos and parked it. "I'm with Bug Limos," Miller announced. The other drivers clustered around, admiring the elegant antique.

When the service was over, Miller picked up his party and headed for the reception at the St. Regis hotel. Boyce Budd had admired Miller's work at the cathedral and decided to challenge him: "You used to crash a lot of events when you were younger. Bet you can't get into this one." "How much," asked Miller. "Fifty bucks," answered Boyce. And Miller was back in the game. Qualitatively, crashing a party calls for the same attributes as scoring in soccer: finely honed skills, sharp timing, anticipation and creativity, unshakable confidence, and a certain degree of luck. And "one touch" it.

The reception was in a second floor ballroom at the St. Regis, accessible only by a single escalator, with a security guard at the bottom, checking invitations and credentials. Miller's technique was flawless. His nonverbal behavior was intimidating, saying in effect: "I work for somebody way higher up the food chain than you. Don't even think of messing with me." In contrast, his smile and charm were magnetic.

The combination of both turned the guard into putty. Miller had parked the limo in a nearby garage and grabbed a box out of the trunk. "I'm running this upstairs for the Kennedys," he said to the guard as he firmly pushed forward onto the escalator. "No problem, buddy," said the guard.

The security at the top was much easier. They assumed that anyone who had gotten onto the escalator had already been cleared. Once in, Miller ditched the box in a coatroom and joined the party. Miller had a wonderful time at the bar talking with Teddy Kennedy, Bobby's kids, Don Meredith, Frank Gifford, Andy Warhol, and Howard Cosell, among many other notables. It was a Kennedy wedding, after all.

When it came time to leave as the guests were going in to dinner, Miller just reversed the process. He grabbed the box, went to the guard at the top of the escalator, and said, "I've got to run this out to my car. I'll be right back," and down he went. Had this been a soccer game, Miller would have been named "Man of the Match." He did collect the $50 from Boyce.

Adventures in **Europe**

The Eiffel Tower

"When I was a young kid," Miller says, "I really wanted to be a Hollywood stunt man."

Instead of becoming a stunt man, Miller's career path led to teaching and coaching. But he didn't lose the desire for outrageous, daring – and usually dangerous – adventures. He might have gotten his inspiration from Reese Williams, Pingry's revered Athletic Director from 1920-1959. Coach Williams liked to take students for walks along the Elizabeth River and amaze them by hopping onto the railing of the rickety Parker Road Bridge spanning the river and walking across it – on his hands. "It's easy," Coach Williams might have said. "All you have to do is maintain your balance and keep moving forward."

So it's completely understandable that one of the oldest, most frequently repeated stories of Miller is that he did a handstand on the top of the Eiffel Tower. From London, there are rumors, as well, of Nelson's column in Trafalgar Square and Big Ben. Who knows if they are true? That is the problem with legends: since they *could* be true, they might as well *be* true.

In actual fact, what happened on his first trip to Europe in 1958 was that Miller got tired of having to pay the constant "fees" for everything in Paris, including simply being seated in the theater, and decided to get some fun for his money. So he climbed to the observation deck of the Eiffel Tower, hoisted himself over the railing, and hung by his hands, dangling 300 feet above the street as startled Parisians in the street below pointed and gasped and the tourists on the deck yelled in alarm. By the time the gendarmes had rushed to the observation deck in puffing panic to prevent what they were sure was an impending suicide, Miller had made his escape.

And thus was born the legend of Miller the acrobatic stunt man. Reese Williams would have applauded. "It's easy. All you have to do is maintain your balance and keep moving forward." In retrospect, Miller's been doing that all his life.

Castles in Spain

Miller's unswerving desire to establish new standards for gymnastic daring was undiminished on his second trip through Spain, Italy, and Greece with Pingry colleague Tom Behr '58 in the summer of 1963. The aerial tramway high over Barcelona harbor, the Coliseum in Rome, the Temple of Delphi in Greece – it didn't matter. There would be Miller, balancing on top of the structure or hanging over a railing at a ridiculous height as passersby gasped and police sirens wailed. If Miller hadn't been under the weather with stomach ailments in Barcelona, he would certainly have scaled Gaudi's *Sagrada Familia*.

Perhaps Miller's most dramatic acrobatic feat was at the beginning of the trip. Miller and Tom had decided to visit the famous castles in northern Spain: Segovia's picture-book Alcazar, Manzanares el Real, Medina del Campo, Burgos, and the less famous castles dotting the plain from Madrid to the north. Miller has always loved history, and this is one of the most ancient places on earth. One feels the presence of an older, darker religion steeped in blood and the worship of the bull god. Its roots go deep into the mists of pre-historic time. Phoenicians, Greeks, Carthaginians, Romans, Visigoths, Moors, and Christians have all battled on these hot, arid plains. This is the mysterious, enchanted land of Don Quixote and Sancho Panza where windmills turn into giants: the perfect place for a magical adventure. But no matter where they went those first few days, they were dogged by busloads of tourists with their tongues and Kodaks clacking like locusts. It did dispel all the romance.

So at the last castle on their agenda that day – it might have been Peñafiel – they climbed to the top as the evening began to paint the ancient stones in gold. Behind them was the unmistakable dust trail of a bus carrying their by now very irritating pursuers.

As the group of tourists started up, Miller mounted the parapet of a prominent turret, grabbed some protruding bars, and swung out of sight, *outside* the castle walls, dangling a couple of hundred feet off the ground. When the tourists arrived, panting from the climb, Tom, pretending he was an expert on the ancient Visigoths who still haunted this castle, steered the tourists so they faced the wall on the other side of which Miller was hanging.

Suddenly Miller sprang up, flinging himself over the wall to alight on the floor of the parapet with fiendish cries – ferocious Visigoth oaths, without question. It was magic! Who would have imagined so many out-of-shape, overweight, shrieking tourists could run so quickly – or fit all at once through the same small door! Sancho Panza would have loved it.

Running the Bulls

On his 1963 trip to Spain, Miller thought it would be exciting to run the bulls in Pamplona. When they arrived at the fiesta, Miller and Tom ran into one of Tom's Pingry classmates, Terry Corbin, with a bunch of his Dartmouth buddies. "Tell me again," someone asked, "Why are you going to try to outrun a half-ton animal that can sprint at 40 mph, has horns as sharp as swords, and can hook you faster than Ali?" "It's a challenge," said Miller. "I haven't done it yet. And it will be fun. You'll see."

If you haven't run the bulls, it's hard to imagine how dangerous it really is. Obviously getting trampled or gored is a distinct possibility. But just as dangerous is the logjam of runners that piles up in front of the entrance to the bullring right before the bulls arrive. The bulls go through it in an explosion of bodies.

Miller got Tom up at 5:00 a.m., after perhaps three hours of sleep. They got their tickets and entered the walled-off streets through which the six bulls to be killed that day run from the pens to the bullring, accompanied by steers who have done the trip before. Even at 5:30 in the morning, the windows on the houses overlooking the street and the viewing spots along the walls were jammed with spectators. Like most of the other runners, Miller and Tom were dressed in white with red bandanas, carrying rolled-up newspapers with which to ward off any bull that came after them. A baseball bat would have been better.

As usual Miller was bright and cheery, rubbing his hands together in excitement in a gesture every Pingry soccer player will recognize; Tom was still hung over from the previous night's partying. Then a rocket was fired by the bull pens to signal the start, the crowd started shouting, and the huge mob started running for their lives. As another visitor to Pamplona, Ernest Hemingway, once wrote: "The world was not wheeling anymore. It was just very clear and bright and inclined to blur at the edges."

Anyone who has watched Miller bench press a heavily loaded bar with just one finger of each hand knows how strong he is. He put that strength to good use, grabbing the runners ahead of him and hurling them aside, carving a tunnel through the crowd like a tank going through a wheat field. Tom just drafted right behind him as bodies of startled Basques and tourists flew by in his wake.

They made it into the arena ahead of the bulls. By now the bullring was filled with spectators, roaring just as loudly as the people on the street. The gladiators in Rome would have recognized the sound.

Gradually, the bulls, led by the steers, worked their way through the arena into holding pens. At one point the guy next to Miller and Tom, a student at Penn they found out later, whipped off his red beret and waved it in front of the nearest bull as a target. The bull hooked at the hat and the Penn guy guided the bull past him in a move that would have made Manolete proud. The crowd went "Ooooohh!" He turned with a triumphant grin – just as the steer he hadn't seen blindsided him from the back and ran over him. He rolled in the dust as the crowd went "AAAAHHHH!" and cheered. For the steer.

Miller and Tom caught their breath by the protective *barreras* next to the bullring walls; then the next bit of excitement started. After the fighting bulls clear the arena, some young bulls are released into the mass of runners. The idea is to get the bulls used to attacking people as part of their education. The young bulls are about half the size of the grown fighting bulls, and their horns are padded, but they still hit like a ton. More fun for Miller: he amused himself by chasing after the young bulls and whacking them on the butt with his newspaper. But that's Miller: he jumps into adventures that would terrify most people.

Good Fortune in Florence

After leaving Spain, Miller and Tom Behr made their way to Florence, Italy. In his turns driving, Tom amused himself by terrorizing other drivers, pedestrians – and Miller – pretending he was the famous Formula One driver Juan Fangio, and their clunky Simca 1000 was a Maserati. So what happened in Florence shouldn't have been a surprise.

Anyone who has traveled in Florence, especially at dinnertime, knows how dark and congested the narrow streets can be. So neither Miller nor Tom saw the guy on a Vespa cut right in front of them from a side street. They broadsided him and sent him airborne – straight at a long sidewalk trattoria table full of diners. The guy hit the table like a 747 crash landing on the runway and slid all the way to the end in an explosion of food, plates, wine bottles, and people.

As soon as the car stopped, Miller jumped out to help the man they'd hit. The fact that the guy was drunk probably saved him – and, as it turns out, saved them as well. Almost instantly, the small square was packed with people – all of them eyewitnesses – gesturing and arguing passionately over whose version of the accident was correct. Happily, their victim wasn't seriously injured. He started complaining loudly about the pain in his back until Miller said, "We have insurance," at which point he sat up with a huge grin and grabbed an unscathed bottle of wine to share in celebration of everyone's collective good luck. *"Beviamo! Noi siamo uomini fortunate!"* And he was absolutely right about the "fortunate" part.

Eventually the ambulance and *Polizia* showed up. Once Miller had seen that the victim was safe inside the ambulance, Miller started to negotiate with the local cops. Two men had been dispatched: a sergeant, who spoke decent English and was pretty sharp, and a lieutenant who spoke almost no English and was considerably less sharp. Doubtless he was some politician's nephew. So of course Miller started with him.

The lieutenant wanted to take them to the station for questioning; Miller talked him out of it. Then he demanded their passports and wallets, to be returned when Miller and Tom showed up the next morning to fill out the accident report. Miller talked him out of that, too. By the time Miller was done with him, the lieutenant had agreed to release Miller and Tom to go on their way. The sergeant just smiled through the whole thing.

During the interview, Miller had noticed the lieutenant's expensive Montegrappa gold pen as the lieutenant filled out the accident report to sign. When the lieutenant gave Miller the completed report, Miller reached over, took the pen from the lieutenant's pocket, and used it to sign the form. When he was done, Miller then nonchalantly put the pen in his own pocket and turned to go.

"Mi scusi, signore," the lieutenant said in astounded anger. "I think you have my pen!" Miller and Tom got back in the car and drove to the hotel with their freedom, their car, their passports, their wallets… and almost with the lieutenant's pen. One more victory for Miller; one more illustration of a fundamental lesson: don't get into a battle of wits with Miller. You're overmatched.

Miller the Chaperone

Anyone who has attempted to chaperone teenage boys on trips away from school and home knows that it's like trying to herd cats… or rhesus monkeys. Miller's baptism of fire as a Pingry chaperone came in 1960, overseeing Pingry seniors on their spring break trip to Bermuda. When the plane landed in St. George's and the kids arrived at their hotel, they promptly staged a jailbreak, scattering in a dozen different directions. The trip had instantly turned into a goat rodeo.

Miller did the only thing he could think of: go from bar to bar, rounding up strays. He got to one elegant restaurant with an outdoor aquarium, one glass side of which spread across the entire back of the bar inside. He joined the Pingry students he'd tracked down in the darkened bar, only to see Rusty Hyde '60 inside the aquarium, mooning his buddies through the glass. That's one antic even Miller never attempted.

Among many other chaperoning adventures, one of the most notable was a ski trip Miller organized in 1964 to Mount Snow in Dover, Vermont. As Steve Newhouse '65 remembers the experience, "Fifteen or so of us signed up, Dick Weiler was recruited as faculty co-leader, and much to my chagrin, my mother, Patty Newhouse, signed on as a chaperone. The lodge selected was the Snow Barn. I recall there were some serious problems with the septic system, but the price was right and the smoke backing up from the dodgy fireplace masked any less fragrant odors.

"It soon became apparent that our leader, Coach Bugliari, was new to the sport. Presumably taking his cues from watching Olympian Franz Klammer streak downhill on Wide World of Sports, Miller had adopted the tightly compressed 'egg' position with skis fairly far apart and pointed straight down the slope. His head was tucked tightly between hunched shoulders. Visibility was very limited. Turning and stopping were not yet part of his repertoire.

"After watching Coach hurtle pell-mell down the trail, the more experienced of us agreed that we needed to protect the innocent and unwary by running interference for him. Skiing ahead of Miller, we cleared the trail of potential obstacles, including small children, elderly skiers, and snow-plowing beginners so Miller managed to ski for the rest of the trip without killing anyone.

"In the evenings, Miller patrolled the Snow Barn to make sure we were abiding by the no drinking rule and not getting into any other forms of mischief. On the third night, Miller was in the lounge with my mother, who then as now was a rather attractive woman, when another guest who introduced himself as Jack from Hudson Valley approached them. After a few preliminaries, Jack asked my mother to go for a drink with him. Miller told Jack that Mrs. Newhouse was not that kind of lady and that he should move on. Jack took umbrage. He told Miller that he was not to be trifled with and produced a tiny Swiss Army knife from his fanny pack to give weight to his warning. Miller stepped up close to Jack and spoke into his ear in a low voice. We couldn't hear exactly what he said but we caught phrases like 'my boys from Jersey' and 'sleeping with the fishes.' Jack turned very pale, quickly tucked his Swiss Army knife back into his fanny pack, and moved off into the crowd. Mother had been rescued from a menacing predator, and we all had another 'Miller Moment' to treasure."

Adventures in Italy with Aldo Tripicchio

Telling all the stories of Miller's trips with his soccer teams over the years would fill a book all by itself. One trip, however, that perfectly captures the wonderful experiences Pingry soccer teams had traveling with Miller would be the team's first trip to Italy in 2000, organized and made possible by Aldo Tripicchio, father of Gianfranco '00, Anthony '02, and Kristen '11. Aldo was a highly respected figure in Italian professional soccer whom Miller had met when the Italian National Team came to Pingry to train for the 1994 World Cup in the United States. In the ensuing years he has become one of Miller's closest, and equally hilarious, friends.

And so, with the help of Aldo's many contacts and the generosity of some Pingry parents, the Italian trip became a reality – or, if you consider their bus rides, an unreality, right out of "Miller Mayhem" from his Springfield College soccer trips. Aldo's and Miller's families both come from Calabria in southern Italy, which means they both love to bet, are highly competitive, and are, some might say, equally stubborn. So the bus rides turned into a running, fiercely contested series of wagers based on cumulative points won and lost.

Pavarotti's Millions

The headline might have read "*Pavarotti deve pagare €20 milioni al Ministero delle finanze dell'Italia per i crediti fiscali fraudolente.*" Miller, whose Italian was good enough to read the Italian papers each morning on the bus ride, turned to Aldo. "Hey, look at this," he said, pointing to the article. "Pavarotti had to pay the Italian Finance Ministry 20 million on a tax evasion charge." "No, Miller," said Aldo. "He didn't pay it, he's just been fined that much." Miller took back the paper and checked each word in the brief story. "Aldo, with all respect, I think you may not be correct. I think it says here he paid the fine." Aldo replied, "Miller, I read the same thing. This is Italy. It's one thing to be fined; actually paying the fine is something different." By now the whole bus was into it. "Bet! Bet!" yelled the crowd. Since Miller refused to concede, Aldo decided to let Eduardo, the bus driver, decide. Eduardo, one eye on the murderous traffic around them, the other on the paper, scanned the story and gave his verdict. "*Sembra proprio di si.* It would seem that he did," he said. Miller triumphantly added 60 more points to his total. Aldo dismissed the ruling: "What does he know?" Aldo argued. "He's only a bus driver."

Eduardo, perhaps feeling guilty, decided to make amends by inviting Miller and Aldo to his house, close to the team's next training facility, to sample his homemade wine and pork sausage. Eduardo was better than his word. His wine cellar not only contained an ample supply of everyday table wine; he also had several thousand bottles of the finest Italian and French wines. So Miller, Aldo, and Eduardo, in the company of the parents and chaperones, continued the debate about Pavarotti, enjoying spicy sausage, bread, cheese, and wine in the cool of Eduardo's cellar while the team sweated at practice in the hot sun.

The Tabiano Terme Hay Wagon Wager

Aldo and Miller bet on *everything*. They were on a bus trip to their hotel in Tabiano Terme when someone asked Aldo, "When do you think we'll get to the hotel tonight?" Aldo thought for a moment about the roads and traffic and then said, "8:15." Miller instantly countered, "No. We'll get there at 8:30." And the battle was on.

With just two miles left to go at 8:00, and an empty stretch of rural road ahead of them, Aldo could already savor the sweet taste of victory and the sweeter savor of gloating over Miller. Then, as so often happens in soccer, when balls take inexplicable bounces or ricochet agonizingly off the goalposts, fate – or something even more insidious – intervened. A hay wagon hooked to a slow tractor pulled in front of the bus, reducing its speed to a crawl. To this day Aldo claims the tractor was a set-up engineered by Miller's son David on his cell phone to ensure his father's victory. But as the large clock on the bus's dashboard inched toward 8:15, the remaining minutes became as tense as a World Cup overtime period. The players and parents counted down and shouted encouragement – or good-natured mockery: "Eight minutes to go! Aldo's got it!" "No! We won't make it. Coach never loses." Then, miraculously, the hay wagon pulled off, and Eduardo accelerated toward the finish. By now the spectators were delirious with excitement, and just as the second hand ticked up to 8:15 the bus pulled to a stop in front of the hotel. Aldo was as triumphantly joyful as he might have been had Roberto Baggio's deciding penalty kick against Brazil in the 1994 World Cup final been driven into the goal instead of arching over the crossbar.

But the bus doors didn't open. Not until 8:16 did the first player step onto the ground in front of the hotel. Once again Miller declared Aldo had lost. Aldo declared "foul" and lodged a protest with the rules committee, which, unfortunately for him, was headed up by Miller.

Aldo's Air Conditioner

In the Italian trip with Aldo, air conditioning was always an issue. According to some reliable sources, Miller refused, on principle, to tip Eduardo, so Eduardo refused, also on principle, to turn on the bus's air conditioning. As a result, the Pingry group spent long bus rides in 90 degree heat.

That summer, a heat wave had settled over Italy and stayed there, so the nights were just as sweltering as the days – except in Aldo's room in Tabiano Terme. The hotel owner, like those in all the hotels where the team stayed, was Aldo's close friend. On his own, knowing that Aldo was traveling with his wife Gloria and their small daughter, he arranged to have a portable air conditioner set up in Aldo's room – an amenity Aldo wisely kept to himself. And he might have gotten away with it. But one evening, Aldo's son Anthony went to get something for his father and stepped into Aldo's gloriously cool bedroom. When he came back downstairs, the coaches and Pingry parent chaperones were at the bar, grousing as usual about the unrelenting heat. "Well at least Dad's better off," announced Anthony. "He has air conditioning." On hearing this, Miller went ballistic. "Air conditioning! Aldo has air conditioning? That's it! THAT'S IT! ... AN AUTOMATIC 10,000 POINT PENALTY!" With the penalty points, Miller now had an insurmountable lead. But as the saying goes, *ride bene chi ride l'ultimo:* Aldo got the last laugh. Miller celebrated his victory that night in Tabiano Terme in stifling heat while Aldo slept in comfort.

Listening to Aldo and Miller now, so many years later laughingly continuing their debate, it's clear that the question of who actually won the week-long battle will never be resolved – Calabrians have a saying: "*A lavare a capu e ru ciucciu, ci perdi a l'isia!* – there's no sense trying to convince a stubborn man." It's also clear that Miller and Aldo share their friendship in the same way that as young men they played the game of soccer they both love: with passion, style, and great joy.

Bugliari Soccer – **The Beginning**

The New Coach

In some ways, soccer was an afterthought in Pingry athletics from the start of interscholastic athletics through the 1950s. As Troupe Noonan wrote in *The Greatest Respect: Pingry at 150 Years*, football under Reese Williams and Mr. Les was "the straw that stirred the sports drink."

When Miller started coaching in 1959, everything changed. His goal was not a winning season – that was a given – it was excellence, as measured in championships. His vision was that Pingry would become not only the leading New Jersey prep school team, it would dominate Union County public schools.

But for Pingry as it entered the 1960s, such aspirations were, well, unimaginable. Pingry was a small school whose students came largely from affluent suburban homes – and who were expected to meet the most demanding academic standards. A "good season" was one in which a team won more games than it lost, or even "tried hard" against tough opponents while winding up with a losing record.

Peter Wiley '60 remembers Coach Frank West, who had guided Pingry soccer for almost a quarter-century, as a deeply caring man with an abiding love for the game of soccer. "But none of us had come even close to experiencing anything like Miller's intensity, energy, and enthusiasm. He was like a big kid. Under Coach West we had practiced, but he didn't really coach us. Miller coached us incessantly – in a different game. For the first time, Miller had us learning and playing tactical soccer – a short passing game completely unlike toe-kicking the ball downfield and scrambling in front of the net."

The October 2, 1959, *Pingry Record* noted: "With the addition of Mr. Miller Bugliari to the coaching staff, a special emphasis has been put on conditioning." Gordy Sulcer '61, a junior on Miller's first team, remembers what "special emphasis" really meant. "We were used to Mr. West conducting practice in the same grey pin-striped suit and wing-tip shoes he taught in. The first day of practice he introduced Miller as 'a former player who was going to help with the coaching.' We looked at him – he was dressed in what amounted to ratty gym clothes, to be kind about it – and we were saying to ourselves, 'Who is this guy?' We found out fast.

"Mr. West just turned the practice over to Miller, who began by saying: 'Gentlemen, we're going to spend time getting in shape' – this to a bunch of guys who had done almost nothing before the season in terms of running. He had us take a lap around the entire field, and when the last player struggled in, Miller said, 'That wasn't fast enough. Do it again.' We ran that second lap a lot harder than the first. That established the tone for the season. Miller drove us incessantly, often taking the lead and setting the pace."

In the Fall 1994 issue of *The Pingry Review*, "Soccer at Pingry," Miller recalled his first years as Pingry's young coach. "I was excited to try my hand at coaching on my own, to try my personal theories about training and fitness as they related to soccer." His first players remember those "personal theories" well: at almost every practice, Miller would have some often bizarre new drill for the team, like dribbling the ball through traffic cones at full speed. Early on, Miller began starting practices with what he told the team was the "Hungarian National Team's Warm-Up Drill," Miller's invention for a series of punishing leg-strengthening exercises that began with hopping, then cariocas at full speed, then lunges – until players' thigh muscles were on fire. He'd have players cool down with jumping jacks, and then start all over again.

That was the foundation on which Pingry soccer under Miller was built: the highest possible expectations, superb conditioning, relentless defense, a total enthusiasm for soccer, and the unswerving commitment to a team-based short passing game.

Mr. West demonstrating proper technique – in his suit!

Miller Playing **Semi-Pro Soccer**

In Miller's first year at Pingry in 1959 as Frank West's assistant varsity coach, a man named Gino, in his late 20s or early 30s, came to the field and asked if he could work out with the team. Miller said, "Sure." As Miller remembers it, "After watching him for just a few minutes, it was clear he was a very skilled player, who, as it turns out, had recently arrived in the United States from Venice. He continued to work out with the team for the rest of the season. The other reason I was fascinated by him was that he was driving a tiny three-wheeled Messerschmitt T-500 Tiger that looked like a frog whose back legs had been bitten off.

"Gino asked me to join his local semi-pro team, the Westfield Lions, playing in the Italian American League. The Westfield Lions were an international bunch: a majority of Italians, two Germans, an assortment of other nationalities, and me. One of our best players was Mario Porchetta, father of the All-State kid who gave us so many problems when Pingry played Westfield. Most everyone spoke two or three languages. We would meet in the Italian American Club in Westfield, where everyone but me smoked. Heavily. You could hardly see the people in the room because the smoke was so thick.

"It was an interesting challenge, because I hadn't played in about three years after graduating from Springfield College. Our home games were in Westfield, but we played all over the state and in New York City. I remember our coach telling us one year, 'Hey. Good news. I just scheduled a friendly match with the Kearny Scots.' They were a notch above us in quality and there was nothing friendly about playing them. Their fans lined the field, often standing over the touchline. You'd let a ball go out of bounds thinking a Scots player had touched it last, and then the crowd would step back, clearing the actual touchline, and a Scots player would go by you to collect the still in-play ball. And you learned very quickly not to bring a ball downfield near the touchline. If you got too close to the crowd, you could get hit with a container of beer, a foot, or an elbow. It was pretty rough soccer. I loved it."

One of Miller's last appearances as a player came with an exhibition team, Vecchie Glorie, that the late Charlie Stillitano, Sr. put together in the mid-1970s for a match against a traveling Italian team, Alitalia. The name of Miller's team, in southern Italian dialect, meant "Old Glory," which sounds about right for Miller at that point in his playing career. The write-up of Vecchie Glorie's 4-3 victory in a New Jersey Italian-language newspaper said: *"La gara é stata giocata con impegno,"* which means Miller and his team played with "commitment and zeal" – which sounds right for Miller, too.

"Vecchie glorie" a suon di gol

Le "Vecchie glorie del N.J." (maglia scura) e la rappresentativa Alitalia (maglia bianca) prima dell'inizio dell'incontro, diretto da Piscopo è terminato a favore del New Jersey per 4 a 3. Al centro della foto, la mascotte dell'Alitalia Michael Zaretti. Sono inoltre nella foto, i fratelli Stillitano, Giorgio Piscopo, Antonio Doria e Osvaldo Mugnai. (Foto Waley).

The 1959 Season

For Miller, the 1959 team captained by Jim Petrie still has, after so many years, the nostalgic appeal of one's first love.

As Miller wrote in the 1994 *Pingry Review* article: "The 1959 season was truly exciting. The players, almost all from the Class of '60...were hard to beat." With over 30 seniors on the team, Miller needed to find a way to get them all involved in the game – and in his vision for the team. So he created "The Bandits," inspired by LSU football coach Paul Dietzel's defensive specialists, the "Chinese Bandits." Miller's "Bandits" weren't the most skilled soccer players on the team. But for five-minute stretches at a time, they ran nonstop and hounded the other team with enthusiastic, relentless energy.

Besides learning to play with Miller's characteristic, game-long hustle, his first team also took on his toughness. Peter Wiley remembers a game against the Hun School in the years when one or another of the Saudi Crown Princes were Hun's most skilled – and dirtiest – players. "One of the Saudis was Bandar Faisal. The other might have been his cousin. It was clear that these two were trying to physically intimidate us. At one point a ball was kicked in my direction. As I focused in on the ball, I could see Bandar headed in my direction with the intention of taking me out with a vicious tackle. So I intentionally kept my leg extended after I kicked and nailed Bandar with my foot, studs up. My spikes ran up in the inside of his leg, tearing his skin. He dropped to the ground in pain. In a flash, a big guy in dark glasses and a bomber jacket – he could have been Faisal's bodyguard – started running from their sideline across the field at me. Then I saw Miller come tearing across the field from our side to head him off. The bodyguard never made it to me. He argued at midfield for a while with Miller then went back to their bench with Faisal." For the rest of the game, the remaining Faisal was better behaved.

The team began the season on a tear, beating Rutgers Prep, Peddie, Bordentown Military Institute (BMI), and Springfield High School by a combined 15-1 margin in goals. After losing to Haverford on a penalty kick, Pingry beat the George School – the first victory against this prep school rival in 11 seasons.

The team fought its way to a successful 9-4-0 season, going on to beat Linden, Edison, Poly Prep, and Staten Island Academy, losing only to Peddie in a rain-soaked rematch, to a postgraduate-stocked Hun on their rutted postage-stamp field, and in arguably their best-played game, to Union County power Thomas Jefferson 1-2 in a near upset.

Post-season county or state honors were awarded to Jim Petrie, Lloyd Barnard, Rusty Hyde, Don West, Pete Coughlin, and Peter Wiley. In the *Pingry Review* article, Miller also recalled his appreciation for the commitment and courage of players like Dave Wheaton, Jim Whitlock, Steve Meyer, Bart Wood, goalie Skip Reitman, and "stalwart substitutes" Jim Eagan, John Rush, Rhett Foster, and Larry Clayton.

So one way to view Miller's first season as Frank West's assistant coach, therefore, would be to see it as a very successful pre-season for the more than half-century of seasons that followed. He was testing not only his players, but himself as a coach – against the highest expectations. And Miller wasn't just coaching a team; he was creating a culture of championship-level soccer.

The 1960 *Blue Book* page summarizing the 1959 soccer team's accomplishments said: "After completing a 9-4 record breaking season, this year's soccer team may well be ranked as one of the three best squads in Pingry's history."

For the players on Miller's first team, that praise was well deserved. It just turned out to be premature.

Miller's First Game

Of course Miller's first game coaching a Pingry team would have a bizarre twist to it. What else would you have expected?

On the way to their opener at Rutgers Prep, one car with five starting players got lost in the wilds of Piscataway; Pingry had to start the game with substitutes hurriedly plugged into the lineup and regulars like Tom Stowe moved to less familiar positions. Fortunately, Don West's early goal, with an assist from Jim Petrie, took away the pressure.

After the missing players finally showed up, the game turned into a 5-0 rout with additional goals from West, Petrie, Rusty Hyde, and Larry Clayton.

At least no one ran across the field wearing a monster mask.

Frank West, *Head Coach*
Miller Bugliari, *Assistant Coach*
Jim Boskey, *Manager*

Barnard, L.	Hughes, J.	Rush, J.
Beinecke, R.	Hyde, R.	Scutro, A.
Boyer, P.	Johannsen, P.	Sloboda, J.
Clayton, L.	Keats, P.	Stowe, T.
Coughlin, P.	MacNeil, D.	Sulcer, G.
Danzig, H.	May, E.	West, D.
Eagan, J.	Meyer, S.	Wheaton, D.
Ellis, W.	Monahon, R.	Whitlock, J.
Erickson, M.	Mook, T.	Wiley, P.
Foster, R.	Petrie, J.	Wood, B.
Gibson, G.	Prevost, R.	Wood, P.
Griepenkel, E.	Reitman, S.	
Hackett, T.	Rogers, D.	

1959 Season
Jim Petrie, Captain
9-4-0

Captain Jim Petrie
All-County outside left

Strong Booters Win Three Scrimmages, Petrie Leads Club Against Rutgers Today

Built around a nucleus of 10 returning lettermen and experienced J.V. players, the Varsity soccer team looks forward to at least equalling last year's 7-2-2 record. The team is

Steve Reitman holds the all-important goalie's position followed by Phil Keats and Gordon Sulcer, who lack Skip's skill and experience.

Coach West

Coach West in the "Elephant Coat."

The 1960s: **The Championship Quest**

> *"Blended into my memories of coaching in the 1960s are recollections of the intensity and nervousness that go with that responsibility."*
> MILLER, 1994

The Challenge

The year before Miller's arrival, Pingry's schedule reflected its prep school identity, with opponents like Poly Prep, Rutgers Prep, Bordentown, Haverford, George School, Staten Island Academy, and Riverdale. Pingry would often measure the success of its season against Blair Academy. But winning repeated prep school championships would mean beating boarding schools like Peddie, Hun, and Lawrenceville, whose teams were stocked with postgraduates, often All-County and All-State players from the previous year, as well as with foreign students who had grown up playing soccer.

Accomplishing that goal against the large Group III and IV Union County public schools was an even more daunting challenge. And it wasn't just the disparity in the size of the schools Pingry competed against. Pingry was located in one of the richest areas of the country in terms of high-level soccer.

In the mid-1800s, the Clark Thread Company from Scotland opened plants in Kearny and Newark, importing hundreds of workers and their families to serve in the factories. The ensuing decades witnessed the opening of the silk mills in Paterson and the rapid growth of industrialized areas throughout Hudson, Union, and Essex Counties. By the late 1920s and 1930s, soccer clubs representing the huge influx of working-class immigrant families had spread throughout New Jersey's industrial cities and neighborhoods: Scots and Irish in Kearny, Harrison, and Paterson; Portuguese and Ukrainians in Newark's Ironbound district; Germans and Italians in Union; Hungarians in New Brunswick; and Spaniards in Bayonne. These clubs evolved into semi-pro soccer leagues such as The American Soccer League, The German American League, The Schaefer League, and the Italian American League, whose players stunned the soccer world by beating England in the 1950 World Cup.

And the challenge Pingry teams faced wasn't just from the descendants of America's earlier immigrants. Through the 1960s, local high school soccer teams were fueled by a steady influx of players whose families had recently arrived in New Jersey. If you look at the All-County and All-State teams in the 1960s, you see names like Kelley, Fiorillo, Porchetta, Russo, Periera, Schiesswohl, Jurczak, Barroquiero, Tsimanides, Dziadosz, Theofilos, and Majkut. These players were skilled soccer players with deep roots in the rich heritage of countries like Ireland, Italy, Germany, Poland, Greece, and Argentina. The instinctive sense of and love for the game was in their blood.

"In my three years on the varsity soccer team, we worked harder than any other sports team at Pingry. The incessant running and relentless conditioning was the 'Red Badge of Courage' that you earned as a Pingry soccer player.

"Two other things really set Miller apart. We realized immediately that he was a really skilled, experienced player who could defend more tenaciously, control the ball better, and kick more accurately and harder than any of us. He modeled for us the kind of player we needed to become.

"And he was 'Italian' – he epitomized all the allure and deep traditions of the European game."

Les Buck '64

Out of gritty dirt fields like Farcher's Grove in Union, the Gunnell Oval in Kearny, Schutzenpark in North Bergen, Hinchcliff Stadium in Paterson, Passaic Sportfreunde Field in Wayne, and the famous old fields on Delancey Street and the Ironbound Stadium in Newark came not only the gifted, superbly skilled players like the United States National Team stars of the 1990s and mid-2000s such as Tony Meola, John Harkes, Tab Ramos, Greg Berhalter, and Claudio Reyna, but also the All-County high school players from Thomas Jefferson in Elizabeth and from Linden, Union, and Edison Tech. They played a different game than Pingry kids and defined the extraordinary level of excellence Miller had to help Pingry players achieve in order to win county championships.

> **"This Is Why We Don't Lose"**
>
> Bob Dwyer '65 remembers a story that has been repeated in different versions so many times it has become an indelible part of the Pingry Soccer legend. "We beat BMI 4-0, but didn't play particularly well, so Coach made us run laps afterwards. An astounded BMI player asked me: 'You just killed us. What do you guys have to do if you lose?' I replied: 'This is why we don't lose.'"
>
> **Bob Dwyer '65**

Becoming Champions

Like a long-distance runner relentlessly, inexorably picking off competitors ahead of him to cross the finish line in first place, Miller's teams worked their way through the prep school competition in the 1960s, relegating Blair and Peddie to also-rans and finally and permanently taking the measure of Hun. That left the reigning pace-setter Lawrenceville, winner of 12 of the past 16 Prep School Championships, so loaded with postgraduate talent that Pingry would never have dreamed of competing against them before Miller's arrival. Pingry's first meeting with Lawrenceville in 1963 inaugurated a bitter but successful rivalry that would last for more than another quarter-century.

Becoming Union County Champions posed a more basic challenge. In 1964 and 1965, Pingry went undefeated against the top Union County teams, but watched teams they had beaten be awarded the championship based on points for wins and losses – and Pingry couldn't get enough public schools on the schedule to qualify. Miller remembers thinking, "What do we have to do to win a championship!"

The following year, working with equally visionary high school coaches like Frank Severage of Clark, Frank Chirichillo of Edison Tech, Herb Kassel of Jefferson, and Jim Jesky of Union, Miller took the initiative to petition the state to establish a Union County Tournament. Convincing the more conservative athletic directors in Union County on the value of innovative change turned out to be a struggle. Miller was successful finally in leveraging the example of the county basketball tournament – since it worked well in that sport, why not give soccer the same opportunity? Miller and his fellow coaches got approval initially for a four-team post-season tournament, but Miller realized that too narrow a field might still leave good Pingry teams out of consideration, so he fought and won the battle to expand the tournament to eight teams.

Building the Sport

Miller's leadership then expanded to embrace the entire state. He was instrumental in helping create the New Jersey Soccer Coaches Association in 1968 and headed up their committee charged with formally ranking the Top 20 teams in New Jersey each week and guiding the selection of players to All-State and All-Group teams.

Looking back, Miller recalls, "In the early 1960s, high school soccer was still largely an ethnic thing limited to a few schools. I believed soccer had a much greater potential value throughout New Jersey as a competitive sport. Done the right way and for the right reasons, soccer – all sports, actually – could offer kids invaluable experiences and lessons they would draw on the rest of their lives. So we needed to find ways to make soccer attractive, get kids interested, and help schools build programs. The tournaments and Coaches Association were ways to achieve that goal. When we started instituting clinics to upgrade the quality of coaching, soccer took off. In retrospect, what we did in Union County in the 1960s with soccer really opened a lot of doors for other emerging sports like hockey and lacrosse, and, just as important, for girls' competitive athletics a few years later."

In September 1959, a young, incredibly intense, and unproven rookie coach stood at the first day of practice looking at a senior-dominated team he didn't know, taking in their curiosity – and skepticism. He must have wondered, "Can they do it?" – and, more importantly, "Can I do it?"

Miller got his answer: his first decade ended with one unofficial and five official Prep School Championships. The goal of winning the Union County Tournament he had created, however, frustratingly eluded Pingry through the 1960s. That would change, in dramatic fashion, starting in 1970.

The 1960 Season

When you look at the team photo from Miller's first year as head coach in 1960, he's there, sitting in the second row, staring into the camera – and into the future – with a grim, intensely determined look on his face. If you didn't have the caption to go by, you might think he was just an especially mature, hard-nosed senior.

Three returning lettermen greeted Miller at the start of that season. This was a team he would have to build from the ground up. Miller later said, "Blended into my memories of coaching in the 1960s are recollections of the intensity and nervousness that go with that responsibility. I was blessed, however, in those early days with some fine athletes who had the ability to make a fledgling coach look good."

As Gary Baum recalls, "Miller was working through the kind of soccer he wanted us to play; the kinds of players, as athletes and people, he needed to make that system work; and the kind of character we would take on as a team. In the process, we were helping him learn how to coach."

What Miller already knew he wanted was a superbly conditioned team that could run opponents into the ground. Imagine a chilly, wet, late Saturday afternoon at Pingry in November. The parents of the football team are already enjoying the warmth of the post-game tea in the Whitlock Room (poured by the Mothers' Association from an elegant silver tea service in fine bone china, of course). The soccer parents are still huddled in the stands as their kids run, after the game, in the cold rain.

Miller was also figuring out which players he needed at various positions to play his kind of soccer. Gordy Sulcer '61 remembers: "As for my place on the team, you gotta love a coach who tells it like it is. Even in 'Millerese.' Early in the pre-season training in September, Coach turned to me one day after practice and said without missing a beat…'Gordy, you've got great hands as a goalie…that's why I want you to play halfback'… OK, Coach!"

The young team of Miller's first season as head coach featured senior captain Tom Stowe and junior John Geddes at fullback, backed up by seniors Pete Benedict and Joe Caruso. Senior Steve Hart narrowly beat out classmate Phil Keats in goal. Seniors Fred Guyer and co-captain Rick Monahon and juniors John Whitmarsh, Roger Herrmann, John Wight, and Tom Carter started on the front line, supported by Doug Leavens and juniors Bill Ghriskey and Bob Scott. The halfbacks were returning senior letterman Dave Rogers, junior Ted Manning, and sophomore Gary Baum, with strong contributions from seniors Al Spalt, Doug Leavens, Gordy Sulcer, and junior Gibby Gibson.

Led by Stowe, Geddes, Manning, Baum, and Hart on defense, Herrmann's record-setting 13 goals and Monahon's 12, Pingry outscored their opponents 31-8 and registered seven shutouts, losing only to Hillside and public and private school powerhouses Thomas Jefferson and Hun, to close Miller's first year as head coach with an 8-3-2 record. The Hillside game was a frustrating but important lesson to the team: a high kick landed in front of a well-positioned Steve Hart and then took a freakish bounce over his head into the goal. Playing on a narrow field that largely nullified the width of Pingry's attack, Hillside then bunkered in. Miller's young team still lacked the composure to overcome that adversity.

The team rebounded with a 2-0 win over Blair at Homecoming on goals by Manning and Monahon. For the past decade, Blair had been a team against whom Pingry measured its success. The 1960 team turned them into what they became for the ensuing decades: one more opponent who couldn't match Pingry's skill, conditioning, and desire. All told, 22 players saw action that year as Miller measured himself and his players against their prep school rivals and county foes. Post-season All-County honors went to Gary Baum, First Team; Roger Herrmann, Second Team; and Steve Hart and Dave Rogers, Honorable Mention.

Playing Well

"I can still recite Miller's mantra: 'If you play well and win, walk off the field graciously. If you play well and lose, walk off the field with dignity. If you play poorly and win, expect extra conditioning after the game. If you play poorly and lose, God help you!' Since 'playing well' was a goal Pingry players could rarely if ever achieve, they ran after every game."

Dave Rogers '61

THE LIFE & TIMES OF MILLER A. BUGLIARI

Frank Romano, *Assistant Coach*
Ed Atwater, *Manager*

Adams, R.	Guyer, F.	Rosenberg, J.
Baum, G.	Hackett, T.	Rubin, R.
Benedict, P.	Harsanyi, Z.	Scott, B.
Bushell, D.	Hart, S.	Snyder, S.
Carter, T.	Hawkins, R.	Spalt, A.
Caruso, J.	Herrmann, R.	Stowe, T.
Chalmers, J.	Jones, C.	Sulcer, G.
Curtis, Z.	Keats, P.	Walter, F.
Delfausse, P.	Leavens, D.	Wendell, G.
Dreyer, G.	Lewis, R.	Whitmarsh, J.
Erickson, J.	Manning, T.	Wight, J.
Evans, B.	Martin, P.	Yuckman, P.
Geddes, J.	Monahon, G.	
Ghriskey, B.	Monahon, R.	
Gibson, G.	Norton, J.	
Greenberg, R.	Rogers, D.	

1960 Season
Tom Stowe, Captain
8-3-2

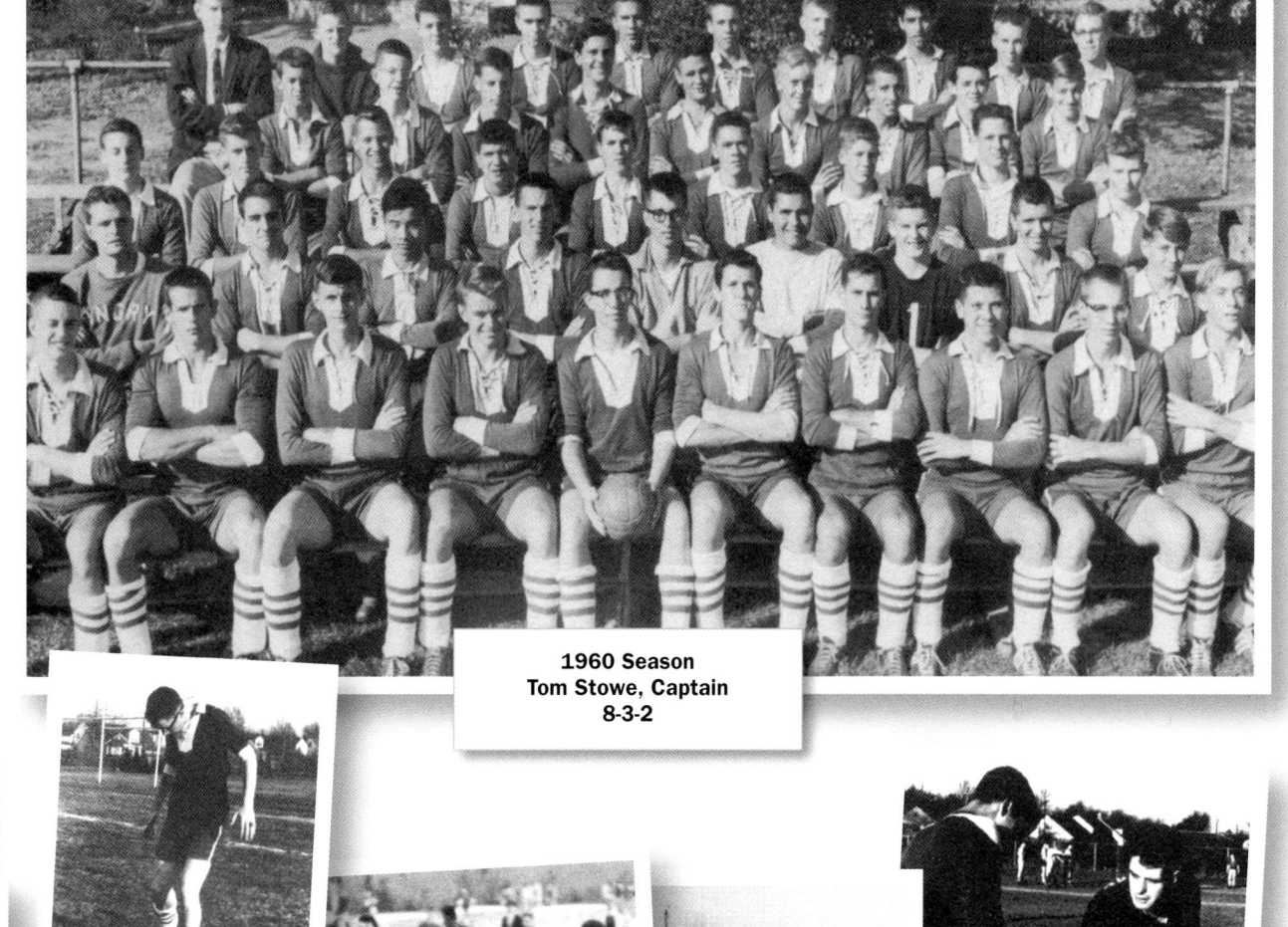

CAPTAIN TOM STOWE

COACH BUGLIARI

The 1961 Season

Many of those on Miller's team in his second full season as the Pingry soccer coach were avid soccer players who had played together since the first grade. John Geddes '62, captain of the 1961 team, and his neighboring buddies in the Westminster section of Hillside adjoining the Pingry campus, Jim Whitlock '60 and Bob Scott '62, practiced soccer incessantly. Their "play" was certainly not the same as one might have seen on the streets and fields of England, Italy, or Brazil – or even Kearny, New Jersey – but the love of the game ran just as deeply. By their junior year at Pingry, John and Bob, and other Pingry classmates like Bill Ghriskey, Roger Herrmann, Ted Manning, Jay Norton, John Whitmarsh, Tom Carter, and John Wight, had been playing together for years. So Miller's arrival at Pingry was not just a shock, it was a gift.

This group, along with newcomers from the previous two seasons, formed the nucleus of the team that achieved a 12-1-1 record. Based on their identical records, Pingry would have earned its first shared State Prep Championship with Lawrenceville had a mechanism for selecting a prep school champion existed. The defense, led by Geddes, and including seniors Ted Manning and Gibby Gibson, juniors Jeff Fast, Gary Baum, Dale Schlenker, Jack Laporte, Kit Kennedy, Grant Monahon, Dick Stickel, and Tom Derr, and sophomore Bob Ziegenhagen, with Dick Manley in goal, set the standard that would characterize Pingry teams over the decades, allowing only three goals all season. The starting line, including seniors Herrmann, Scott, Ghriskey, Wight, and Carter, and the "Bandit Line" led by Norton, wasn't prolific. But it was timely, and their 30 goals, often scored in the final quarter as opponents wore down, were enough.

After a frustrating 1-0 loss to Peddie in which Pingry dominated the game but couldn't overcome a fast first-period goal by Peddie, they avenged Pingry's previous season loss to Hillside, and then went unscored on for the next 10 games. Their victories included the first over Pingry's early nemesis Hun, on a goal by Bob Scott and a defense that clamped down on their star player Bander Faisal, and a sweet revenge win over Peddie on a wet, overcast Pingry Homecoming Day on John Wight's fourth-quarter header.

They also established themselves as a force to be reckoned with against the strong Union County teams they faced, beating top-ranked Linden 2-0 on goals by Herrmann and Jack Laporte, gaining Pingry's first victory over a typically physical, talented Thomas Jefferson team on scores by Herrmann and Scott, and in the season final, fighting to perserve a tie against a loaded Edison team on a rain-soaked, sloppy field after Herrmann's opportunistic goal five minutes into the game.

One incident tells the story of Pingry soccer in those first years. John Geddes remembers watching Jefferson's star player Joe Fiorillo running down the field in warm ups, keeping the ball in the air by alternating left and right kicks, the ball seemingly tethered to his feet. "I've never seen that before!" John thought. "He's really good. But we're in much better shape. So we'll just play him tough until he tires and gives up."

Gary Baum was selected for the second year to the All-Union County First Team.

When the *Star-Ledger* presented its All-Star team for the past 50 years, Dick Manley '63 was honored as the top goalkeeper of the 1940s through 1960s decades.

Dick Manley recalls: "I was an OK player on the JV at a line position, but Miller saw the potential in me I didn't know existed. At the end of my sophomore year, Miller told me: 'I'd like you to be a keeper.'

"I spent more hours than I can think about in the sawdust of the high-jump pit with Miller and goalie coach Frank Romano. They had a spectacular tool kit of drills.

"I practiced diving for low balls and then instantly recovering to extend for high shots from every angle on the goal until I didn't even need to think about stopping a tough shot; I would just react instinctively.

"I got a lot of accolades as a goalkeeper, but in fact the line in front of me was so good that the other team rarely got a good shot – which made it all that more important that I save the shots that did get through."

Dick Manley '63

THE LIFE & TIMES OF MILLER A. BUGLIARI

Frank Romano, *Assistant Coach*
Ed Atwater, *Manager*

Baum, G.	Herrmann, R.	Rodgers, C.
Bethune, W.	Ibsen, M.	Rosenberg, J.
Boyer, B.	Kennedy, K.	Schlenker, D.
Brown, J.	Laporte, J.	Scott, B.
Carter, T.	Manley, D.	Somers, P.
Cornwall, T.	Manning, T.	Stickel, D.
Curtiss, T.	Mayer, J.	Teague, G.
Dean, J.	McCreery, R.	Van Wyck, B.
Derr, T.	Meyer, G.	Waterman, J.
Fast, J.	Monahon, G.	Whitmarsh, J.
Ganz, F.	Moser, H.	Wickenden, T.
Geddes, J.	Muvumba, J.	Wight, J.
Ghriskey, B.	Neunert, D.	Wilson, J.
Gibson, G.	Norton, J.	Ziegenhagen, B.

1961 Season
John Geddes, Captain
12-1-1

CAPTAIN JOHN GEDDES

COACH BUGLIARI

The 1962 Season

The 1962 team, captained by Gary Baum and co-captain Grant Monahon, picked up the unbeaten streak begun by the 1961 team and ran it in dominating fashion to 25 games on the way to a 10-0-3 season. They captured Pingry's first official Prep School State Championship – and raised the bar for excellence by which subsequent Pingry teams would be measured.

The offense, led by Monahon and seniors Jack Laporte, Pete Somers, Fred Ganz, and junior Tim Cornwall, with strong contributions from foreign exchange student Gabriel Pinhiero, seniors Dale Schlenker and Dick Stickel, and juniors Todd Barber and Les Buck, was opportunistic, setting a new team season record of 37 goals.

The defense, anchored by senior goalkeeper Dick Manley and backs Baum, Bronson Van Wyck, Tom Derr, Kit Kennedy, Jeff Fast, and junior Bob Ziegenhagen, was stifling. Over 13 games, Dick Manley registered nine clean sheets in goal, surrendering just four goals to Hillside, Edison Tech, Linden, and Thomas Jefferson. When you consider the quality of the offensive players Pingry faced, it was a remarkable effort.

Those were the days when games were officiated by a single referee and before red and yellow cards. After a player had been fouled, his team was just awarded a direct or indirect kick depending on the foul, so the middle of the field was "no-man's-land" – especially when the referee was looking elsewhere. Baum recalls that the public schools thought Pingry were just a bunch of prep school wimps who could be physically intimidated. "That was a mistake in judgment on their part," Baum recalls. "Miller taught us to play through the ball – hard."

The team's first serious challenge came against Peddie, which, along with Hun in those years before the start of the annual Lawrenceville wars, was the toughest prep school competition Pingry faced. Peddie's 1-0 victory had been the 1961 team's sole loss. This year was a different story. After three well-contested scoreless quarters, Pingry put the game out of reach. Gabriel Pinhiero blasted the ball from 10 yards out to take the lead. Minutes later, Les Buck converted on a pass from Jack Laporte. Pingry's final score came on Claude Rodgers' wide-open shot on a pass from Bronson Van Wyck. Peddie's one real scoring opportunity, threatening Manley's string of 13 shutouts, came on a dangerous penalty kick in the fourth quarter from two yards out. Lacking the appropriate soccer terminology for the wall Miller established on the goal line in front of Manley, the *Pingry Record* article called it an "unprecedented goal-line stand." In any case, the unnerved Peddie penalty kicker drove the ball harmlessly into the Pingry defense.

Pingry's unstoppable march to its first Prep School Championship concluded with a 2-0 victory over Hun on goals by Pinhiero and Monahon, assisted by Buck, and a similar 2-0 shutout of Peddie in the rematch, Pingry's third game in four days. Tim Cornwall's score off Buck's assist was the game winner, followed by Monahon's fourth-quarter insurance goal. Miller described the game as "one of the best ever played by a Pingry team."

At the end of the season, Baum was selected to the Union County All-Star First Team for his third consecutive year and to the All-State Second Team. Monahon, Ziegenhagen, and Manley also received post-season recognition. Looking back on that season, Miller called Baum "a grown man playing among boys."

The hallmark of this team was its toughness. A signature play came against Hun, in those years a contender for best prep school team in the state. Hun was led by yet another of its perennial Saudi Crown Prince postgraduates, a skilled player who made Honorable Mention on the 1962 All-State Team – and the kind of viciously dirty player who could seriously injure a teammate. Baum and Manley decided to take matters into their own hands.

Dick Manley remembers the play as if it were yesterday. The moment came on a second-quarter corner kick. "We knew they'd try to get the ball to Faisal in the box, so I told Gary, 'You take him low and I'll take him high.' The kick was well struck, a high, looping ball with a little slice on it that drifted into the upper corner of the near post. As I jumped up, I punched the ball away with one fist. My other fist landed squarely on Faisal's chin as Gary ran underneath at full speed and submarined the guy as he came down. He was definitely through for the day. Problem solved!"

Gary Baum and Dick Manley '63

Frank Romano, *Assistant Coach*
Ed Atwater, *Manager*
Bill Lord, *Manager*

Barber, T.	Hoyt, E.	Poster, M.
Baum, G.	Hyde, A.	Rodgers, C.
Buck, L.	Johnson, D.	Schlenker, D.
Christensen, D.	Kennedy, K.	Somers, P.
Cornwall, T.	Laporte, J.	Stavenick, E.
Derr, J.	Logan, W.	Stickel, D.
Erickson, G.	Manley, D.	Tracy, C.
Erickson, R.	Mayer, J.	Van Wyck, B.
Fast, J.	Meyer, P.	Whitlock, D.
Gale, L.	Monahon, G.	Ziegenhagen, B.
Ganz, F.	Neebe, A.	
Gleason, D.	Pinhiero, G.	

Varsity Soccer Squad Undefeated; Wins Prep School Championship

By JERRY S. HUBENY

On November 7, the varsity soccer team defeated Hun by the score of 2-0 for its ninth victory of the

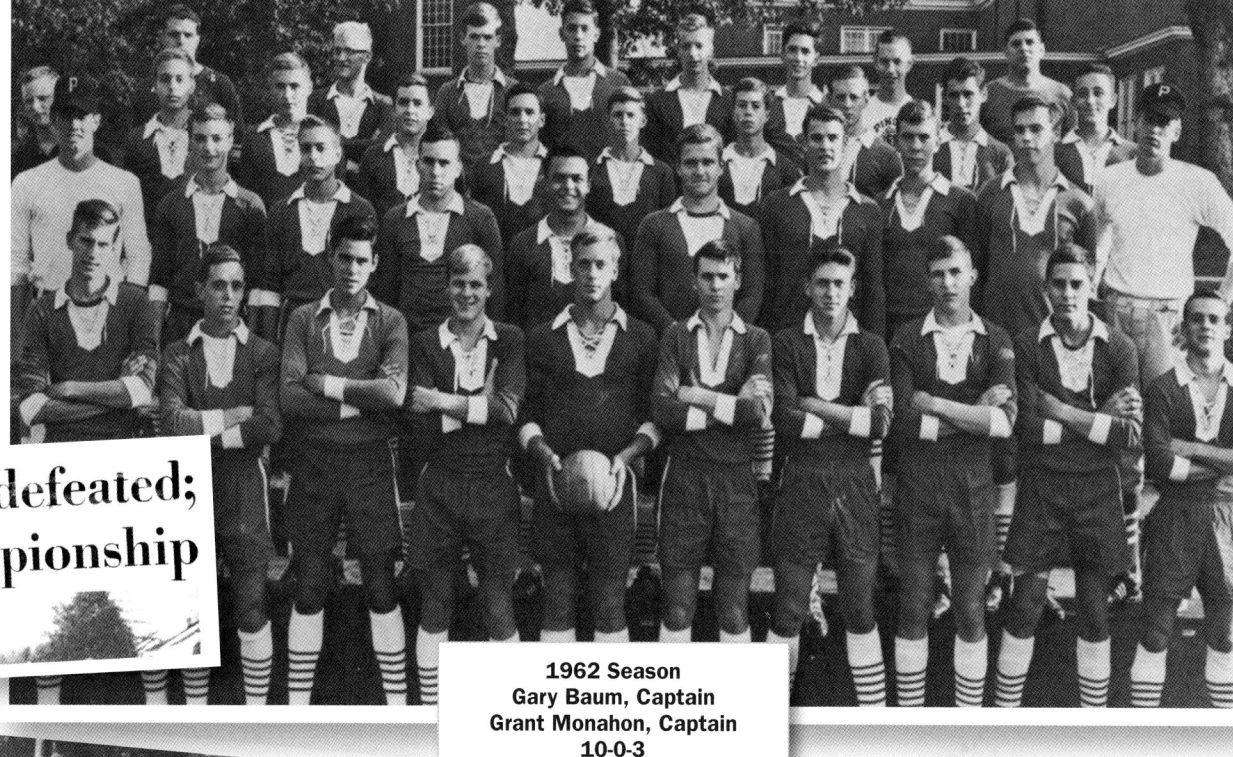

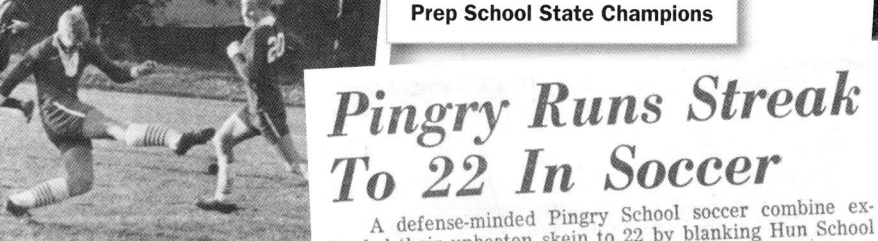

1962 Season
Gary Baum, Captain
Grant Monahon, Captain
10-0-3
Undefeated Season
Prep School State Champions

Pingry Runs Streak To 22 In Soccer

A defense-minded Pingry School soccer combine extended their unbeaten skein to 22 by blanking Hun School of Princeton, 2-0, yesterday at Pingry.

Goal line stand against Peddie

The 1963 Season

When is a 7-1-3 season disappointing? When you go undefeated in Union County competition with the best record in the county, but fail to win the county championship because you haven't played enough qualifying games.

The 1963 team scored 13 goals while yielding just four in taking the measure of the best Group III and IV teams in Union County. Comfortable victories over Berkeley Heights, Springfield, and Linden set the stage for Pingry's first game in what would be a legendary 20-year rivalry against Watchung Conference champion Westfield – a 1-0 win on Charlie Tracy's score off a Les Buck cross. Miller singled out the defensive play of goalkeeper John Sterner, captain Bob Ziegenhagen, and Tom Melin in contributing to the shutout.

Pingry then met eventual Union County champion Thomas Jefferson in a hard-fought physical game one commentator called "one of the biggest and most exciting soccer games in the county for many years." Jefferson's All-County forward Bill O'Donnell managed to score in the third quarter, but his goal wasn't enough to overcome a Pingry first-half lead built on Ray Erickson's conversion of a pass from Bob Ziegenhagen and Ed Hoyt's goal on a cross from Les Buck. The only blemish on Pingry's record against county opponents came in their last game against a strong Edison Tech team. The team fought to preserve the 2-0 lead created by Todd Barber's and Glen Erickson's third-period goals, but Edison Tech's All-County forward Frank O'Donnell's two fourth-quarter scores led to the final 2-2 deadlock.

When is a 7-1-3 season disappointing? When you play your hearts out against a postgraduate-loaded Lawrenceville on their field in a game that would decide the 1963 Prep School Championship – and lose 0-1. The loss kept Pingry from repeating as prep champions and snapped an undefeated streak of 33 games going back to the 1961 loss to Peddie.

Lawrenceville, champions 12 times in the past 16 years, came into the game unbeaten against prep school competition. Lawrenceville's Scott Robertson scored the game's only goal, in the second quarter. Led by Bob Dwyer and captain Bob Ziegenhagen, Pingry controlled the run of play and threatened throughout the second half on breakaways triggered by crosses by Les Buck and attacks by Tim Cornwall '64, but couldn't finish. Goalie John Sterner '65 registered 10 saves.

Naturally, the players were nervous on the bus ride home about Miller's reaction to the end of the streak. Junior starter Bob Dwyer remembers, "All he said on the bus back to Pingry was, 'Time to start another streak.' And so we did. It was 41 games, long after my graduation, before Pingry lost again. I learned from that experience not to worry about the momentary stumble, but to get focused on the next opportunity, and the next, and the next."

Starters for the 1963 team were Sterner, fullbacks Dwyer and Art Kurz '65, senior halfbacks Tom Melin, Ziegenhagen, and Don Gleason, and senior forwards co-captain Tim Cornwall, Ray Erickson, Todd Barber, Charlie Tracy, and Buck, and junior Ed Hoyt. Key contributions were made by substitutes Glen Erickson '64, Geoff Goodfellow '65, and Alan Gibby '66. At the end of the season, Les Buck and Bob Ziegenhagen were selected for the All-Union County First Team.

Tim Cornwall '64

Pingry's field for junior varsity soccer and girls' varsity lacrosse and the adjacent pavilion are dedicated to the late Timothy Clift Cornwall '64, who starred as a soccer and lacrosse player and received The Class of 1902 emblem award.

His brother Joe '67, an architect who designed the pavilion, describes him as a gifted athlete who thrived on competition and challenges, and relates that Tim earned the nickname "Clutch" because of his performance under pressure.

"Tim entered Pingry in grade 5. He liked to say that his classmates felt sorry for his new and awkward standing and so, in an effort to make him feel at home, made him President of the class," Joe says. "Tim was elected President of the class every subsequent year and, in his senior year, his classmates elected him President of the school."

Fred Walters, *Assistant Coach*
Bill Lord, *Manager*
Doug Hardin, *Manager*

Ackley, G.	Erickson, R.	Melin, T.
Barber, T.	Fisher, G.	Meyer, P.
Barrett, R.	Fitzpatrick, E.	Mueller, J.
Borden, P.	Gale, L.	Pedrick, W.
Buck, L.	Gibby, A.	Rafferty, J.
Cali, J.	Gleason, D.	Rettig, J.
Cassidy, D.	Goodfellow, G.	Roos, R.
Connor, G.	Griesemer, J.	Sterner, J.
Cornwall, T.	Guijarro, A.	Tracy, C.
Dudley, R.	Hoyt, E.	Wachter, K.
Duncan, B.	Johnson, D.	Ziegenhagen, B.
Dwyer, B.	Kurz, A.	
Erickson, G.	Logan, W.	

1963 Season
Bob Ziegenhagen, Captain
Tim Cornwall, Captain
7-1-3

Soccer Streak Hits 31 For Pingrians

The 1964 Season

How do you improve on the stellar performance of a team that only lost one game the previous season? Run the table the next year.

The 1964 team finished up undefeated, winning Pingry's first Union County Championship on points over runner-up Springfield and sharing the Prep School Championship with Lawrenceville based on a 0-0 tie. As usual, the defense was suffocating, led by First Team All-County seniors Bob Dwyer and co-captain Art Kurz, and Honorable Mention goalkeeper John Sterner and halfbacks Pete Meyer, along with Geoff Goodfellow, Jim Mueller, Jim Matthews, and senior goalkeeper Pete Borden. As Bob Dwyer recalls, "Those were truly glory days, and I know that our defensive success and the feeling of accomplishment I got came from two tenets I learned from Miller: they can't score if they don't have the ball; and keep attacking on defense – they won't beat you six times in a row. Miller was also a step (or two) ahead in tactical thinking. For example, we played 4-2-4 or 4-3-3 in '63 and '64 with overlapping fullbacks when our opponents were playing 2-back (or 3-back), which gave us a real advantage. He taught us how to out think, not just out play, the opposition."

Pingry's defense recorded 10 shutouts in a row and only allowed two goals all season, one to Cranford in the opener, won by Pingry 4-1 – the only score allowed all season in the run of play. Following in the tradition of Gary Baum and Bob Ziegenhagen, Art Kurz was an intimidating force in the middle. Art had grown up playing skilled, hard-nosed soccer at Farcher's Grove in the rough world of the German American League. In today's soccer terminology he would be called "a destroyer." He led the effort that closed down Lawrenceville star Scott Robertson and some of the most dangerous offensive threats in the county, like Edison Tech's Stan Dziadosz and Jim O'Donnell, Westfield's Nick Delmonaco, and Linden's Leon Stawicki – while the offense outscored seven Union County opponents by 18 goals.

This was a team that simply refused to be beaten. After surrendering the penalty kick against Thomas Jefferson, Pingry took over the game. Art Kurz's penalty kick near halftime knotted the score, and Ed Hoyt headed in the game winner on a rebound off the goal post on John Cali's shot in the third period.

The 2-0 effort against a dangerous Edison Tech team was even more dominating. In the second period, Jeff Rettig drilled home a cross from junior Alan Gibby. Art Kurz's penalty shot provided the insurance goal. It was Pingry's 28th consecutive game against Union County teams without a loss.

The 1964 team had great balance throughout their lineup. The offense led Union County in scoring, setting a new Pingry record of 43 goals, with 10 players scoring at least once.

The pace-setter was First Team All-Union County senior captain Ed Hoyt, who finished second in Union County scoring with 11 goals, followed by juniors Alan Gibby (eight goals) and John KixMiller (seven goals), and Art Kurz's conversion of five penalty kicks. The other offensive contributors included seniors Bob Barrett, Jeff Rettig, and John Cali; juniors Rick Roos and Dave Rath; and sophomore Bill Rosenberg. Looking back on this season, Miller said: "This was the most skilled team I ever had.'"

> "My sophomore year, Miller threw me out of JV basketball practice when I had the misfortune to be at the bottom of the pile and didn't get up soon enough. Miller didn't want to listen to my excuses (I couldn't get my teammates off of me). He made me understand that excuses are no substitute for performance.
>
> "My senior year against Peddie on a rainy day, I headed the ball over a Peddie player and was called for a foul. The referee told me I'd have to leave the game, and remembering back to the JV basketball incident, I refused to leave, saying it wasn't that egregious a foul. Only after Miller came out and I started bleeding on his white raincoat did I realize that I had a serious cut above my eye. I guess that was the one occasion on which I was tougher than he wanted me to be. Coach allowed me to play the next two games, since he knew how much that season meant to me. I was moved from sweeper to outside back because I couldn't head the ball – the stitches in my forehead were padded and wrapped with gauze."
>
> **Bob Dwyer '65**

Fred Walters, *Assistant Coach*
Bill Lord, *Manager*
Doug Hardin, *Manager*
Adam Rowen, *Manager*

Adams, B.	Fisher, G.	Mueller, G.
Auerbach, B.	Fitzpatrick, J.	Plum, T.
Barrett, R.	Fleming, D.	Rath, D.
Borden, P.	Gibby, A.	Rettig, J.
Brewer, F.	Goodfellow, G.	Rettig, T.
Cali, J.	Griesemer, J.	Roos, R.
Carter, W.	Hoyt, E.	Rosenberg, B.
Cornwall, J.	Jensen, B.	Satulsky, L.
Cumpton, J.	KixMiller, J.	Sterner, J.
Dixon, D.	Kurz, A.	Witte, J.
Dudley, R.	Matthews, J.	
Duncan, B.	Meyer, P.	
Dwyer, B.	Mitchell, T.	

1964 Season
Ed Hoyt, Captain
Art Kurz, Captain
11-0-2
Undefeated Season
Union County Champions
Prep School State Champions

Pingry Booters Win Title

Pingry School's hustling soccer team completed another undefeated campaign and captured its first Union County Conference championship yesterday.

Coach Miller Bugliari's booters turned back Edison Tech, 2-0, to win the UCC crown by one point in a home tussle. Pingry, which hadn't met enough loop foes in the past, finished second private school crown since the loop was started in 1949. Pingry had captured honors outright two years ago.

Pingry also was the only area crew to finish with an undefeated record, winning 11 games besides the deadlocks with Lawrenceville and Springfield. The Big Blue allowed only two goals while scoring 11 shutouts.

Rettig, Kurz Tally

Jeff Rettig launched Pingry's scoring in the second period. He took a corner kick by Al Gibby and drilled it home from the goal mouth. Art Kurz's penalty boot in the third session added an insurance tally.

Lawrenceville last year interrupted combine was in 1960 to Jefferson, 3-0.

The Union County Conference soccer loop was organized in 1959. Jefferson won four of the first five years with Berkeley Heights capturing the 1961 crown.

PINGRY — Sterner, g; Goodfellow, rfb; Dwyer, lfb; Rettig, rh; Meyer, ch; Kurz, lh; Rettig, or; Cali, ir; Hoyt, cf; Lich, il; Gibby, ol. Substitutes— Barrett, Kissmiller, Mueller, Roos, Rosenberg.

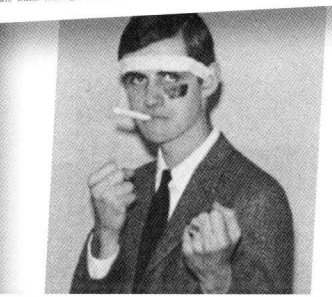

V. Soccer Team Shuts Out Four Foes In Boosting Record To 7-0-1

By DOUG FLEMING

The Varsity Soccer team, during the last two weeks, increased its number of victories to seven. Meeting Westfield, Peddie, Linden, and Blair, the squad gave no goals to their opponents. With the record of seven wins, no losses, and one tie, the team faced its toughest opponents. Jim Matthews, Jeff Goodfellow, and Pete Meyer, held the Peddie offense.

3 Pingrians On Soccer All-County

OUTSTANDING BOOTERS: These seven players were among 11 named to The Daily Journal's All-Union County scholastic soccer team. In photo above are three Pingry School stars, left to right: Art Kurz, halfback; Ed Hoyt, forward, and Bob Dwyer, fullback.

The 1965 Season

As the 1965 season began, captain Alan Gibby '66 was carrying the weight of all the sacrifices that had gotten him and his teammates to this point. As rare sophomores on the Pingry varsity, he and classmate Bill Duncan had received "the treatment," wearing the dreaded lead vest and spats while running laps, continuously being challenged to become physically tougher (Miller's favorite nickname for Alan that year was "dish rag"), and in Alan's case, having to dribble the five leather practice balls home each night to clean and saddle soap them for the next day's practice.

The larger burden he shared with the entire team was the challenge of continuing "the streak" of the previous year's undefeated team and repeating as Prep School Champions. The 1965 team responded to that challenge with a 12-0-1 season, setting a new scoring record with 45 goals and crushing Union County Champion Westfield 3-0. Led by Dave Rath's 12 goals and Alan Gibby's 10, Pingry topped the county in total scoring for the second straight year and placed six players on the Union County list of Top 15 scorers. Union and Springfield each had two. No other Union County team had more than one.

At the start of the season for a relatively young team, Miller had observed that "Providing the defense progresses, the future has possibilities." Surrendering only four goals all season long might meet even Miller's standards for "progress." Pingry's stellar defense was led by junior goalkeeper Larry McClure, fullbacks Bruce Adams and Gene Mancini, and halfbacks Bill Duncan and co-captain Jim Matthews – the only returning lettermen on defense – and junior John Witte. Mancini remembers, "The back four knew exactly what Miller demanded: Nobody gets behind you, ever."

Lawrenceville had been a thorn in Pingry's side since they first began playing in 1963, snapping the previous undefeated streak in 1963 and battling the unbeaten 1964 team to a 0-0 tie. This year was a different story. After a tense first quarter in which each team tested the other, John KixMiller opened the scoring on a cross from the right wing. Lawrenceville countered with a goal to start the second half following a scramble in front of Pingry's net. After that it was all Pingry. Gibby put Pingry back in front again with a rocket on a penalty kick, followed by third-period goals from Bill Rosenberg and Dave Rath and KixMiller's second tally of the game in the fourth quarter. The local Lawrenceville paper said it best: "Pingry's main assets: organization, precision, experience, and an urgent drive to win, were too much for Lawrenceville."

At the end of the season, Alan Gibby and Jim Matthews were both selected for All-Union County First Team honors.

> "Our final game – for the Prep Championship – was against Hun, a team comprised, as usual, mostly of foreign-born players and postgraduates. We were playing on their small, rough, poorly lined field with no clear penalty areas, and Hun faculty members, not sanctioned officials, for referees. When we got off the bus, Miller's shoulders were hunched, his face grim and his eyes narrowed into a thousand-yard stare.
>
> "Coach had reason to be anxious. Ten minutes into the game, Hun was awarded a penalty shot on a phantom hand ball call against Jim Matthews – and scored. Down by a goal, we knew we weren't playing well but just couldn't seem to get untracked. At halftime Miller told us: 'Lose and you walk home,' but we understood his real message: 'You're better than this. Play the way you know how to play.'
>
> "We responded with an explosion of scoring in the second half that left Hun stunned. Rick Roos tied the game early in the third period followed by my go-ahead goal. A little over a minute into the fourth quarter, I scored again on an assist from Jim Matthews, and Doug Fleming finished the 4-1 rout on an assist from Dave Rath. It was a good bus ride home.
>
> "The point of all the hard work Coach had put us through during the season was that he understood what we didn't: that we needed to be strong enough individually and as a team to win on the road, on a bad day, and with everything going against us. If we hadn't deeply believed in him, that victory, the unbeaten season, and the Prep Championship we earned would never have happened."
>
> **Alan Gibby '66**

Fred Walters, *Assistant Coach*
Steve Hart, *Assistant Coach*
Adam Rowen, *Manager*
Dick Harris, *Manager*

Adams, B.	English, B.	McKay, K.
Aibel, J.	Fleming, D.	Monroe, P.
Birkhold, J.	Freeman, B.	Nebel, J.
Blair, J.	Gibby, A.	Plum, J.
Bye, R.	Gilbert, S.	Rath, D.
Carter, W.	Gustafson, G.	Robinson, R.
Colford, B.	Jennings, R.	Roos, R.
Cornwall, J.	KixMiller, J.	Rosenberg, B.
Cumpton, J.	Long, B.	Sterns, W.
Cunningham, G.	Mancini, G.	Talbot, J.
Dolan, J.	Matthews, J.	Witte, J.
Duncan, B.	McClure, L.	

V. Soccer Team Posts Greatest Record Ever

By JOHN WITTE

On Friday, the varsity soccer team terminated Pingry's second consecutive undefeated soccer season after having beaten its last three oppo-

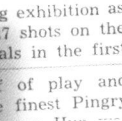

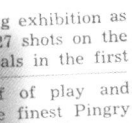

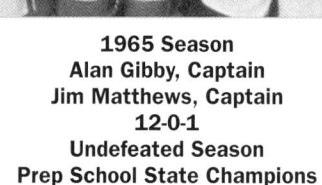

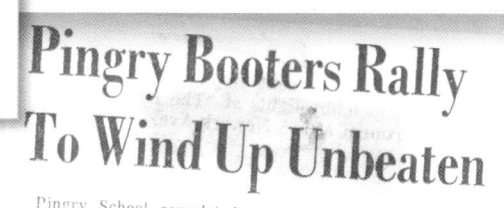

1965 Season
Alan Gibby, Captain
Jim Matthews, Captain
12-0-1
Undefeated Season
Prep School State Champions

Pingry Booters Rally To Wind Up Unbeaten

Pingry School completed another undefeated soccer season yesterday by defeating Hun's...

Pingry record by making tact with the ball 90 times Billy Rosenberg and Fleming tallied the other P markers and Jimmy Mat and Dave Rath were cre with assists.

Jeff Ties Linden
Jefferson High, victor in one game this fall, held vi

The 1966 Season

Ray Robinson, starting fullback on the 1966 team, remembers clearly the awards ceremony at Pingry when the team was honored for winning its third straight state Prep School Championship. The team presented Miller with a necktie, then said, "Read it, Coach." On the tie was written "0-0" – a scoreless tie.

To paraphrase Sepp Herberger, National Team Coach of Germany's 1954 World Cup Champions, sometimes "the round thing just won't go into the square thing." Some soccer games can be an agony of headers that sky over the goal, drift wide by inches, or hit the post. Pingry's offense in 1966 had a season full of those heartbreaking disappointments in recording seven ties against six victories and just one loss. Over a season, teams facing that kind of sustained frustration can fall apart. To the credit of the 1966 team, they never stopped working for each other. In that respect, they may have been one of Miller's most courageous squads.

And the same courage was needed on defense. When you have a dominant team conditioned to put unrelenting pressure on opponents all game long, a 1-0 lead in soccer is usually safe and a 2-0 lead is almost insurmountable. The 1966 team's defense, ranked first in Union County at the end of the season, needed to be consistently brilliant because of the offense's difficulty in finishing scoring opportunities.

The defense was up to that challenge, led by a season full of spectacular saves by second-year starting goalkeeper and First Team All-Union County selection Larry McClure. Fullbacks Ray Robinson and Rob Jennings, halfbacks John Witte, Bud Coughtry, and First Team All-Union County captain Bruce Adams, provided the wall in front of him. All but Coughtry were seniors.

In seeking to repeat as prep champions, the title came down to the annual encounter with arch-rival Lawrenceville. Pingry took an early lead when Gordie Cunningham collected a well-weighted cross from Angus Paul. Unfortunately, Lawrenceville salvaged a tie in the last six minutes with their final shot.

But a tie was enough, and Pingry was awarded its fourth Prep School Championship based on comparative season records.

In the inaugural year of the Union County Championship Tournament started by Coach Bugliari, Pingry won its first-round game, blistering Scotch Plains 5-0, on two goals by Bill Rosenberg and one each from Bruce Adams, Joe Cornwall, and Paul Monroe. In retrospect, they might have saved two of them for their next game.

Pingry was eliminated in a heartbreaking 1-0 quarter-final upset loss to Westfield, ending the second unbeaten streak of the decade at 41 games. The game's only score came when Westfield knocked in a rebound of a direct kick. Pingry outshot Westfield 16-10, but couldn't make any of their shots count.

A tie is no substitute for victory, but it's a whole lot better than a loss. The 1966 Prep Champions ran Pingry's three-year regular season undefeated streak to 41 games and preserved their seven-year invincibility in home games.

An integral part of Pingry soccer that doesn't show up in the win/loss records is what it meant for players to be part of what Miller was building – not just championship teams, but the experience of aspiring to play at a championship level. If you worked hard and committed to the goal of excellence, you got a Pingry shirt. And regardless of ability or how often you actually played in games, you got to share in that life-shaping experience. Jim Stearns '68 was one of those unheralded players.

"I remember throwing up during the long runs and wind sprints of the first day of practice because I had goofed off the summer before and had not trained as he urged us to do. But I also remember continuing to run. I remember the season-long effort to become stronger and better. I remember the tough goals that Coach set for the team and each individual on the team.

"What I took away and bring forward from Coach is a conviction in the importance of hard work and high standards. I have achieved a modest measure of success in my life: a happy marriage, a productive engineering career. They required hard work and high standards. Coach Bugliari helped me learn their importance, and I am grateful to him."

Jim Stearns '67

Fred Walters, *Assistant Coach*
Geoff Archer, *Manager*

Adams, B.	Gilbert, S.	Robinson, R.
Aibel, J.	Gustafson, G.	Rosenberg, B.
Berger, A.	Hanger, W.	Sarkin, R.
Birkhold, J.	Jennings, R.	Simson, P.
Blair, J.	McClure, L.	Staehle, R.
Bonn, H.	McKay, K.	Stearns, J.
Burt, D.	Mindnich, J.	Szarko, F.
Colford, B.	Monroe, P.	Weltchek, T.
Cornwall, J.	Monroy, C.	Whyte, S.
Coughtry, B.	Nebel, J.	Wilson, D.
Cunningham, G.	Paul, A.	Witte, J.
English, B.	Plum, J.	

1966 Season
Bruce Adams, Captain
Bill Rosenberg, Captain
6-1-7
Undefeated Regular Season
Prep School State Champions

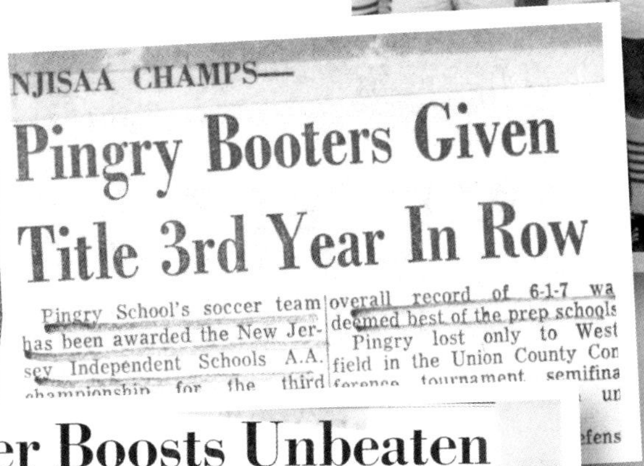

NJISAA CHAMPS—
Pingry Booters Given Title 3rd Year In Row

Pingry School's soccer team has been awarded the New Jersey Independent Schools A.A. championship for the third

overall record of 6-1-7 was deemed best of the prep schools. Pingry lost only to Westfield in the Union County Conference tournament, semifina

Varsity Soccer Boosts Unbeaten Skein To 29

BEAT BERKELEY IN SEASON'S OPENER

The Varsity Soccer team stretched its unbeaten streak to 29 games after a 2-0 win over Berkeley Heights on Friday, September 23. The starting lineup was Senior-dominated. Jim Aibel, Joe Cornwall, Greg Gustafson, John Blair, and Bill Rosenberg held positions on the starting line. Captain Bruce Adams, Bob Jennings, Bud Coughtry, John Witte, and John Plum were the defensive starters. Larry McClure was opening in the goal for the second consecutive year.

The first quarter was a scoreless tie, although the excitement of it was not altered by this fact. Bill Rosenberg, at center forward, came close three or four times, and only the strong defensive play by Berkeley Heights thwarted a score. The scoreless tie was broken at 7:25 of the second period when Joe Cornwall took a Gustafson pass

Returning nucleus of lettermen. Kneeling (from left

Co-captain Rosenberg passes to inside John Blair during 2-0 victory over Kenilworth. (Photo by Forbes)

The 1967 Season

Pressure, in important ways, was the constant, abiding character of Pingry soccer under Miller. Other teams felt it in the game-long effort just to pierce Pingry's defense and the constant barrage of shots they would have to endure until the final whistle. Pingry players felt it in the challenge of having to compete against many of the best teams in New Jersey – by the mid-1960s in high-stakes, single-elimination post-season tournaments. But the greatest pressure was internal – meeting Miller's expectations at a level of intensity no other Pingry athlete had to contend with.

The 1967 team facing those challenges was one of the youngest, least experienced teams Miller had ever put on the field. Only two senior starters from the 1966 team returned: captain Bud Coughtry and co-captain John Blair. The team powered through its first four games, easily disposing of Union County foes Berkeley Heights and Kenilworth and scoring 18 goals, led by junior John Mindnich's seven goals and strong efforts by junior Fermo Jaeckle and seniors Alan Berger, Angus Paul, and Rich Sarkin.

Their first real test came next against Westfield, essentially the same team that had snapped Pingry's unbeaten streak the previous year. Until deep in the fourth quarter, Pingry fought to maintain a one-goal lead on a second-period goal by junior Paul Simson, assisted by Angus Paul. The team's bid for revenge was spoiled by Dino Magliozzi's header with seven minutes left, giving Westfield a tie.

Pingry polished off its next two prep opponents, Peddie and Blair, before meeting Lawrenceville in a game that would decide the Prep School Championship. In what was already evolving into a bitter, fiercely contested, and often ugly rivalry, Lawrenceville's second-period goal on a penalty shot was the only score in the game. It was Pingry's first regular season loss in 47 games.

Only a 1-1 tie against a surprisingly tough Hillside team marred Pingry's record over its last five games of the season. Along the way,

Pingry beat Cranford 1-0 on Angus Paul's first-period goal on an assist from Alan Berger. The high point was a very physical 3-2 victory over traditional rival Thomas Jefferson in which Pingry's defense closed down Jefferson's junior scoring ace Phil Russo. Again, the offensive edge – and the winning goal with 3:30 left in the fourth quarter – was provided by John Mindnich, with an assist and goal from Angus Paul.

The season ended in an upset, and Pingry's second loss of the season, in the first round of the Union County Tournament. Pingry may have been looking ahead to a semifinals return match against Westfield. Scotch Plains wasn't. Scotch Plains's first-period goal stood up for the rest of the game in spite of Pingry's desperate attempts to equalize the score.

Over the 1967 season, Pingry's young, unproven defense met the test, repeating as Union County's top defensive unit, led by seniors Coughtry, Hans Bonn, and Bart English, and juniors Don Burt, Tom Weltchek, and goalkeeper Jim Corbett.

Offensively, John Mindnich's 12 goals tied Dave Rath's one-season scoring record, and both Alan Berger and Angus Paul tied Alan Gibby's assist record. Captain Bud Coughtry was selected to the Union County All-Star First Team.

"I still vividly remember the long bus ride home following the Lawrenceville loss that gave them the championship and ended a regular season winning streak of 47 games. Being teenage kids, after all, we were laughing and joking when Miller stood up at the front of the bus and roared: 'I can't believe you're laughing! There is nothing to be laughing about!' Then he sat down.

"All of us were just terrified. The rest of the two-hour bus ride was spent in utter silence. We were afraid to even breathe. Looking back, I realize now he was still teaching us. We hadn't brought our best game to one of the most important matches of the season. He was angry because he cared so deeply about us – how we did in school and what kind of men we were growing up to be. He wanted us to be the best we could be, and certainly better than we imagined we could be."

Alan Berger '68

Fred Walters, *Assistant Coach*
Dan Phillips, *Assistant Coach*
Ed Deren, *Manager*
Bryan Shelby, *Manager*

Berger, A.	Fitzpatrick, B.	Nelson, C.
Blair, J.	Ford, J.	Paul, A.
Bonn, H.	Hamann, C.	Pfister, K.
Bristol, B.	Jaeckle, F.	Sarkin, R.
Buchner, L.	Jakobsen, G.	Sharts, A.
Burt, D.	Knetzger, T.	Simson, P.
Connell, J.	Lerman, M.	Slauson, H.
Conway, B.	Leverich, D.	Szarko, F.
Corbett, J.	Maass, B.	Weltchek, T.
Coughtry, B.	Marzak, J.	Whyte, S.
English, B.	Mindnich, J.	

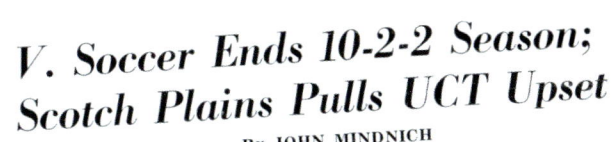

1967 Season
Bud Coughtry, Captain
John Blair, Captain
10-2-2

V. Soccer Ends 10-2-2 Season; Scotch Plains Pulls UCT Upset

By JOHN MINDNICH

The Varsity Soccer concluded the year with a 10-2-2 record. An early loss to Lawrenceville destroyed Pingry's opportunity for state honors and a defeat by Scotch Plains spoiled the Big Blues bid for a […] Nevertheless, the over-all record was a decided improveme[…] Coughtry and Blair did an outsta[…]

The 1968 Season

One dramatic statistic tells the story of the 1968 team: they came from behind in the fourth quarter or overtime to win eight of their 11 victories. The most hair-raising came both against Cranford: a goal by John Mindnich with 15 seconds left in the regular season game, and Don Burt's score in the opening round of the county playoffs – another 15 seconds from the end of the second overtime.

In the course of their 12-2-3 campaign, Pingry also evened some old scores. They held Westfield, spoiler of Pingry's undefeated streak in 1966, to a 1-1 tie, and battled to a 0-0 deadlock against a typically strong Lawrenceville team, setting up Pingry's 2-1 victory over Hun to earn Pingry its fifth Prep School Championship of the decade. The sweetest victory, however, may have been the 6-1 destruction of Scotch Plains, upset winners in the previous year, this time in the semifinals of the Union County Tournament.

In the finals, Pingry met yet another familiar adversary, Edison Tech. Edison entered the finals on a tear, demolishing defending county champion Union 5-0 and Jefferson 7-0. The game quickly turned into a typical Edison Tech–Pingry defensive struggle, with Pingry backstopped by senior Jim Corbett, and Edison by their equally talented goalkeeper Jack Russo, who just nudged ahead of Corbett for the All-Union County First Team.

Pingry's defense was tenacious – and needed to be. Edison's Argentinian-born three-time All-County forward Richie Majkut had been terrorizing Union County opponents since his sophomore year. His hat trick against Union and his four goals against Jefferson in the county tournament brought his season total to 35 goals and his career total to 101 – but in three years of play against Pingry, Majkut scored only one goal.

Unfortunately, that came in the first quarter of the 1968 finals on a breakaway from midfield and a booming opposite-corner blast from 30 yards out as the Pingry defense collapsed around him. And that one goal was enough. Pingry pressed a tiring, bunkered-in Edison Tech relentlessly in the second half, outshooting them 15-3 in the fourth quarter and 22-8 for the game, only to watch shots sail wide of the goal, hit the post, or get turned away by Russo. For the first and only time all season, Pingry's late-game magic deserted them.

The 1968 team was deluged with post-season honors. Captains Don Burt and John Mindnich were named First Team All-County players by the *Elizabeth Daily Journal*, the *Newark Evening News*, and Union County soccer coaches. Jim Corbett joined Burt and Mindnich as First Team players on the inaugural Parochial and Prep All-Star teams, and Burt became the first Pingry player to be named as a starter on the All-State, All-Groups team. Six other players – Claus Hamann, Paul Simson, Bill Maass, Dick Leverich, and Hank Slauson – all received post-season honors.

Throughout the 1968 season, senior co-captain John Mindnich, in his second year as Pingry's leading scorer, set new school records for most goals in a season (18), most goals in a career (30), and trailed record-breaking Fred Szarko for most assists in a season (8). Mindnich's highlight was a three-game stretch in which he scored nine goals, starting with a hat trick against Kenilworth, two goals against Springfield, and a four-goal outburst against Peddie – the single-game record for a Pingry player.

Sometimes in the toughest games, individual players step up and lead. In the Prep School Championship game against Hun in 1968, Claus Hamann '69 had just that kind of gutsy performance.

"I think I scored just two goals all year as a halfback. The first was in our 6-1 rout of Scotch Plains in the county semifinals. I still remember the goal against Hun – one of those times when timing, technique, and perhaps a little luck all come together. The result was a 30-yard rocket into the upper right corner."

It could not have come at a better time, with Pingry tied 1-1 against Hun. Near the end of the first half, captain Don Burt was ejected for protesting the referee's call on a penalty kick. Junior starting defender Bill Maass was already out of the game with an injury. Early in the third period, another Pingry defender was thrown out for fighting. So Claus took over, leading the defensive effort that shut down Hun for the rest of the second half, and winning the game with his fourth-quarter goal.

Claus Hamann '69

Dan Phillips, *Assistant Coach*
Peter Blanchard, *Manager*
Ed Deren, *Manager*
Bryan Shelby, *Manager*

Adams, R.	Heins, W.	Murphy, J.
Biedron, M.	Hodge, J.	Nelson, C.
Burt, D.	Homer, S.	Pfister, K.
Conway, B.	Jaeckle, F.	Seaman, B.
Corbett, J.	Kallop, P.	Sharts, A.
Costa, M.	Knetzger, T.	Shrank, I.
Cox, C.	Lerman, M.	Simson, P.
Errington, J.	Leverich, D.	Slauson, H.
Fitzpatrick, B.	Lowish, R.	Smith, M.
Ford, J.	Maass, B.	Sprague, J.
Glascock, S.	Miller, B.	Szarko, F.
Gustafson, T.	Mindnich, J.	Zoephel, J.
Hamann, C.	Mindnich, P.	

1968 Season
Don Burt, Captain
John Mindnich, Captain
12-2-3
Prep School State Champions

Pingry Soccer Team Wins Independent School Crown

Soccer Squad Edges Riverdale; Burt Leads Pingry Defensive Unit

Mindnich's Record 13th Sparks Pingry Booters

The 1969 Season

But for an out-of-position referee's blind, impulsive, and utterly wrong call of a goal for Lawrenceville, the 1969 team would have become the fourth Pingry team in the decade to go through the regular season undefeated on their way to repeating as Prep School Champions.

One game, however, shouldn't dim the luster of the 1969 team's defensive effort. As captain Bill Maass recalls, "The thoroughly strong 1968 team was very much a team of seniors, with 10 of them starting most games. However, this meant the 1969 team lacked varsity experience. Robbie Adams was the only member of the 1969 team who had scored in a varsity game – and he had scored just once. Then, at the start of a pre-season game against the Penn freshmen, we lost John Ford for the season – a three-year varsity player Miller was counting on to solidify the midfield. While this seemed the low point of the young season, it was also the turning point. Miller took the players he had and turned them into a tough, resilient team. I don't recall when Coach did it, but very early in the season he began to start four sophomores, which was totally unheard of for a Pingry team. They were Ian Alexander and Scott MacLaren in midfield, and Paul Ciszak and Jimmy Betteridge up front."

Throughout the 1960s, Pingry had established itself as the dominant defensive team in the county and prep school ranks. Even by those standards, arguably, the 1969 team's accomplishments were spectacular. In addition to the Lawrenceville "non-goal," only one other team scored on Pingry in 1969. Linden's Miro Jencick put them unexpectedly ahead with three and a half minutes to go in the fourth quarter. Brian Fitzpatrick's penalty shot, 45 seconds before the end of the game, preserved a tie.

And Jencick's goal was it for the season. Junior Bob Stephens, following a decade of outstanding goalkeepers beginning with Dick Manley '63 and including John Sterner '64, Peter Borden '65, Larry McClure '67, and Jim Corbett '69, put his own stamp on the record book, recording 15 shutouts in 17 games.

Robbed of a Prep School Championship with the Lawrenceville loss, Pingry's last chance for a title came in the Union County Tournament. After a first-round bye as the top-seeded team in the tournament, Pingry met Clark in the semifinals. The two teams battled evenly for four quarters, then through two overtime periods, to end the game tied 0-0. Pingry allowed just one corner kick the entire game, which Stephens and the defense easily turned away. But that one corner kick – the tie-breaker – was all it took for Clark to claim victory after six quarters of scoreless play.

At season's end, Bob Stephens joined captain Bill Maass on the Union County All-Star First Team, with co-captain Brian Fitzpatrick, Tim Gustafson, Ian Shrank, Brad Seaman, and Robbie Adams also receiving All-County recognition. Both Stephens and Maass were selected for Third Team All-State honors.

Ian Shrank, a junior stalwart on defense, can still relive the "non-goal" by Lawrenceville clearly, all these years later. "I was right there, back on defense. I saw it all. Lawrenceville won a corner kick, and sent a high, looping cross into the penalty area. Bobby Stephens tracked it all the way, and standing inside the goal, reached out and cleanly grabbed the ball, holding it with his arms stretched out well ahead of the goal line. His back was to the referee, blocking the referee's view completely.

"In the millisecond after thinking, 'He got it!' I heard the referee's whistle blow and saw his hands signal a goal. When the save was called a goal, I went berserk, screaming at the referee.

"In an instant, Coach was on the field next to me. I would have expected him to be all over the referee, too, but instead, he pulled me aside. I can't remember exactly what he said – I was too upset really to listen – but I got his message: 'Calm down. Get yourself under control. We still have over a half to play. We can come back – and we need you!' We fought for the equalizer the rest of the game, taking 17 shots to Lawrenceville's 11, but the result was still a 0-1 brutal – and tainted – loss."

Ian Shrank '71

Dan Phillips, *Assistant Coach*
Peter Blanchard, *Manager*
Chris Colford, *Manager*
Bryan Shelby, *Manager*

Adams, R.	Ford, J.	Morgan, J.
Alexander, I.	Glascock, S.	Nelson, C.
Betteridge, J.	Grippo, J.	Parker, G.
Biedron, M.	Grover, J.	Penney, J.
Ciszak, P.	Gustafson, T.	Rooke, B.
Connell, M.	Homer, S.	Sacks, D.
Cox, C.	Lowish, R.	Schmidt, R.
Downs, G.	Maass, B.	Seaman, B.
Duncan, B.	MacLaren, S.	Shrank, I.
Engel, Rick	Mading, O.	Slobodien, D.
Engel, Rob	Mindnich, P.	Stephens, B.
Fitzpatrick, B.	Monroe, B.	Walbridge, J.

1969 Season
Bill Maass, Captain
Brian Fitzpatrick, Captain
11-2-4

The 1970s: Union County Dominance

"What's the secret of anything? It's hard work and the attempt to be ready for every game... and we try to keep it fun."

MILLER, 1975

Throughout his career as a player, from his sophomore year at Pingry through Springfield College and his years playing semi-pro soccer with the Westfield Lions, Miller had followed a simple, fundamental principle: to win consistently against top competition you have to continuously improve your skills and understanding of the game. The best way to do that is by practicing and competing against players who are better than you. Each season, Miller used pre-season games to set players' expectations for the level of soccer they needed to reach. Opponents included not only top-rated high school teams not on Pingry's schedule, but also the Penn freshman team.

Miller's successful efforts in the 1960s to grow the sport of high school soccer in New Jersey had the inevitable consequence of increasing the caliber of play of the teams Pingry needed to beat to win championships.

That meant finding ways to continuously lift the level of the game for Pingry players. Miller needed not just dedicated, tough, hard-working athletes who would never quit; he needed soccer players. But you can't develop a soccer player in a couple of weeks of pre-season practice and a 12-week season. Pingry's rise to become the dominant soccer team in Union County was forged by the commitment of the players to work at their game during the off season.

For many players in the mid to late 1960s through the 1970s, the "off season" was spent at Miller's Camp Waganaki in Maine. Younger campers gained the experience of competing against and learning from older, more experienced often All-County and All-State players. For members of Miller's team, a summer at Waganaki was spent as counselors-in-training or as members of the infamous "kitchen crew." Pete Borden '65 remembers almost developing a hernia lugging rocks off what would become the soccer field – when he wasn't humping 50-pound potato sacks for Waganaki "chef" Larry Karet.

Even though the Pingry soccer players called Waganaki "Miller's illegal soccer camp," Miller was careful to follow the state athletic association's rules and restrictions on formally coaching his players in the summer. That doesn't mean they didn't work hard on developing new skills and getting in shape – often until 9:00 at night.

But competing against your teammates wasn't enough. In order for them to not only play the game at a higher level but actually feel the game of soccer, Miller knew his kids needed to develop against the best soccer talent in New Jersey.

The Waganaki Soccer Camp

Rob Curtis started as a camper at Waganaki as a nine-year-old – which means that's also when he started playing soccer. "Compared with the professional quality of Pingry soccer, Waganaki was pretty rough. We played on a rock-strewn field wearing soccer cleats or sneakers, shorts or cut-off jeans, tube socks, and the Waganaki T-shirts we were supposed to save for Sunday. And Waganaki was a small camp; putting age-group teams together for games and tournaments with other camps was a challenge. It was typical to have nine- and 10-year-old kids playing on the 12-and-under team. So growing up, you were competing with and against older players. And for young Pingry kids, our coaches were Miller's varsity stars – players we idolized. Then, as an older camper myself, it became part of my job to get younger kids involved in the game and make them feel a part of the team.

"The biggest impact on my growth as a player, however, was when Miller brought in two counselors from England, Roger Bruce and Mike Prideaux, both of whom were soccer coaches with a whole new approach to the game. It certainly helped me when I and the other Waganaki kids returned to Pingry each fall. We were in good shape, our skills had developed, rather than becoming rusty, and we were mentally ready to start the season at a high level. It gave Pingry a big, early edge on most of the teams we played."

Rob Curtis '79

In the mid-'70s, Miller initiated the Pingry Soccer Camp – the first such camp in New Jersey. Run by assistant coach Dan Phillips '59, and now in its 42nd year, the camp exposed young players to some of the best coaches in the country – and to the benefits of attending Pingry.

Farcher's Grove

But developing highly skilled players ultimately meant winter soccer on the frozen field of Farcher's Grove in Union and the other tough fields of the German-American Soccer League. Art and Robbie Kurz's father was a member of the Elizabeth Sport Club and a sponsor of their semi-pro team, which would change its name in 1982 to the Union Lancers. His sons had played at Farcher's Grove in the youth programs since they could first kick a soccer ball. He helped Miller, starting in the mid-1960s, get his best kids onto league teams – the first prep school coach to start formally developing players out of season. Miller's model was the public school stars who played soccer year-round because that's just what they did – they were soccer players.

Sean O'Donnell '75, who captained the 1974 team and went on to star at the University of Pennsylvania, was just such a "soccer player." He began playing at Farcher's Grove with his buddies as a little kid, using empty beer kegs from Farcher's bar for goals. "There was nothing even close to fancy about Farcher's," Sean remembers. "The dirt field was bounded on one side by the train tracks and on the other by the river, with the PSE&G substation in the rear. The far side of the field was fenced in – right next to the field. If you overran the touchline you smashed right into the chain link fence. On the other side by the clubhouse they had raised wooden bleachers, but people didn't usually sit there. They lined the field. You learned to be really careful when you were playing the ball next to the other team's fans. If you lofted the ball over the 20-foot-high fence at one end, it could bounce through the Sunoco station next door and start rolling downhill on the street.

"We got a lot of conditioning just sprinting after balls to keep them from getting run over in the traffic. And the 'locker room,' if you can call it that, was a cinder block building that hadn't been painted – or cleaned – for decades. The shower room had three shower heads…and lots of mold. Getting to the bottom of it would have been like an architectural dig."

Christopher Merrill's *The Grass of Another Country* is a fascinating history of the growth of soccer in New Jersey and the United States leading up to the 1990 World Cup – and a must-read for fans of both the U.S. Men's National Team and Pingry soccer. In it, he relates his own experiences playing at Farcher's when he was Sean's Pingry teammate. "I remembered training here under the lights in midwinter: how the cleat marks, divots, and holes in the mud would freeze until the field was harder and rougher than a cobblestone street. Good players like Sean learned to run with short strides, moving their feet constantly, hoping not to turn an ankle. They learned to trap the ball with a minimum of effort, dribble it close to their feet so that it would not get away from them, adapt instantly to balls ricocheting off the ground, deliver to their teammates quick, accurate passes, and pray for the best." Brian O'Donnell '81 remembers watching the old New York Cosmos with their team of international stars play an exhibition at Farcher's. "Pelé handled the ball on the rutted field easily. That wasn't a surprise. But Franz Beckenbauer had a nightmare game of bad passes."

Grass couldn't grow on Farcher's field, but something else did: Pingry's 1970s dominance as Union County champions.

Mighty Sean O'Donnell shows off a little style.

The Puma Soccer Camp

The other foundation for Pingry's dominance in the '70s and succeeding decades came in the unrelenting heat of the Puma soccer camp in Lawrenceville – three to five weeks of practicing and competing against soccer standouts from across the country, including junior national team players and prospects.

Hubert Volgelsinger, or, as players called him, "Hubie," the Austrian-born former Yale coach and director of the Puma All-Star Soccer School, believed with the fervor of religious commitment in the value of relentless conditioning, incessant skill drilling, and intense practice. He saw to it that the soccer players who attended his three-week school got a big dose of all three. Hubie may have borrowed a lot of his philosophy and approach from Dutch coaching legend Weil Coerver, but he added his own special touch as well. Hubie's mantra was "Learn under stress, condition under stress, and you learn to play at a peak level under stress." Two generations of Pingry soccer players can attest to the positive impact of that experience on their success.

> ### Winter Soccer
>
> "One night, the Newark Sport Club played an indoor match in the Elizabeth Armory, a dilapidated (and now boarded-up) building in the heart of the city....[The balcony] stands were full. Down on the floor, my teammates and I heard Latinos shouting from one side of the stands, Scotsmen and Irishmen from the other; the smell of beer, sangria, and a variety of fried foods mingled in the air. 'Whatever you do,' said one of my friends, 'don't mess up.' 'What do you mean?' I asked. 'You'll see,' he replied.
>
> "And I did....I was running down the court, veering in from the wing to take a ball rolling across the floor. The goalkeeper had been drawn out of position, and I had an open shot at an empty net. I struck the ball with the outside of my foot, determined to keep it low. But it sailed over the goal. Crestfallen, I ran back up the court, shaking my head – and then I was soaking wet. An old Scotsman was leaning over the railing of the balcony, waving his empty beer mug at me. 'Keep your head down, laddie!' he roared. The crowd laughed and clapped. I smelled like a tavern the rest of the game."
>
> **Christopher Merrill '75**

> ### "Soccermasochism"
>
> Tom Trynin '79, who was team co-captain his senior year, still remembers the Puma regimen: "Each day started at 6:00 a.m. with 'Soccernastics' (players called it 'Soccermasochism'): physical torture thinly disguised as fitness training, then a half hour of dribbling practice on the cold, wet field – in bare feet. Then shower and breakfast before the real work of the day began. An hour of strategy discussions, then on the field for three hours of drills. Shower, then lunch, followed by a 20-minute 'rest period.' By the third day we were setting our alarm clocks to make sure we could wake up after 15 minutes. Back on the field for three hours of practice games, with additional drills thrown in just in case we weren't tired enough. Shower, then dinner, followed by soccer movies. At 10:00 we'd set the alarm again for 5:30 and collapse into bed. When I got home, I was so exhausted I think I slept for two days straight. But I knew I was twice the player I had been before I left for soccer camp."
>
> **Tom Trynin '79**

The payoff for this sacrifice and effort is now a matter of the record books: Pingry won its first Union County Championship when the undefeated 1970 team tied defending champion Scotch Plains 0-0 after two overtime periods in the final, and the school went on to win or share successive titles from 1974 through 1977 and again in 1983. The teams of the 1970s included four undefeated squads and won five Prep School Championships, scoring a total of 459 goals over the decade while yielding only 77 and registering 89 shutouts.

Miller was named Coach of the Year by the New Jersey College and High School Soccer Officials Association for the 1972 season and the Central New Jersey Coach of the Year in 1975. To cap an extraordinary decade, Miller was selected as Soccer Coach of the 1970s for the *Star-Ledger's* "Team of the Century."

Miller Bugliari Field Dedication

When Paul Ciszak '72, co-captain of the 1971 team, first broached the idea of naming Pingry's soccer field after Miller, George Christow, Miller's close friend and Pingry's Athletic Director, asked jokingly, "Aren't people supposed to be dead before something is dedicated to them?" In Miller's case the answer is a resounding "No," and in fact Miller has had the Pingry varsity soccer field dedicated to him not once, but three times.

Initial credit for this gesture of love and appreciation goes to co-captains Ciszak, Ian Alexander '72, and the entire 1971 team. As Ciszak described it, "I cannot recall who actually came up with the idea of dedicating the field to Miller, but I do vividly recall the first substantive discussion of the notion being at a study hall with fellow senior Ralph Warren, so I am quite willing to give Ralph credit. Since we knew that the school was planning to move, we decided this dedication would go with the school, dedicating the varsity soccer field 'to Coach Bugliari in perpetuity, wherever the location.'

"Fortunately for us, Ian Alexander was also the President of the Class, Student Council, and Student-Faculty Assembly. Ian suggested we speak with English teacher Jack Dufford about how to proceed, and Mr. Dufford was instrumental in helping us word a formal proposal to be ratified by the Board of Trustees. The Board of Trustees did endorse the proposal at their next meeting and made special note of the 'perpetuity clause,' which we were very happy about.

"Classmate Bill Weldon's father, owner of Weldon Materials, helped us select the original stone, installed the plaque into the stone, and set the stone at the Hillside campus field. The formal dedication of the field took place at the 1972 Pingry Reunion on a beautiful spring day. As we were getting ready for the ceremony, I noticed a figure laboring across the fields from Master's Square, struggling to walk in our direction. I suddenly realized it was Mr. Les. In what was probably his last public appearance before his passing from pancreatic cancer, Mr. Les wanted to be there for this dedication. I went out to meet him, tried to help him, and in typical Les fashion he said, "Leave me alone, Paulie!" I know his presence meant a lot to both me and Coach Bugliari. The picture of the dedication has me, Ian Alexander, Coach Bugliari, and Mr. Les. It could not have been a more perfect moment.

"So why did we do it? As simply as I can state it, we felt we had something special in Coach Bugliari. This was the late '60s and '70s. A difficult time for many. But Miller showed us and taught us some universal principles: responsibility, self-discipline, reliance on others, caring about others, and learning from both winning and losing with integrity and dignity. And we had fun doing it. This was much more than the 'sports can teach you about life' cliché. This teacher taught every bit as effectively as any academic, both the subject content as well as the bigger picture. We didn't do it for the 1971 team, but for Miller's impact on us. And we wanted everyone associated with Pingry, present and future, to know it."

(Left to right): Ian Alexander '72, Headmaster Cunningham, Miller, Mr. Les, Paul Ciszak '72.

The 1970 Season

In the 1970 Union County Championship final against Scotch Plains, the two undefeated teams played four scoreless quarters, with Pingry's All-State goalkeeper Bob Stephens making a brilliant save on a penalty kick in the last minute of regulation time to preserve the tie.

As the Pingry team gathered around Miller in midfield prior to the first overtime to decide the winner, team captain Ian Shrank remembers, "It seemed as if the entire Scotch Plains school was on their sideline chanting 'We will, we will, rock you! Rock You!' The noise was deafening. Miller was kneeling in the center of the team, his voice almost gone, pounding on the ground with his fist, pleading in a hoarse near-whisper: 'You can do this! YOU CAN DO THIS!' The stress was so great I could barely breathe."

Two scoreless overtime periods later, Pingry won its first Union County Tournament as co-champions with Scotch Plains, inaugurating a run of five county championships through the decade of the 1970s.

As expected, Pingry met Lawrenceville to decide the Prep School Championship. A typically hard-fought, physical battle against Lawrenceville ending in a scoreless tie earned Pingry its sixth Prep School Championship. Pingry might also have claimed itself to be the New York City prep champions by virtue of their 2-1 triumph over previously undefeated Horace Mann on a tap-in by Paul Ciszak and a stunning half-field volley by Ralph Warren, plus their 3-0 demolition of the eventual champion Riverdale on two goals by Jay Morgan and one by co-captain Peter Mindnich '71, brother of Pingry's scoring record-holder John Mindnich '68. All told, over the season 10 players contributed to Pingry's 40 goals, led by seniors Mindnich, Morgan, Gates Parker, and co-captain Tim Gustafson; juniors Ciszak and Jim Betteridge, with assists from juniors Warren, Craig Johnson, and Ian Alexander; and sophomore Robbie Kurz.

When you dominate opponents as Pingry had done through the 1960s, they lift their own game in response. Pingry's defense – fullbacks Oliver Mading '71 and Gary Giorgi '72, and halfbacks Shrank, Rudy Schmidt '71, Scott MacLaren '72, and Ian Alexander '72 – met that challenge head-on, surrendering just three goals all season, and again shutting out such All-Star scorers as Hillside's Bob Boehm, Edison Tech's Jack Russo, Berkeley Heights' Ron Steel, and Scotch Plains' Greg Frey.

Without question, however, the leader of Pingry's defense was All-County goalkeeper Bob Stephens '71. Sports reporters exhausted the resources of the Thesaurus with words like "insuperable" in attempting to describe Stephens' heroics. Over a two-year career spanning 34 games, Stephens surrendered just five goals, recording 31 shutouts – 16 of them in his senior year, including the last 13 games in a row. At season's end he was selected for the second time as Union County's top goalkeeper, joining Ian Shrank on the All-Star First Team and becoming the second Pingry player, after Don Burt '69, to be named to the All-State First Team.

The 1970 team's accolades included what would become yet another continuous hallmark of excellence for Pingry soccer: In the inaugural listing of the Top 20 teams in the state by the New Jersey Soccer Coaches Association, Pingry ended the season ranked No. 2 in the state behind undefeated Kearny.

"The most memorable games my senior year were both against Westfield, our big rival along with Lawrenceville. We beat them twice, both times 1-0, once at home during the regular season and then on the road in the county tournament. They put tremendous pressure on us both games, but we got a goal in each game and made it stand up both times. I know Coach was very proud of us for our toughness. He loved beating the big high schools. He was definitely focused and more intense than usual in the week leading up to these games and during them.

"It was a great team effort as we withstood their relentless attack together. Tim Gustafson was magnificent in the first game, and put himself into the action all over the field. Gates Parker scored a stunning goal in the county game, as he one-timed a cross into the corner. Their goalie had no chance. I still remember after both games the Westfield players sat on the ground watching us run after the game, thinking 'WTF! We outplayed these guys, lost to them, and now they're running sprints!' The Westfield players were exhausted and frustrated, but full of respect for their adversaries."

Peter Mindnich '71

Dan Phillips, *Assistant Coach*
Chris Colford, *Manager*
Gerald Garafola, *Manager*
Bob Nelson, *Manager*

Alexander, I.	Hall, K.	Penney, J.
Bartenstein, J.	Homer, C.	Sacks, D.
Betteridge, J.	Johnson, C.	Schmidt, R.
Ciszak, P.	Kurtz, R.	Shrank, I.
Conway, G.	Kurz, R.	Stephens, B.
Cunningham, G.	MacLaren, S.	Warren, R.
Davis, B.	Mading, O.	Weldon, B.
Fraites, J.	Marano, F.	Zahodiakin, P.
Giorgi, G.	Mindnich, P.	Zenker, D.
Grover, J.	Morgan, J.	
Gustafson, T.	Parker, G.	

1970 Season
Ian Shrank, Captain
Tim Gustafson, Co-Captain
Peter Mindnich, Co-Captain
14-0-4
Undefeated Season
Union County Champions
Prep School State Champions

Pingry Moves Up To 2nd In Soccer Rankings

Pingry Is Second To None In Art Of Soccer Defense

FACES IN THE CROWD

MILLER BUGLIARI, coach of the Pingry School soccer team in Elizabeth, N.J., this season led his players to their sixth state title in 11 years. Pingry has never lost a regular-season home game, and its overall record under Coach Bugliari stands at 116-12-33.

Stephens Of Pingry Gets 14th Shutout

The 1971 Season

For the 21 seniors on the 1971 team, their soccer career at Pingry had been a long and exciting ride. As sophomores, captain Paul Ciszak and co-captain Ian Alexander, along with Jim Betteridge and Scott MacLaren, had made strong contributions to the 1969 team's 11-2-4 season and suffered through the bitterly contested loss to Lawrenceville. As juniors, joined by classmates Craig Johnson, Gary Giorgi, Ralph Warren, and David Zenker, they had savored the triumph of the 1970 team's undefeated season and dual State and County Championships.

Led by its seniors, now including John Bartenstein, Granville Conway, Bruce Davis, Joe Fraites, Kip Hall, Rob Kogan, and Dave Poppick, with powerful support from juniors Kevin Briody, Jim Gibby, Rich Kurtz, Robbie Kurz, Rich O'Connor, and Greg Whitehead, and sophomores Andy Lawson and Mike Mindnich, the 1971 team ran Pingry's regular season undefeated streak to 39 games, obliterating 14 opponents by a combined score of 38 goals to 3, with senior goalkeeper Gardner Cunningham and the defense recording 12 shutouts.

They entered the last game of the season, the Union County finals against Berkeley Heights, with a 1-0 Prep School State Championship already to their credit. Against Lawrenceville in the finals, Ciszak's hard-hit full volley off a cross by Betteridge slammed off the post, fortunately right back to Ciszak, who rammed home the rebound for the game-winning goal. Cunningham made a spectacular save on a Lawrenceville penalty kick minutes later to preserve the victory.

To get to the final against Berkeley Heights, Pingry had to beat arch-rival Westfield in the semifinals not once, but twice. The first game ended in a 2-2 deadlock after six quarters of regulation and overtime play, Pingry's goals coming on Rich O'Connor's second period goal and Robbie Kurz's electrifying bicycle kick off a cross from Ralph Warren. Because both teams were tied in corner kicks, they had to replay the semifinal four days later. This time, Paul Ciszak's third quarter goal erased a 1-0 Westfield lead, and after two more scoreless overtimes, Pingry was declared the winner on a 2-0 margin of corner kicks.

Pingry's reward for fighting through the semifinal against Westfield was a repeat confrontation with similarly undefeated nemesis Berkeley Heights, whom Pingry had tied in the regular season 0-0. For 56 minutes, in front of a crowd of 3,000 spectators, both defenses dominated once again, Gardner Cunningham turning away 13 shots. But this time, an unmarked Gary White's first-time kick with four minutes left eluded a diving Cunningham. It was only the third loss Pingry's seniors had suffered over a 38-game career.

Gary Giorgi and Paul Ciszak were named to the 1971 All-Central Jersey and All-Prep First Teams. They were joined on the Union County First Team by Jim Betteridge, whose 17 career assists set a new Pingry record. Union County post-season honors also went to Ian Alexander and Scott MacLaren. Pingry ended the season ranked fifth in the state.

"I still call it 'The Greatest Pingry Game Nobody Ever Saw.' We played the Prep championship game at Lawrenceville on a gray, overcast day in front of perhaps 10 spectators. We dominated the first half, yet held only a 1-0 lead. Midway through the third quarter, we lost our star winger, Jim Betteridge, to injury, but Craig Johnson came in and played the game of his life, keeping our attack alive. Then with about five minutes remaining, Lawrenceville was awarded a penalty kick. Up stepped Mike Pico to take the shot, an All-Group first string All-State player the year before. He smashed a low hard shot and in a blur, Gardner Cunningham was parallel to the ground and got a hand on it... the ball went flying out of bounds and we were ecstatic!

"Until the whistle blew. And the referee decided one of us had stepped into the penalty area before the ball was struck, and awarded Lawrenceville another penalty kick! As captain, the only player given the privilege to 'speak' to the referee, I went sprinting toward the ref to 'have a discussion' with him when Coach Bugliari grabbed me and threw me aside. Coach knew I would probably get ejected from the game. So, at the top of my lungs, I yelled, 'Do it again Gardner! He can't shoot that well twice!' Pico stepped up, agitated, and drilled a shot high over the crossbar. We held on to become sole State Champions."

Paul Ciszak '72

Dan Phillips, *Assistant Coach*
Chris Colford, *Manager*
Bob Nelson, *Manager*
Skip Slauson, *Manager*

Alexander, I.	Fraites, J.	MacLaren, S.
Ambrose, W.	Gibby, J.	Martin, J.
Bartenstein, J.	Giorgi, G.	Mindnich, M.
Betteridge, J.	Hall, K.	O'Connor, R.
Briody, K.	Hurri, H.	Poppick, D.
Ciszak, P.	Johnson, C.	Reisner, D.
Colter, C.	Kogan, R.	Warren, R.
Conway, G.	Kurtz, R.	Weldon, B.
Cunningham, G.	Kurz, R.	Whitehead, G.
Davis, B.	Lawson, A.	Zenker, D.

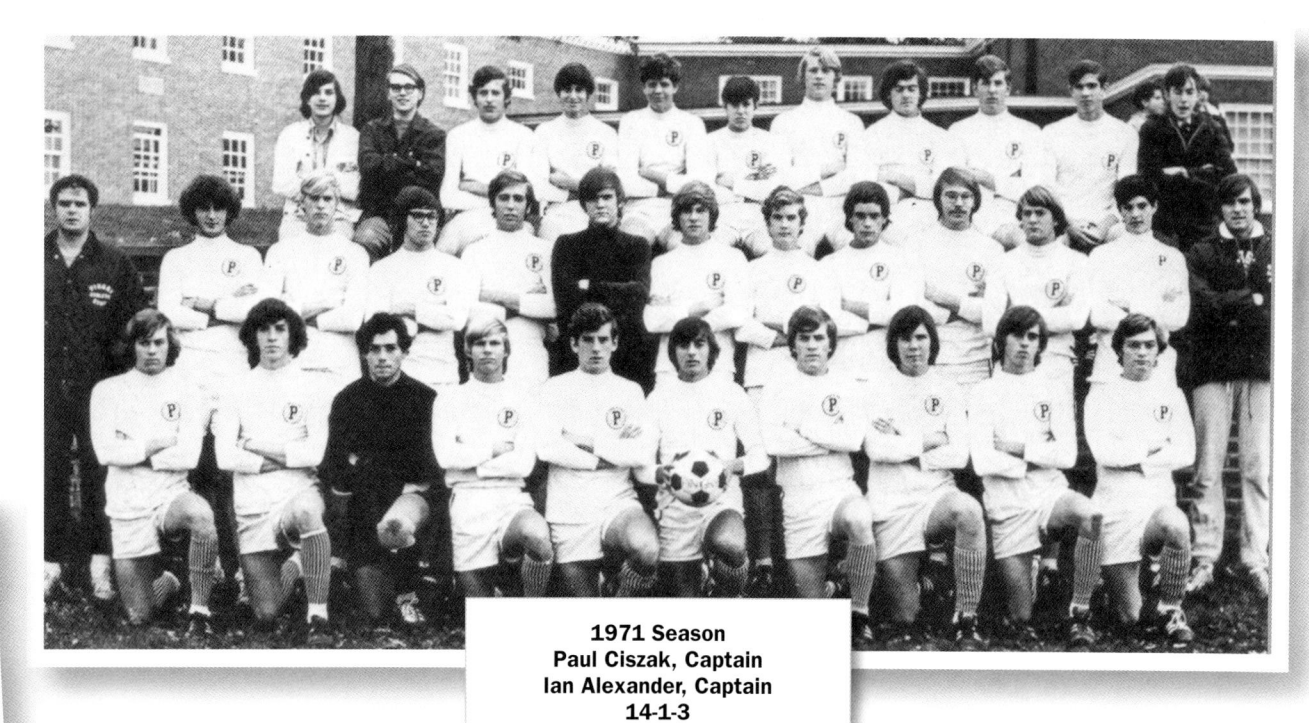

1971 Season
Paul Ciszak, Captain
Ian Alexander, Captain
14-1-3
Undefeated Regular Season
Prep School State Champions

The 1972 Season

In spite of returning only two starters from the previous year's team – co-captains Rich Kurtz, a three-year letter winner, and Robbie Kurz, a two-year starter – the 1972 squad had high expectations: claiming its third straight Prep School Championship, this year in the inaugural "A" Division prep school tournament; gaining revenge for the preceding year's 1-0 loss to Berkeley Heights in the Union County Tournament finals; and preserving Pingry's undefeated regular-season streak of 13 years.

The 1972 squad was both untested, and uncharacteristically young for a Pingry team. Besides Kurtz and Kurz, seniors included Rich O'Connor and Jim Gibby on the line, halfback Kevin Briody, defenders Dave Gernert and Greg Whitehead, and goalkeeper Jim Page. The bulk of the team consisted of juniors Mike Mindnich, Dave Lerman, Dave Reisner, John Shelby, Andy Lawson, Tom Briody, Chris Scott, and sophomore Sean O'Donnell.

Given the team's relative inexperience, their offensive explosion may have surprised Miller; it certainly shocked Pingry's opponents. Their 55 goals shattered the previous record set by the 1965 team. On their way to recording 16 victories – the highest number of wins ever to that point for a Pingry team – they finished the regular season undefeated, crushing Lawrenceville 4-0, and stunning Westfield 1-0 on a throw-in goal by Kevin Briody. Except for a scoreless tie against old rival Edison Tech after two overtime periods, they overwhelmed the rest of their prep school and high school opponents.

The young defense started off skittishly. Pingry had to come back against Horace Mann 3-2 on Lerman's goal with three minutes left and recover from a two-goal halftime deficit against Montclair Academy on Lawson's hard volley in overtime. After an early goal by traditional "across the fence" rival Hillside in a game won by Pingry 3-1, they reeled off nine straight shutouts, concluding the season with a 5-1 trashing of Cranford. At the conclusion of the season, Pingry had risen to No. 5 on the NJSCA's Top 20 state ranking.

The 1972 team's surge continued through the playoffs with a solid victory over Hun on a rain-soaked, muddy Wardlaw field, followed by a dominating second half against Lawrenceville in the finals at Rutgers University to win 2-1 on goals by Mindnich, assisted by Kurz and O'Connor on Mindnich's corner kick.

In the Union County Tournament, second-seeded Pingry easily eliminated Kenilworth 4-0, setting up a semifinal match against sixth-seeded Clark. Against Pingry in 1972, Clark brought its "A+" game, playing courageous soccer to stunningly upset an equally determined Pingry team. An own-goal by Pingry after a scramble in front of the net in the second period, plus Clark goalkeeper Cliff Platt's 15 saves, ended Pingry's hopes of a county championship.

The local Rahway paper summed up the game's aftermath: "A jubilant Clark team was sobered momentarily at the approach of the entire Pingry squad for the after-game congratulatory routine. They clasped hands, some embraced, and all of them had tear-streaked faces."

Following Pingry's 16-1-1 season and final No. 10 state ranking, Rich Kurtz and Robbie Kurz were selected to the Union County All-Star First Team.

"It was the summer of my senior year – August 1972 – in pre-season practice at the Hillside campus in the sweltering heat. The team was coming off an excellent season the prior year but had lost the bulk of its starters. After one particularly upsetting practice (to the Coach) – Robbie Kurz suffered an uncontrollable fit of dribbling; Rich O'Connor arrived late due to a 'project' with a Vail-Deane student; and for the final straw, our trainer ran out of Life Savers – Coach B, in some choice words, told us we were one of the weakest teams he had coached and that we would be lucky if we finished with a .500 record (that's the polite version). The challenge worked, as those words struck to our core and we felt an incredible motivation that carried us through the season. We still remember that speech and until this day talk about proving the Coach wrong – the team went on to a 16-1-1 record, the state championship, and the Pingry Hall of Fame."

Kevin Briody '73

Dan Phillips, *Assistant Coach*
Richie Thomas, *Assistant Coach*
August Wooter, *Assistant Coach*
Bob Nelson, *Manager*
Skip Slauson, *Manager*

Ambrose, W.	Kietzman, K.	Parker, P.
Briody, K.	Kurtz, R.	Pell, T.
Briody, T.	Kurz, R.	Reisner, D.
Cipriano, G.	Lawson, A.	Schoch, J.
Dormont, P.	Lerman, D.	Scott, C.
Gatto, J.	Mindnich, M.	Shelby, J.
Gernert, D.	Monroe, C.	Spurr, G.
Gibby, J.	O'Connor, R.	Whitehead, G.
Hanson, J.	O'Donnell, S.	Whitlock, C.
Houston, A.	Page, J.	Williams, D.

1972 Season
Robbie Kurz, Captain
Rich Kurtz, Captain
16-1-1
Undefeated Regular Season
Prep School State Champions

Booters Crush Lawrenceville, 4-0; Conclude Regular Season at 13-0-1

By DAVE REISNER

After having tied Edison on Friday the 13th of October, a somewhat disgruntled Pingry soccer team transcended its frustration and finished the season victoriously. At Linden, Richard O'Connor, "the icebreaker," put Blue on the scoreboard with an intended cross that sailed into the left-hand corner of the goal. Andy Lawson followed in the second quarter with a turn-and-shoot and soon after, Kevin Briody assisted Bob Kurz for the third tally. Mr. Bugliari gave a few words of encouragement to the team, ("I have nothing to say. You guys play the game your way!"), and Pingry was back on the field ready for blood. The subs all got chances to show off rainbows and Tasmanian Swirls before Richard Kurtz sealed the victory with a score in the fourth quarter. At this point, Linden players were getting rowdy as catcalls began to emanate from their bench.

On Saturday, the 21st, Pingry ho

year's team had learned to know and love. Pingry meant business and eagerly showed it. Excellent ball control and team spirit paved the way to a 4-0 shutout. O'Connor, on the heels of his past Westfield glory, put in two goals in the third and fourth

semble themselves on dry land and went into calisthenics. Delbarton, upon swimming to the field, appeared to be tired by the time the game started. Dave Lerman watched the game from a bathyscope as Kurz, playing more brilliantly every time he touched the ball, netted the game's only two goals.

Varsity Soccer Remains Unbeaten; Briody's Throw-in Edges Westfield

By GUY CIPRIANO

The Varsity Soccer team continued it's winning ways on October 11, when the Big Blue triumphed over Westfield's Blue Devils, or Whirling Dervishes. In the opening minute of the game, the Blue massed for a score, but shots by Mike Mindnich and Rich O'Connor went just wide. The visitors bounced back, and by the end of the first quarter were playing even

Booters Maul Union Catholic, 7-0; Win Twice in Thrilling Comebacks

By GUY CIPRIANO

September 1 marked the beginning of another Pingry soccer season. This year, led by Captains Robbie Kurz and Rich Kurtz, the Big Blue was looking to maintain the fine records of past teams. Three multi-team scrimmages prepared the Blue for its opening contest against Horace Mann. Pingry started off quickly, barely missing two opening minute tallies. But a defensive lapse allowed the New Yorkers to convert a loose ball in the goal area. Fired up, Pingry came back in the second period on a penalty kick by Rich Kurtz, equalizing the score just prior to the half.

A few adjustments were made during the intermission by coaches Bugliari, Phillips, and Mr. August Wooter, and Horace Mann had no serious offensive threats through the rest of the game. With the Big Blue

Sean O'Donnell, Pingry's sophomore soccer sensation, dribbles as three defenders pursue him.

In the second game, versus Montclair Academy, a feeling of euphoria had engulfed the team, and by game time, the Blue was expecting an easy win.

After Mr. Bugliari was revived and the team calmed down, a pattern of all-out attack was formulated in which to get two goals in the remaining thirty minutes

The 1973 Season

Entering the 1973 season, Pingry was ranked No. 10 in the state off the previous year's 16-1-1 season and the return of seven experienced starters on the line and midfield. Once again, the defense was new, with Rick Raabe, Dave Gernert, and Steve Spurr as fullbacks and Guy Cipriano in goal. Seniors Jon Shelby, Andy Lawson, and Tom Briody started in midfield; Mike Mindnich, Chris Scott, and Jim Hoitsma manned the wings; and the attack was led by Sean O'Donnell, Dave Lerman, and John Hanson. Pingry breezed through the first half of their schedule, outscoring opponents 20-3 and registering six shutouts. One of those shutouts, however, against perennial Union County championship contender Berkeley Heights, should have sounded a warning note.

Coach Ralph Bianchi of Berkeley Heights came up with a defensive scheme to blunt Pingry's attack. Against Pingry, Bianchi fielded a hybrid 2-4-4 defense that had four interior players in a diamond shape, with the critical front and back of the diamond manned by two junior All-State players, Fred Vitollo and Pete Dellmono. The strategy blunted Pingry's passing game, and both sides fought to a tough 0-0 tie. And Westfield coach Jim Geohegan paid attention.

Geohegan used the same formation against Pingry. "If it was good enough for Berkeley Heights," he said, "I figured it was good enough for us." The result was an offensive barrage of 21 shots by Westfield. Cipriano was inspired in the goal, making acrobatic saves to keep Westfield scoreless until just before the end of the first half, when, following a flurry of shots, Westfield's Phil Carragher found the ball at his feet to the left of the goal. Cipriano, now lying on the ground, managed to get a hand on Carragher's shot, but the ball trickled into the corner of the net to give Westfield a 1-0 lead. A third-period penalty kick gave Westfield its 2-0 victory, Pingry's first regular-season loss since 1969, going back 58 games. Pingry dropped from seventh in the state ranking to 20th.

The team rebounded to win its next four games with 0-0 ties against Lawrenceville and Cranford and headed into the Union County Tournament as a hungry, fourth-seeded team. Then disaster struck. In the opening game, a short-handed Pingry met a deep, talented Jefferson squad. For most of the season, co-captains Jon Shelby and Mike Mindnich had been hobbled by injuries. Against Jefferson, they were joined on the sidelines by starters Rick Raabe and Jim Hoitsma.

As Cipriano remembers, "Coach wouldn't abide any excuses. We played with the players we had without whining. We learned that nobody gives a tinker's damn about excuses – all that matters is RESULTS. We had to carry on without our full squad, and we did, without complaint."

Courage can keep you in a tournament game; talent – and luck – often wins it. A rebound off yet another Cipriano save hit a Pingry player's hand, and the resulting penalty kick by John Avila, who had not missed one in his three-year varsity career, gave Jefferson a 1-0 lead. Jefferson's second score came on John Riggi's opposite-post blast that just eluded a diving Cipriano.

Pingry's final shot at a championship came in the Prep School Tournament. After disposing of Hun 2-1, a courageous 1-1 tie with Lawrenceville earned Pingry its ninth, and fourth consecutive, State Prep Championship. Cipriano and Mindnich were selected for the All-Union County First Team, with Andy Lawson, Chris Scott, Sean O'Donnell, Dave Gernert, John Hanson, and Dave Lerman also gaining recognition.

"Honestly, in 1973 Lawrenceville was a better team than we were – the game was played mostly in our half. However, Sean O'Donnell pinched an early goal against the run of play. That was a boost for us and a shock for Lawrenceville. The game turned into a shooting gallery for our opposition, but I and the rest of the team set our minds to not allowing a goal. Finally, near the end of the game Lawrenceville equalized on a lucky shot, but we held on for the draw. I was mighty glad we didn't play extra time that day! That draw provided some consolation, but in our hearts we were glad to escape with a share of the title. I also learned that, in life, things don't always go your way, and that hard work, determination – and a little luck – can carry you through."

Guy Cipriano '74

THE LIFE & TIMES OF MILLER A. BUGLIARI

Dan Phillips, *Assistant Coach*
Rob Nelson, *Manager*

Aibel, B.	Gatto, J.	Merrill, C.
Allan, D.	Gernert, D.	Mindnich, M.
Baldwin, D.	Hallett, L.	O'Donnell, S.
Bartenstein, T.	Hanson, J.	Parker, P.
Baxley, J.	Higgins, B.	Raabe, R.
Betteridge, D.	Hoitsma, J.	Schwartz, M.
Boozan, J.	Homer, B.	Scott, C.
Briody, T.	Kietzman, K.	Shelby, J.
Chwazik, G.	Lawson, A.	Spurr, S.
Cipriano, G.	Lerman, D.	Whitlock, C.
DiBuono, B.	Levinson, B.	Zashin, M.

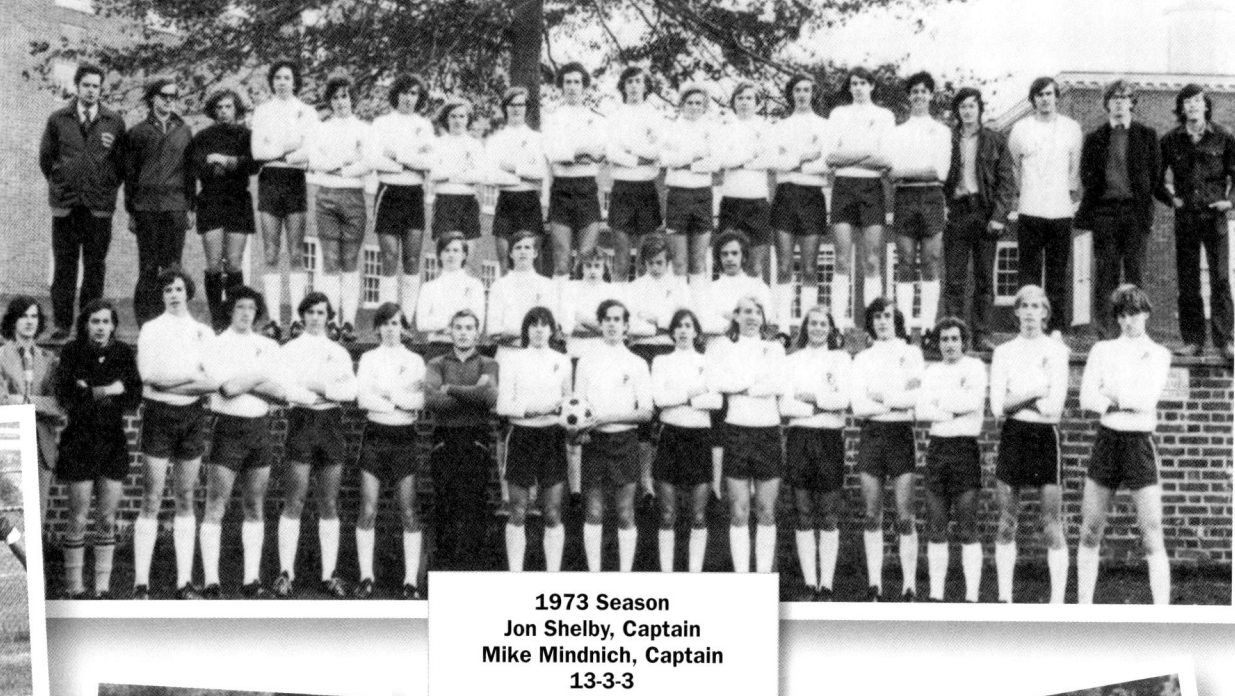

1973 Season
Jon Shelby, Captain
Mike Mindnich, Captain
13-3-3
Prep School State Champions

The **1974** Season

Westfield coach Jim Geohegan stood in the freezing rain in the Union County Championship finals at Pingry, raising his hands in amazement at Sean O'Donnell's winning goal, a lunging tap-in off Kim Kimber's direct kick that hit the left post and careened into the net. "Like, what the hell just happened? Who missed him? We were covering O'Donnell man-to-man all day. There's no way in hell that boy should have been able to turn like that."

The 1974 team rode an explosion of offense all year on the way to a 17-1-2 season, outscoring opponents 54-12 and capturing both the Union County title and the Prep School Championship. Senior captain O'Donnell's 22 goals, backed up by 14 assists, tied John Mindnich's single-game tally of four goals and broke Mindnich's single-season and total career scoring records. The other offensive pacesetters for Pingry were senior Jim Hoitsma, junior Brian Briody, sophomore Charlie Stillitano, and junior Warren "Kim" Kimber III, whose astounding total of 28 assists, to go along with 14 goals, shattered the previous single-season record of 11 set in 1973.

Pingry's senior-dominated defense featured fullbacks co-captain Rick Raabe, Bill Higgins, Bill DiBouno, and Bob Homer; halfbacks Larry Hallett, Gary Chwazik, Bill Levinson, Tom Ward, Dave Allan, Mark Zashin, and Mark Schwartz; plus junior Leo Stillitano. In goal, Miller alternated two goalkeepers: senior Peter von der Linde usually starting games, and junior Sean Mullen coming in for the second half.

They captured the Prep School Championship over Lawrenceville on O'Donnell's two third-period goals in a two-and-a-half-minute span that brought Pingry back from a 0-1 halftime deficit. It was the fifth straight year Pingry had won or shared the championship with Lawrenceville.

Pingry entered the Union County Tournament as the fourth seed. To get to the semifinals, Pingry had to beat a fired-up Kenilworth team not once but twice. The first game ended in a 0-0 tie, and since both teams had four corner kicks, there was no tie-breaker, and they had to replay the game three days later. This time, sophomore Charlie Stillitano converted a rebound off an O'Donnell close-in shot. Briody headed in what turned out to be the winning goal off a cross from Kimber, and Kimber made an 18-yard blast that sealed the victory.

In the Union County finals in the driving rain, after O'Donnell's stunning second-period goal gave Pingry the only score in the game, Westfield fought back ferociously – but unsuccessfully – to regain the lead. "Mullen played a nice game, especially at the end, and we got big plays from Rick Raabe, Bill Higgins, and Leo Stillitano," Miller said after the game. As he stripped out of his soaked clothing, he concluded, "My superstitious socks can go home now. It's time to start a new superstition."

Sean O'Donnell came to Pingry with a rich soccer heritage. His father starred for the Elizabeth Sport Club in the German-American League, and his uncles Frank and Billy O'Donnell, who had so plagued Pingry in the 1960s, went on to play for the Elizabeth Sport Club team that in 1970 won the National Challenge Cup for American professional teams.

So, starting as a five-year-old, Sean grew up playing soccer at Farcher's Grove in Union. Ten years of working to control the ball on the rutted dirt field had given him an uncanny touch. His sense of the game and anticipation was in his genes. As Miller described him: "Sean waits for what he wants and then goes when he has to. He'll play part of a quarter where it doesn't seem that he's going on offense, then he'll get two shots – two goals – bang, bang."

But even the most skilled striker needs good service, and that was provided by Kim Kimber, about whom Miller said, "He's so good with either foot it's hard to tell which one is natural." Kimber was just the opposite in background from his scoring partner. Rather than immersing himself in soccer, he loved all sports. Blessed with superb eye-hand coordination (and, for soccer, eye-foot coordination), he starred in basketball in the winter and excelled at golf in the spring.

Together, the two of them were as lethal an offensive threat as Pingry ever put on the field.

Sean O'Donnell '75 and Kim Kimber III '76

Dan Phillips, *Assistant Coach*
Bennett Baker, *Manager*
Lewis Gastorek, *Manager*
Leslie Walters, *Manager*
Scott Alenick, *Manager*

Allan, D.	Hoitsma, J.	Seabrook, C.
Bartenstein, T.	Holtzman, M.	Schwartz, M.
Baxley, J.	Homer, B.	Siegel, A.
Boozan, J.	Kimber, K.	Sokich, J.
Brenner, A.	Levinson, B.	Sperling, K.
Briody, B.	McLendon, J.	Stillitano, C.
Chwazik, G.	Merrill, C.	Stillitano, L.
DiBuono, B.	Mullen, S.	von der Linde, P.
Fields, J.	O'Donnell, S.	Ward, T.
Giorgi, D.	Raabe, R.	Williams, B.
Hallett, L.	Robson, K.	Zashin, M.
Higgins, B.	Russell, S.	

1974 Season
Sean O'Donnell, Captain
Rick Raabe, Captain
17-1-2
Union County Champions
Prep School State Champions

Pingry Finishes No. 1 In Soccer

After weeks of constant upheaval, The Daily Journal's final top 10 Union County big school soccer rankings show only one change.

That is Summit jumping over Berkeley Heights into second place. Summit last five teams, Je Union, Kenilworth, Catholic and Edison T all finshed their seaso last week.

Pingry scored game's only goal in second period when Sean O'Donnell (10) deflected direct kick by Kim Kimber (not shown) off left post and past Westfield goalie Pete Nostrand (center). Brian Briody (25) of Pingry watches ball head for goal.

Pingry Gets A Big Kick Out Of Little O'Donnell

By TOM MONIGAN
Journal Sports Writer

O'Donnell Goals Give Prep Title To Pingry

The 1975 Season

After winning their first Union County Tournament in 1970, Pingry had gone through a three-year drought in hard-fought losses to Clark, Thomas Jefferson, and Berkeley Heights before the 1974 team regained the trophy. The returning veterans from that team – seniors Andy Brenner, Brian Briody, Ed Nelson, Scott Russell, Connor Seabrook, Tom Ward, Sean Mullen, and co-captains Kim Kimber III and Leo Stillitano – were determined to claim that honor for themselves as well.

Led by Kimber's 18 assists and eight goals, Briody's 17 goals and six assists, junior Charlie Stillitano's six goals and nine assists, and junior Chuck Allan's six goals, the 1975 team continued the offensive onslaught of the previous year, scoring 51 goals. On the way to an eventual 13-3-3 season, the defense peaked for the Union County Tournament at the right time. Pingry defeated Kenilworth and old nemesis Scotch Plains to meet another familiar foe, Clark, in the final.

The Clark game marked Leo Stillitano's return from a thigh injury. "We were very happy to have him back at full strength," said Miller. "He's the leader out there. Before the game it was just Leo and the team for 15 minutes in the locker room." Clark had recorded 12 shutouts that year and had only been held scoreless twice. None of that mattered. Brian Briody scored in the first half on an assist from Charlie Stillitano, who also added an insurance goal in the second half. The defense and goalkeeper Sean Mullen did the rest for a 2-0 Pingry victory. "We did what we had to do," said Miller after the game. "It's probably more satisfying because we didn't have as strong a team as last year."

That left the Private School A Division tournament. After eliminating Hun, Pingry met fourth seed Newark Academy, upset winners over Lawrenceville 2-1, in the finals. Pingry had easily handled Newark Academy 3-1 in the regular season. "Pingry's a Top 20 team in the state," commented Newark Academy coach Bruce Goddin. "They play big time. The odds of us beating them are 15 or 20 to one." Sometimes, however, the one odd card comes up. Newark needed to play a gritty, inspired game to win, and they did, 3-2, for their first victory ever over Pingry. In front of a crowd of over 1,000 at Pingry's field, Newark's Don Savoy tied the game after a first-period Pingry goal by Scott Russell, and Bill Bradford's two ensuing goals put the game out of reach.

For Pingry's seniors, the season's luster was somewhat dimmed by the loss to Newark Academy, but they still ended their career as champions, recognized again as a Top 20 team in the state. Kim Kimber and Leo Stillitano were chosen for the Union County All-Star First Team, with honors also going to Brian Briody and Charlie Stillitano. Both Stillitanos and Kimber were selected to the A Division All-Prep Team, with Honorable Mention earned by Brian Briody, Sean Mullen, and Tom Ward.

The late Leo Stillitano, who died far too soon at age 55 in 2014, was the kind of Pingry player Miller loves: a tough guy who could impose his will on a game. His lifelong friend Sean O'Donnell remembers him as someone who "took on life the way he played – no fear – he never backed down from a single tackle." After leading Pingry to a Union County championship, Leo went on to star as an All-Ivy player at Columbia, and he continued to compete in semi-pro soccer after college. Then tragedy struck. On a business trip to Georgia, he got into a car accident that left his left leg so badly mangled that the doctors had to remove it below the knee. Through four years of painful struggle, and with the help of friends like Santiago Formoso, who played professionally with the New York Cosmos, Leo rebuilt his life.

There's another part of the story, however, that illustrates another reason why Leo Stillitano was "Miller's kind of player." Jason Evans from Killeen, Texas, was another kid who loved soccer – until he lost a leg to osteosarcoma. But Jason still wanted to play. Jason was fitted with a special prosthetic leg that allowed him to continue with his dream. And that's where Leo comes in. Leo and Santiago found Jason and started working with him through his successful efforts to play high school soccer. Because Leo had battled the same loss, he knew exactly what Jason was going through. "Leo was a world-class player until he lost his leg in a car accident," Jason said in a 1997 interview. "He taught me a lot of things I needed to be doing. He was great. He cared. Leo got me to be able to kick out the first ball at the first MetroStars game. Right now I'm doing it for him and Formoso. I will succeed because I'm doing it for them." It sounds a lot like a Pingry player talking about Miller.

Leo Stillitano '76

THE LIFE & TIMES OF MILLER A. BUGLIARI

Dan Phillips, *Assistant Coach*
Scott Alenick, *Manager*
Jean Amabile, *Manager*
Larry Kaufman, *Manager*
Jude Schneider, *Manager*
Leslie Walters, *Manager*

Allan, C.	Kimber, K.	Russell, S.
Bald, M.	Lieb, R.	Seabrook, C.
Boozan, J.	Louria, C.	Siegel, A.
Brenner, A.	Macrae, D.	Sokich, J.
Briody, B.	McLendon, J.	Sperling, K.
Daeschler, T.	McKeown, B.	Stillitano, C.
DeLaney, F.	Meyer, C.	Stillitano, L.
DeBlecourt, J.	Moser, R.	Tomlinson, B.
Fields, J.	Mullen, S.	Ward, T.
Haselton, K.	Nelson, E.	Warren, H.
Hiscano, D.	O'Connor, M.	Williams, B.
Hutchison, C.	Procopio, F.	
Johnson, R.	Robson, K.	

1975 Season
Leo Stillitano, Captain
Kim Kimber, Captain
13-3-3
Union County Champions

125

The 1976 Season

Assistant Coach Dan Phillips '59 still remembers the sound: "We thought it was a whistle blown by the official Lawrenceville had hired, right in front of the Pingry net." The Pingry players stopped playing; the Lawrenceville kid with the ball didn't. His goal won the game for Lawrenceville in spite of Pingry's impassioned protests. But that loss was the only disappointing result in a wonderful season, highlighted by Miller's 200th victory.

The 1976 team was led on offense by senior captain Charlie Stillitano, whose 24 goals set new Pingry season and career scoring records, classmates Chuck Allan, Jamer Boozan, and Ted Daeschler, and junior Chuck Pepe. Defensive leadership was provided by seniors Chuck Louria, Richard Lieb, goalkeeper Chris Meyer, and co-captain Frank DeLaney, and by juniors Rad Lovett and Chuck Dooley.

Pingry began the season strongly, demolishing its first three New York City opponents, Horace Mann, Riverdale, and Poly Prep, by a combined 22-1 margin, and climbing to No. 12 in the state rankings. Their conference battles started with a familiar opponent, Berkeley Heights, who hadn't been scored on in running their regular-season unbeaten streak to 38 games. That streak was shattered by Pingry's complete 3-0 triumph.

After disposing of Peddie 3-1 and gaining a 2-0 revenge win for Newark Academy's upset victory in the previous year's prep championship, Pingry hammered another traditional Union County rival, previously unbeaten Westfield. The score, 1-0, doesn't tell the story of Pingry's suffocating dominance of the run of play. Pingry held possession for 46 of the game's 72 minutes. Stillitano's third-period goal off a throw-in by Doug Hiscano provided the margin of victory.

The regular season ended in glorious fashion. Pingry's 4-1 rout of Cranford set the stage for Pingry's unstoppable march to its fourth consecutive Union County Championship.

Pingry knocked off Clark 2-0 and No. 1 seed Union 3-1, before meeting emerging county powerhouse Summit in the final. Stillitano's penalty kick with four minutes to go knotted the game, and after two scoreless overtimes marked by tremendous saves by both goalkeepers, Pingry gained its fourth consecutive Union County title as co-champions with Summit. Pingry came up short, however, in the prep championship game against Lawrenceville, a 1-0 loss in the "phantom whistle" game.

Year-end honors went to Charlie Stillitano, who was named to the First Team All-County, All-Prep, and All-State squads and was rated as the top player in the county by the Union County coaches. In his Pingry career he played in 10 Union County Tournament games and never lost. Stillitano also received Honorable Mention on the *Star-Ledger's* "Team of the Century" for the 1970s decade.

He was joined on the 1976 All-County First Team by Allan and Boozan. Louria and DeLaney also received All-County honors.

"We were leading our arch-rival (and host) Lawrenceville 1-0 in the waning moments of the state prep school tourney finals when one of their attackers was fouled. To this day I swear I heard a whistle blow, but the Lawrenceville player continued to play and shot the ball past me. I protested to no avail. We went on to lose the game in overtime, 2-1. On the long trip home, Coach came up to me with a half-smile and said, 'One day you are going to pick up the phone and hear a long whistle...that will be me on the other end.' My first instinct was to sink further into depression, but my second, more mature and lasting impression was more philosophical. By injecting humor at a very sensitive moment, Mr. Bugliari (I can't help but still refer to him by his formal name) taught me that it is still just a game, and to gain perspective through laughter is a life lesson learned well. It wasn't complete absolution. He was also telling me that I should have played through, despite hearing the whistle, until it was really clear play had stopped – but his words helped me get through that night and the next few days. And I remember the conversation as if it were yesterday."

Chris Meyer '77

Dan Phillips, *Assistant Coach*
Scott Alenick, *Manager*
Jean Amabile, *Manager*
Larry Kaufman, *Manager*
Jude Schneider, *Manager*

Akins, J.	Hiscano, D.	Quaas, K.
Allan, C.	Johnson, R.	Schrader, B.
Boozan, J.	Lieb, R.	Scrudato, P.
Carro, P.	Louria, C.	Siegel, S.
Dackerman, R.	Lovett, R.	Stillitano, C.
Daeschler, T.	Macrae, D.	Tant, D.
DeLaney, F.	Meyer, C.	Tomlinson, B.
Donahue, J.	McCarthy, S.	Tweedie, T.
Dooley, C.	McKeown, B.	von der Linde, E.
Echikson, B.	O'Connor, M.	Walbridge, T.
Haselton, K.	Pepe, C.	Warren, H.

1976 Season
Charlie Stillitano, Captain
Frank DeLaney, Captain
14-3-3
Union County Champions

The 1977 Season

Pingry entered the 1977 season with just one returning starter, captain Chuck Dooley. "We started off slowly," Miller said in summing up the season. "By the time you get to the tournament and the younger kids have 10 or 15 games under their belt, you've got an experienced player." In its first three games, Pingry ripped through the New York City part of its schedule, beating Horace Mann, Riverdale, and Poly Prep by a combined score of 12 goals to 1. Then they ran into a brick wall, losing to Berkeley Heights 1-0.

Pingry fought its way through the rest of a 9-3-2 regular season, led by captains Dooley and Chuck Pepe, and first-year senior starters Tom Tweedie, Ray Dackerman, Ken Quaas, Teddy Walbridge, Paul Scrudato, Peter Carro, Jeff Akins, Rad Lovett, and Scott Siegel. Juniors Leighton Welch, Robbie King, John Michaud, Rob Curtis, and Tom Trynin and sophomore Josh Gradwohl rounded out the team. Goalkeeping duties were shared by senior John McLaughlin and junior Todd Cunningham.

In the Prep School semifinal against Newark Academy, Pingry, seeded first, again discovered what it was like to face a determined underdog. As they had done in 1975, Newark Academy upset Pingry 3-1, in spite of Pingry's 7-0 advantage in corner kicks and 33 shots to Newark Academy's nine. Pingry's championship hopes now rested on the Union County Tournament, with Pingry seeded fifth – as it turned out, right where a hungry, determined underdog team needed to be.

Pingry beat fourth-seeded Kenilworth to then meet top-seeded and undefeated Union, ranked 11th in the state, in the semifinals. Rad Lovett's third-period corner kick and Chuck Dooley's denial of a corner kick by All-State forward Ed Donahue gave Pingry the tie-breaker over Union on corner kicks 3-2 after the two teams fought to a scoreless tie in regulation play. "I think this was one of the biggest tournament upsets in a long time," said Miller. "Union was just an excellent team, and for us to beat them, everything had to go right."

High-scoring Scotch Plains hadn't been shut out in 18 games. But Pingry needed a shutout to beat them – and that's exactly what goalkeeper John McLaughlin and the defense led by Chuck Dooley were able to do. The winning goal came on junior Tom Trynin's one-time blast into the upper right-hand corner of the goal. After gaining the lead, Pingry's defense shut down Scotch Plains' frantic efforts to equalize, and Rob Curtis's insurance goal with two minutes left sealed the 2-0 victory and Pingry's fifth consecutive Union County title.

Dooley was named to the All-Union County First Team, with honors also going to Pepe, Carro, and Curtis. Dooley, Pepe, and Carro were also named to the Prep School A Division First Team.

Both Miller and the opposing coach, Tom Breznitsky, described Tom Trynin's winning goal in the 1977 team's Union County Championship game against Scotch Plains as "a beautiful goal" – a 20-yard one-time rocket into the upper right corner. In Breznitsky's words, "I don't think any goalie in the state could have stopped that shot."

As Trynin recalls of his game-winner many years later, "Well, it really was a pretty goal. The ball and I arrived in the same moment. Without thinking, I just turned, planted my foot and shot. But you have to remember where that goal came from. Practice after practice, week after week, season after season, Coach put us through pressure drills in the critical situations and skills that could make the difference in a game. The move was just instinctive. It might be fair to say that goal was as much Coach's as it was mine."

"Miller's coaching made a big difference," recalls Leighton Welch '79, thinking about his junior season. "Chuck Dooley was a mainstay on our defense, and Miller prepared him to guard a Scotch Plains player, one of the top scorers in the league, who had a patented move of juggling the ball from one foot to the other several times before volleying it from around the top of the box into the back of the net. He tried that move on Dooley, and Chuck stepped into his juggle and boomed the ball to half-field. NICE!! I don't think the kid tried it again. That was Chuck for us all season long."

Chuck Dooley '78 and Tom Trynin '79

Don Burt, *Assistant Coach*
Jean Amabile, *Manager*
Larry Kaufman, *Manager*
Jude Schneider, *Manager*

Akins, J.	Gradwohl, J.	Quaas, K.
Allan, C.	King, R.	Raabe, C.
Bartlett, C.	Lovett, P.	Scrudato, P.
Brainin, J.	Lovett, R.	Siegel, S.
Brody, M.	Mamangakis, S.	Teixeira, M.
Bunn, C.	McCarthy, P.	Trynin, T.
Carro, P.	McLaughlin, J.	Tweedie, T.
Cunningham, T.	Meyer, H.	von der Linde, E.
Curtis, R.	Michaud, J.	Walbridge, T.
Dackerman, R.	Monaghan, J.	Wegryn, K.
Dooley, C.	Paglia, A.	Welch, L.
Friedman, S.	Pepe, C.	Ziobro, P.

1977 Season
Chuck Pepe, Captain
Chuck Dooley, Captain
12-4-2
Union County Champions

Goalie Joe Gillikin of Scotch Plains comes out to stop shot while Tom Trynin (23) of Pingry and Henry Janssen (24) of Scotch Plains tangle in front of net.

One goal's all it takes for Pingry

The 1978 Season

Since Miller's third year as head coach in 1962, seven Pingry teams had gone through the regular season without a loss. The 1978 team set a new standard, finishing the regular season with a sparkling 13-0-0 record that included a 4-1 demolishing of Westfield and a solid 2-0 win over Lawrenceville. Except for late-season struggles against Edison Tech and Blair, Pingry's defense was rarely tested in recording 10 shutouts.

Senior tri-captain Todd Cunningham had shared goalkeeper duties with John McLaughlin as a junior and now owned the position all to himself. Rob Curtis, also a senior tri-captain, was described by Miller as "our best-skilled all-around player. He plays just about anywhere on the field – wherever we need him most." John Michaud was given the responsibility of shutting down each opponent's top scorer. Robbie King, Mike Brody, Peter Ziobro, Mario Teixeira, and Josh Gradwohl at sweeper anchored the defense.

Offensively, Pingry fielded a more veteran team, and their production showed it. A month into the season, with 10 victories already in hand, Miller had characterized the team as "a lot of good players who play well together." The offense was led by returning starter and tri-captain Tom Trynin, who averaged a goal a game, but Pingry's balance was evident in the fact that 13 different players contributed to the team's average of four goals a game, including the second-highest scorer Leighton Welch, plus fellow seniors Phil Lovett, Chris Allan, Chris Bartlett, Pete McCarthy, juniors Alex Topakas and Bobby Jenkins, the team's assists leader and an All-Morris County junior transfer from Chatham Township High School, and sophomore Brian O'Donnell.

Against Linden in the Union County Tournament opener, the newspaper article called it "a questioned official's call," but the ejection of Pingry's playmaker Jenkins for challenging a harsh yellow card forced Pingry to play with 10 men for most of the second half. Trynin's 16th goal of the season with 10 minutes left to play, assisted by Brody, answered Linden forward Scott Morrow's second-period goal. Pingry outshot Linden 29-16, but the statistic that mattered was Linden's 5-1 advantage in corner kicks that gave them the win.

That left the prep final, predictably against a typically strong, fast, experienced Lawrenceville, very much Pingry's equal in terms of talent. The roughly contested game came down to just a few plays, and on this day, Lawrenceville made them and Pingry couldn't. With 30 seconds left in the fourth quarter and Pingry trailing 4-3, Chris Allan won the ball and chipped to a wide-open Trynin. His shot maddeningly just nicked the goal post and popped out – to an unmarked Bobby Jenkins, who fired a perfect shot at point-blank range. It hit a Lawrenceville player and ricocheted back into the penalty area. The Pingry players were still scrambling to get to the ball when the whistle sounded. Looking back on the season, Rob Curtis recalls, "I think we peaked too soon. Somehow, at the end of the season we just ran out of gas."

Many of the seniors on the 1978 team had started playing together as members of a really good freshman team. Dave Allan, senior Chris Allan's dad, watching them play said, "these kids will be Pingry's next dual State and County champions." Besides possessing a tremendous amount of team speed and athleticism, players like Tom Trynin, Rob Curtis, Chris Allan, Chris Bartlett, and Leighton Welch were, by nature, very competitive – they liked to win. Tough, physical players like seniors Pete McCarthy and John Michaud added another important dimension to the team.

Rob Curtis remembers, "Our senior year, Bobby Jenkins joined the team as a junior transfer from Chatham. When a new kid shows up the first day of practice with an experienced bunch of seniors, you first ask 'Who is this guy?' Then we watched him play and started asking, 'Who IS this guy?' His speed and skill on the wing opened things up for all the rest of us. He collected a lot of key goals and assists that year (to go along with some pretty impressive red cards!). So we knew we were good – and played that way. Looking back now, however, what persists most from the season isn't the wins and losses, as exhilarating or disappointing as they were at the time. It's the lifelong friendships that we still treasure. Coach molded a team of players who wound up caring about each other a whole lot."

Rob Curtis '79

THE LIFE & TIMES OF MILLER A. BUGLIARI

Don Burt, *Assistant Coach*
Kathy Baxley, *Manager*
Kathy Coffey, *Manager*

Allan, C.	Humphrey, A.	Rentzepis, M.
Barg, S.	Jenkins, B.	Shinn, A.
Bartlett, C.	King, R.	Teixeira, M.
Bosland, J.	Lovett, P.	Topakas, A.
Brainin, J.	Mamangakis, S.	Trynin, T.
Brody, M.	McCarthy, P.	Vimond, R.
Cunningham, T.	Meyer, H.	Walters, D.
Curtis, R.	Michaud, J.	Wegryn, K.
Dennison, P.	Minter, T.	Welch, L.
Ferry, T.	Mullen, K.	Ziobro, P.
Gradwohl, J.	Norman, M.	
Hensten, D.	O'Donnell, B.	

1978 Season
Tommy Trynin, Captain
Rob Curtis, Captain
Todd Cunningham, Captain
16-1-1
Undefeated Regular Season

TWENTY-EIGHT — THE DAILY JOURNAL, FRIDAY EVENING, OCTOBER 13, 1978

Tops soccer ratings

Another great Pingry team

By JIM OGLE Jr.
Journal Sports Writer

The Pingry School is getting to be synonymous with good soccer.

Miller Bugliari, the veteran coach, has had many great teams over the years and he rates this year's 10-0 unit right up with the best.

"I had a feeling we'd be good because we have six or seven starters back and excellent speed," Bugliari said. "This is one of the quickest teams I've had."

The 10-0 start is the best since 1972, and that team finished at 17-1.

The Big Blue easily held onto the No. 1 spot in The Daily Journ...
remained the same,...
by Summit, Gov. Li...
Scotch Plains m...
followed by Linden,...
Roselle, which crac...
time this season.

"Last year we w...
county, even thoug...
nament," Bugliari...
peak at the right ti...
"This year we c...
time will tell. We d...

Soccer Top 10
1-Pingry..........(10-0)   6-Scotch Pl'ns..(7-3)
2-Union...........(7-0-3) 7-Linden..........(3-2)
3-Summit.........(7-1-1)   8-Westfield......(6-3-1)
4-G. Liv'ston...(8-1-1)   9-Elizabeth......(6-3)
5-Carteret......(8-1-2)   10-Roselle........(6-1-1)

Tom Trynin, the senior striker, leads the team in goals with 11, including two Thursday in the victory over previously unbeaten Princeton Day...

last year, but he has the job all to himself this time around. He has six shutouts (three in a row) and has allowed only five goals all year.

John Michaud is the point man and always defends against the top scorer on the opposition. Robbie King and Mike Brody are the fullbacks, while Josh Gradwohl plays sweeper. Phil Lovett has done a good job at left wing, while Chris Bartlett and Pete McCarthy are solid halfbacks.

As proof of their great balance, Bugliari points to the fact that 13 different players have scored goals for Pingry this year. And the Big Blue is averaging a shade under four goals a...

(Right): Richard Gradwohl, "Pingry's Most Dedicated Fan."

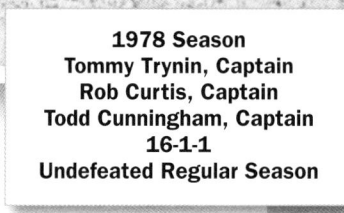

131

The 1979 Season

By 1979, Pingry's position in Union County was clear. "Everybody wants to beat Pingry," Miller remarked at the end of the season. "What makes it interesting is that the best team doesn't always win. That's what makes tournaments special. In 1977 we certainly weren't the best team in the county. We just happened to peak at the right time. Last year, based on head-to-head records, we were the best, but we lost on corner kicks. You just have to play the season, get into the tournament, and give it your best."

Pingry was led by returning starters and co-captains Bob Jenkins, the team's leading scorer, and halfback Josh Gradwohl. Contributing to the offense's record-tying 58 goals were seniors Alex Topakas, Paul Dennison, and Andy Humphrey; junior Brian O'Donnell, brother of 1974 scoring leader Sean O'Donnell, who, in Miller's words, "makes it go up front"; sophomore Rob Macrae; and Belgian exchange student Peter DeGraef. The defense featured Topakas, Gradwohl, and fellow seniors Mike Rentzepis, Doug Hensten, and Tom Minter; and juniors Geordie Kline and sweeper Drew Kronik. Senior goalkeeper Tom Ferry, backed up by John Sisto, recorded 11 shutouts.

The team swept their Union County opponents, including a gratifying revenge win over Westfield 1-0 with Jenkins' 18-foot drive off a cross by Alex Topakas that caromed off the left goal post and into the net past helpless Westfield goalkeeper Pete Kellogg. Pingry got a wake-up call, however, from two Prep School A Division opponents it could expect to meet in post-season, getting shut out by Peddie 2-0 – their first win over Pingry since 1961 – and having no answers for an especially experienced, skilled, and quick Lawrenceville team in a 3-0 defeat.

In the Union County Tournament, Brian O'Donnell's first-quarter goal was all Pingry needed in a revenge win against last year's upset winner Linden. Next up, and then down, was a scrappy Kenilworth team. Jenkins' 20th goal of the season, off fullback Stu Ward's picture-book assist, was enough for the 1-0 win and yet another date with Westfield in the semifinals.

Westfield's Joe DiBella broke Tom Ferry's string of five consecutive shutouts in the second quarter, beating his defender to the ball and hammering in a shot to the right corner of the net from 20 yards out. Jenkins' 21st goal of the year tied it before halftime. Ultimately, the game came down to defensive heroics by Westfield goalkeeper Kellogg, who robbed Pingry of a sure goal when his full-length dive and outstretched hand flicked Topakas' ground-level bullet away from the left side of the net. And once again, a tie game was decided by corner kicks, with Westfield's 5-1 edge sending them into the finals.

In the Prep School tournament, Pingry handled Newark Academy easily, 3-0, and humiliated Peddie in another revenge win 6-0, setting up yet another grudge match with Lawrenceville for the championship. Pingry controlled the run of play early, and Topakas' goal put Pingry ahead 1-0. Jenkins added what should have been an insurance goal at the start of the second half. Then it all fell apart for Pingry. Lawrenceville's superior size, speed, and experience were too much. Lawrenceville drew even, and then won the game, with a three-goal explosion in the fourth quarter against a tiring Pingry defense.

"Against Linden in the County Tournament my junior year, I let my temper get the better of me. I remember that I hadn't really found my rhythm in the game and was getting frustrated. Early in the 2nd half, I miscontrolled a ball into my arm and was called for a handball. It was a good example of how the game was going for me. I took out my growing frustration from my performance on the ref. I'm not sure what I said to him, or if I had a yellow card already, but I do remember slapping a card out of his hand and realizing – at that point – my day was finished. I was out of the game, leaving my teammates a man short for the rest of the game. That was one long walk to the sidelines. When I got to the bench, I fully expected Coach Bugliari to unleash on me. But you know what I got? Not a word. He just let me sit and consider what I had done. Later, when we talked about it, he approached it in terms of a life lesson. He didn't blame me for playing with passion. He understood that. In effect, what he told me was 'It was a mistake, not the end of the world. Learn from it.' He made it easy for a teenage kid to start thinking like a man."

Bob Jenkins '80

John Hutchison, *Assistant Coach*
Steve Samson, *Assistant Coach*
Leo Stillitano, *Assistant Coach*
Amy Ehrlich, *Manager*
A. Copeland Eschenlauer, *Manager*
Sloan Seymor, *Manager*

Allen, M.	Hiscano, D.	Quinn, P.
Barg, S.	Humphrey, A.	Rentzepis, M.
Bent, J.	Jenkins, B.	Schoen, B.
Bosland, J.	Kline, G.	Sisto, J.
Brisgel, S.	Kronick, A.	Stanton, D.
DeGraef, P.	Macrae, R.	Topakas, A.
Dennison, P.	McCormick, D.	Vimond, R.
Eisenbud, G.	Minter, T.	Walters, D.
Ferry, T.	Mullen, J.	Ward, S.
Gradwohl, J.	Norman, M.	
Hensten, D.	O'Donnell, B.	

1979 Season
Josh Gradwohl, Captain
Bob Jenkins, Captain
14-3-1

The 1980s: Challenge and Change

"I like the kids. At the high school level you try to teach more than soccer. You can't coach for this many years and do it just for victories and losses."
— MILLER, 1983

The decade of the 1980s was a time of accelerated growth for high school soccer in New Jersey – and challenging change for Pingry.

Starting in the mid-1960s and escalating rapidly through the 1970s, suburbia had discovered soccer. The first of generations of "soccer moms" began lugging kids to youth soccer programs. At the start, kids may just have been playing "cluster ball." It wasn't long before parents started demanding better coaching – and better results.

Suburbia Discovers Soccer

In *The Grass of Another Country*, Christopher Merrill quotes Miller as saying, "Once we rise above this ethnic thing," referring to soccer's roots in the immigrant communities of Northern New Jersey, "soccer will take off." By the 1980s, that had become a matter of "be careful what you wish for." In the 1960s, the top teams and players in New Jersey high school soccer typically came from towns like Kearny, Harrison, Bloomfield, Elizabeth, Union, and Newark with strong ethnic populations. In the 1970s Pingry's major opponents in Union County now included suburban towns like Westfield, Cranford, Scotch Plains, Berkeley Heights, and Summit. Ten years later, soccer had spread to Central and South Jersey, with teams like Bridgewater East and West, Hillsborough, Ridge, and Bernards Township in Somerset County and Shore teams like Jackson, Brick, Toms River, Cherry Hill, and Shawnee achieving Top 20 ranking.

By the 1980s, the larger Group III and Group IV teams Pingry would need to beat, with student populations three to five times greater than Pingry's, had well-established community feeder programs beginning in the lowest grades and coordinated, well-coached freshman and JV programs. Not surprisingly, Miller played a role in that growth as well, helping develop community programs and improve youth coaching in Summit after he and Elizabeth moved there following their marriage in 1965.

The Growth of Professional Soccer in High Schools

In 1977, the US Youth Soccer Olympic Development Program was formed "… to identify a pool of players in each age group from which a National Team will be selected for international competition; to provide high-level training to benefit and enhance the development of players at all levels; and, through the use of carefully selected and licensed coaches, develop a mechanism for the exchange of ideas and curriculum to improve all levels of coaching."

The program continued to expand and become more efficient through the early 1980s with the development of State Associations working closely with four Regional Programs and a National Program. Trials and player pool selections for five age groups led to substantial increases in international events, so that a dedicated, talented 16-year-old player might find himself on a national team competing against kids of similar ages from Europe and Latin America. The impact on Pingry soccer was once again a numbers game. While increasingly Pingry's best players in the 1980s came from the ODP process, the large schools Pingry needed to beat in order to win a county championship had that many more similarly talented players to draw from.

A Changing Pingry

Pingry underwent dramatic change in this decade as well. Co-education, from both a school community and educational perspective, was a wonderfully positive, enriching step for Pingry. But it had the effect of significantly reducing the number of male students available for Miller to draw from. In 1975, Pingry had graduated 89 seniors – all boys. In 1989, the senior class had expanded to roughly 120 students, half of whom, however, were girls. And the "Country Day School" requirement that all students play after-school sports had long since gone the way of Chapel and the coat-and-tie dress code for students. Some percentage of each senior class consisted of splendidly talented students who never set foot on an athletic field except as spectators.

New Rivals

In terms of competition for county championships, Pingry's move from Union County to Somerset County was like going from the frying pan into the fire. By the 1980s, Somerset County Group III and IV teams had developed strong soccer programs, fueled by robust youth programs and players competing on ODP select teams. While they may not always have possessed the skill level of Pingry players, they more than made up for that deficiency with physical size, speed, rough play, and sheer numbers. Pingry's relocation to Basking Ridge meant just exchanging one set of Union County powerhouses as opponents for another in Somerset County.

Anything But "Parochial" Soccer

And a new group of competitors had emerged. Through the late 1970s and into the 1980s, soccer's growth exploded as well among parochial schools, which decided perhaps it was time for leadership from "soccer Fathers" as well as "soccer moms." Catholic schools started appearing on lists of All-County and All-State teams. And ominously, in 1981 a still-growing St. Benedict's made its first appearance as the 10th ranked team in Essex County with a 15-5-1 record. By 1989, The NJSCA's list of Top 20 teams in the state included seven parochial schools.

In 1987, perhaps the greatest change in competition took place: Pingry's switch from the NJSIAA Independent Schools league to the Non-Public league (in those days called "Parochial Schools"). The move ended what had been, in effect, a 25-year war against Lawrenceville. It also meant going from battling the best New Jersey boarding school to competing against the best team in New Jersey, St. Benedict's, well on its way to becoming a top-ranked team nationally.

Like Lawrenceville, St. Benedict's recruited top players, but its players from throughout the U.S. and Latin America came to St. Benedict's and coach Rick Jacobs to prepare for Division I colleges and potential professional careers. Over the years, 17 St. Benedict's players have represented the United States on the National Men's team.

In taking on St. Benedict's, by now one of the top prep school teams in the nation, Pingry would be going up against high school and college All-Americans, United States ODP National Team players, and future professionals like Scott Schweizer, Pedro Lopes, Dominick Bucci, Bill Bustamente, Petter Villegas, and arguably the best international professional soccer player America has ever produced, Claudio Reyna.

"I would never take anything away from what St. Benedict's has accomplished," said Miller. "We're talking about a great program with great players who deserve all the accolades they've won. But their recruitment and graduation standards put them in a completely different league than high school soccer. But we still scheduled them and played to win."

It would be the mid-1990s before Pingry cracked the Umbro and ESPN/Adidas national rankings of Top 20 teams, and the 2000s that Pingry started competing in games and tournaments against national powerhouses like Chaminade. Not until 1996 did Pingry dethrone St. Benedict's as the No. 1 team in the state, but Pingry's early battles against St. Benedict's were some of the finest and most courageous games any Pingry team has ever played.

A Different Kind of Welcome Wagon

Over the years, Basking Ridge had develped a robust youth soccer program – and a passionate pride in its varsity soccer program. Pingry's arrival in Basking Ridge, however, brought a new level of competition – not just for Somerset County championships but for top players. Attracted by Pingry's excellent academics and stellar reputation as a soccer power, some parents decided to send their children to attend Pingry – and play for Miller.

Basking Ridge greeted the appearance of a new rival next door by burning Miller in effigy – not exactly "Hi. I live next door; welcome to the neighborhood. I've baked some cookies for you." The houses and cars of families who had decided to send their children to Pingry were egged, and their kids became "traitors" to their friends. Boys who had played together as friends and teammates on age-group teams from first grade until high school became bitter enemies.

Different Players – An Evolving Approach

Through this decade of change, Miller was evolving as well – as were the kinds of players he coached. Pingry's Gen X students were more likely to value their own independence and freedom from authority. Having experienced the aftermath of the Kennedy and King assassinations, Watergate and the Nixon resignation, and the Clinton impeachment, they tended not to idealize leaders; having lived through change, they were more adaptive to it in their own lives.

All of that made it difficult for Miller to motivate players to sacrifice to reach the level of excellence he expected and wanted for them. The key to Miller's ability to help his teams succeed in the new world Pingry entered in the 1980s was his flexibility, his passion for learning, and above all his unchanging values. As he remarked on the team's 300th win in 1983, "I like the kids. It's a constant challenge. At the high school level you try to teach more than soccer. You can't coach for this many years and do it just for the victories."

Not Quite Over the Hill

Rob Macrae, a three-year varsity player, captain of the 1981 team and four-year player at Wesleyan, returned to coach at Pingry in 1988. He noticed the cultural difference immediately – and Miller's response. Miller's role was evolving into developing and mentoring young assistant coaches while still setting the same absolute, uncompromising standards and expectations for achievement. Macrae laughs when he remembers what a Pingry Assistant Athletic Director said to him his first year coaching at Pingry. "Rob, it's great that you've come back here as a former Pingry and college player. Miller's getting a bit old. Pretty soon he'll be over the hill. He will probably be retiring soon. Pingry's fortunate you'll be able to take over where he left off."

Macrae, well established in his own career as a Headmaster, now at the New Canaan Country School, still laughs today at the idea of Miller being "over the hill" in 1988: 19 years ranked among the Top 10 teams in the state, over 450 victories, 11 state or sectional championships, and 18 county championships later.

Rob Macrae '82

Not Exactly a "Bermuda Buggy Ride"

In the 1970s and 1980s Miller took the team to Bermuda in August, ostensibly for training, although players may have had other motivational goals as well. The Bermuda trips were a different kind of experience. For one thing, the players could rent motorbikes to get around, which provided lots of opportunities to replicate their favorite scenes from movies like "The Wild One," "Knightriders," "Mad Max," or "Easy Rider." For another, there was no legal drinking age restriction in Bermuda. The instruction letter to parents included the disclaimer: "We will have to assume that your son has your permission to have a beer unless we hear directly from you to the contrary. … Generally, we expect all of the students to act as adults on the trip, and further trips depend on reasonable behavior. Perfection is hardly expected, but we reserve the right to send home any student who cannot conform to these few necessities."

It has always been hard for kids to outwit Miller, and his assistant coaches often included former players who were well familiar with the outrageous stunts they had attempted. But veterans of the Bermuda trips will tell you they may have practiced hard in the day, but they played just as hard at night.

Miller (right) showing the effect of taking the team to Bermuda.

Brian O'Donnell '81 accompanied the team as a coach to Bermuda several times. "We had some real characters on those trips," he recalls. "Some of the stories can't be included in a family publication, but one of the best ones I can tell was a motorbike escapade. Our trips from our hotel, Harmony Hall, to the practice field took a while because of the traffic. Typically, the team would be stretched out in line on their motorbikes, following each other like a camel caravan. But one year we had a terrific player who was also really unpredictable. You never knew what he would do. But we still couldn't figure out how he got lost on the way to the practice field. No one actually saw him leave the rest of the group, but when we started practice, he wasn't there. Then we heard the roar of a motorbike coming full speed through the park next to the practice field. This kid was scattering families and small kids in terror, ripping up flower beds, and digging big chunks out of the carefully manicured lawn. But what he hadn't figured on was our practice field was four feet lower than the park, so he went flying over the retaining wall at the edge of the park like a motocross rider and splattered his landing. We were impressed with his driving. Miller decided the kid needed to do some extra running."

Signature Victories

300th – 1983

It started out as yet another tense game against a Union County rival, 7-5 Edison Tech. The first half ended with the score knotted 0-0. Then, in the second half, Pingry took over. The first goal came early in the third period when Don DiChiara finished on a cross from Dave Freedman. Freedman scored next in a breakaway on a through ball from Chris Welch, followed by Chris Jenkins' solo shot. Anthony Clapcich's hat trick in the fourth quarter completed the 6-0 rout that gave Miller his 300th victory in Pingry's last year in Union County.

"Some coaches sent me notes after I got the 300th victory," said Miller. "I guess some of them are glad we're out [of Union County], but I think we added a nice dimension to the county." The "nice dimension" included seven championships and Miller's leadership in initiating both the Union County Tournament and the formation of the Soccer Coaches Association of New Jersey.

The 1980 Season

Soccer is a team game in which special individuals can sometimes make a big difference. In senior Gary Eisenbud, Pingry's basketball captain, the 1980 team featured the kind of player Miller loves: a big, fast, natural left-footed wing who could penetrate or cross the ball. Captain Brian O'Donnell remembers, "We were really excited by how Gary could stretch defenses vertically with his speed and spread them with his ability to attack from the left side. We worked hard in preseason to develop our offense to take advantage of his capabilities – and then he collided with Union's goalkeeper in our last scrimmage and was gone for the season with a broken leg." His injury turned Pingry from a very dangerous offensive team to one that would have to fight to score goals.

Starting forwards included juniors Ron Weller and Dave Bent. Midfielders included O'Donnell and a strong group of juniors: Geordie Kline, Mark Telling, Rob Macrae, Miles Welch, John Russell, and John Rachlin. Defensively, four seniors started: captain Drew Kronick, Andy Ehrlich, Scott Stratton, and Jim Mullen, with sophomores Jim Gensch and Nick Ward also making valuable contributions. Senior Stu Ward wound up playing wherever Miller needed him most, as a striker or as a man marker against the opponent's best player. Senior John Sisto and junior Ralph Kunzmann shared goalkeeper duties.

Recalling the season, Miller says, "We counted on Brian O'Donnell to manage our offense. He had grown up playing soccer as a little kid in Farcher's Grove like his brother Sean, Art and Robbie Kurz, and the Stillitanos. He had that one-touch skill and the ability to see the field and know where the ball needed to go. Defensively, Jimmy Gensch played the same role. He had come from an excellent soccer program in Chatham, and had that public school toughness that was so important, given the teams we played."

"We had some really talented soccer players on our team," O'Donnell recalls, "but frankly we didn't have the speed and overall athleticism of the big teams we faced like Westfield, Scotch Plains and Lawrenceville. We worked hard for our 13 wins, and fought just as hard in our four losses." The county tournament game against Westfield capsulized the season. Westfield went up early on a fast restart of a direct kick before Pingry could set up a wall. That goal energized Pingry, who controlled the run of play in the second quarter, tying the game on Geordie Kline's 40-yard blast. In the second half, Westfield's speed and strength started to take its toll.

They regained the lead and in the fourth quarter scored again. Macrae's long pass to Gensch with seven minutes left gave Pingry a second goal, but Westfield dominated the rest of the game for a 3-2 victory.

"In my coaching career, I've been blessed to have worked with and observed five of the most successful professional coaches in the world: Bora Milutinovic, Carlos Quieroz, Carlos Alberto Parreira, and Sir Alex Ferguson. They all share two critical qualities with Miller. First and foremost, like Miller, they care deeply about all their players as athletes and as people – it doesn't matter if the player is a star, or a reserve that rarely gets into a game. My first insight into this quality in Miller came when, as a freshman, I was allowed to dress for a Pingry Alumni game, and heard Miller describe each of the alumni players. I remember being amazed and thinking at the time, 'Is he making all this stuff up?' and then realizing that Miller really did remember all these details about kids who might have played twenty years before. The second quality Miller shares with these great coaches is the high standard of excellence he helps players reach. Like them, Miller believes that his players can improve and become better – and holds them to that expectation. 'Good enough' is never good enough. Players make the sacrifice to be better because they know Miller cares."

Brian O'Donnell '81

Steve Samson, *Assistant Coach*
Henry Ziegler, *Assistant Coach*
Motria Huk, *Manager*
Denise Cohen, *Manager*

Bent, D.	Kronick, D.	Sisto, J.
Campbell, A.	Kunzmann, R.	Steinberg, G.
Clarick, G.	Macrae, R.	Stratton, S.
Curtis, J.	Mullen, J.	Telling, M.
Ehrlich, A.	O'Donnell, B.	Walder, S.
Eisenbud, G.	Rachlin, J.	Ward, N.
Gensch, J.	Russell, J.	Ward, S.
Jaffee, T.	Schoen, B.	Welch, M.
Karp, J.	Schoen, K.	Weller, R.
Kline, G.		

1980 Season
Jim Mullen, Captain
Brian O'Donnell, Captain
Drew Kronick, Captain
12-4-4

The 1981 Season

Even in a Pingry vs. Lawrenceville rivalry marked by violent battles and nasty play, the 1981 game at Lawrenceville midway through the season set a new standard for viciousness.

Co-captain Rob Macrae still remembers the play. "They simply were a much better team, but more than that, it was the nastiest – really the dirtiest game I ever played in. A brawl broke out after one of their players clobbered our goalkeeper Ralph Kunzmann. The Lawrenceville player took two steps at a full run after Ralph had fairly caught the ball and hit him in the face, knocking him unconscious – and no penalty was called. For a few moments, we weren't sure he was still breathing. From then on the rest of the game was marred by fights and yellow cards." A cold Matt Feigenbaum was called in to play in the goal and Pingry finished the game with Macrae and co-captain Geordie Kline ejected from the game. The final score was Lawrenceville 4, Pingry 0.

There was a reason Lawrenceville targeted Ralph Kunzmann. Going into the game he had registered 10 shutouts, with only a 1-0 loss to a greatly improved Delbarton and a 1-1 tie against eventual county champion Westfield marring Pingry's record. With Kunzmann sidelined for a month recovering from the broken jaw suffered against Lawrenceville, Matt Feigenbaum took over in goal, recording four shutouts and 22 saves, including a 2-0 win against Oratory in the opening round of the Union County Tournament. The heart of the defense was Kline, a three-year starter, at sweeper. "He just doesn't make mistakes. He's consistently good," Feigenbaum commented. The rest of Pingry's defense, including seniors Macrae, Miles Welch, and Cliff Ruprecht, plus juniors Sander Friedman and Jimmy Gensch, shut out 13 opponents on the way to a 14-2-1 season.

Offensively, Ron Weller's 11 goals and 16 assists led a collective effort of 45 goals for the season, with 13 Pingry players scoring, including seniors Macrae and Dave Bent, juniors Friedman and Gensch, and sophomores Anthony Clapcich, Dave Freedman, and Don DiChiara.

In the semifinals of the Union County Tournament against familiar opponent Scotch Plains, Weller's fourth-period goal forced a tie after Scotch Plains had taken a 1-0 lead. With the score still knotted after two scoreless overtimes, Scotch Plains' two-corner-kick advantage made them the winner. For the Pingry seniors especially, it was a hard defeat. "For them to beat us was an upset," Macrae commented after the season. "I think we lost to them because we took them too lightly. Maybe we played so hard against Lawrenceville in the prep championship finals because of that loss. We were determined that this time, Lawrenceville wasn't going to out-work us – mentally or physically."

Against an older, bigger, and heavily favored Lawrenceville team, it helped that both Macrae and DiChiara were back in action after missing games with injuries and Kunzmann had returned, but Miller summed up the effort when he said, "Hustle and determination kept us in this game." The resulting 0-0 tie meant that once again, Pingry were co-champions with a dejected Lawrenceville. "The tie?" said Miller, with a slight smile. "I guess it was more satisfying to us than it was to them."

Ralph Kunzmann and Geordie Kline were named to the All-County First Team, and Kline and Miles Welch to the All-Prep First Team, with post-season honors also going to Rob Macrae, Ron Weller, and Jim Gensch.

The picture of Ralph Kunzmann in the *Elizabeth Daily Journal* article "Pingry Goalie Beaten Up But Never Beaten" shows just his gnarled, taped-up fingers – hallmarks of the trade in the days before goalkeeper gloves became commonplace. " 'Right now,' Kunzmann is quoted, 'I'm playing with three broken fingers on my left hand. And the fingers that aren't broken are deformed. When I make a fist, I can't even see the knuckle on my middle finger. It's just flat. I broke it a while back and the doctor told me to wear a splint. But I can't block shots with a splint. So because I didn't use it, the break never healed. And it's really tough when I have to hold a girl's hand,' he added, chuckling." In commenting on Kunzmann's selection as *Elizabeth Daily Journal* Athlete of the Week, Miller added, "It doesn't matter if Ralph has a bruised hand, cut legs, or bad knees. He always plays. It's not so amazing that he plays with pain, but that he plays well with pain. That is the mark of a champion."

Ralph Kunzmann '82

THE LIFE & TIMES OF MILLER A. BUGLIARI

Steve Samson, *Assistant Coach*
Henry Ziegler, *Assistant Coach*
Denise Cohen, *Manager*
Motria Huk, *Manager*

Bent, D.	Gensch, J.	Ruprecht, C.
Birotte, A.	Jaffe, T.	Russell, J.
Clapcich, A.	Karp, J.	Stifel, H.
Clarick, G.	Kline, G.	Telling, M.
DiChiara, D.	Kunzmann, R.	Ward, N.
Donohue, G.	Lee, L.	Warlick, P.
Feigenbaum, M.	Macrae, R.	Welch, M.
Freedman, D.	Mahr, G.	Weller, R.
Friedman, S.	Rachlin, J.	

Varsity soccer ties Lawrenceville; shares crown

by JOSH LEVINE

Varsity Soccer fought to a scoreless tie with Lawrenceville to gain a share of the Prep State Championship.

"Hustle and determination were what kept us in the game," commented Coach Bugliari. "We were as aggressive as we were all year, and taking this title is an appropriate reward for this hard-working team.

The title match was the second encounter between the two teams, with Lawrenceville handily winning the first game by a score of 4-0.

Co-Captain Rob Macrae commented, "Maybe we played so hard in the Lawrenceville game to make up for our loss to Scotch Plains." The Blue lost to Scotch Plains in the semi-finals of the Union Tournament in a shootout

All-County goalie Ralph Kunzmann goes for the ball against Lawrenceville as Mile and Rob Macrae look on.

Pingry notches its 8th shutout

Another game and another shutout for Ralph Kunzmann and the Pingry soccer team.

The latest whitewash was a 2-0 triumph over Montclair-Kimberley Monday in a contest played in Hillside.

In other games Cranford trimmed Union Catholic, 2-1, in Scotch Plains, beat Edison Tough in Scotch Plains, 2-0 and Seton Hall Prep stood firm against Bayley Ellard-Madison, 1-0 in Madison.

Pingry 9-0, which has been scored upon in only one game this year, allowed just three of its on goal. Kunzmann was required to make two saves.

The Big Blue scored the two tallies in the first and second periods. Antiano Clapcich scored the first marker off an assist from

Mark Telling and Robbie Macrae added an insurance score by following up a rebound.

The loss dropped Montclair-Kimberley to 0-6-1.

1981 Season
Geordie Kline, Captain
Rob Macrae, Captain
14-2-1
Prep School State Champions

The 1982 Season

By any coach's reckoning, let alone Miller's, the 1982 team was a young team. It was also a very talented team with highly competitive, strong-willed players. That combination can produce exciting soccer – and lots of headaches for a coach. "Sometimes talented players don't want to shoot until they get the perfect shot. So I tell them to shoot more often," Miller said, following a tense 1-0 win over Peddie. When asked by a reporter how his players responded, Miller replied, "They sure don't shoot." "I repeat myself a million times," Miller told his team after Pingry's victory against Union in the Union County semifinals, "then you get mad at me. So listen the first time I tell you something."

The 1982 team's stability came from its senior-led defense, spearheaded by co-captains Jimmy Gensch, Nick Ward, and Sander Friedman, along with junior starters Geordy Mahr, Chris Salibello, Geoff Solomon, Jay Wood, and goalkeeper Steve Platzman. With the exception of a frustrating meltdown against Westfield in the Union County semifinals, they held opponents to a total of 10 goals, many of them in the waning moments of 5-1 or 6-1 blowouts, while registering nine shutouts on the way to a 14-2-2 season.

Offensively, the firepower came from the "kids" on the team: juniors Don DiChiara, Dave Freedman, and Anthony Clapcich, and sophomores Mike Canavan and Chris Jenkins. Freedman's 15 goals and Clapcich's 14 topped the team's 50-goal scoring total. Gensch, Freedman, DiChiara, and Jenkins led the team in recording almost as many assists as goals.

With only a 3-1 loss to Westfield and a 0-0 tie against Lawrenceville marring the regular season's record, the team, seeded third, fought its way into the Union County finals, shutting out New Providence, Edison Tech, and Union by a combined 10-0 margin. Then in the championship rematch with Westfield, everything fell apart. Miller has always preached playing wide in order to create space for scoring opportunities, then finding the open man. But young players under pressure can get fixated on attacking the goal straight ahead and holding the ball too long in the effort to make something happen.

That inexperience played directly into the strength of a very talented, experienced Westfield defense. "Not to take anything from Westfield," Miller said after a devastating 3-0 loss to Westfield, "but we had our worst game. I don't think we distributed the ball well and our best players had bad days. We wanted to work the ball to the wings more and we didn't do it."

That loss may have been a wake-up call for the team. In the Prep School Tournament, Gensch's strong run into the penalty and feed to an unmarked Clapcich provided the 1-0 victory over Peddie, and Clapcich's unassisted goal after a scramble in front of the net following a corner kick from Jay Wood equalized the score in a bruising fight against a typically tough Lawrenceville team. Seniors Gensch and Ward led the defensive effort, helped by several clutch saves by Platzman that preserved the tie through overtime and earned Pingry another a Prep School co-championship with its perennial rival. The best that Lawrenceville coach John King could say was, "It's a little frustrating, but it's better than a loss." "I thought you saw a good ball game," was Miller's assessment. He might have added, "The kids finally listened."

"Looking back on our team, it's fair to say we were a pretty wild bunch, I think Coach enjoyed our enthusiasm and appreciated that we knew how to fly under the radar. Nevertheless, in some ways I think we tortured Miller. For just one example, we had the same bus driver, Bob, to all our away games. Most of the seniors would sit in the back. Jimmy Gensch and I would get right behind Bob, in his ear, we would coax him to 'Pick it up!' 'We'll never get there on time!' 'Come on, Bob, put the hammer down!' Coach found it amusing until Bob listened to us and sped up. We went around an exit ramp off the highway on two wheels and almost rolled the bus over. Coach's standard refrain all season long was 'You guys are killing me!' Even if we won a game on the road, if Coach felt we were not playing to his standards, he'd tell us to 'take a lap' after the game. As seniors we knew he expected us to lead by example and we were always the first on our feet. I always loved the look on our opponents' faces when they saw us running after they lost. You just wanted to play hard for Miller. He is that kind of coach."

Sander Friedman '83

THE LIFE & TIMES OF MILLER A. BUGLIARI

Steve Samson, *Assistant Coach*
B. Samson, *Assistant Coach*
Ken Thibault, *Assistant Coach*
Brian O'Donnell, *Assistant Coach*
Lauren Bockskopf, *Manager*
Barbara Coffey, *Manager*
Adrienne Cohen, *Manager*
Alison Little, *Manager*

Abbott, C.	Fuller, R.	Platzman, S.
Bent, S.	Gensch, J.	Reiken, R.
Birotte, A.	Jenkins, C.	Rentzepis, J.
Canavan, M.	Lee, L.	Salibello, C.
Clapcich, A.	Levine, J.	Solomon, G.
DiChiara, D.	Liotta, S.	Ward, N.
Donohue, G.	Mahr, G.	Warlick, P.
Edwards, T.	Mullett, C.	Welch, C.
Freedman, D.	Osmun, T.	Wood, J.
Friedman, S.	Perlman, B.	

1982 Season
Jimmy Gensch, Captain
Nick Ward, Captain
Sander Friedman, Captain
14-2-2
Prep School State Champions

Once again, Pingry and Lawrenceville must share crown

By JOE TINTLE
Journal Sports Writer

PRINCETON — As the sun sank slowly in the west late Monday afternoon, so did the hopes of Pingry and Lawrenceville...

The 1983 Season

For the seniors on the 1983 team, winning the Union County Tournament was a long-distant story from an earlier season. They were 7th graders when Pingry last beat Westfield 2-0 in 1978. They and the other seniors on the 1983 team were determined that their year would be different.

Led by co-captains Don DiChiara and Jay Wood IV, the 1983 team achieved the best season yet for Pingry soccer: an 18-1-1 record and sole possession of both the Union County and Prep titles. Offensively, they tore apart opponents – and the Pingry record book – their 78 goals for the season completely eclipsing the 1976 and 1979 teams' season total of 58 goals. The leaders were Anthony Clapcich, with 19 goals and 13 assists, and Dave Freedman, with 20 goals and 11 assists. DiChiara added 11 goals from his midfield position, as did junior Chris Jenkins. Seniors Tom Osmun and Conor Mullett also contributed to the scoring deluge. Junior Mike Canavan's 14 assists led the team in that category.

The defense, led by seniors Wood, DiChiara, Geoff Solomon, Chris Salibello, Geordy Mahr, and Chris Welch, and goalkeeper Steve Platzman, was just as much a headache for other teams, shutting out their first nine opponents until the team's only loss in midseason, 2-1 against Lawrenceville. The only tie in 1983 was with undefeated Prep School B Champion Princeton Country Day, 0-0. "We had a very diverse group of personalities on that team," recalls Freedman, "but we came together like no team I ever played for before or since."

Entering the Union County Tournament as the top seed with a 9-1-1 record, Pingry easily disposed of Linden 8-0. A much tougher fight with Union resulted in a 2-1 victory.

That brought yet another final encounter with Westfield, in what would be Pingry's final appearance in the Union County Tournament Miller had initiated 17 years before. Pingry's last appearance, however, may well have been its best.

Freedman's first goal came at 8:19 in the second period, off a perfectly weighted pass from Clapcich. Pingry's second goal, 12 minutes into the third quarter, came when Jenkins followed up Freedman's point-blank shot. Platzman's try for a 15th clean sheet for the season was spoiled by a penalty kick in the final period.

After dumping Peddie 4-0, Pingry met Lawrenceville again. As in their regular season win, they took the initial lead. But that triggered perhaps the best 40 minutes of soccer a Pingry team ever played. "We couldn't do anything to stop them," said Lawrenceville coach John King. Freedman's first-quarter shot from deep in the right corner curled into the net to tie the game, and DiChiara's follow-up of a Clapcich shot halfway through the second period iced it. At the end of the game, Tom Hoffman, the Lawrenceville goalkeeper, summed it up perfectly. "I think they wanted us more than we wanted them."

Post-season honors appropriately reflected the balance and strength of the 1983 team. Chapcich and DiChiara were named to the Union County All-Star First Team, with Platzman, Freedman, Wood, and Solomon also being honored. Freedman joined Clapcich and DiChiara on the All-Prep First Team.

In describing Anthony Clapcich's three-year varsity career and his role in the 1983 team's dual championships, Miller said, "He knows where the ball has to go. His contributions are very essential – his scoring, his passing, his leadership – he really made us go."

Clapcich came from a soccer family. His father, Eligio, played an attacking midfielder for Libertas in Italy. "My pop built a full-size goal in my back yard," Clapcich remembers. "He said, 'There it is; see what you can do with it.' When it came to the fundamentals, he was there." Clapcich's game was polished in his years playing in Farcher's Grove under Manfred Schellscheidt, who also coached the U.S. Pan American Team. "He really helped me with one-touching the ball and doing things quickly."

But the reason he came to Pingry from New Providence in his sophomore year was Miller, and the combination of first-class soccer and strong academics the school provided. "It was probably the best move I ever made." It was a good move for Pingry as well. Arguably, his greatest contribution was his commitment to a winning team effort. Speaking after the Lawrenceville game, Clapcich said, "A co-championship is pretty cheap…. It's like the World Cup. How can you have two World Cup Champions?" He made sure there was only one winner in 1983 – Pingry.

Anthony Clapcich '84

Brian O'Donnell, *Assistant Coach*
Lauren Bockskopf, *Manager*
Margaret Humphrey, *Manager*
Melinda Tucker, *Manager*

Abbott, C.	Fair, D.	Mullett, C.
Becker, D.	Feigenbaum, J.	Osmun, T.
Bent, S.	Freedman, D.	Platzman, S.
Canavan, M.	Fuller, R.	Reiken, R.
Clapcich, A.	Garrow, A.	Rentzepis, J.
Croke, D.	Jenkins, C.	Salibello, C.
DiChiara, D.	Jentis, S.	Solomon, G.
Edwards, T.	Lewis, S.	Welch, C.
Eisenbud, D.	Mahr, G.	Wood, J.

1983 Season
Don DiChiara, Captain
Jay Wood, Captain
18-1-1
Union County Champions
Prep School State Champions

The 1984 Season

The 1984 season was a difficult transition for captains Mike Canavan and Chris Jenkins. They were the only two returning starters from the senior-led championship 1983 team. Tez Abbott, Steve Bent, Anthony Clapcich, Don DiChiara, Dave Freedman, Geordy Mahr, Conor Mullett, Tom Osmun, Steve Platzman, Chris Salibello, Geoff Solomon, and Jay Wood had all graduated. Pingry would need to rebuild around a group of largely untested underclassmen and discover its own identity as a team.

After decades playing against Union County powerhouses, Pingry had to define itself against unfamiliar competitors and develop new rivalries, including physical battles against its very unfriendly new neighbor, Ridge High School. Canavan remembers Pingry's first season on the Basking Ridge campus as a strange, almost disorienting experience. They had gone from playing on one of the most beautiful, regulation soccer pitches in New Jersey, the Miller A. Bugliari Varsity Soccer Field in Hillside, to a rough, poorly sodded rock garden of a new field. The new campus, still very much in an uncompleted stage, was yet another strange transition, like going from a stately Georgian mansion to the Pompidou Center in Paris – what some disenchanted alumni called "the pink Attica." Because of the condition of the field, Pingry was forced to play a lot of games on the road, including a rare night game under rented lights against Chatham.

Tom Johnson '59 remembers: "While I was athletic director at Pingry, I scheduled a night soccer game with Chatham High School at Chatham on their football field. When I told Miller, he wasn't exactly happy. Chatham was a very strong team and Miller hated the thought of playing soccer on a small football field. However, somehow I convinced him the game would be great for Pingry. The night of the game, all I heard were complaints from Miller and his assistants about the poor lighting and size of the field. To Miller's surprise, and as I had predicted, Pingry dominated the game. They won 3-0 and probably should have won 5-0. That's one of the few times I got one-up on Miller."

Joining Jenkins at forward were juniors Mike Coughlan and Rob Katz. Depending on the opponent, Canavan, juniors Boyce Bugliari, Matt Welch, and sophomore Todd Gibby alternated between forward and midfield. Mike Pizzi became the first freshman to start for a Pingry varsity team.

Senior Dave Becker led a defensive group that included senior Dave Croke, juniors Gil Lai and Bob Lavitt, and sophomore Steve Johnson at sweeper. Seniors Digger Fair and Dave Eisenbud along with first-time goalkeeper Jesse Feigenbaum and juniors Kirk Parker, Peter Tulloch, and Matt Welch rounded out the squad.

The 16-4-2 season was a story of feast and famine. Pingry had no trouble beating Bound Brook twice, and Blair, Edison Tech, Oratory, Montclair Kimberley, Union Catholic, and Horace Mann by a combined score of 45-0. They worked hard to claw out victories against the Morris County champion, Chatham, and against old foes Union and Peddie. But they struggled to score in losses to Hun, Berkeley Heights, and Ridge in the Somerset County Tournament. In one of their best games, they tied Lawrenceville 1-1 in the regular season. In the Prep Championship rematch, however, they were stymied by Lawrenceville in a 3-0 loss.

> "Chris Jenkins and I had played major roles as sophomores and juniors on two strong Pingry teams, and had enjoyed the championship run of the 1983 team's last year in Union County. Our senior year was all new for us. We were a young team, in an unfamiliar home, who had to figure out who we were. At the time, missing out on the county and prep championships, in spite of our 16 wins, was disappointing. Looking back after all these years, what stands out now, is that it was a fun season with some great guys as teammates."
>
> **Mike Canavan '85**

Bob Jenkins, *Assistant Coach*
John Alfano, *Manager*
Andrea Splan, *Manager*

Adams, B.	Eisenbud, D.	Lavitt, R.
Becker, D.	Faherty, P.	Parker, K.
Bugliari, B.	Fair, D.	Pizzi, M.
Campbell, J.	Feigenbaum, J.	Tulloch, P.
Canavan, M.	Gibby, T.	Waterbury, D.
Coughlan, M.	Jenkins, C.	Welch, M.
Croke, D.	Johnson, S.	White, M.
Donohue, C.	Katz, R.	Wixom, C.
Dougherty, K.	Lai, G.	

1984 Season
Chris Jenkins, Captain
Mike Canavan, Captain
16-4-2

The 1985 Season

For the team's tri-captains, Boyce Bugliari, Matt Welch, and Mike White, along with the rest of the seniors, it had been two years since Pingry had won a championship. As sophomores, they had shared in the elation of Pingry's final Union County title. They had yet to make their mark on Somerset County, as their neighbors from Ridge High School were only too happy to point out.

On their way to a 15-3-2 record, Pingry started off as they often did by ripping through their first nine opponents in a season in which 16 different players accounted for Pingry's 63 goals and 10 shutouts. Mike Pizzi and Mike White led the team in scoring, with senior Rob Katz and juniors Jamie Eldon and Peter Faherty also contributing strongly. White, Bugliari, and junior Todd Gibby were the assist leaders. Midfield and defensive standouts included seniors Peter Tulloch, Mike Coughlan, Kirk Parker, and Welch. Miller used two goalkeepers, veteran Kevin Dougherty starting games and newcomer Vik Kapila finishing them.

Pingry gained the "A" prep school finals by beating Peddie 1-0 after a two-game, 10-quarter marathon. In the replay of the scoreless first game, a foul against Todd Gibby with slightly over four minutes left set up Mike White's winning penalty kick. In the finals, Lawrenceville, led by postgraduate standouts Pete Harris from Madison and Brian O'Reilly from Notre Dame, were clear favorites, but the regular season means nothing in tournament play – especially against Lawrenceville. "We're real rivals," said White. "We don't like each other very much." Pingry controlled the run of play and finally took the lead with 3:29 left in the third quarter when Gibby's header found an unmarked White three yards in front of the goal. It wasn't enough. O'Reilly scored with 3:16 left in the game. "We put up the sandbags after we scored our goal, but we collapsed," said Gibby after the tie gave Pingry another shared championship with Lawrenceville.

That left a meeting with Ridge in the Somerset County finals, after Pingry's 1-0 victory over Hillsborough in the semis on Pizzi's first-period goal. In the first overtime period following a 0-0 regulation deadlock, Pingry threatened repeatedly – but couldn't find the net. Then, a minute into the second overtime, disaster struck. Steve Archer's 19th goal of the season gave Ridge its first lead. With less than a minute to go, their bench was already celebrating the championship. They were 17 seconds premature.

Sixteen different players had scored for Pingry during the season; junior Chris Wixom wasn't one of them. But he made his first varsity goal memorable when he collected Gibby's 10-yard cross off an indirect kick and drove it into the right corner of the goal to tie the game and make Pingry co-champions with Ridge.

First Team All-County and All-Prep honors went to White, Parker, and Gibby, with Bugliari, Welch, Steve Johnson, and Pizzi also receiving recognition.

"My most vivid memory happened when we were playing at Lawrenceville my senior year. I was going up for a head ball when a defender came from behind and head-butted me. I continued to play as Miller yelled at me to get down on the ground. I kept looking over at him like he was crazy and refused. He then started walking out on the field and forced me to get down. It was then that I realized I had been busted up. I got 50 stitches over the eye. Three days later, we were to play Union under the lights and I didn't want to miss the game. Mr. Bugliari and Mr. Lalley came up with this contraption including gauze, foam, and a very thick headband so I could play. Mr. Bugliari before the game came over to me and said I would have no problem tonight because I never used my head when I played anyway. It was just another example of how he was able to get me to play my best for him.

"I was back at Pingry in May for our 20th reunion and he took my twin 5-year-olds down to his office and showed my kids pictures of me and our team on his wall. He told my kids and my wife that he never had to worry about me playing hard and tough. My son Leo was so impressed that he takes pride in being tough on the soccer field now. It was a great moment for my family and I am truly honored to have played for a great coach with a great heart."

Michael White '86

THE LIFE & TIMES OF MILLER A. BUGLIARI

Bob Jenkins, *Assistant Coach*
Tom Alfano, *Manager*
Jennifer Chiaramonte, *Manager*

Adams, B.	Dougherty, K.	Lai, G.
Becker, M.	Dunlap, D.	Lavitt, R.
Braun, M.	Dziadzio, J.	Padulo, D.
Bugliari, B.	Eldon, J.	Parker, K.
Cooper, P.	Faherty, D.	Pizzi, M.
Coughlan, M.	Faherty, P.	Salibello, P.
Crabtree, S.	Gibby, T.	Schwarz, E.
Curtis, P.	Johnson, S.	Tulloch, P.
D'Costa, M.	Kaimer, F.	Welch, M.
DiChiara, J.	Kapila, V.	White, M.
Donohue, C.	Katz, R.	Wixom, C.

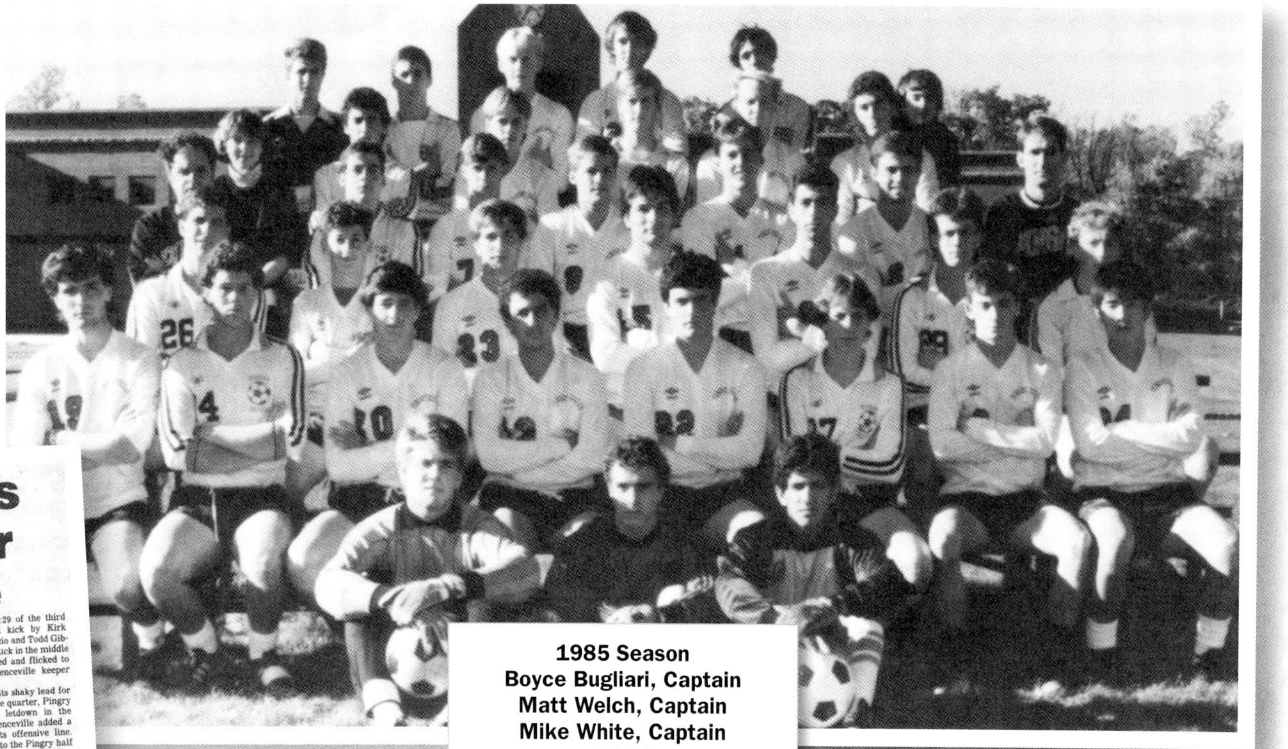

1985 Season
Boyce Bugliari, Captain
Matt Welch, Captain
Mike White, Captain
15-3-2
Somerset County Champions
Prep School State Champions

Pingry ties for soccer state title

By JOHN KELLY
Courier-News Staff Writer

PRINCETON — In what has become an annual rite of the fall season, Pingry School and Lawrenceville Prep battled to their third Independent Schools "A" soccer co-championship in five years yesterday with a 1-1 tie on Princeton University's Bedford Field.

It was the fifth consecutive meeting in the final round between the two teams. Pingry and Lawrenceville finished as co-champs in 1981 and 1982 seasons. Pingry won the championship, 2-1, in 1983; Lawrenceville answered with a victory last year.

"In reflection of the championship, it's easy to see that the Lawrenceville tradition has gone further than five years. The all-round matchup has occurred with such frequency that they prepare themselves for it with certainty even at the beginning of the year."

"Always in the finals against the kind of expect it," said Pingry striker Mike White, who scored a 1-0. "We don't really expect much, but it's always something to look forward to at the end."

White scored at 3:29 of the third period off a direct kick by Kirk Parker. Mike Dziadzio and Todd Gibby both headed the kick in the middle before White trapped and flicked to the right of Lawrenceville keeper Pete St. Phillip.

After protecting its shaky lead for the remainder of the quarter, Pingry suffered a severe letdown in the fourth when Lawrenceville added a fourth player to its offensive line. Play was confined to the Pingry half of the field and it was only a matter of time before Lawrenceville tied it.

At 3:16 of the final quarter, Lawrenceville's Brian O'Reilly took the ball down right wing and slipped it on the left past the charging Pingry keeper Vic Kapila.

"We wanted to apply a lot of pressure in the fourth quarter," said Lawrence coach John King. "We wanted to do it sooner but were forced to wait a little. But when we went to four forwards, it was one of those things where you could sense that something was going to happen."

Lawrence (11-2-2) fired eight shots on goal in the fourth while holding Pingry to none. Pingry returned to its early-game form and created some opportunities during the two overtime periods, but it was too little too late. Gibby expressed what most of the Pingry team must have felt...

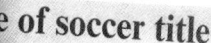

Keeping Possession — Steve Archer of Ridge attempts to dribble past the outstretched foot of Pingry's Chris Wixom during the finals.

In The Air — Pingry's Mike White, wearing white, and Ridge's Paul Feldman crash in midair in a battle for possession of the ball during the Somerset County Tournament championship game Saturday. The two teams will share the trophy after tying 1-1.

A HEAD START — Pingry's Matt Welch (17) gets a head on the ball as Lawrenceville School's Chris Lugossy (16) waits for the rebound during the half of yesterday's NJISAA Class A title contest.

149

The 1986 Season

Looking back on their senior season 25 years later, what co-captains Todd Gibby and Steve Johnson remember is the expectation going into the campaign: "We knew we had a really good team – seven of the eleven starters our year went on to play Division I soccer." Along with Gibby and Johnson, the 1986 team was led by seniors Geoff Arlen, Drew Dunlap, Jamie Eldon, Peter Faherty, and Chris Wixom; juniors Mike Becker, John Dziadzio, Mike DiChiara, Mike Pizzi, and Gardiner Welch; and sophomores Scott Aimetti, Tom Logio, and Mike Pence. "And we weren't just good players," Gibby adds. "We were a really tight-knit group. We wanted and expected to be one of the great Pingry teams."

Then, in the very first game, it all came crashing apart. Pingry was upset by Peddie on a day when good shots missed by inches to bang off the goal posts, skittered wide of the goal or sailed maddeningly over it. "It was a huge blow mentally," both Gibby and Johnson recalled. The players had to pick up the pieces and discover what kind of team — and men — they would actually be.

Sixteen of their opponents found out just what kind of team they were the hard way. Mike Pizzi followed up his dazzling sophomore season with another 15 goals, and newcomer Scott Aimetti added 12. Gibby led the team with 21 assists along with 10 goals.

In the Prep School championships they ran into a Lawrenceville team that was just too strong and loaded with postgraduates even for this gifted a Pingry team. "I was playing against some of the same kids who had graduated from high school my junior year," Gibby remembers. "It was like playing a college freshman team – we worked hard but could never manage to get in the game."

Defending co-champion Pingry earned a spot in the Somerset County finals with a thrilling 3-2 double overtime victory against Bridgewater on DiChiara's clutch goal off a pass from Pizzi with 1:40 remaining. The championship game against very unfriendly rival Ridge was another physical battle marked by hard fouls and yellow cards. Unfortunately for Pingry, Dziadzio's second yellow card for unavoidably running into a referee forced Pingry to play a man down for most of the second half. Ridge's goalkeeper Eugene McInerny made some huge saves to preserve Ridge's 1-0 victory.

Against St. Benedict's in the Parochial B final, Pingry faced an even rougher challenge. Gibby had played for St. Benedict's coach Rick Jacobs on the Millburn Strikers. "Rick loved to play mind games against opponents, so when we stepped on the field against St. Benedict's, it was the same old thing. They came out nonchalantly sucking on blow pops tossing balls around in a choreographed routine. We weren't impressed – and certainly not intimidated." With goalkeeper Arlen making some clutch saves, Pingry fought St. Benedict's to a standstill in regulation, but in the second overtime, after Pingry's defense had cleared a direct kick, the referee called Pingry for pushing, and this time, Rory McCauley's shot ended the game. "What can you say?" commented Miller after the game. "We just couldn't get the ball to bounce our way."

Gibby and Johnson were named to the All-County and All-Prep First Teams for the second year, joined in 1986 by Pizzi, with DiChiara and Wixom also being recognized in post-season honors.

"What I appreciated most about playing for Coach were two things. He was the first coach I'd met who loved to compete and put it all on the line. That quality really appealed to me. It became the way I played and how I've lived my life since Pingry. Beyond that, Steve Johnson and I were best friends as kids, playing together in Chatham, and for both of us, becoming Pingry co-captains was a special honor, and also provided another important Miller lesson: 'With great privilege comes great responsibility.' It was our job to ensure that the team lived up to the expectations that go along with playing soccer for Pingry – in daily practice, in games, around the school, and socially, and in the off-season. You understand that there's a 'right way of doing things' – being accountable to ourselves, to the school, to Coach, and to the legacy of the program."

Todd Gibby '87

Bob Jenkins, *Assistant Coach*
Tom Alfano, *Manager*

Aimetti, S.	Dziadzio, J.	Padulo, D.
Arlen, G.	Eldon, J.	Pappas, W.
Becker, M.	Faherty, D.	Pence, M.
Bourne, M.	Faherty, P.	Pizzi, M.
Choe, C.	Gardner, T.	Rusen, T.
Cooper, P.	Gibby, T.	Southworth, N.
DePalma, G.	Gibson, J.	Welch, G.
DiChiara, M.	Johnson, S.	Wilmerding, H.
DiMartino, J.	Kaimer, F.	Wixom, C.
Dunlap, D.	Logio, T.	

1986 Season
Todd Gibby, Captain
Steve Johnson, Captain
16-3-1

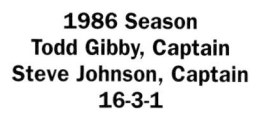

The 1987 Season

In describing the team midway through the season, Miller said, "We're a young team, and sometimes it shows. But then most of the time we've played very well."

That assessment captured the up-and-down fortunes of the 1987 team. Offensively, "very well" translated into a new scoring record of 85 goals and 91 assists. Leaders were senior forwards Mike Pizzi, whose 16 goals and 18 assists capped a four-year career with a new Pingry career scoring record of 42 goals, and John Dziadzio, halfback and co-captain Mike DiChiara, and juniors Scott Aimetti and Tom Logio. Eight other Pingry players scored at least once during the season.

Defensively, while the team got consistent leadership from seniors co-captain Mike Becker and Gardiner Welch, it was an unusually young group, with juniors Will Pappas, Tom Rusen, and Mike Pence as new starters and a sophomore, Mike Coughlin, starting in goal.

Pingry finished the regular season 12-2-1 entering into the Somerset County Tournament, seeded fifth. After disposing of previously unbeaten Bernards 4-2, Pingry faced defending champion Ridge, this time in the semifinals, their fourth meeting in the tournament in a row. Ridge had bested Pingry in the finals in 1984 and 1986, and tied them as co-champions in 1985. This year it was a different story. Logio's first-period score stood up until Aimetti's insurance goal with 45 seconds left sealed the victory. Dziadzio added two more assists to match his total in the Bernards game. Coughlin repeatedly frustrated the Ridge players with whom he had grown up in the Basking Ridge youth leagues by recording 14 saves to earn his clean sheet.

Against high-powered and undefeated Bridgewater-Raritan, a questionable early penalty and a defensive lapse were enough to send Pingry home with a 2-0 loss. Bridgewater's tough, experienced defense throttled Pingry's high-powered offense all game long.

That left Pingry one last shot at a trophy – in the A Division Prep Finals against Lawrenceville, who earlier in the season had demolished Pingry 5-1 – its worst beating in Miller's career as a coach. Miller's pre-game analysis was succinct and, as it turned out, prophetic. "To win next Monday, we're going to have to hustle to the ball and make things happen." They did. Pingry's unrelenting pressure prevented Lawrenceville from getting into the flow of the game and led to the first goal, an Aimetti header off a cross by Dziadzio at 11:45 in the first period.

But Miller, with so many crazy Lawrenceville games burned into his memory, didn't start to relax until Mike DiChiara's penalty kick in the fourth quarter sealed Pingry's stunning upset and championship. "It was an excellent team effort for the guys to come back after that earlier beating," Miller said after the game. "I'm happy for them because they deserved it."

Post-season All-County and All-State Prep honors were awarded to Scott Aimetti, John Dziadzio, Mike Pizzi, Mike DiChiara, and Mike Becker. Scott Aimetti was named the Somerset County Boys Soccer Player of the Year.

In the Prep School finals against Lawrenceville, a penalty kick was going to put Pingry up by two goals with only eight minutes or so left in the game. Mike DiChiara still remembers the moment. "I'll never forget the other players shouting, 'Me, coach! Me, coach! Let me take it! Miller, let me take it! I'll put it in, I'll put it in!!!' Well, Miller scanned the scene with that all-knowing look as though he had made up his mind the day before the game just in case a dire, last-minute situation like this did indeed arise… and he waved me on, 'Deech, take the kick.'

"Needless to say, I was unbelievably nervous! Here was a chance not just to win a game, it was a chance to exact revenge upon a team that had taken us apart 5-1 in the regular season. One of the roughest, most aggressive games I'd played in my entire career came down to this one unbelievably tense moment. It wasn't a pretty shot…it wasn't that postage stamp you always hope for and seemingly always hit when you're in practice but it went in. It squirmed by the keeper and the team piled on top of me. We stunned Lawrenceville and, I'm pretty sure I can speak for anyone there that day, we stunned ourselves."

Michael DiChiara '88

Brian O'Donnell, *Assistant Coach*
Jennifer Hartstein, *Manager*

Ackerman, P.	Dziadzio, J.	Pence, M.
Aimetti, S.	Faherty, D.	Pizzi, M.
Becker, M.	Gardner, T.	Rosenbauer, P.
Bourne, M.	Gibson, J.	Rusen, T.
Bugliari, A.	Hilgendorff, N.	Southworth, N.
Choe, C.	Logio, T.	Welch, G.
Coughlin, M.	Merrill, D.	Wilmerding, H.
Crosby, B.	Mulvihill, C.	
DiChiara, M.	Pappas, W.	

1987 Season
Mike Becker, Captain
Mike DiChiara, Captain
14-3-1
Prep School State Champions

Mike Pizzi
...helps Pingry finish 14-3-1

Pingry foils Lawrenceville for 'A' title

Scott Aimetti, Mike Pizzi and Mike DiChiara scored a goal each to give Pingry a 3-1 victory over Lawrenceville and the state prep schools A Division boys' soccer championship

BOYS' SOCCER

yesterday at Raritan Valley College in Somerville.
 Pingry (14-3-1) avenged a 5-1 loss to Lawrenceville (14-3-1) earlier in the season.
 Aimetti, a junior forward, scored the first goal 9:45 into the first quarter on an assist from John Dziadzio. Dziadzio also assisted on Pizzi's goal early in the second quarter, staking Pingry to a 2-0.
 Scott Coleman scored for Lawrenceville midway through the second, cutting the lead to 2-1, but DiChiara converted a penalty kick late in the

Miller Bugliari...4th winningest high school soccer coach in New Jersey history

Bridgewater-Raritan West's Brain Lockwood, right, heads the ball away from Pingry's Gardiner Welch yesterday during the Somerset County finals. West won, 2-0

Bugliari has formula for success

Entering 27th season as Pingry soccer coach

By CHRIS BRIENZA

Miller Bugliari teaches biology in Pingry High School classroom, but strategy may be one of the biggest reasons for his success on the soccer field.
 "I like to have everyone get a feel for scoring when they're young, then I can always move a player back," said Bugliari, who will enter his 27th year as head coach at the prep school in Martinsville. "That way, I can interchange a lot of players at different positions and not lose anything in the process."
 That method, along with a tireless work ethic, has helped Bugliari become the fourth winningest soccer coach in state history with a record of 347-49-36. He is second among active coaches, behind only George Stiefbold of Verona.
 Bugliari's soccer theory may have been developed in his days as both a midfielder and forward at Springfield (Mass.) College in the mid-1960s and during the school year.
 Bugliari's Pingry Soccer Camp runs from Aug. 17-22 and will be the third camp he has coached in this summer. He worked at the Puma Soccer Camp at Rutgers last month and in April he coached a benefit camp run by Rutgers raised more Jersey Speci "I expe their game

As if he weren't working enough, Bugliari was recently named to the Governor's Council on Fitness.
 "I'm really excited about that," he said. "I'll be working with soccer programs, the Special Olympics and also with baseball, which I used to coach at

he helped the Pingry expansion committee raise more than $30 million when they were moving from Hillside. He's very well-rounded.
 Bugliari also doubles during the soccer season as an official at Giants football home games. He works the sidelines keeping track of penalties and moving the chains.
 All Bugliari's extra activity doesn't keep him from one of his biggest jobs — finding players for his Pingry program. Unlike public schools the prep school doesn't have the luxury of community recreation programs to provide future talent.
 "We can't recruit," said Bugliari "because it's both illegal and unethical So we have to hustle to find players attract some good job got a pretty good pro

153

The 1988 Season

The poster on Scott Aimetti's bedroom wall read: "Happy are those who dream dreams and are ready to pay the price to make them come true." That motto could have served as well for the courage of the 1988 team, captained by Aimetti, Tom Logio, and Mike Pence, and including returning fellow senior defenders Tom Rusen, Brian Crosby, Ned Southworth, Will Pappas, Ned Hilgendorff, and goalkeeper Doug Proudman.

The result was a 17-1-2 season and a Somerset County co-championship with Ridge. With strong support from juniors Peter Ackerman, Jake Angell, Anthony Bugliari, Mark Donohue, Rob Range, and goalkeeper Mike Coughlin, who split duties all season with Proudman, Pingry demolished its prep school opposition, scoring 57 goals and recording 7 shutouts on the way to an undefeated regular season. The only blemish was a hard-fought 1-1 tie in double overtime against old Union County foe Union High School. In the rematch, Pingry gained revenge in a 2-0 victory.

Aimetti broke the Pingry single-season scoring record with 35 goals on his way to a career best 63 goals. Fifteen different players contributed assists during the season, led by Ackerman's 16 and Bugliari's 12.

In the Somerset County Tournament, Pingry blistered Bernards 7-1 and Bridgewater East 4-0, including a run of three goals in 50 seconds, to set up yet another rematch with Ridge in the finals. Aimetti opened the scoring in the first quarter with a 25-yard free kick. Ridge knotted the score with 3:00 to go before the half. Then the game turned against Pingry. Three minutes into the overtime period, Ridge converted an indirect kick to give them their first lead in the game. Moments later, Aimetti collided with Ridge's Johnny Green, sending Pingry's leading weapon to the bench with a game-ending ankle injury. But Pingry had fought too hard to get to this point and leave with a loss. With two minutes left in overtime, Ackerman evaded two defenders in the penalty area to center a ball that Hilgendorff headed in to regain the final tie.

In the Parochial B Tournament, Pingry easily disposed of Marist 5-0 and beat previously undefeated Don Bosco 1-0 on Aimetti's penalty kick to gain a rematch with St. Benedict's in the final. Pingry fought St. Benedict's to a 3-3 tie, only to lose 4-3 in the game-deciding shootout.

Aimetti was named to the All-Central Jersey, All-State Parochial, and All-Somerset County First Teams along with Logio and Rusen. Post-season honors also went to Bugliari, Pence, and Coughlin. Miller was similarly honored by his induction into the New Jersey Youth Soccer Association's Hall of Fame.

At the start of the 1988 season Scott Aimetti had said, "I hope we can get some respect in my last year here. We haven't gotten any since we've been in Somerset County." Ironically, that respect came in Pingry's only loss in 1988, against St. Benedict's.

Undefeated St. Benedict's had not been scored on in 20 straight games. Pingry's players embraced the challenge. With 11:55 left in the first period, Ackerman converted a pass from Aimetti for a 1-0 lead, which grew to a shocking 2-0 edge on Aimetti's 25-yard bullet on a direct kick early in the second quarter. St. Benedict's had too much talent and pride to surrender meekly. They pulled within a goal and then, with 2:05 left in the period, equalized when high school and college All-American Pedro Lopes' 22-yard direct kick just cleared the Pingry wall and dipped under Doug Proudman's dive. With their confidence restored, St. Benedict's continued to pressure Pingry's defense until All-American Scott Schweitzer hit a rolling shot past Mike Coughlin, now in the goal, for St. Benedict's first lead in the game. And it might have ended there, in a gallant defeat.

But Pingry wasn't finished either. In a scramble in front of the St. Benedict's goal, Ackerman alertly headed the ball to Aimetti, whose tap-in tied the game again with 1:31 left to play. After two 10-minute scoreless overtimes, highlighted by tremendous defensive efforts by Bugliari, Rusen, and Southworth, and by key saves by Coughlin, the game went into a shootout, and finally turned against Pingry. Three players scored for St. Benedict's, while Coughlin rejected the attempt by St. Benedict's third All-American, Bill Bustamente. But Mike Pence was the only Pingry player to score, and St. Benedict's preserved its undefeated season in a 4-3 shootout victory.

It would take a few years longer for Pingry to earn respect as one of the dominant teams in Somerset County, but they certainly earned St. Benedict's respect on that day.

Scott Aimetti '89

Rob Macrae, *Assistant Coach*

Ackerman, P.	Goldstein, J.	Pence, M.
Aimetti, S.	Hilgendorff, N.	Proudman, D.
Angell, J.	Jentis, R.	Puleo, F.
Baird, D.	Lee, E.	Range, R.
Bourne, M.	Levy, B.	Rosenbauer, P.
Bugliari, A.	Logio, T.	Rosenthal, P.
Coughlin, M.	Loikits, S.	Rusen, T.
Crosby, B.	Neary, O.	Southworth, N.
Donohue, J.	Pappas, W.	Welch, S.
Donohue, M.		

Bugliari hopes to build on legend as he starts 29th year at Pingry

The winning never stops
Pingry boys soccer riding another unbeaten streak

Pingry Ends Lawrenceville Win Streak

1988 Season
Scott Aimetti, Captain
Tom Logio, Captain
Mike Pence, Captain
17-1-2
Undefeated Regular Season
Somerset County Champions

Boys Soccer #1 in N.J.
Ranked 1st in Preps by Star-Ledger

The 1989 Season

The 1989 team seemed destined for greatness. As in the previous year, they blasted through the regular season without a loss and headed into the county and parochial tournaments confident of success.

The 1989 Pingry soccer team's confidence was well placed. Its leaders were co-captains and returning Second-Team All-County selections Peter Ackerman, whom Miller described as "very fast and strong, and hard to knock off the ball," and Anthony Bugliari, one of the most versatile players in Somerset County, who understood and could play every position on the field. Joining them was a group of veteran seniors: Jake Angell, Mike Coughlin, Jamie Donohue, Owen Neary, and Rob Range; juniors Jeremy Goldstein, Andy Gottlieb, Jack Meyercord, Frank Puleo, and Spencer Tullo; along with newcomers sophomore Chris Pearlman and freshman Andrew Lewis. All told, 10 different players scored for Pingry, headed by Bugliari's 19 goals and 8 assists and Ackerman's 15 goals and 11 assists.

Over the regular season, in allowing just four goals, their only blemish was a tie against Peddie. For good measure, they disposed of two old opponents from Pingry's Union County years, ninth-ranked Summit 3-0 and fifth-ranked Union 2-0.

In the opening round of the Somerset County Tournament Pingry defeated Bridgewater West 2-1 to again meet Ridge in the semifinals.

By 1989, the ill will between Pingry soccer players and their former Basking Ridge youth soccer teammates, with whom Mike Coughlin and Rob Range used to play, had become a hot flame. Games against Ridge were wars, not soccer matches. "We know those guys pretty well," recalls Range. "I broke my arm in a collision with Rich Swift, and finished the season wearing a soft cast."

Ridge jumped out early with 9:25 left in the first quarter on Rich Swift's drive into the opposite corner. Pingry pressured repeatedly in the opening half and into the third quarter until Ackerman seemed to have gained the equalizer at the end of the third period, when he collected a through pass, held off a defender, and found himself with an open goal six yards out.

But before he could shoot, he was pulled down roughly by a Ridge defender – and no foul was called. Pingry's outcry of protest from the bench earned a caution for dissent from the referee. Then the tight match fell apart. Pingry goalkeeper Mike Coughlin was cynically fouled by Ridge's Swift on a challenge for a high ball in front of the goal. The referee missed that foul, too, but didn't miss Coughlin's impulsive retaliation. The resulting penalty kick, against a cold Pingry substitute goalkeeper, put Ridge safely ahead 2-0, and Bob Parisi's goal with 7:34 remaining closed out a bitter loss for Pingry.

That left the Parochial Championship and a rematch against top-seeded St. Benedict's as Pingry's remaining opportunity for a championship. The rematch never took place. In the opening round, Morris Catholic scored with 2:03 left in the fourth quarter to forge a tie, and then won the shootout for another disheartening Pingry loss. In the 1989 team picture, there are no smiles on the faces of the team's seniors. But denied a championship, the 1989 team could still take pride in a stunning undefeated regular season.

Somerset County First Team selections included Bugliari, Ackerman, and Neary, with Angell, Coughlin, Goldstein, Gottlieb, Lewis, Range, and Puleo also receiving honors.

"My senior year I'd suffered a knee injury earlier in the season – and all my one-time buddies at Ridge knew it. So during the 1989 county championship game, they kept running into my legs, trying to take me out. Finally Rich Swift, one of their best players, and a guy I'd known and played with growing up, deliberately kicked me in my bad knee. I just snapped, and as he lay on the ground, I kicked him back. The ref didn't see his foul, but instantly gave me a yellow card for my retaliation. By the rules, I had to leave for the next play – a penalty kick – and my backup, Jamie Donohue, had to come in cold off the bench to play in the goal. They scored and that was the turning point of the game."

After the game, Ridge coach Rick Hildebrand said it best: "Coughlin went to school with all our guys. It's become more than a soccer game. It shouldn't be; it should just be soccer."

Mike Coughlin '90

THE LIFE & TIMES OF MILLER A. BUGLIARI

Rob Macrae, *Assistant Coach*
Leo Stillitano, *Assistant Coach*
Adam Rohdie, *Assistant Coach*
Hunter Hulshizer, *Manager*

Ackerman, P.	Gardner, A.	Neary, O.
Angell, J.	Goldstein, J.	Pearlman, C.
Bugliari, A.	Gottlieb, A.	Puleo, F.
Cameron, C.	Krantz, C.	Range, R.
Corbin, C.	Levy, B.	Range, S.
Coughlin, M.	Lewis, A.	Smart, A.
Donnelly, A.	Loikits, S.	Tullo, S.
Donohue, J.	Londa, P.	Weldon, W.
Donohue, M.	Lucas, S.	
Gardiner, T.	Meyercord, J.	

1989 Season
Anthony Bugliari, Captain
Peter Ackerman, Captain
13-3-1
Undefeated Regular Season

Pingry registers behind Bugliari

Anthony Bugliari scored twice to spark unbeaten Pingry to a 6-0 boys' soccer victory over Montclair-Kimberley yesterday in Martinsville.

Jake Angell, Sam Welch, Frank Puleo and Jeremy Goldstein added a goal apiece for Pingry (3-0-1). Montclair-Kimberley is 1-1.

Pennington 5, Doane Academy 0: Peter Cook connected for three goals and Trip Stephanelli put in two shots in Burlington. Derek Landry of Pennington (2-1) made five saves to halt Doane (1-3).

Shawnee 2, Lawrenceville 1: Scot McFadden snapped a 1-1 tie when he scored on an assist from Dave Sallade at 2:41 of the fourth quarter in Lawrenceville. Lawrenceville (2-1) had tied it, 1-1, on Judd Lando's goal at 6:39 of the third period. Sallade opened the scoring for Shawnee

Tullo helps Pingry gain county final

Spencer Tullo came up with a goal and an assist when top-seeded Pingry, 15th in The Star-Ledger Boys' Soccer Top 20, defeated fourth-seeded Hillsborough, 3-1, yesterday to gain the final round of the Somerset County Tournament in Martinsville.

Peter Ackerman and Anthony Bugliari also scored for Pingry (11-0-1), which opened a 3-0 lead in the second period. Matt Rose had the goal for Hillsborough (9-3-1).

THE COURIER-NEWS CENTRAL JERSEY BOY SOCCER TOP 10

1. **WESTFIELD (8-0):** Westfield, last season's top-rated team, piled up four more victories since the first rating week.
2. **SCOTCH PLAINS-FANWOOD (6-1):** Scotch Plains is on a collision course with Westfield, which it meets next Tuesday in a key Watchung Conference clash.
3. **RIDGE (5-0):** Ridge has quickly established itself, once again, as one of the premier teams in Somerset County.
4. **PINGRY (6-0-1):** Ten players have gotten into the scoring act for coach Miller Bugliari's well-balanced team.
5. **HILLSBOROUGH (5-1-1):** Hillsborough has gotten off to a good start in the very tough Mid-State Conference, where every game is an adventure.
6. **SOMERVILLE (5-1):** Only 5-4 loss to Hillsborough last week stands between Somerville and a winless season.
7. **HUNTERDON CENTRAL (3-1-1):** Central has eked out stirring two victories in

Pingry's Bugliari sets the pace among high school soccer coaches

By RON JANDOLI

Miller Bugliari, the legendary soccer coach at the Pingry School in Martinsville, added another honor to his list of achievements last month when he was recognized as the 1989 national boys' private-parochial school coach of the year by the National Soccer Coaches Association of America.

Bugliari, whose name is almost synonymous with New Jersey soccer, was noted nationally in 1983 when he was elected the overall national high school coach of the year by the association.

He served as an officer for the NSCAA from 1974 through 1980, including the presidency in 1978 when the convention keynote speaker.

"Winning coach of the year honors shows that I had a reasonable" said Bugliari, whose 1989 team posted a 13-3-2 mark.

The coaches from around the country voted for me, and that carried nationally for the award," he said.

The senior member of the association among New Jersey coaches, the 61-old Bugliari has been the head at Pingry for 31 of its 61 years of and has a career record of 1-38. In 1988, his team went 17-1-0

plays on a field bearing his name. It was dedicated to him when the school was located in Hillside in 1971. Pingry moved to its present location in 1964.

Bugliari plans to stay with his players for a long time. "I will continue to coach as long as I can relate to the players and the people involved in the game," he said.

In 1966, Bugliari founded the Union County Tournament, the first county tournament in the state. His teams won it seven times, and added two Somerset County co-championships after the school moved in 1964.

The coach also helped found the New Jersey Soccer Coaches Association in 1968.

"Starting the coaches association and the county tournament really took a lot of work and time," reflected Bugliari, who was also voted into the New Jersey State Youth Soccer Hall of Fame in December.

"You go through your ups and downs putting things like that together, but, in the long run, it's worth all the effort."

Bugliari, an alumnus of Pingry and Springfield College in Massachusetts, has produced nine undefeated teams. In the early '70s, his clubs produced a 58-game regular-season unbeaten streak. From 1962-66, his teams

Miller Bugliari
National coach of the year

The oldest boy, Boyce, co-captained the Pingry soccer team in 1985, and Anthony, 17, captained the team last fall and was selected to the All-Somerset County Team by The Star-Ledger. David, the youngest at 10 years of age, will most likely carry on the strong family tradition in the sport.

How long will the Bugliari coaching legacy continue?

"Right now I'm just one of the coaches and will continue to do my job until it's no longer fun," he said.

"After all, the kids keep me young and the enthusiasm that they show year after year always rubs off on me and keeps me going."

157

The 1990s: County Dominance – National Prominence

> *"I'm going to continue coaching until I start to fall apart. It keeps me young and enthusiastic and is still very exciting and challenging to me."*
>
> MILLER, 1991

Finding Opponents to Play Against

When you look at Pingry's opponents through the 1990s, it's hard to get a solid picture of the character of Miller's teams. Through the first half of the decade, Pingry's regular season schedule included opponents whom players from the 1960s and 1970s would instantly have recognized: prep schools like Newark Academy, Blair, Hun, Peddie, and Lawrenceville, and old Union County foes like Union, Scotch Plains, and Clark (now Johnson Regional High School). Marred only by a 1991 loss to Lawrenceville and a 1994 upset versus Peddie, Pingry's record against these teams during this period was a stunning 40-2 domination, but since Pingry no longer played in the Prep A league or Union County, these were all just well-earned victories, not championships.

In the middle years of the 1990s, it looked as if Pingry scheduled anyone who would give them a game. Teams like Good Counsel, Collegiate School, Emerson, Academic, Brooklyn Friends, Belvidere, Solomon Schechter, and Wayne Valley added Pingry for a year or two, absorbed a beating, and then dropped Pingry.

Finally, in 1995, as part of a statewide league reorganization by the NJSIAA, Pingry found a new home in the Colonial Hills Conference, which brought a whole new list of opponents from Morris and Essex Counties, including Chatham, a soccer power in its own right and one of the top Group II teams in New Jersey.

The State Championship Challenge

At the same time, in state competition Pingry also became part of a reorganized Parochial (and later Non-Public) group including Morris Catholic, St. Augustine, Bishop Eustace, Immaculata, Bergen Catholic, and a new nemesis in Delbarton. In effect, in the 1990s Pingry competed against some of the very biggest and best teams in Union, Morris, and Somerset counties and against the top Parochial teams statewide.

With its entry into the Parochial/Non-Public group, Pingry's quest for state championships became extraordinarily harder. In the years from 1960 to 1987, a state championship meant a head-to-head battle with Lawrenceville. In the Parochial/Non-Public competition, Pingry first had to win its North Sectional title, usually in a four-round tournament, before taking on the South Sectional Champions for the state title. It was like moving from winning the Ivy League championship to trying to win the NCAA tournament. Pingry's two titles in the decade came when the 1995 and 1996 teams compiled back-to-back undefeated seasons. The rest of the decade was marked by often heartbreaking last-minute or overtime losses to Morris Catholic, Immaculata, Delbarton, or Bergen Catholic. But there's great accomplishment in getting to the finals in the first place, and Pingry's accomplishments in the 1990s included winning three titles.

County Championships and National Recognition

When you look at Pingry's record in Somerset County, however, the team's identity snaps into sharp focus. Starting in 1991 and for the next 10 years, Pingry owned Somerset County, winning the title outright five times, including a four-year run of consecutive titles from 1994 through 1997, and sharing the title in 2000 with Bridgewater.

The other lens through which to view Pingry's teams in the 1990s is in competitive rankings. By the 1980s, Pingry was regularly ranked among the Top 20 teams in the state. Through most of the 1990s, it had risen to a Top 10 team, dethroning St. Benedict's as the number one team in the state in 1996. Foreshadowing seasons to come, Pingry gained the tremendous prestige of being recognized as the 10th-best high school team in the United States in 1995 and the seventh-best team in 1996. Given Pingry's size, it was a remarkable achievement. Among the schools ahead of Pingry in the rankings, Quaker Valley had over 2,000 students enrolled in grades 9-12, Stillwater High School 2,036 in grades 10-12, and St. Thomas Aquinas over 1,000. Calvert Hall's enrollment was 1,200 – all boys.

Miller also continued to build the talent available to him at Pingry through the Pingry soccer camp and through a strong development program coordinated with Middle School, freshman, and JV coaches like long-time assistant Manny Tramontana. Promising freshmen like David Fahey and Steve Lewis also joined the "taxi squad," JV starters who also practiced with the varsity to gain maturity.

What's most startling about Miller's rosters in the 1990s, however, is the number of freshmen who made an impact on the team. Miller had always counted on seniors to serve as team leaders, modeling how players should practice, compete, and conduct themselves in school. And especially in the early years, the rare sophomores on the varsity team were definitely rookies. They were expected to respect the older members of the team, and were subjected to additional chores like shining the seniors' shoes and carrying team equipment.

By the 1990s some 14-year-olds had been playing very high-level competitive soccer on community, regional, and age-group ODP teams for almost a decade. Their skills and game sense were years ahead of what one might expect in a ninth grader. In the 1990s, Miller wouldn't start a freshman – that honor still went to an older player. But ninth graders like Andrew Lewis, Mike DeGrande, Mike Roberts, Kris Bertsch, Gianfranco Tripicchio, and John Rhodes embraced the challenge of playing on a big stage immediately, and they logged significant minutes in making key contributions to the team's success.

UMBRO high school boys soccer rankings

Voted by the National Soccer Coaches Association of America
Final fall ranking

Rank, School, city, state	Record	Prev.
1. Quaker Valley (Leetsdale, Pa.)*	26-0-0	1
2. St. Charles, Ill.*	29-0-2	4
3. Calvert Hall (Baltimore)	21-0-1	5
4T. Guilford, Conn.*	21-0-0	12
4T. Stillwater, Minn.*	23-0-0	7
6. St. Thomas Aquinas (Overland Park, Kan.)*	19-1-1	8T
7. Pingry (Martinsville, N.J.)*	18-0-1	8T
8. Haverling Central (Bath, N.Y.)*	25-0-0	20
9. Weymouth North (Weymouth, Mass.)*	22-1-0	NR
10. J.O. Sanderson (Raleigh, N.C.)*	20-1-1	NR
11. Regis Jesuit (Aurora, Colo.)*	17-2-1	13
12. Bethel, Conn.*	21-0-0	6
13. St. Mark's (Wilmington, Del.)*	19-0-1	11
14. Herricks (New Hyde Park, N.Y.)*	17-2-1	15
15. Thomas Stone (Waldorf, Md.)*	17-0-0	16
16. Crescent Valley (Corvallis, Ore.)*	18-0-1	NR
17. John Jay (Hopewell Junction, N.Y.)	22-1-0	3
18. North Olmsted, Ohio*	18-1-4	19
19T. Strath Haven (Wallingford, Pa.)*	25-1-1	25
19T. Jesuit (Carmichael, Calif.)*	21-1-2	17T
19T. Gilford (N.H.) Middle*	19-0-0	17T
22. Lakeland (Fla.) Christian*	26-0-0	NR
23. Cathedral (Springfield, Mass.)	20-1-0	2
24. Centerville, Ohio	21-1-1	22
25T. La Cueva (Albuquerque)*	16-3-0	24
25T. Marquette (Milwaukee)*	24-2-1	NR

Building Toughness

In his first year of coaching, Miller had discovered two critical elements for beating bigger, often better teams. One was fitness: making sure his kids were in better shape than their opponents so that Pingry teams would just run opponents into the ground. The second was mental and physical toughness. From the earliest days in the 1960s, high school opponents had counted on intimidating the "wimpy preppies" with rough physical play. One would think that after losing so many times, high school kids would have figured out this wasn't a winning strategy. But through the 1990s, Miller and his assistant coaches still had to ensure that Pingry players didn't play like "prep school kids."

Compounding the problem was the fact that kids who grew up playing soccer in community and academy programs were much better skilled than their predecessors, but not ready for the wars that took place against Somerset County and Parochial teams in tournaments. A game between two club teams might be really skilled, attractive soccer, but there rarely was any blood spilled.

The Ring

Bullying has become a serious concern in sports, from peewee leagues to professional teams – as it should be. Abuse of younger, weaker or "less popular" students or players, at Pingry or any other school, is wholly unacceptable. So one could look at the Pingry soccer tradition of "The Ring" and call it "bullying." Every week or so through the 1990s, players, without their coaches, would jog to a spot out of sight of the school and practice fields, form a circle, and then the captains would call two players into the circle to battle it out until one player got the other on the ground. But what set this ritual apart from what we rightly condemn as "bullying" are two critical elements: players chosen to enter "The Ring," always veterans at the beginning of the season, were matched against opponents of comparable strength; it was never a matter of pitting strong against weak, or "popular" against "unpopular." Those discriminatory biases could never exist on a Miller-coached team. But even more important, in Pingry Soccer, "The Ring" was a way to unite all players, seniors and underclassmen, starters and bench warmers, as one team, one family. While certainly a tough, physical ritual, it was, in fact, the diametric opposite of bullying. Pingry players don't perform "The Ring" today, but the sense that "we are a family" is no less strong.

So Miller and his assistants still paid attention to "fitness" – coming up with diabolically challenging conditioning exercises and drills like "Orcas" and "Christopher Street Pushups" until kids' arms and shoulders were on fire and their legs were ready to drop off. When you've pushed past the limits of physical strength, you have to reach deeper in order to go on, or you quit. Since it was unthinkable that a kid wearing a Pingry shirt would ever give up, players found that deeper place in themselves.

Building Skill

There was another, unexpected and less desirable characteristic of the players who came to Pingry with years of club soccer experience: some of the best players had surprising gaps in skill ability, like no left foot or an inability to control the ball with a single touch. Club coaches, fixated on winning games (and thus attracting more top players), all too often leveraged a physically dominant player's athletic ability, such as speed, height, or a strong shot, at the expense of developing a real soccer player. When Claudio Reyna took over as United States Soccer Federation Technical Director in 2012, reflecting on his own career, he observed: "I think the winning aspect is what has caused some really ugly youth soccer. When I grew up, you played a lot of games but there was less training. The training has to be better and there has to be more of it." Throughout the late 1980s and 1990s, Miller and his assistants provided that training. As Miller remarked in 1988, "Our practices are light on scrimmages and heavy on technique and instruction, especially concerning the team's weak spots."

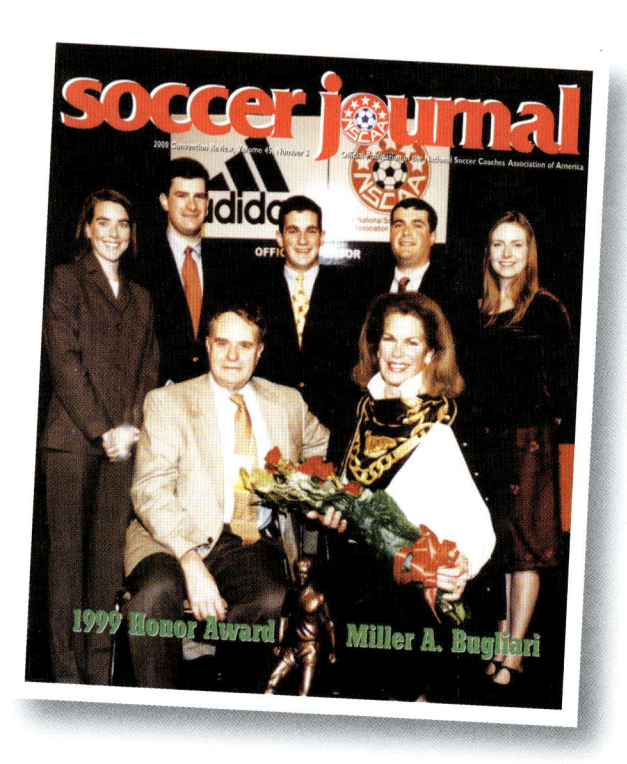

Father Time

Most sports writers don't have a whole lot of good questions to ask, so lots of writers just channel the same question over and over again in interview after interview. Through the 1990s, now at an age when most men worry about how to handle the wicked dogleg on the 14th hole rather than winning a state championship, Miller had to continuously answer the question: "You're turning 60 now (or 63 or 65). How long do you expect to keep coaching?"

In 1988 Miller had said, "I really enjoy the camaraderie with the kids. When you're not going out to practice with a lot of excitement, it's time to leave." His answer through the '90s was the same: "If I keep the enthusiasm, I'll stay." In a 1999 interview he looked back on the decade by saying, "I'm not in it to set any records. As long as I am still effective and relate to the kids I'll be here."

The history of sports is filled with the sad stories of once-successful coaches who stayed in the game too long, or their wiser colleagues who acknowledged the emotional and physical wear and tear of coaching at a high level and retired when it was time. Once they lost the enthusiasm and could no longer reach their players, it was time to surrender to age and change. Miller, however, reversed the equation. As values and cultural norms changed, and kids' needs, expectations, and problems kept evolving, Miller simply changed with them. And his secret for staying young in the game was simple: "I always look forward to the give-and-take with players. That's the best part of the job. That's where I get my energy from, and that's what makes it so exciting." If you recharge your enthusiasm each season, you never lose it.

So Miller's friend and NSCAA colleague C. Clifford McGrath was just being truthful when, in his speech honoring Miller with the NSCAA's Lifetime Achievement Award in January 1999, he said: "The final Honor Award winner of the 1990s is truly a man for the ages. He is the millennium man. He is Father Time."

Signature Victories

400th - 1990

Miller had been working on the sideline crew at Giants Stadium since 1974. So he was there in 1986 when Harry Carson dumped the first Gatorade bucket on Coach Bill Parcells' head after the Giants' 17-3 victory over the Washington Redskins. As that victory celebration became a ritual in the Giants' Super Bowl run of 1986, Miller probably got spattered a few times.

On October 3, 1990, against Wardlaw-Hartridge, he got drenched when members of the 1990 team dumped their water bucket on top of Miller in celebration of his 400th victory. "One of my friends joked that it seems like it took me 400 years to get my 400th victory," Miller said after the game.

Alan Donnelly and Frank Puleo scored two goals each in an 8-0 romp with Julian Ackerman, Seth Berry, Matt Hinton, and John Lee also scoring. Jeremy Goldstein had four assists.

Cold Shower
Pingry School boys soccer coach Miller Bugliari got an unexpected cold shower courtesy of his team after the coach posted his 400th victory last Wednesday in Bernards Township. He has been coaching the team for 31 years. For a story on the historic win please see page 21 in today's sports section.

500th - 1996

The 1996 team was one of the most successful in Pingry's history, winning its conference, the Somerset County title, and the Parochial B state championship and finishing the season ranked the No. 7 team in the nation. But for the players, the most satisfying victory was Miller's 500th win.

Kris Bertsch scored twice, and Nick Ross and Brian Hirsch also scored in a 4-0 whitewashing of previously undefeated Bernards. "A lot of years and a lot of games," Miller laughed. "You've got to win some games when you've been here this long."

Co-captain Chris Marzoli said, "To be honest, the state title is the most prestigious title you can win, but emotionally this one is so much higher."

On November 2, 1996, Miller was honored at a career dinner at Pingry.

EXTRAORDINARY PEOPLE

Staying young by keeping up with athletes
Name: Miller Bugliari
...and started this season with a record of 494 wins, 66 losses and 75 ties.

You and your guests are cordially invited to attend a Celebration in honor of

Miller A. Bugliari and his 500th Career Soccer Victory

Saturday, November 2, 1996
6:00 p.m. reception
7:00 p.m. dinner

The Pingry School
Martinsville Road
Martinsville, New Jersey

Reservations are limited
$60.00 per person

Please reply on the enclosed card by October 23rd

The 1994 World Cup

When FIFA, the governing body of international soccer, decided to have the 1994 World Cup played in the United States, it was a huge leap of faith in the potential for the sport in this country. Interest in soccer in the U.S. was still in its infancy, and the United States Men's Team had yet to even qualify to appear in a World Cup. One commentator described the decision as equivalent to "holding a major skiing competition in an African country." But if the United States was wholly unqualified as a soccer power, we were experts at hosting profitable, successful major sporting and entertainment events. The 1994 World Cup turned out to be a great success and launched this country's growth as a respectable international soccer competitor. An important part of that triumph, which led to the creation of the Miller A. Bugliari World Cup Field in Basking Ridge, were the contributions of Charlie Stillitano, Sr., Pingry soccer's Technical Director, his son Charlie Jr. '77, and Miller. Following his graduation as an All-Ivy and All-American player at Princeton in 1981, Charlie Stillitano, Jr. coached at Princeton under Bob Bradley and later served as New Jersey Soccer Association Vice President for Officials. When the 1994 World Cup planning committee began planning its sites for the series of games that would be played across the nation, Charlie was selected as the New York/New Jersey venue Executive Director for the games to be held at Giants Stadium. Miller, in collaboration with his friend Bob Reasso, Rutgers' soccer coach at the time, was appointed Director of Volunteers for the New York/New Jersey venue.

"Being named venue director was a huge career jump for me," Charlie recalls, "and one that led to my being selected as Vice President and General Manager for the New York/New Jersey MetroStars of Major League Soccer when the league debuted in 1996. But at the time, I realized I was taking on a much bigger challenge than I really was ready for. Without Miller's constant support and wise advice, I might never have been able to pull it off."

Charlie and Miller worked together to have Pingry selected as a potential team training site for the World Cup, along with local colleges. Arranging for the Italian National Team, the Azzuri, to practice at Pingry, however, was primarily the work of Charlie Sr. Every national culture has its own style of negotiation. With some countries negotiation is a battle; with others it's a chess game.

"Negotiating with the Italians," Miller remembers, "was all drama. No one else but Big Charlie could have pulled it off."

For the Pingry players, when the Azzuri practiced at Pingry it was like taking part in a master class. "We got to watch Franco Baresi, Paolo Maldini, it was great for us," remembers Mike Crandall '95. "We even got to play goal against Roberto Baggio and Giuseppi Signorini. Their organization was phenomenal. They had super skills and were super athletes, but how they were coached and how they were organized, it was like a machine."

The Miller A. Bugliari World Cup Field

When Pingry moved from Hillside to Basking Ridge in 1983, the team played on what amounted to a rock garden at the barely finished Basking Ridge campus. It wasn't until a decade later in 1994, when a new field was constructed as the World Cup training site for the Italian National Team, that Pingry championship teams actually got to play on a championship-quality pitch. Thanks to the foresight of the 1971 team, the new field would be called the "Miller A. Bugliari Field," but it was dedicated to the late Charlie Stillitano, Sr., a passionate friend of Pingry soccer and the man who had arranged for the Italian National Team to practice at Pingry.

"Big Charlie" was born in Italy in 1929 and began playing professional soccer at age 14 for his local team, AC Gioiese. When he was 18, his family emigrated to America, and Charlie brought his love of the game with him, playing on many teams in New Jersey and New York, such as Calabria of New Rochelle, Inter Giuliana, Torino of the Bronx, Calabria of New Jersey, and Roma Soccer Club. After his playing career ended, he became one of the most highly respected high school referees in New Jersey and served as the president of the Referee Association of New Jersey. It was through his officiating that Charlie came to know and respect Miller's soccer program, and he eventually sent both of his boys, Leo and Charlie Jr., to Pingry.

Given Charlie's love of the game, it was inevitable that he would become involved in Pingry's program, serving as Pingry's Technical Director for more than a dozen years. "Big Charlie was an incredibly dynamic, invaluable asset to the Pingry program and to me personally," says Miller. "Most Pingry kids, coming from suburban homes, had never met anyone like him. He didn't have a formal education, but kids quickly grasped that he was one of the most innately smart people they had ever encountered, with a total mastery of the game, who was intensely committed to helping them improve. He taught kids the essential geometry of soccer – the critical importance of maintaining offensive and defensive shape – and was a master of the nuances of tactical soccer."

Big Charlie was also very definitely "old school." His sharp-edged comments to kids, coming from a real sense of love, were priceless. "You turn like a bus," he commented to Chuck Louria '77. Tom Trynin '79 was a center midfielder pressed into service as a forward, and was more of a "poacher" than a classic striker. His independent, freewheeling play drove the disciplined Charlie crazy. "You're setting center forward play at Pingry back 10 years," he remarked at one point to Trynin in frustration. But his best comment may have been, in assessing the tentative play of one team, "You attack like Mussolini, side to side. Attack like Patton! Straight forward." Big Charlie's untimely death in a car accident in 1991 robbed Pingry soccer of one of its dearest and most valuable friends.

Charles Stillitano, Sr.

The 1990 Season

How do you slow down a racehorse? Clamp a bulldog to its leg. In the Parochial semifinals at the conclusion of a 14-2-1 season, Pingry met St. Benedict's, the No. 1 ranked team in the nation, led by All-American Claudio Reyna. Miller's answer to Reyna was 1990 co-captain Andy Gottlieb. He wasn't Reyna's match in terms of soccer ability – nobody really was. But Gottlieb, co-captain Frank Puleo, and the rest of the team fought St. Benedict's to a standstill in a game that captures the toughness and tenacity of the 1990 Pingry squad.

In addition to Puleo and Gottlieb, seniors Jeremy Goldstein, Spencer Tullo, and Jack Meyercord, along with sophomore Andrew Lewis, returned as starters in 1990 from the preceding year. Facing the challenges and high expectations of the season were seniors Crico Krantz, Woody Weldon, Tom Kuchler, Stew Range, Andrew Smart, and goalkeepers Peter Londa and Cort Corbin; juniors Alan Donnelly and Chris Pearlman, along with newcomers Eric Miller (a transfer student from J.P. Stevens), Julian Ackerman, and John Lee; and freshman Mike DeGrande.

Prior to the semifinals of the Somerset County Tournament, the *Bernardsville News* said, "Something has to give when the undefeated Bernards High and Pingry boys' soccer teams meet." The only blemish on Pingry's 13-0-1 regular season record was a tie against Wayne Valley. Included in that successful stretch was the elation of beating Wardlaw-Hartridge 8-0 for Miller's 400th career victory.

In getting to the semifinals, Pingry had demolished Bridgewater West 4-0 on Ackerman's two scores and goals by Miller and Goldstein. Bernards, the Group I state champion the preceding year, was a tougher challenge. After Bernards jumped out to a 2-0 lead in the third period, Puleo's two goals on assists from Pearlman and Gottlieb knotted the score at the end of regulation. But that's as close as Pingry could get. Dave Kertesz's goal with just 52 seconds left in overtime sent Bernards to the finals.

Pingry regrouped for the Parochial B state championship run by beating Oratory and Roselle Catholic by identical 4-0 scores. As they had done all season, Puleo, Ackerman, Miller, Lewis, and DeGrande provided the offensive firepower.

Woody Weldon remembers the tension of the semifinal battle with St. Benedict's: "It was the biggest game of my life, and Coach took me out because my nervous energy was tripping me up. He had Coach Macrae do some basic ball-skill drills behind the bench to loosen me up so I could return as sweeper."

It was a terrific defensive struggle: Weldon, Lewis, Meyercord, Tullo, DeGrande, and Londa in the goal constantly turned away the St. Benedict's attacks. Gottlieb was all over Reyna, constantly frustrating and denying him the ball. In the second period, they both went up for the ball, and after a hard but clean challenge, Reyna went to the bench, bleeding from a head wound that required stitches to close.

Unfortunately, the Pingry kids weren't the only courageous players on the field that day. With nine minutes left in the 0-0 game, Reyna came back on the field, and his goal with five minutes left, on a ball that bounced off his thigh in a scramble in front of the net, was the winning score. Years later, in a conversation with Pingry Assistant Coach Adam Rohdie, Reyna praised Pingry as the toughest, most physical team he had faced in his high school career. The 1990 team played the game with heart and courage. That's a trophy you can carry inside you for the rest of your life.

All-State Prep honors went to co-captains Puleo and Gottlieb.

"Miller had the greatest impact on me of anyone that I encountered in my academic and sports career, which includes Pingry, Williams College, and Columbia University. He helped me realize that grades and academics created opportunities and that I was quickly closing my window by not applying myself in school. This was my freshman year. I was a solid C-D student and perfectly content to continue that performance. Miller opened my eyes to the happiness of excelling on all levels at Pingry, and creating the opportunity to attend Williams and all the great things that would come from college. Miller is a once-in-a-lifetime individual and someone I feel very lucky to have as a friend and mentor."

Frank Puleo '91

Rob Macrae, *Assistant Coach*
Adam Rohdie, *Assistant Coach*

Ackerman, J.	Hinton, M.	Pearlman, C.
Baird, D.	Krantz, C.	Puleo, F.
Berry, S.	Kuchler, T.	Range, S.
Bevill, S.	Lee, J.	Rothman, H.
Corbin, C.	Lewis, A.	Sachs, K.
DeGrande, M.	Londa, P.	Sharma, H.
Donnelly, A.	Lucas, S.	Smart, A.
Gardner, A.	Malo, J.	Thomas, C.
Goldstein, J.	Marchese, A.	Tullo, S.
Gottlieb, A.	Meyercord, J.	Weidknecht, F.
Grandis, M.	Miller, E.	Weldon, W.

1990 Season
Frank Puleo, Captain
Andy Gottlieb, Captain
14-3-1

Skying For A Save
Pingry goalkeeper Peter Londa, right, leaps up to make a save during last Saturday's Somerset County Tournament semifinal boys' soccer game against Bernards at Gill St. Bernard's. Pingry's Chris Pearlman, left, and Bernards' Eric Hains look on.

Miller Time
Miller Bugliari picked up his 400th victory as Pingry boys' soccer coach last Wednesday, Oct. 3, when the Big Blue blanked Wardlaw-Hartridge, 8-0, in Bernards Township. Bugliari has been the head coach at Pingry for 31 years.

Bugliari gets 400th Pingry win

By TOM IERUBINO
Sports Editor

BERNARDS TWP. — By the time the fourth quarter rolled around, there was little doubt who was going to win the boys' soccer game between Pingry and Wardlaw-Hartridge last Wednesday, Oct. 3, as the host Big Blue led 8-0.

However, there was some suspense left, and it involved how the Pingry players would celebrate coach Miller Bugliari's 400th win at the school. The Big Blue players did it in a fashion made popular a few years back by the Pingry's head coach.

The victory raised Bugliari's coaching record to 400-53-43 as Pingry moved to 7-0-1 on the season. A lot of players have contributed to the record, Bugliari pointed out, and some of them were on hand to see the historic win.

"A lot of the alumni came back. I didn't even realize it until after the game," he said. "We had a little get-together afterwards. It brought back some great memories."

The memories include winning four streak.

More recently, Pingry won the Union County and state titles in 1983. The team continued its success when the school moved to Somerset County in 1984. The Big Blue have reached the finals of the Somerset County Tournament five straight years. Twice they have shared the title with Ridge, twice they have lost to the Red Devils, and once they have lost to Bridgewater-Raritan West.

Pingry is seeded second in this year's tournament and will host B-R West in a quarterfinal game at 2 p.m.

The 1991 Season

The hungry, deeply talented 1991 team simply devastated opponents. Under co-captains Alan Donnelly and Chris Pearlman, they were undefeated in the regular season against high school competition, outscoring opponents 71-13. Their 19 wins for the season included victories over tough former Union County opponents Summit, 12th ranked Union, and Group III State Champion Scotch Plains, and, in the Somerset County Tournament, Group II State Champion Somerville. Their only regular season loss was to an exceptionally strong Lawrenceville team in a match that Miller described as "like playing against a college team."

The Pingry offense, driven by the punishing partnership of senior striker Eric Miller (24 goals and 8 assists) and sophomore Mike DeGrande (18 assists and 13 goals), played "Bugliari soccer" with style and enthusiasm. Center midfielder Donnelly, classmates Matt Hinton and Justin Malo, and newcomers sophomore Harlan Rothman and juniors Bert Kwan and Jon Pascale, helped frustrate opponents all season long with tight, crisp passing and ball control.

The defense was spearheaded by returning stopper Chris Pearlman and All-State sweeper junior Andrew Lewis, who, along with senior John Lee, not only closed down opponents' best scorers, but relentlessly initiated attacks from the backline. The one exception to this veteran group was the team's goalkeepers, seniors Hemant Sharma and David Baird.

Twice before, Pingry had shared the Somerset County championship with Ridge. The 1991 team was not in a sharing mood. Eric Miller's two goals and DeGrande's and Pearlman's solo shots led the 4-0 rout of neighboring rival Ridge. After disposing of a stubborn Franklin in the semifinals 1-0, Pingry met 13-2 Somerville for the title. In a typically bruising SCT championship game, during which a dozen yellow cards were handed out, Pingry earned sole possession of the Somerset County title in a dominating 3-0 victory on goals by Lewis, Malo, and Miller.

Pingry's second championship came when Eric Miller's clutch overtime goal against Roselle Catholic earned Pingry its first-ever Parochial B North Jersey title.

Pingry's loss in the State Championship game, against 21-1 St. Augustine, was heartbreaking in many ways. The Pingry team, wearing black armbands in tribute to former assistant coach Charlie Stillitano, Sr., who was tragically killed in an auto accident just a few days before the game, came out on fire. DeGrande's second-half goal on yet another assist from Miller gave Pingry a 1-0 lead. Pingry lost a potential second goal when the referee refused to call an obvious handball in St. Augustine's penalty area. But then the game slipped away from Pingry. St. Augustine's Matt Miles tied the score with his 39th goal of the season with 20 minutes left in the game, and then it all fell apart. After a hard collision with a St. Augustine player in the box, Sharma had to leave the game, replaced by senior backup David Baird. With less than two seconds left in the game, St. Augustine stunned Pingry with the game-winning goal. "It was almost like after we scored, we lost track of what we had to do," said DeGrande. "When they scored the winner… I just looked at the clock and knew it was over. It was like a Hail Mary pass in football."

The team's post-season honors reflected its two championships. Miller, Lewis, and DeGrande were selected to the All-County First Team, with Donnelly, Pearlman, Lee, and Sharma also being recognized. Miller was again named the *Star-Ledger* Coach of the Year.

"In analyzing my performance following my first varsity game, early in my sophomore year, Coach told me this was not only my first time seeing the field as a player for him, it could be the last time. Needless to say, I realized I had some work to do. I spent the next three years working tirelessly to earn Coach's respect and approval. Win or lose, my goal every game was to have Coach's post-game comment on my performance be a positive one.

"There aren't many people in life who truly make everyone around them better. Coach Bugliari is one of those people. That's why so many people stay in touch with Coach long after graduating from Pingry."

Chris Pearlman '92

Rob Macrae, *Assistant Coach*
Adam Rohdie, *Assistant Coach*
Brian O'Donnell, *Assistant Coach*
Frank Liberato, *Manager*

Baird, D.	Korn, K.	Pascale, J.
Burani, M.	Kwan, B.	Pearlman, C.
Crandall, M.	Lee, J.	Rothman, H.
Cuaycong, M.	Lewis, A.	Sharma, H.
DeGrande, M.	Malo, J.	Ulz, C.
Donnelly, A.	Mandelbaum, J.	Ulz, M.
George, S.	Marchese, A.	Wittmann, R.
Hinton, M.	Miller, E.	Yook, J.
Khawaja, S.	Molloy, R.	Zigmont, M.

1991 Season
Alan Donnelly, Captain
Chris Pearlman, Captain
19-2-0
Undefeated Regular Season
Somerset County Champions
Non-Public B Sectional State Champiions

The 1992 Season

The returning nucleus from Pingry's 1991 championship team picked up where they had left off the preceding year, crushing opponents in the regular season and repeating as Somerset County champions. Among Pingry's 18 wins in 1992 were victories over former Prep rivals Peddie and Lawrenceville, the latter in a bitterly contested game in which Andrew Lewis's fourth-quarter goal off an assist from Mike DeGrande produced the 1-0 win. Pingry's only regular-season loss came against the No. 1 team in the state, Scotch Plains.

For three years, co-captain Lewis had been a headache for other teams, anchoring Pingry's defense and igniting scoring attacks with hard, penetrating runs from his sweeper position. As a senior in 1992, he was opponents' worst nightmare in a season that ended with his being named the Soccer Coaches Association of New Jersey Player of the Year and selected as a High School All-American by both the NSCAA and *Parade* magazine.

But Lewis wasn't opponents' only problem. The preceding year, Pingry's offense had largely been a two-man effort between Eric Miller and DeGrande. As a junior in 1992, DeGrande continued to rewrite the Pingry record book for goals and assists, but 14 other players contributed to Pingry's season total of 78 goals, led by co-captain Jon Pascale's 10 goals and 10 assists and senior Burt Kwan and juniors Anthony Marchese, Jeff Mandelbaum, and Ryan Molloy, and sophomore Mike Crandall. Defensively, junior Kevin Korn took over duties as goalkeeper behind a front line of Lewis, juniors Harlan Rothman and Andrew Legge, and sophomore Chris Runnells.

The 1991 team's march to the Somerset County championship had been an unstoppable surge. In defending that title, the 1992 team had to claw its way to the top. Against Hillsborough, Pingry's initial 1-0 lead on Mandelbaum's third-period goal evaporated when Hillsborough evened the game with 3:30 left. In the resulting shootout following a scoreless overtime period, Lewis, DeGrande, Pascale, and Rothman all converted for Pingry for the 4-1 edge that gave Pingry its quarter-final win. In the semifinals Ridge and Pingry battled to a 2-2 tie in regulation; DeGrande's third score of the game and an insurance goal from Crandall gave Pingry the overtime win.

Gill St. Bernards was a newcomer to the SCT Championships. But coming off a 17-1 season, in which they scored 85 goals, they gave Pingry all they could handle, going in front 1-0 in the first half. "We had an answer for everything Pingry had today," commented Gill's coach Tony Bednarsky, "except Andrew Lewis." Two minutes after Gill scored, Lewis converted a pass from Mandelbaum to tie the game and, in the second half, put Pingry ahead on a pass from Ryan Molloy. Rothman's alert steal of a careless pass and his relay to Kwan provided the insurance goal in Pingry's second consecutive county championship.

The 1992 team fought just as hard to repeat as sectional champions, but after convincing wins over Oratory and DePaul, Pingry once again came up tragically short against a senior-laden Delbarton team. Pingry had fought back to a 1-1 tie on Pascale's goal off DeGrande's assist. But in a frustrating rerun of the 1991 loss to St. Augustine, Chris Gannon's screaming liner with a minute left just eluded a diving Kevin Korn and gave Delbarton the championship.

In addition to Lewis's county, state, and national honors, DeGrande and Pascale were selected for the All-County and All-Central Jersey First Teams and were joined on the Prep All-State team by Korn.

Jon Pascale grew up playing on a top club team with Mike DeGrande '94, and Mike essentially "recruited" him to come to Pingry to play soccer for Miller. Jon became a key player in Pingry's back-to-back county championships his junior and senior years. Adjusting to a new school as a 16-year-old kid, however, was much harder. "I'd left all my friends at Immaculata behind, and Pingry socially was a completely different world. And nothing had prepared me for just how tough the academic part of it would be. I really struggled, and might not have made it except for Coach. Miller immediately made me 'part of the soccer family.' The two hours of practice each day and the countless hours I spent with him in his amazing sanctuary and shrine of an office, just talking about how I was handling things, were what really helped me get through it all."

Jon Pascale '93

THE LIFE & TIMES OF MILLER A. BUGLIARI

Rob Macrae, *Assistant Coach*
Adam Rohdie, *Assistant Coach*
Frank Liberato, *Manager*
Tim Parliman, *Manager*

Alford, S.	Huang, A.	Molloy, R.
Benjamin, T.	Hughes, D.	Newhouse, J.
Burani, M.	Khawaja, S.	Pascale, J.
Crandall, M.	Korn, K.	Rothman, H.
Cuaycong, M.	Kwan, B.	Runnells, C.
DeGrande, M.	Kwei, S.	Slater, A.
Emmitt, P.	Legge, A.	Ulz, C.
Friedland, D.	Lewis, A.	Ulz, M.
Fritsche, H.	Lucas, J.	Wittmann, R.
Gormley, T.	Mandelbaum, J.	
Hoffman, C.	Marchese, A.	

1992 Season
Andrew Lewis, Captain
Jon Pascale, Captain
18-2-0
Somerset County Champions

Pingry School's Bugliari will be honored Sunday

By The Courier-News Staff

Miller Bugliari, the long-time soccer coach at The Pingry School, will be the recipient of the College Soccer Coaches Association of New Jersey Lifetime Merit Award for his contributions to New Jersey soccer.

Bugliari will be honored at the CSCANJ's eighth annual all-state awards banquet Sunday at the Somerset Marriott.

A native of New Jersey, Bugliari has long been considered one of the outstanding prep coaches in the nation.

He has compiled a 444-59-45 record in 33 years at Pingry and has twice (1983, '89) been named the nation's "High School Coach of the Year."

Under Bugliari, Pingry has won 16 state championships, six Union County (when the school was located in Hillside Township) and four Somerset County (since the school moved to Bernards Township) titles and had nine undefeated seasons.

In 1988, Bugliari was inducted into the New Jersey Youth Soccer Association Hall of Fame and he was named to The Pingry School Hall of Fame in 1990.

In addition to his coaching responsibilities, Bugliari has served on numerous athletic committees. He was the past president of the National Soccer Coaches Association of America and is currently the coaching administrator for the New Jersey State Youth Soccer Association and the coordinator of volunteers for New Jersey/New York venue for World Cup '94.

Bugliari graduated cum laude from Springfield College in 1957, with an award for excellence in journalism. Since 1959, he has worked at The Pingry School as both a teacher and Director of Alumni Activities. In 1964, he earned his master's degree from New York University.

Bugliari and his wife, Elizabeth, reside in Westfield with their three sons, Miller, Anthony and David.

DeGrande hat trick propels Pingry, 5-0

BOYS' SOCCER

Mike DeGrande scored three als to lead Pingry, No. 11 in The ar-Ledger Boys' Soccer Top 20, to a) victory over Rutgers Prep yester-y in Franklin.

Pingry successful in defense of crown

BOYS SOCCER

By BRIAN LEWIS
Courier-News Staff Writer

PEAPACK-GLADSTONE — Pingry Pride just wouldn't let the Big Blue fold. Seniors Andy Lewis and Burt Kwan capped personal comebacks of their own to lead Pingry to a come-from-behind 3-1 victory over Gill St. Bernard's Saturday in the Somerset County Tournament championship game.

Todd Moore put Gill ahead 1-0, but Lewis shook off a nagging injury to score twice and give Pingry the lead, while Kwan shook off a sub-par game to

"It's fine now," Lewis said. "I'm back in shape and it doesn't bother me. The important thing is that we got the back-to-back titles, which is always nice."

Kwan, also a sprinter on the Pingry track team, put his speed to good use Saturday. While his shots were just a bit off, and his passes just a bit astray, he made up for it with hustle, speed and a flair for the dramatic.

"This wasn't my best game of the season," Kwan said. "It was probably my worst game. I just didn't feel sharp at all."

Pingry's Lewis honored

■ Senior sweeper will be named to Parade Magazine All-America Soccer Team this Sunday.

By BRIAN LEWIS
Courier-News Staff Writer

Two weeks after being named to the National Soccer Coaches' All-America Team, the Pingry School's Andy Lewis has garnered yet another national honor. Sunday, the senior sweeper will be one of four defensemen named to the Parade Magazine All-America Team.

Lewis was a first-team Courier-News All-Area pick last fall and led Pingry to the Somerset County title. Lewis said his selection by Parade was exciting, even though he doesn't play to make all-star teams or trophies.

"It's certainly a great honor," said Lewis, who lives in the Murray Hill section of Summit. "They do a great job of getting the best kids. It's a true All-America team."

Parade's All-America team is selected by a panel that includes the coaches of the National and Regional all-star teams. Those coaches come from elite

After running the 400-meter leg on one of America's best high school distance medley relays in the spring, Lewis pulled both hamstrings over the summer. He missed the early part of the scholastic soccer season, and spent the middle part of the season working his way back into shape. By the end of the season, Lewis' defense, speed and passing were all back to their old levels. His performance at the end of the season was enough to earn him Player of the Year honors from both the Somerset County and New Jersey Coaches Associations.

"Andrew had an amazing year," said Pingry coach Miller Bugliari. "Because of the (hamstring) pulls, he really couldn't practice. He just was able to play with a lot of inspiration even though, in many cases, his leg bothered him. He's just been great."

After fielding letters from universities all across the country vying for his athletic services, Lewis finally decided on Princeton. Lewis chose the Tigers over Rutgers and Virginia, saying the combination of academics and great coaching convinced him.

"It's an honor to be recruited by Princeton," Lewis said. "They usually just figure out what positions they need, go after the best guys in the country at those positions and usually get them."

As long as Lewis' athletic resume is, his academic one is longer: he is a perennial honor-roll student.

Lewis has the maturity to keep the student ahead of the athlete while staying competitive as both.

"You can't beat Princeton as a school," Lewis said

The 1993 Season

Before the start of the 1993 season, Miller said, "We've got good balance and some depth, but I don't know if we're as skilled as last year. I don't know if we can recover from our losses. We're pretty good, but not super."

The one "super" aspect of the season was Mike DeGrande's culminating achievement as Pingry's all-time leading scorer. Scott Aimetti had held the record, averaging 21 goals a season from 1986 to 1988. Ten years on, Kris Bertsch would equal Aimetti's total of 63 goals over a four-year career from 1995 to 1998. But DeGrande's 64 career goals still stands as the target for future players to aim at.

When you have a relatively new, untested team, "pretty good but not super" can translate into a 14-5-1 season, which most teams would celebrate. For this team's tri-captains, DeGrande, Kevin Korn, and Harlan Rothman, and fellow senior starters Andrew Legge, Ryan Molloy, and Joe Marchese, who had tasted championships, the 1993 season was a frustrating one of encouraging victories mixed with adversity and hard-fought battles lost.

The team's first taste of adversity came in an early, unexpected upset loss to Montclair Kimberley Academy 2-3 in overtime. The team regained confidence in a well-earned defeat of Union and a sweep of its historical Prep opponents Hun, Blair, Peddie, and Lawrenceville by a 10-1 scoring margin. In prior decades, that would have earned Pingry another Prep championship. In 1993, St. Benedict's had moved from the Parochial to the Prep ranks, and in Pingry's reappearance in the Prep A finals nationally ranked St. Benedict's had far too much firepower for Pingry's less experienced team. DeGrande's direct kick from 30 yards out gave Pingry a short-lived lead. That lead disappeared, under a subsequent five-goal onslaught that a heroic, 18-save effort from Korn couldn't prevent.

There's a reason players and coaches hate to have a championship decided by a shootout: it turns a soccer game into a guessing game.

In the Prep School semifinal, Peddie's goalkeeper guessed wrong on shots by DeGrande, Mike Crandall, Molloy, and Rothman, and Korn stuffed two out of Peddie's first three shots. Against Watchung Hills in the opening round of the county tournament, Pingry's luck didn't hold. Rothman, Crandall, and Molloy converted for Pingry in the shootout, but all five of Watchung Hill's players scored to give them a 1-0 upset victory. The season ended, after a promising start in the Parochial B tournament with shutout victories over All Saints and Essex Catholic, with a loss to 13-1-5 Morris Catholic 1-0 in overtime.

At the end of the season DeGrande was honored on the All-County First Team. But there was another epilogue to the disappointments of the 1993 season. The underclassmen on that team – juniors Stu Alford, Peter Blanchard, Mike Crandall, Blake Jarrell, David Margolis, Jamie Newhouse, Scott Nettune, and Chris Runnells, plus sophomores Colin Bennett, Jeff Boyer, Jake Ross, and Jared Wilkinson – formed the nucleus of a lineup that over the next three years would result in some of the most successful seasons ever for Pingry soccer.

Mike DeGrande's Pingry teammates knew him as a wonderfully outgoing guy, in the mix of everything that was going on at school. Like Miller in his years at Springfield College, Mike was the kind of leader who brought everyone on the team together and made them feel like part of the family. And like Miller, he was hilariously funny. Teammate Jake Ross remembers Mike and Howard Rothman constantly busting up practices with their comedy routines and crazy sense of humor.

Mike DeGrande's opponents, however, knew him as a lethal scorer with a great first step and an uncanny nose for the goal. "He was all about scoring," Jon Pascale '93 remembers. "He wasn't a big guy, maybe 5 foot 5 on a good day, but his size actually helped him: it made him a pain to mark and try to stay with. And the bigger the game, the bigger he played."

DeGrande's four-year scoring record of 64 goals still stands as the career mark just ahead of Scott Aimetti '89 and Kris Bertsch '99. What sets DeGrande apart as a complete offensive player is that he also holds the career record for assists with 57.

Mike DeGrande '94

Rob Macrae, *Assistant Coach*
Adam Rohdie, *Assistant Coach*
Frank Liberato, *Manager*
Tim Parliman, *Manager*
Tucker Siler, *Manager*

Alford, S.	Gormley, T.	Margolis, D.
Benjamin, T.	Hirsch, B.	Molloy, R.
Bennett, C.	Hoffman, C.	Nettune, S.
Blanchard, P.	Hughes, D.	Newhouse, J.
Boyer, J.	Jarrell, B.	Parliman, T.
Crandall, M.	Korn, K.	Pinkin, D.
Daglaroglu, R.	Legge, A.	Ross, J.
DeGrande, M.	Lewis, M.	Rothman, H.
Emmitt, P.	Mandelbaum, J.	Runnells, C.
Franklin, C.	Marchese, J.	Wilkinson, J.

1993 Season
Mike DeGrande, Captain
Kevin Korn, Captain
Harlan Rothman, Captain
14-5-1

Sports

Pingry boys soccer may be as powerful as 1992 squad

By MIKE D. SKARA
THE PRESS

Before the first few games of the season, almost every coach in high school sports plays down the prowess of their current team and guardedly praises the opposition. The coaches also often speak about how many outstanding seniors they have lost due to graduation.

While it is true many times these coaches have a valid point, but in some instances coaches are playing down their teams too much.

It seems Pingry Head Coach Miller Bugliari is currently riding the line between the two extremes.

It is very true three outstanding Pingry players, defender Andrew Lewis, midfielder Jon Pascale, and Bert Kwan, are no longer with the Big Blue team. And it is easy to find support in the belief these three athletes helped to catapult the Big Blue to the final game in the Somerset County Tournament and the semifinals of the Prep B state tournament.

On the other hand the Pingry club does have its leading scorer, senior striker Mike DeGrande, returning and has many solid players to fill the holes left by the graduates.

Most likely Bugliari, who has 30 years of head coaching experience, is wise for only being cautiously optimistic about the 1993 squad, and not predicting it to surpass last year's 18-2 record. That would be risky for any coach even if they had Pele on their team.

"We've got good balance and some depth," said Bugliari, "but I don't know if we're as skilled as last year. I don't know if we can recover from our losses. We're pretty good, but not super."

If the Pingry squad is to win it must get production from DeGrande, who had 24 goals last year.

"Mike's one of our key players," said Bugliari.

Pingry's midfield should also be very strong this year. Seniors Harlan Rothman and Ryan Malloy each already have three years of varsity experience. A solid junior, Stewart Alford, will also be playing in the middle of the field.

"Harlan has a good touch and Ryan is solid," said Bugliari.

Defensively the Big Blue will be lead by senior goalkeeper Kevin Korn and versatile junior sweeper Mike Crandall. Joining DeGrande up front will by Andrew Legge, who has a good header, and Jeff Mandelbaum, who knocked in six goals in '92.

"We move the ball very well," said Bugliari, "and our defense is new but full of good athletes."

Pingry opened its season after press time Tuesday evening against Newark Academy at the Livingston school's field.

Pingry junior sweeper Mike Crandall and the rest of the Blue soccer team looks to keep their eyes on the ball and pick up some wins during the upcoming season.

Pingry 3, Lawrenceville 0

Stu Alford, Mike Crandell and Mike DeGrande each scored goals for the Big Blue, who improved to 11-3-1.

Kevin Korn made eight saves to earn his seventh shutout of the season.

Ryan Molloy and Jeff Mandelbaum each had assists for Pingry.

Pingry boys soccer goalkeeper Kevin Korn is about to snatch up another save during Big Blue practice.

Bugliari gets 450th

BOYS SOCCER

Pingry soccer coach Miller Bugliari registered his 450th victory in Pingry's 6-1 win over Blair Academy yesterday.

Long Valley native Mike DeGranded scored a hat trick and Mike Crandall added two goals for the Big Blue 6-3-1

The 1994 Season

There have been some great defensive teams in the 50-plus years of Miller's tenure as head coach, but none has equaled the achievement of the 1994 team, which shut out 15 of the 18 opponents it faced, yielding only an astounding three goals all season long on the way to an undefeated regular season, a 16-2-0 record, and another Somerset County championship.

Montgomery coach Charlie Webb captured the tenacity of this team after losing 4-0 to Pingry: "They control the ball well offensively, which keeps the pressure off the defense. And when you do get the ball down there, it doesn't stay there long."

In 1994, co-captain Mike Crandall put his own impressive stamp on how the sweeper position should be played. His supporting cast included seniors Scott Nettune, Jamie Newhouse, Drew Pinkin, and co-captain Stu Alford, and junior Jared Wilkinson. Blake Jarrell had spent his junior year playing behind Kevin Korn. In his senior year, like Crandall, he made the position his own. The offensive output of 66 goals was less prolific than in other years; when you have a stifling defense, it doesn't need to be prolific. Seniors Alford, Jeff Boyer, Peter Blanchard, and juniors Jake Ross, Colin Bennett, and Casey Cotton, and sophomore Brian Hirsch contributed clutch goals. Tellingly, the scoring often came from the midfield and from penetrating runs by defenders like Alford and Crandall, who led all scorers in 1994 with 10 goals each.

Pingry's march to its fifth Somerset County championship in 10 years was as unstoppable as its formidable defense. After ripping through Montgomery, Pingry met rising Somerset County opponent Gill St. Bernard's in a collision of styles. Gill's explosive offense was led by All-County forwards Brent Malo and Steve DeLuca. But against Pingry in the semifinals, they and their teammates rarely saw the ball. With that kind of defense, all Pingry needed was a single goal. They got it from Jake Ross, who, with four minutes left in the game, capitalized off a sharp through ball following a deep run by David Margolis to freeze Gill's goalkeeper and put away the game winner.

Pingry met familiar and bitter rival Ridge in the finals. Led by All-State forward Stu Hulke's 33 scores, Ridge had blistered opponents for 92 goals over an 18-1 season.

Pingry had surrendered just one goal in 16 games. After defeating Watchung Hills to gain the final, Ridge coach Rick Hildebrand had said, "Watchung was the physically toughest team left in the tournament." He had to revise that assessment after Pingry's 1-0 victory. Ridge's only real chance in the game came when Hulke won a ball in Pingry's penalty area and pushed it past Jarrell toward the empty net. But this was a Pingry team that forced opponents to beat the entire team and not just a single player. Stu Alford, tracking back from upfield, cleared the ball. "We had chances," said Hildebrand after the game, "but couldn't get it done. They just shut us down." Pingry's game winner came at the 31 minute mark when Bennett took a pass from Blanchard and slipped it past Ridge's goalkeeper.

Two teams had scored against Pingry heading into the Parochial B final against Immaculata. John Grey's direct kick in overtime was the third, as once again Pingry fell just short of winning a state title. First Team All-County and Parochial All-State honors for 1994 went to Crandall, who was also named the *Courier News* Player of the Year, and to Jarrell and Jake Ross, with Newhouse, Alford, Bennett, Nettune, Blanchard, and Runnells also receiving recognition.

The honor of scoring the first goal on the Miller A. Bugliari World Cup Soccer Field went to Chris Runnells '95, a three-year varsity player whose senior season was cut short by a mid-season injury.

Mike Crandall was a ball boy as a freshman on the Pingry varsity. In three years, Crandall developed into the best defender on the best defensive team in the state. "He's a fierce competitor on the field," Miller said. "Off the field he's very pleasant and mild. But on the field he doesn't take any prisoners."

Jake Ross grew up playing soccer on club teams with Crandall. "He always played like he was on fire," Ross remembers. "His influence on the team was huge; he drove everyone around him to be better than they thought they could be, whether they liked it or not. And he loved being the underdog fighting against the threat of defeat – not an easy thing to do playing for Pingry. His standard line before a big game was, 'We'd better win this one. We won't win another after it.'"

It was almost like having a younger version of Miller the player on the team.

Mike Crandall '95

Rob Macrae, *Assistant Coach*
Adam Rohdie, *Assistant Coach*

Alford, S.	Fitzgerald, J.	Parliman, C.
Bennett, C.	Franklin, C.	Phillips, D.
Blanchard, M.	Hirsch, B.	Pinkin, D.
Blanchard, P.	Jarrell, B.	Ross, J.
Boyer, J.	Lewis, M.	Ross, N.
Bugliari, D.	Margolis, D.	Runnells, C.
Cotton, C.	Marzoli, C.	Schmidt, K.
Crandall, M.	Nettune, S.	Wilkinson, J.
Crosby, J.	Newhouse, J.	

1994 Season
Mike Crandall, Captain
Stu Alford, Captain
16-2-0
Undefeated Regular Season
Somerset County Champions

The 1995 Season

Many coaches will tell you: "speed kills." In assessing the 1995 team's potential, Miller said, "Defensively, we're not as complete as we were last year. We're blessed with some good players and some speed. I'll tell you, we have a lot of speed. When you play against big schools, speed allows you to do some different things."

What the 1995 team did that was different was to complete the season undefeated, successfully defend its county championship, win Pingry's first Parochial B championship, and get selected as the 10th best high school team in the country in the Umbro Top 25 national poll.

Team speed can create breakaways, stretch the defense, and open up space for quality shots. It did all of that for the 1995 team, whose season total of 98 goals set a new Pingry scoring record. Up front, Pingry's offense was led by senior captain Jake Ross, junior Brian Hirsch, sophomore R.T. Treveloni, and freshman Kris Bertsch. As a senior, Jake Ross was asked to score more, and he did. His 31 goals represent the second-highest single-season total behind Scott Aimetti's 35. But defending against Pingry's offense in 1995 was a matter of picking your poison. Sixteen different players scored for Pingry, nine of them multiple times.

Speed translates into dominating possession and limiting opponents' time on the ball. At midfield, the run of play was controlled all season long by senior captain Jeff Boyer and co-captain Colin Bennett, senior Mike Lewis, and juniors David Bugliari, Bobby Corvino, and Chris Marzoli.

Speed also nullifies an opponent's scoring chances, and here, too, Pingry was dominating – its 15 shutouts matching the achievement of the 1994 team. The defense of senior co-captain Jared Wilkinson; juniors Patrick Reid, Corey Simonson, and Nick Ross at sweeper; freshman Mike Roberts; and sophomore goalkeeper Kevin Schmidt was rarely tested. Only a 3-3 tie with Bernards spoiled Pingry's perfect season on its way to Pingry's first Colonial Hills Conference championship.

For Pingry, a county championship usually means another battle with Ridge. After getting past Hillsborough 4-1, Pingry jumped ahead of Ridge 2-0 on Jake Ross's goals in the first four minutes. Boyer's score on a pass from Roberts iced the victory. Pingry captured its fourth county championship in five years when it brought Bridgewater-Raritan's 12-game winning streak to a halt in a convincing 2-0 victory. "I thought we played hard," said Bridgewater coach Rick Szeles, "but they kept beating us to the ball."

In the Parochial B State Championship game, North Sectional winner Pingry met Bishop Eustace. Treveloni's 15-yard shot under the crossbar with just 7:47 gone in the first half on a sharp build-up from Marzoli and Lewis came much too early in the game for Miller, who knew all too well that early leads can disappear in the last minutes of a game. "It was pretty nerve-wracking," commented Jake Ross after Pingry had successfully defended its one-goal margin of victory for nearly 48 minutes. "But we had Kevin Schmidt in net, and he played well. Some people say our defense last year was better, but we went all the way." At season's end, Jake Ross was named to the All-State All-Groups First Team. Jeff Boyer joined him on the Parochial All-State and Somerset County First Teams, and Schmidt, Wilkinson, and Hirsch also received commendations.

When you talk with Pingry Athletics Hall of Fame member Jake Ross about his experience at Pingry, he doesn't dwell on his accomplishments: captain of the Pingry soccer, hockey, and baseball teams; repeated All-County and All-State awards in three sports; and comparable achievements in soccer and baseball at Lafayette College, including winning the Hall of Fame Award and being named to the Patriot League All-Star Team in soccer. He talks about the closeness of the soccer teams he played on at Pingry. "We had freshmen playing a lot of minutes. On some teams, that could have led to tension and jealousy, but not on our team. We respected how they helped us win."

Jake Ross '96

Adam Rohdie, *Assistant Coach*
Mike Coughlin, *Assistant Coach*
Jay Crosby, *Manager*

Bennett, C.	Franklin, C.	Ross, J.
Bertsch, K.	Hirsch, B.	Ross, N.
Blanchard, M.	Lewis, M.	Santoriello, A.
Boyer, J.	Marzoli, C.	Schmidt, K.
Brauman, J.	Parliman, C.	Simonson, C.
Bugliari, D.	Phillips, D.	Stevens, G.
Corvino, B.	Pratt, D.	Treveloni, R.
Cotton, C.	Reid, P.	Umbdenstock, T.
Fitzgerald, J.	Roberts, M.	Wilkinson, J.

1995 Season
Jeff Boyer, Captain
Colin Bennett, Captain
Jake Ross, Captain
Jared Wilkinson, Captain
20-0-1
Undefeated Season
Conference Champions
Somerset County Champions
Non-Public B State Champions

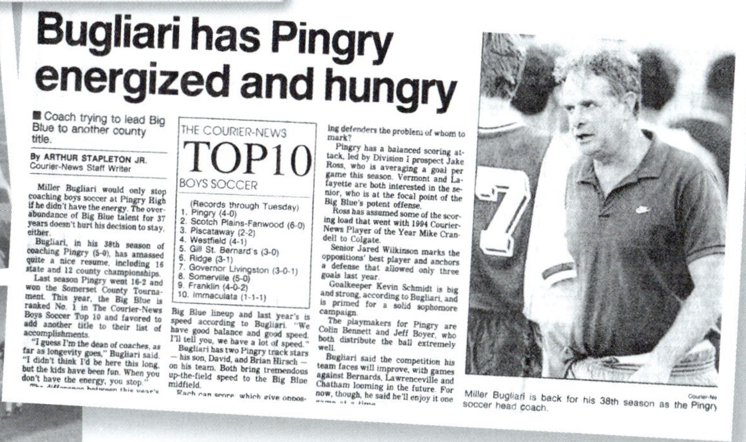

The 1996 Season

Through the decades, Miller has seen it all: some seasons can be heartbreaking, some enormously satisfying. And once in a while, as in 1996, a season is just magical.

St. Benedict's had been named the No. 1 team in New Jersey in 1992, and for an amazing four uninterrupted years had held that title against all challengers until 1996, when a new No. 1 team took their place – The Pingry School. The 1996 team had announced their intention to rule as the best team in the state when they beat St. Benedict's 2-0 in a pre-season scrimmage – a result that immediately caught the attention of every other major team in New Jersey. In an 18-0-1 season Pingry extended the previous year's unbeaten streak to 40 games, successfully defended its conference, county, sectional, and state championships, and at the end of the season was ranked the top team in New Jersey and the seventh-best team in the nation. "Being No. 1 is something everyone in the state strives for," Miller said before the Somerset County finals. "It would mean a lot for me, but it also means that everything just happened to line up the right way for this particular year."

And it did line up. As has been the case every year, Miller had to replace the productivity of some terrific departed players. But he started with as strong a nucleus of returning players as he's ever enjoyed. Pingry didn't have a single player who could equal Jake Ross's 31 goals from the previous year – they had three: returning senior striker Brian Hirsch, whose breakaway speed led to 11 goals; junior R.T. Treveloni, with 14 goals and 11 assists; and sophomore Kris Bertsch, who led the team with 22 goals and 18 assists.

The midfield consisted of senior tri-captains David Bugliari and Chris Marzoli, senior Tyler Umbdenstock, and sophomore David Fahey, with sophomore Heath Freeman and freshman Gianfranco Tripicchio playing supporting roles. Besides controlling the ball and blunting opponents' attacks, they contributed an additional 20 goals for the season.

The veteran defense of tri-captain Nick Ross, seniors Corey Simonson and Pat Reid, and sophomore Mike Roberts formed the shield in front of senior goalkeeper Dan Phillips, who shut out six opponents before Kevin Schmidt returned from an ankle injury to record eight more shutouts, while the team conceded only six goals against 19 opponents.

In winning the Somerset County, Parochial B North sectional, and state championships by a 23-3 goal margin, Pingry was tested just once – against a big, strong Bridgewater-Raritan team in the finals. "Everybody knows how good they are," said Bridgewater's All-County goalkeeper Dan Luongo, "with their national rankings and everything, but we have confidence we can take them." In a predictably bruising game, marked by more injuries than goals, Pingry finished the game with Hirsch, Fahey, and Simonson on the bench and Bridgewater playing the second half and overtime without its leading scorer, Eric Leininger. Ross's header off a Bertsch cross in the second overtime with 5:46 to go earned Pingry its seventh county title. And that was the last time the 1996 team would be threatened. Bertsch's hat trick ignited a 6-0 rout over 20-1-3 Wildwood Catholic in the state championship match. "Soccer-wise," said Wildwood coach Gerry Macfarlane, "they're as good as any Division III college team."

At year's end, Ross was named to the All-State First Team and was honored as the New Jersey Boys' Soccer Player of the Year. He and Bertsch were selected for the All-County First Team, and Bugliari, Hirsch, Marzoli, Schmidt, Reid, Phillips, and Treveloni also received post-season honors.

Miller has always liked to initiate attacks from the back line and create mismatches with overlapping runs. In 1996, no one was better than Nick Ross from his sweeper position. "Nick was what made us go," said Miller after the season. "I liked to have the luxury of having him in back, but when necessary, we moved him up and he just took charge by always looking for someone to fill the space on the open side of the field." His leadership made the difference in the county final against Bridgewater-Raritan. The picture of his winning goal shows him sandwiched between two Bridgewater defenders, willing the header into the net past a well-positioned Dan Luongo. "I didn't want a scoreless tie," Nick summed up after the game. "We wanted to get it for ourselves, because being co-champs isn't the same."

Nick Ross '97

Adam Rohdie, *Assistant Coach*

Bertsch, K.	Heller, G.	Ross, N.
Blumenstyk, M.	Hirsch, B.	Sarro-Waite, N.
Boyer, G.	Lewis, S.	Schmidt, K.
Boylan, T.	Marzoli, C.	Simonson, C.
Brauman, J.	Monaco, C.	Stevens, G.
Bugliari, D.	Parsons, C.	Treveloni, R.
Fahey, D.	Phillips, D.	Tripicchio, G.
Ferraro, J.	Pratt, D.	Umbdenstock, T.
Feuer, J.	Reid, P.	Wilkinson, D.
Freeman, H.	Roberts, M.	

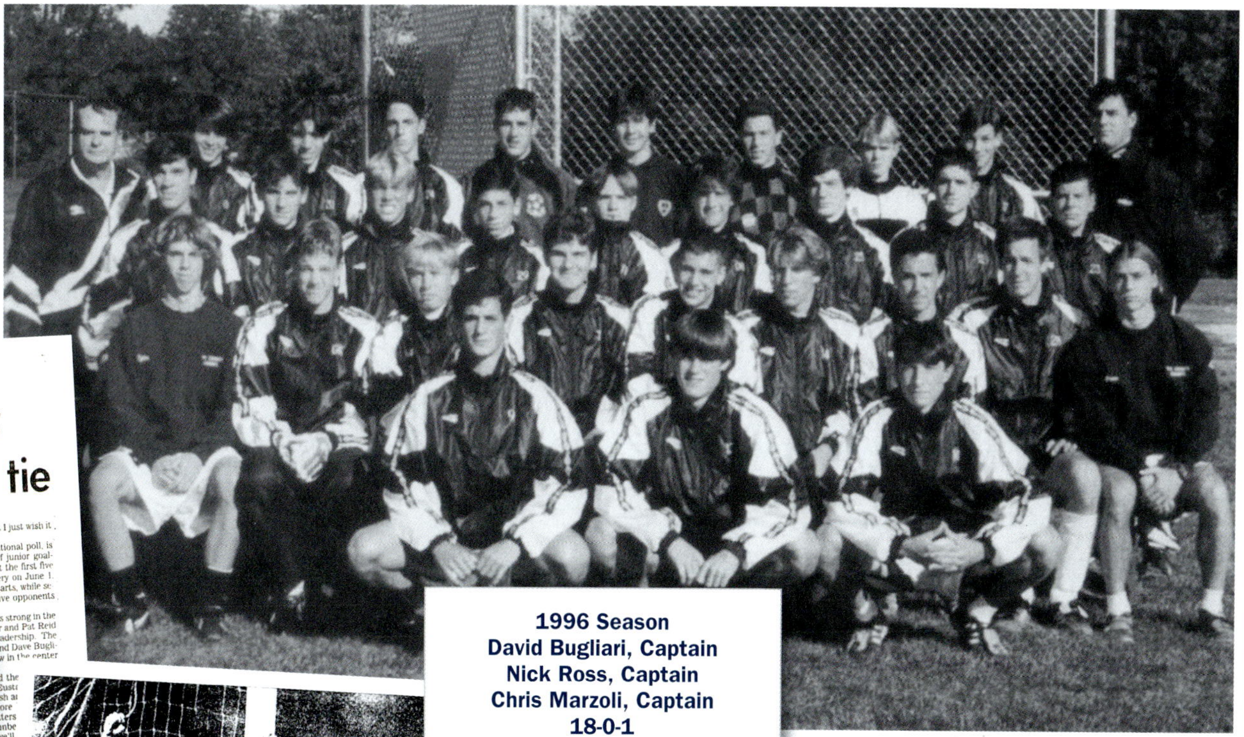

1996 Season
David Bugliari, Captain
Nick Ross, Captain
Chris Marzoli, Captain
18-0-1
Undefeated Season
Conference Champions
Somerset County Champions
Non-Public B State Champions

Bridgewater-Raritan's Brian Chartowich, at left on top photo, wins the fight with Pingry's Brian Hirsch for a ball. However, Pingry won the game when Nick Ross, center in above photo, scored on this header.

The 1997 Season

A Morris County Group II power for decades, Chatham High School had ruled the Colonial Hills Conference until Pingry joined the conference in 1995 and relegated them to also-rans. But in 1997 two goals by Chatham's Mike Walsh brought an end to Pingry's 46-game unbeaten streak and dethroned Pingry as conference champions. After the game, Miller said, "I thought we played well and I thought Chatham played better. It's bittersweet. It was great to have the streak, but now we know we have to grind it out every game and not take anything for granted. We're going to have to work harder than we have the last couple of years."

The team that sought to rebound from this discouraging loss still had plenty of scoring power, with returning All-County striker Kris Bertsch and new starters junior Paul Anderson and sophomore Nick Caiella as forwards, and returning veteran offensive threats co-captain R.T. Treveloni and equally dangerous sophomore Gianfranco Tripicchio, seniors Josh Feuer and Heath Freeman, juniors Matt Margolis and Steve Lewis, and sophomore Dave Alchus in the midfield.

Returning senior Kevin Schmidt gave Pingry a strong, reliable presence in goal, but the group in front of him was relatively inexperienced and untested. A player on whom Miller had counted to anchor the defense, returning junior starter Mike Roberts, was gone for the season with an ACL tear, so starting midfielder David Fahey was moved back to sweeper, along with new starters senior Todd Boylan and juniors Nick Sarro-Waite, Todd Kehoe, and Matt Blumenstyk, who was given the responsibility of shutting down the other team's most dangerous scorer.

Through the balance of the regular season, Pingry lost only one other game, another 2-0 setback to Chatham, as it prepared for its second season of county and state tournaments. Pingry routed North Plainfield 5-0 in the opening round. In the second round, Bernards jumped to a 2-0 lead before Treveloni narrowed the margin in the second half on a pass from Fahey. But Pingry still trailed Bernards by a goal heading into the final 48 seconds, when Bertsch evened the game with a clutch score. The overtime was all Pingry on Bertsch's and Treveloni's second goals and Dave Alchus's insurance score.

In another predictably hard, physical game against second-seeded Hillsborough in the semifinals, Anderson drove home the rebound of his own shot on an assist from Treveloni in the first half, and Pingry's defense and Schmidt held on to send Pingry into the finals against heavily favored top seed Somerville. Freeman had been part of all three of Pingry's previous county championships, and he had no interest in breaking the string. "It feels really good," he said after his opportunistic strike, on a classy buildup from Margolis and Treveloni in the 56th minute of play, gave Pingry its fourth consecutive county championship and its sixth in seven seasons. Again, Pingry's defense made the single goal stick, with Blumenstyck again stopping Somerville's leading scorer Steve Dussan in his tracks and Schmidt making 11 tough saves.

Pingry was rated an underdog going into the defense of its Parochial sectional title, which suited the 1997 team perfectly. Then it all fell apart. Kevin Schmidt had starred in goal for Pingry for three years as a hard-nosed, aggressive player. But when that same aggressiveness led to a fight in gym class, he was suspended for the opening Parochial B game against Morris Catholic. Backup goalie Carl Monaco played well in his place, but his eight saves and Bertsch's and Treveloni's goals weren't enough to prevent the 3-2 loss that ended Pingry's season.

Bertsch was named again to the Somerset County First Team, along with Schmidt and Treveloni.

Even on the impressive roster of Pingry's many All-County and All-State goalkeepers, Kevin Schmidt stands out. In his three years as a varsity starter, Pingry won 53 games versus just three losses, with Schmidt registering clean sheets in 41 of those victories. He received All-County recognition in each of his three seasons, being named to the All-Somerset County First Team as a senior.

Schmidt continued his career at Top 10 NCAA team Maryland, recording an impressive 0.72 goals against average in two seasons as a starter. Maryland coach Sasho Cirovski praised him for his leadership abilities and said of him, "Distribution of the ball is a strength of his game. Kevin is courageous, physical, and a very good shot stopper."

Kevin Schmidt '98

Adam Rohdie, *Assistant Coach*
Mike Coughlin, *Assistant Coach*

Alchus, D.	Fahey, D.	Monaco, C.
Anderson, P.	Feuer, J.	Pekarsky, J.
Appelbaum, M.	Fisher, D.	Roberts, M.
Askin, S.	Freeman, H.	Sarro-Waite, N.
Bertsch, K.	Gittes, D.	Schmidt, K.
Blumenstyk, M.	Haverstick, S.	Scurci, J.
Boylan, T.	Kaplus, J.	Siegel, R.
Caiella, N.	Kehoe, T.	Treveloni, R.
Chernoff, M.	Lewis, S.	Tripicchio, G.
Corliss, B.	Locke, K.	Wilkinson, A.
Croke, D.	Margolis, M.	

1997 Season
R.T. Treveloni, Captain
Kevin Schmidt, Captain
15-3-0
Somerset County Champions

Pingry tops Somerville for SCT title

By JEFF GOLDMAN
GANNETT NEWS SERVICE

BOUND BROOK — In his each of his first three years at the Pingry School, Heath Freeman helped the Big Blue win the Somerset County Boys' Soccer Tournament championship. Freeman took center stage again last night at LaMonte Field, scoring in the 56th minute to give Pingry a 1-0 victory over top-seeded Somerville in the 1997 tournament final.

"I've dreamed about this my whole life," Freeman said after the Big Blue annexed the county title for the fourth straight year and sixth time in seven seasons.

"It feels really good. I was praying that I'd actually get a chance to score in the counties and I did."

"I thought we had maybe a couple better...part of his body," Freeman said. "I just happened to be there. The goalie came near post and I just put it behind him."

Pingry extends streak to 42 victories in row

Kris Bertsch and R.T. Treveloni connected on penalty kicks to help Pingry defeat Princeton Day, 3-0, and extend the state's current long winning streak to 42 games yesterday in Princeton.

Treveloni leads way as Pingry soars, 5-0

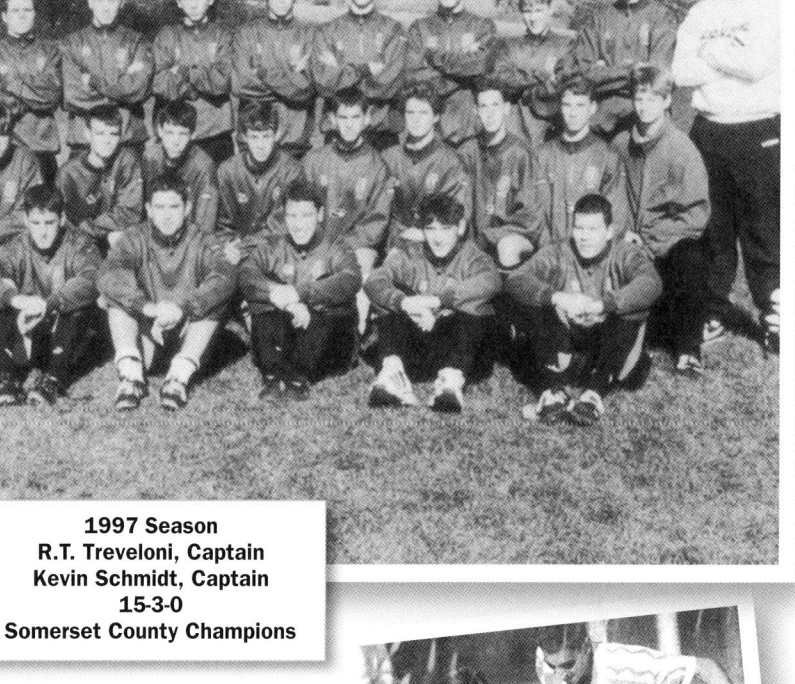

R.T. Treveloni scored twice when Pingry, No. 14 in The Star-Ledger Boys' Soccer Top 20, rolled to a 5-0 victory over North Plainfield in a Somerset County Tournament first-

HIGH SCHOOL SOCCER
Pingry sweeps

Both the boys and girls win Somerset tournament titles with victories over Somerville and Ridge, C-1

The 1998 Season

For the 1998 team, the entire season was a tough uphill battle. Pingry started the season without tri-captain Mike Roberts, whose recovery from an ACL injury his junior year was tragically ruined when he tore up the ACL again before the start of the season. Miller had been counting on freshman John Rhodes, already a polished player with his club team, to anchor the midfield. He, too, was lost for the season with a broken bone. The loss of key players rippled through the rest of the team. Tri-captain Kris Bertsch, instead of playing striker, had to play the role of a distributor in the midfield, and fellow captain David Fahey, slotted to play center midfielder, had to return to play sweeper. "Before the season," says Fahey, "we really wanted to take the team to prominence. As it turned out, with some key guys missing, we just didn't have the horses."

In spite of the loss of key players, the 1998 team was able to put together a successful 16-3-1 season. As expected, the offense was led by Bertsch's 12 goals and 15 assists and Gianfranco Tripicchio's 14 goals and 15 assists, but they had strong support from returning senior starters Paul Anderson, juniors Nick Caiella and Joe Pekarsky, and sophomore Rob Siegel up front, and senior Steve Lewis, junior Dave Alchus, and sophomore Kevin Locke alongside Bertsch and Tripicchio in the midfield. Seniors Fahey, Nick Sarro-Waite, Todd Kehoe, and Matt Margolis and junior Matt Blumenstyk returned on the back line, with first-year starter Mike Chernoff in goal.

Their only regular-season loss came against their Colonial Hills nemesis Chatham, when Mike Walsh's goal with 36 seconds left in regulation forged a tie and his game-winner with 40 seconds remaining in overtime sealed the win. In their second meeting, Pingry came back from a two-goal deficit on Caiella's one-time left-footed blast and Bertsch's conversion of a long throw-in from Fahey. Despite being a man down after Caiella's harsh expulsion for running into a referee, Pingry hung on for a tie, with Blumenstyk silencing Walsh for the rest of the game.

In the Somerset County semifinals against Watchung Hills, highly favored Pingry, which started the game without three key players because of a team rules violation, ran into two obstacles they couldn't overcome. Watchung Hills' goalkeeper Joe Coletti was truly inspired, stopping 21 shots, and what Coletti didn't block, the woodwork did, as two point-blank shots by Pingry late in the game clanged off the goal posts. Pingry's defense made only one misplay all game long, but that lapse, in overtime, gave Watchung Hills a 1-0 victory. The same misfortune haunted Pingry again in the Prep A semifinals against Delbarton. Bertsch and Tripicchio had given Pingry a 2-1 lead at the end of the first half. In the second half, Pingry twice scored in a bid to break the game open, only to have both goals inaccurately called back for off sides. The game went into overtime when Delbarton scored with 1:30 left in regulation, and then won the game when Mike Kaag's poorly hit slow roller somehow trickled through the defense with 4:20 left in the second overtime.

Both Bertsch, whose outstanding four-year career was highlighted by 63 goals, just one behind all-time scoring leader Mike DeGrande, and fellow three-year defensive standout Fahey were selected to the Somerset County All-County First Team.

Soccer, like any other competitive sport, can be pitiless. Mike Roberts, tri-captain of the 1998 team, found that out the hard way. As a freshman, he had contributed strongly to the 1995 team's undefeated season and started as a sophomore on the No. 1 ranked 1996 team. After a torn ACL had sidelined him for the 1997 season, he worked relentlessly through the off season and the summer to get back at full strength for his senior year. But it wasn't to be. In pre-season, he again tore his ACL and then had to live through the misery of helplessly watching his teammates and close buddies battle through the season. "Miller always introduces me to alumni as 'a player who never lost a game he played at Pingry,' which is true, but also really caring – the way Miller is. He knew how hard it was for me not to be part of the team my last two years."

Mike Roberts '99

Adam Rohdie, *Assistant Coach*
Mike DeGrande, *Assistant Coach*
Mike Coughlin, *Assistant Coach*

Alchus, D.	Ellis, T.	Margolis, M.
Anderson, P.	Fahey, D.	Pekarsky, J.
Appelbaum, M.	Gittes, D.	Rhodes, J.
Askin, S.	Haverstick, S.	Roberts, M.
Bertsch, K.	Kaplus, J.	Sarro-Waite, N.
Blumenstyk, M.	Kehoe, T.	Siegel, R.
Caiella, N.	Lewis, S.	Tripicchio, A.
Chernoff, M.	Locke, K.	Tripicchio, G.

1998 Season
Mike Roberts, Captain
Kris Bertsch, Captain
David Fahey, Captain
16-3-1

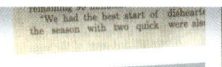

The 1999 Season

Thinking back on the 1999 season, Pingry's long-time revered assistant coach Adam Rohdie said, "Sometimes I hate the game of soccer." Part of that could be the nature of the game itself. When two talented, well-organized defenses go against each other, a split second of indecision or a bad bounce can decide an otherwise tight game. But part of it is that referees can sometimes take the game away from players with a bad call.

When Pingry protested Bergen Catholic forward Alecko Eskaderian's handball that preceded his winning goal in the Parochial A semifinals, the official ruling was that the foul was unintentional – as if that mattered. Only after the game did the officiating crew admit that Eskaderian had used his hand to knock the ball to himself. Courage and tenacity can accomplish a lot of things in a soccer game, but getting some officials to own up to a mistake is beyond the realm of will power.

Miller had assessed the team's chances at the start of the season by saying, "We're certainly not loaded, but we can be competitive. Some years we can just breeze by people, but this year I think we'll be in every game." It was an accurate prediction. The 1999 team ended what had been a decade of huge success for Pingry soccer with a 17-4 season marred only by the frustration of coming up short in its quest for championships. With one exception, Pingry ripped through its Colonial Hills Conference schedule as expected.

That exception was a regular-season confrontation with arch-rival Chatham. Over the years covering the late 1990s and early 2000s, Pingry wound up seeing more of the Walsh family of Chatham than it might have wished for. In 1999, Pingry had to deal with two Walshes: striker Dave Walsh, and his older brother and Chatham's new coach, Billy Walsh, who doubled as a player for the MSL's MetroStars. Because the Chatham contest had been scheduled on the same day as the MetroStars' home game against the San Jose Clash, Billy Walsh asked the MetroStars' management if the Pingry-Chatham game could be played at the MetroStars' home field, Giants Stadium. The MetroStars' general manager, Charlie Stillitano '77, was happy to oblige. In a difficult game played in the infamously blustery, unpredictable Giants Stadium winds, Chatham made more of their chances than Pingry, with Dave Walsh's goal providing Chatham's 2-1 victory.

The players on the 1999 team represented an unusual dichotomy of seniors and sophomores. The team's success was driven by a strong group of seniors – captains Gianfranco Tripicchio and Matt Blumenstyk, and co-captains Dave Alchus and Nick Caiella – along with juniors Sam Haverstick and goalkeeper Steve Askin. In addition to returning junior starters Rob Siegel, Nathan Bragg, and Tommy Ellis, an unusually strong group of sophomores gained experience in 1999 that would translate into a 36-1 record their last two years at Pingry.

Looking back at the season, and the team's struggles against adversity, Coach Rohdie said, "I am as proud of this team as I have ever been of any other team in my ten years of coaching."

Tripicchio and Caiella were selected for the All-County First Team, and Alchus, Askin, Blumenstyk, Kevin Locke, John Rhodes, and Siegel were also honored with post-season awards.

Over the years, Pingry has had a number of potent scoring partnerships. Few were as dangerous as Gianfranco Tripicchio and Nick Caiella in 1999. Caiella came back from a badly broken ankle as a sophomore to lead the 1999 team with 15 assists in addition to his 15 goals. "Fifteen goals is normal for me," Caiella commented at season's end, "but I'm always looking to pass the ball. I guess it's just my nature." On the receiving end of many of those assists was Tripicchio. "Gianfranco and I have a connection. We read each other very well." Tripicchio's 32 goals in 1999, along with 15 assists, topped off a stunning four-year Pingry career of offensive leadership and clutch play.

Nick Caiella and Gianfranco Tripicchio '00

Adam Rohdie, *Assistant Coach*
Mike DeGrande, *Assistant Coach*
Mike Coughlin, *Assistant Coach*

Alchus, D.	Ellis, T.	Siegel, R.
Appelbaum, M.	Gittes, D.	Susko, M.
Askin, S.	Haverstick, S.	Thiam, C.
Barsamian, C.	Holland, A.	Tripicchio, A.
Blumenstyk, M.	Lan, T.	Tripicchio, G.
Bragg, N.	Locke, K.	Wilkinson, W.
Caiella, N.	Miller, J.	Yeomans, C.
Davich, E.	Oh, R.	
Elkins, A.	Rhodes, J.	

1999 Season
Gianfranco Tripicchio, Captain
Matt Blumenstyk, Captain
Dave Alchus, Captain
Nick Caiella, Captain
17-4-0

Big Blue oust defending SCT champion

By JEFF WEBER
Staff Writer

PINGRY 2
B'WATER-RARITAN 0

BERNARDS — The defending county champion is gone.
Pingry got two second-half goals and used solid defensive play to oust 1998 Somerset County champion Bridgewater-Raritan, 2-0, in a controversial quarterfinal game Saturday in Bernards.
Pingry (11-2) scored its first goal on a penalty kick three minutes into the second half. John Locke was awarded...

some opportunites as well, but we certainly had the better chances."
The Panthers (7-4-2) had their best chance with 13 minutes remaining. Greg Natale apparently had scored the game-tying goal off a beautiful pass from Eric Brown when he was whistled for knocking the ball into the net with his hand.

up front."
Pingry got the ball possession it desired and the ... from its other forw... away the game v... two minutes left, knocked home a that had come of Bridgewater-Ra Pete Brozyna. B strong game in saves.
Panthers coac was visibly upse game but was po team's play. Sze ly was pleased...

Trippichio's hat trick lifts Pingry to 2nd victory

BERNARDS — Led by senior midfielder Gianfranco Trippichio's hat trick, The Pingry School boys soccer team cruised to a 6-1 win over Mountain Lakes in a Colonial Hills Conference game Wednesday.
Junior forward Robby Siegal added two goals for Pingry.

The 2000s: New Opponents

> *"It's been a nice ride for 50 years, and I hope I made soccer a little better. I'm not in it for the wins or the awards. It's about the players and the team."*
> — MILLER, 2009

For years Miller had taken the soccer team for a pre-season trip to develop skills and team chemistry. In 2000, when the Pingry team got off the airplane, the welcoming sign said "*Benvenuto all'aeroporto di Milano Malpensa.*"

Aldo Tripicchio suggested that Miller bring the team to Italy for pre-season training. One can almost hear Aldo say, "Miller, you want your players to get better at football and you take them to Canada? Come to Italy, where we really know how to play the game."

Thanks to Aldo's contacts, the team spent 10 days in Italy practicing, usually in double sessions, but also experienced the highlights of cities like Florence and Rome. The players trained with professional coaches Enrico Connata of Parma AC and Stephano Donatti of Salsomaggiore and played against professional Under-17 teams, tying Bologna 0-0, and playing well, even in defeat, against Piacenza and Parma.

Aldo Tripicchio with Miller.

In 2001, the team returned to Italy and this time competed against the Piacenza and Perugia Under-20 teams. The games were very rough, and the Pingry players had to respond with equal toughness. One 6'4", 29-year-old Piacenza player, who had played for Inter Milan, was rehabilitating with the junior team. During the game a Pingry player knocked him down, and then instinctively said, "Sorry." The Italian pro jumped to his feet, pulled the Pingry player's ear, and yelled, "What is *sorry!*"

Summer 2000 Trip to Italy

Chaperons:
Miller Bugliari
David Bugliari
Aldo Tripicchio
Gianfranco Tripicchio
Gerard Pascale
Daniel Siegel
Richard Locke
Libero Saraceno

Players:
Michael Appelbaum
Charles Barsamian
Kevin Boova
Nathan Bragg
Eric Davich
Alex Elkins
Tommy Ellis
Andrew Holland
Peter Jeydel
William Kovacs
Travis Lan
Kevin Locke
Ari Marciscano
James Miller
Robert Oh
John Porges
John Rhodes
Leonardo (Lenny) Sara
Daniel Scher
George S
Robert S
Mark Su
Amadi
Anthony
Matthe
Matthe
Christo

2010 BIG BLUE SOCCER
ITALY

Boys' Soccer Plays Local Opposition in Germany and the Netherlands

By IAN MARTIN-KATZ (VI)

The soccer team left for Germany on August 9th for its annual training trip. Players, coaches, and chaperones arrived in Cologne, where they boarded a bus to Leverkusen, the team's main training center and residence for the next eight days.

On the first day in Germany, the team attended a match between the Bayer Leverkusen and Koblenz U-18 squads. "Bayer dominated the game," Conor Starr (VI) observed, "and the skill level of these athletes was higher than that of most similarly-aged players in the US." The game gave Big Blue a [taste of things] to come.

Pingry's first game of the trip was against Troisdorf football club. "We had to adapt," Kevin McNulty (VI) said, "since they played defensive-minded soccer." Captain Will Stamatis (VI) agreed that "They had a different style of play [over] there." The game, wh[ich] ended in a 2-2 tie (Sta[matis] scored both goals for [Pin]gry), was a good experi[ence] for the team. "Both t[eams] played really well an[d we] learned a lot," said Da[vid of some] kind (VI).

The team's secon[d op]ponent was SSG Ber[gisch.] Tyler Smith (V) sco[red to] start Pingry with a 1-[0 lead], captain — followed with goals of their own. The match, whose score remained close throughout, tested the team's abilities as a group and put to practice the changes that they had made since their tie against Troisdorf. Ultimately, Pingry's efforts earned them a 3-2 victory over Bergisch.

[In between training ses]sions, club Patrick Ladru, AJAX's assistant academy director, took the team through a training session. "We were disappointed that we didn't get to play the AJAX amateur team, but it was cool to practice in their complex and train with their coach," Eric Opplinger (VI) said.

Thus started what became a new ritual for Pingry soccer: taking the team to Europe to learn from and compete against some of the best youth clubs in the world.

Whether they were competing against teams from England, Holland, Mexico, Germany, Italy, Spain, Croatia, Portugal, or the Czech Republic, Pingry kids weren't just representing their school; they were representing their country as well. Their shirts said "Pingry Soccer," but they could also have said "USA."

As the scrapbook from the 2003 trip to England tells it, Pingry fought a rough, physical game against a Cottesmore (Leicestershire) team that had previously mauled another American team. Miller played all the kids, not just the starters. He wanted a great learning experience for everyone on the team, but he wanted the team to play well and get a result, too. Pingry equalized against Cottesmore at 2-2 in the second half before bowing 3-2 in the final minutes. The second game, against Oadby Town, also in Leicestershire, was just as physical. But this time the Pingry players did themselves, the program, and their country proud with a 3-0 win, and they established well-earned respect between two hard-playing teams.

While the focus of the trips to Europe was soccer, Miller made sure there were other learning experiences as well.

As the 2003 scrapbook tells it, "In addition to the professional tour guide assigned to each bus, Coach had many personal favorite places he pointed out to the team, notably the old and current homes of Scotland Yard. …Westminster Abbey had something for each of us, from the architecture and antiquity of the cathedral, to Winston Churchill's exceptional place of honor, to the impressive decorations and inscriptions for Shakespeare, Newton, Mary Queen of Scots, etc."

But kids are kids. The scrapbook also described how "…we struck GOLD, disguised as Lili White's, a uniform emporium. [We] found incredibly discounted jerseys, shirts and jackets. Fortunes were exhausted; desperate trades of prior purchased items for cash advances and loans were negotiated. [It was] a fantastic place."

Somerset County Dominance… Again

Clearly, that higher level of training and competition paid off. In the 1990s Pingry had dominated the Somerset County Tournament, winning seven titles over the decade. In the 2000s, Pingry owned the tournament, winning eight titles, including an unprecedented six consecutive championships from 2004 to 2010. As Matt Fechter, co-captain of the 2008 team, exclaimed after Pingry's victory, "It's the Pingry County Tournament. The name's been changed." Through the 2000s Pingry also dominated the Colonial Hills Conference, winning the championship based on regular season play nine times.

Winning a state title still proved to be a daunting challenge, however, as the teams in the 1990s had discovered. The tournament was grueling: Pingry first had to get through three or four rounds of elimination games against larger Catholic schools to win the Non-Public North Sectional title, then face the South winner in order to claim the state title. Pingry won the North title four times, and emerged as the state champions three times in the decade.

Pingry's regular season performance during this decade was stunning. Seven teams in the 2000s completed their regular season undefeated; the 2001 team was named the second best in the state; and the 2008 team won the *Star-Ledger* trophy as the best team in the state and was recognized as the 11th-ranked team in the country.

Signature Victories

600th - 2001

2001 was another special year for Miller and for Pingry soccer. On their way to a perfect 21-0 season, Pingry defeated Seton Hall 2-0 for Miller's 600th win in defending its Parochial A North Jersey title. John Rhodes set up the first score off an own goal and assisted Mark Susko with a picture-perfect cross for the insurance goal. The 2001 team wound up winning their conference, the Somerset County title, and the Parochial A state championship to earn a ranking as the No. 9 team in the nation.

As usual, Miller made light of the accomplishment. "I guess it means I've been around awhile. Reaching 600 means that I've had the opportunity to coach a lot of quality soccer players over the years." Rhodes was happier about the milestone victory than the state sectional title. "I personally have a lot of respect for him. I gave everything I can – and so did the team for him today."

700th - 2008

Miller's 700th win was a 5-1 thrashing of Newark Academy at Pingry's 2008 Homecoming. It was another banner year that saw the team finish the season undefeated, win conference, county, and state titles and wind up ranked No. 11 in the nation. But it didn't start out looking like a victory. Newark Academy jumped out to a 1-0 lead, which held up until Matt Ryback's equalizer near the end of the first period. Tyler Smith acknowledged that the pressure of the milestone caused the team to play tight in the first half. At halftime, be recalled, "The coaches got our heads in the game and set us straight. Once we started scoring goals in the first 10 minutes of the second half, we dominated play."

In the second half, co-captain Brendan Burgdorf took over, assisting Randy Falk for the first goal, scoring himself two minutes later on a cross from Andrew LaFontaine, and adding a solo goal, then assisting on the final goal by Will Stamatis.

In the post-game celebration, the team put on T-shirts with Miller's name on the back. "It's a big day for Pingry soccer," Miller observed, "and it's a big day for me." It was also a big day for the players. Smith said the milestone victory "was like winning the states or counties. We were really happy for Coach."

Pingry Athletics Hall of Fame

Miller's selection to the Pingry Athletics Hall of Fame in 2006 was celebrated by dozens of alumni, friends and colleagues, but one of the most poignant tributes came from someone who wasn't there, former Headmaster John Hanly:

45 West 67th Street,
New York,
NY 10023

10th August 2006

Dear Miller,

This is the sort of letter which I would always have written in longhand, but, thanks to Parkinson's, my writing is illegible and so I am reduced to using the word processor. I enclose a card to give it the "personal" touch"!

I am sorry that I was unable to attend the Hall of Fame ceremonies last Saturday; but I want you to know why I would like to have been there. It is probably fair to say that we have had our disagreements over the years, - who hasn't? - but I learnt very quickly that your views on any issue were astute and never to be ignored. But more importantly, you embody two qualities - actually, many more than two, but I have limited space!! – which are so significant to the life of Pingry. First is your personal kindness, courtesy and compassion. I cannot remember ever seeing you strike a false note, and as one of the many people who have benefited from your decency, I thank you. The second gift that you have given your players – and I'll bet that you heard this a million times at the Hall of Fame – is to teach them about life. Coaching soccer is just the tool that you use; producing good human beings is your goal. (No pun intended.) I've said many times that students very quickly forget what they have learnt, but they never forget the people who taught them. That is why it is so important to have a faculty of honorable, principled men and women, men and women for whom at Pingry, you have set a magnificent example.

Someone once asked me what Pingry would be like if populated by Miller-clones. A gruesome thought!!! But much more frightening is the concept of a Pingry without Miller because to lose you, the school would be losing its heart and soul and guts. I don't want to be around to see that happen, and so if I had been at the Hall of Fame dinner, I would have proposed the toast: "Miller: To the next 50 Years."

With Warmest Wishes,

J L Hanly

Miller Magic

The Xavier University soccer program Kris Bertsch and Head Coach Andy Fleming took over in 2011 was in the cellar. They were the doormats of the Atlantic 10 Conference, winning only five games the preceding two years while losing 29. Bertsch's official title at Xavier is now "Assistant Head Coach," but from the start he and Fleming were tightly aligned in their commitment to turn Xavier soccer into a championship team. They succeeded beyond their wildest expectations, achieving the biggest one-year turnaround in the history of NCAA soccer. And significantly, Miller and Pingry soccer played a decisive role in that stunning transformation.

As Bertsch tells it, "We were told we should bench the holdover kids, play the new recruits we'd brought with us, and gradually work to improve the program. We had a different idea, based on what I'd learned at Pingry – build a winning soccer culture first, based on values every Pingry player will recognize: high expectations, hard work, commitment to the team, and meeting one's school, soccer and social responsibilities.

"The kids bought into the challenge to 'board the success bus.' We battled through early injuries to key players, picked up some big wins, and by the end of the season were 3-1 and ranked second in our conference. Then, kids being kids, the players started to think they were better than they really were and we dropped two conference games in a row, the last one a demoralizing 0-3 pasting. Just to qualify for the Atlantic 10 Tournament, we had to win the next three games in a span of five days. It was a tough spot.

"We were right down the road from Pingry, so I called Miller and asked if we could practice at Pingry and if he might talk to the team. Of course he said 'yes.' I remember when the team bus pulled up to the school, and the players got out and walked onto the World Cup Field, with all those championship banners hanging on the fence. I'd shared a little of my experience with Pingry soccer with them, and it's a little strange to say, perhaps, but I know they could feel the power of that tradition of excellence around them. Miller spoke to the team about expectations and effort and commitment to each other – he knew exactly what they needed to hear – and the players had the best practice they, or we as coaches, had ever experienced. It was transformational. That momentum continued into a magical run culminating in qualifying for the Atlantic 10 Tournament, winning the championship as an unranked 'Cinderella team,' and making the NCAA Tournament. The Pingry soccer tradition Miller has created changed their lives just as it had mine all those years before."

Kris Bertsch '99

The 2000 Season

Payback can be sweet. The 1997 headline had read: "Pingry Streak Stopped at 46 Games by Chatham." In 2000, it was Pingry's turn. Goals by Mark Susko and John Rhodes ended Chatham's 39-game undefeated run. "This was a really big win," said junior goalkeeper Anthony Tripicchio about Pingry's Colonial Hills Conference title. "We haven't beaten them for two and a half years."

It was a season of big wins. Pingry finished an undefeated regular season, sharing the Somerset County title with Bridgewater-Raritan, winning the Non-Public A North Jersey tournament, and ending the year ranked as the No. 6 team in the state.

Captains Kevin Locke and Rob Siegel led the offense with 42 goals between them. They received strong scoring support all season long from junior midfielders Rhodes and Susko and fellow seniors Mike Appelbaum and Condi Thiam, whose clutch scores won tournament games against Hillsborough, Hudson Catholic, and Pope John.

Defensively, juniors Matt Wilkinson and Rhodes took over the assignment of shutting down opponents' top threats. The rest of the defense was anchored by seniors Tommy Ellis, Nathan Bragg, and Andrew Holland, and junior Alex Elkins. Tripicchio earned the start in goal, backed up by classmate Kevin Boova. In recording 11 clean sheets for the season, Tripicchio was at his best in the county championship game against Bridgewater.

With 17 minutes left Locke evened the score at 1-1. Bridgewater hotly protested the score, claiming the ball hadn't crossed the line. Locke disagreed: "I knew when I hit it that it was going in." The referee agreed with Locke, but the call triggered a desperate, sustained assault by an aroused Bridgewater team. In recording a season-high 17 saves, Tripicchio repeatedly turned aside a barrage of shots to preserve the tie, somehow twice making fingertip saves on point-blank opposite-corner shots. "You've got to give all the credit in the world to Anthony," remarked Locke after the game. "He was tremendous."

Heading into the state tournament, a team wants to have all its key players available, not sitting on the bench with red cards. The Pingry team managed to accomplish that goal; its coach didn't. In what he still claims was an unwarranted call by an overly emotional referee, Miller was thrown out of the sectional semifinals against Hudson Catholic, forcing him to miss the sectional finals and the state championship game.

With Assistant Coach Adam Rohdie now in charge, Pingry won its first Non-Public B North Jersey championship against Pope John 2-0 on Thiam's game-winner and Locke's insurance goal. "There need to be asterisks after some of Miller's championships," joked Rohdie. "I won a couple of them while he was banned from the games."

In the state final against Christian Brothers Academy, Pingry twice forged leads on goals by Locke and Elkins. But in the second half, both the weather and the game turned against Pingry. With a strong, gusting wind at their backs, CBA's pressure resulted in Pingry's first loss of the season by a 3-2 score. "You have to give CBA credit," Rohdie said after the game. "They knocked us around a bit and were tough on 50/50 balls."

Locke and Siegel capped an outstanding year by being selected for the All-County First Team, with Ellis, Thiam, and Rhodes earning Second Team honors. Locke was honored as the *Star-Ledger* Player of the Year, Pingry was named the Team of the Year, and Miller was the Coach of the Year.

In 2000, Pingry was faced with the challenge of replacing the 1999 scoring duo of Gianfranco Tripicchio and Nick Caiella. Seniors Kevin Locke (23 goals and 17 assists) and Rob Siegel (19 goals and 10 assists) picked up the slack with a vengeance. "Rob and I have been playing together since our freshman years for Pingry and in the off-season for the Chatham Cobras," noted Locke after the season. "We have developed a great rapport which translates into knowing what the other one is going to do before we do it. Rob and John Rhodes took the pressure off me. The three of us couldn't be stopped, which allowed me to score more often."

Kevin Locke and Rob Siegel '01

Adam Rohdie, *Assistant Coach*
Jake Ross, *Assistant Coach*
Miles Dickson, *Manager*

Alam, Z.	Lan, T.	Scopelianos, G.
Appelbaum, M.	Locke, K.	Siegel, R.
Boova, K.	Marciscano, A.	Spano, K.
Bragg, N.	Oh, R.	Susko, M.
Davich, E.	Penrose, D.	Thiam, C.
Elkins, A.	Porges, J.	Tripicchio, A.
Ellis, T.	Rhodes, J.	Weil, M.
Holland, A.	Salerno, D.	Wilkinson, M.
Kehoe, B.	Saraceno, L.	Yeomans, C.
Kovacs, B.	Scher, D.	

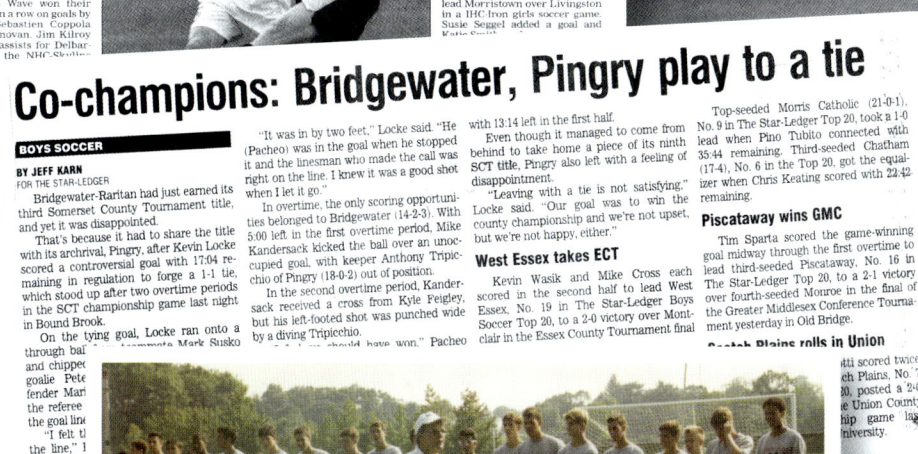

2000 Season
Kevin Locke, Captain
Rob Siegel, Captain
20-1-2
Undefeated Regular Season
Conference Champions
Somerset County Champions
Non-Public A Sectional Champions

The 2001 Season

On the first day of the 2001 pre-season, Assistant Coach Adam Rohdie showed up with a T-shirt bearing the message "CBA 3 Pingry 2." For the players who, as underclassmen, had watched a championship disappear in the gusting winds of the 2000 state title game, the message was clear. "I didn't need to be reminded," said co-captain John Rhodes. "That loss made the whole team angry. I don't want to feel like that again."

Rhodes, tri-captains Anthony Tripicchio and Matt Wilkinson, and their 2001 Pingry teammates made sure that didn't happen. In a 21-0-0 perfect season, Pingry won their conference championship, the county tournament, the Non-Public A state sectionals, and the Non-Public A state championship on their way to a ranking as the No. 2 team in the state and the ninth-best high school team in the nation.

Once again, Pingry's opponents had to deal with a deep, versatile offense led by Rhodes (13 goals and 15 assists) and senior striker Alex Elkins (14 goals and 11 assists), with timely contributions from juniors John Porges, Amadi Thiam, and Robert Oh. In the midfield, seniors Rhodes and Mark Susko and junior Billy Kovacs were joined as the season progressed by freshmen Will Munger and John Stamatis. Defensively, Wilkinson, charged with marking opponents' top scoring threat, worked with senior Travis Lan, sophomore Kenny Spano, and freshman Kevin Vieira to form a wall in front of senior goalkeeper Anthony Tripicchio, who followed up his 2000 heroics in goal with a season full of sparkling saves.

Against Bernards in the Somerset County final, in spite of controlling the run of play, Pingry fell behind near the end of the first half when goalkeeper Tripicchio was caught off his line. Tripicchio made up for that goal midway through the second half by scoring the equalizer on a penalty kick. Although he excelled as a goalkeeper, Tripicchio grew up as a field player – he buried his penalty kick in the right corner. Six minutes later Oh converted a pass from Vieira, and with seven minutes left in the game Elkins' direct kick put the game out of reach.

The road to the state championship was just as dramatic. Immaculata, in the semifinals, was led by Jamie Granger, the state's leading scorer with 34 goals. As he had done with opponents' top scorers all season long, Wilkinson shut Granger down. Pingry's 2-0 victory came on Rhodes' one-time rifle shot into the right corner and Thiam's heads-up conversion of a pass from Porges in the box.

Pingry successfully defended its state sectional championship in a 2-0 victory over Seton Hall, for Miller's 600th career win. That brought up the long-awaited rematch with Christian Brothers Academy. As it had the previous year, Pingry jumped to an early 1-0 lead on Porges' conversion of a Thiam pass. Christian Brothers equalized with 40 minutes to go, as they had in 2000, but then the Pingry defense took over the game. The game-winner, earning Pingry its first state championship since 1996, was a bending right-footed blast from Munger. After the game, John Rhodes recalled Coach Rohdie's motivational T-shirt from the beginning of the season. "It worked…we'll probably give him some grief about it…and get him a new shirt."

Rhodes was selected for the All-State First Team and was named Central Jersey Player of the Year. He joined Elkins and Wilkinson on the All-County First Team, with Tripicchio and Susko also receiving post-season honors.

John Rhodes' illustrious soccer career started in St. Louis. When his family moved to New Jersey when he was 11 years old, Pingry was the obvious choice. In addition to starting for Pingry for three years after missing his freshman year due to injury, he also captained his club team, PDA Dalglish, to state championships in 2000, 2001, and 2002. After a stellar four-year career at Penn he was named to the All-Ivy Second Team. But his best soccer experience was his senior year at Pingry. "We had some great players, but what set this team apart was its incredible chemistry. We genuinely cared about each other. Nobody put themselves ahead of the team. We all knew our roles and executed them together. And we were never satisfied with what we accomplished."

John Rhodes '02

THE LIFE & TIMES OF MILLER A. BUGLIARI

Adam Rohdie, *Assistant Coach*
Jake Ross, *Assistant Coach*
Miles Dickson, *Manager*

Alam, Z.	Kovacs, B.	Saraceno, L.
Aquino, M.	Lan, T.	Scher, D.
Boova, K.	Leonard, T.	Scopelianos, G.
Burgess, J.	Marciscano, A.	Spano, K.
Callaghan, M.	Munger, W.	Stamatis, J.
Davich, E.	Oh, R.	Susko, M.
DiLeo, L.	Papasikos, J.	Thiam, A.
Elkins, A.	Penrose, D.	Tripicchio, A.
Fechter, B.	Porges, J.	Vieira, K.
Hirsch, D.	Rhodes, J.	Wilkinson, M.
Jeydel, P.	Salerno, D.	

2001 Season
John Rhodes, Captain
Anthony Tripicchio, Captain
Matt Wilkinson, Captain
21-0-0
Undefeated Season
Conference Champions
Somerset County Champions
Non-Public A State Champions

Pingry caps perfect season with 1st Parochial A state title

Defense propels Pingry

Wilkinson shuts down Granger as Pingry reaches sectional final.

The 2002 Season

Looking at the strength and talent of the 2001 graduates who had led Pingry to a 21-0-0 perfect season, Miller agreed, "We're in a rebuilding season. The best we can do is contain teams." But for the senior starters on the 2002 team, tri-captains Billy Kovacs, Robert Oh, and John Porges, plus classmates Amadi Thiam, Lenny Saraceno, George Scopelianos, and Dave Salerno, the goal during their final season in a Pingry uniform was the same as that of any senior class: win the conference, win the county, win the state. Unfortunately, that was also the goal of Pingry's Colonial Hills and Somerset County opponents, all of whom had scores to settle. Joining the seniors on the 2002 team were four juniors, Kenny Spano, Liam Griff, Seth Flowerman, and Alex Tuller, and four talented sophomores who as juniors and seniors themselves would form the nucleus of championship teams: Brad Fechter, Will Munger, John Stamatis, and Kevin Vieira.

Pingry split the series with Group II powerhouse and Colonial Hills rival Chatham, losing the first game 1-0, then coming from behind to win the rematch, in one of Pingry's most complete games all season, 5-3, on Porges' hat trick and Thiam's goal in the second overtime. Against perennial Group I leaders Bernards and Whippany Park, however, similar 2-1 losses ended Pingry's chance for a Colonial Hills title that year. Whippany Park, the 2001 Group I state champion, had managed a 0-11-1 record against Pingry since 1995, the year Pingry joined the conference. They relished the experience of revenge, as did Bernards. "Everybody says how bad they are this season," said Bernards coach Joe LaSpada, "but they are still a tough team to face every season, and our game with Pingry was a true test for us."

In the Somerset County tournament quarter-finals, Montgomery had its own bitter memories to erase. In 2001, they had jumped to a 2-0 lead in the first half only to wither under a second-half Pingry onslaught of five unanswered goals. This year they made their initial lead stand up for an eventual 3-1 victory. "One of our goals was to make it to the county final," remarked Montgomery senior midfielder Adam Hyncik. "Beating Pingry is something you have to do to get there."

The returning players from Pingry's undefeated 2001 team struggled to understand how their season got away from them. "We just don't flow together like we usually do," said three-year letterman Billy Kovacs. What stands out about a disappointing season, however, is that the team never stopped believing in itself, and going into the Non-Public A tournament still had dreams of repeating as champions. "I know we definitely can make a run," Kovacs added before the start of the state tournament. "It all depends if we work hard and play together." The first step toward realizing that dream came in Pingry's opening-round 5-0 whitewashing of Hudson Catholic in what Miller called "one of the best games we've played." Sophomore Will Munger, whose game-winning goal had given Pingry its 2001 Non-Public A championship against Christian Brothers, was the offensive sparkplug, with assists on three of Pingry's first four goals. But against Bergen Catholic in the semifinals, once again, Pingry couldn't find the net, and ended up on the short end of a hard-fought but disappointing 2-0 loss.

"Billy, Amadi, Robert, and I enjoyed a lot of success as juniors because, frankly, we had great players around us. But if I assess our senior year team fairly, we didn't have a standout scorer who could create goals when we needed them. We knew the sophomores on the team were really talented, but they also hadn't yet matured physically and were a year away from reaching their potential. So from a Pingry perspective, at 10-6-3, we had a 'bad year,' although lots of teams would call that record a successful season. My senior year was a lesson in humility. We got knocked down a peg – and it hurt. We were in every game we played; it was frustrating not to be able to close the deal.

"But Pingry soccer isn't just about the season, it's about the total experience. You grow up in a tradition of excellence – the sense that you're 'special,' not in any egotistical way, but as an expectation. Pingry soccer's history of success breeds a culture of success. You realize that you need to constantly commit to getting better, giving 100% in practice, staying after practice to work on something you need to improve. If you don't put in the work, you won't be the best. As a kid in the Pingry soccer program, you really don't know how good you have it. Even for the guys who go on to college soccer, your athletic career is short. But the lessons are life lessons to treasure – and so are the friendships."

John Porges '03

Adam Rohdie, *Assistant Coach*
Jake Ross, *Assistant Coach*
Ranzato, *Assistant Coach*
Miles Dickson, *Manager*

Aquino, M.	Kovacs, B.	Saraceno, L.
Burgess, J.	Leibowitz, A.	Scopelianos, G.
Callaghan, M.	Leonard, T.	Silbermann, M.
Dilio, L.	Magrane, R.	Spano, K.
Dwyer, S.	Marciscano, A.	Stamatis, J.
Fechter, B.	Munger, W.	Strackhouse, T.
Flowerman, S.	Oh, R.	Thiam, A.
Gandolfo, J.	Papasikos, J.	Tuller, A.
Garcia, M.	Parrondo, J.	Vieira, K.
Griff, L.	Porges, J.	
Hirsch, D.	Salerno, D.	

Pingry rebounded well from tournament loss

BOYS SOCCER NOTEBOOK
By JIM GREEN
Staff Writer

2002 Season
Billy Kovacs, Captain
Robert Oh, Captain
John Porges, Captain
10-6-3

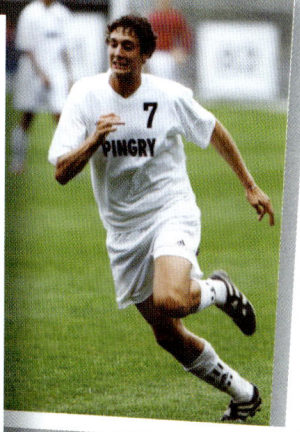

The 2003 Season

At the end of the 2003 season, Miller remarked, "I thought we'd be competitive." "Competitive" translated into an undefeated regular season, an overall 15-2-1 record and a Colonial Hills Conference title. Pingry's four captains, seniors Kenny Spano, Liam Griff, Seth Flowerman, and Alex Tuller, may not have been the most talented players on the team – but they were certainly the team's leaders. Joining them as starters and key players were junior midfielders Will Munger, John Stamatis, and Brad Fechter; junior forward Rob Magrane and junior defender Kevin Vieira; sophomores Len Coleman, Mark Garcia, Jack Gandolfo, and Peter Cipriano; and freshmen Warren "Kim" Kimber IV and Jeff Zimering.

The newspaper sports articles' headlines tell the story of Pingry's offensive depth: "Late goal by Stamatis lifts Pingry," "Tuller leads Pingry past Chatham," "Munger's goal lifts Pingry by Bernards," "Vieira leads Pingry by Hillsborough," "Munger, Zimering boost Pingry," "Stamatis stars, propels undefeated Pingry."

Against Colonial Hills Conference opponents, Pingry opened the season with a 3-2 victory over Chatham, with Stamatis' free kick in the 76th minute providing the winning margin. Pingry followed that up with a six-game sweep of conference foes in which they scored 24 goals to their opponents' one.

Entering the Somerset County tournament, top-seeded Pingry at 12-0-1 won a spot in the finals thanks to a Zimering overtime goal against Somerville in the semifinals. Pingry started the Ridge game on fire, Munger repeatedly breaking free only to have balls skim over the top crossbar or agonizingly miss wide by inches. Late in the first period, Munger was fouled hard on the line, but the ensuing free kick was shot right at Ridge goalkeeper Chris DeAngelis. Unfortunately, Ridge made more of the few chances Pingry's defense gave them and opened up a 2-0 lead. Pingry fought back in the second half, Stamatis' conversion of a perfect Fechter cross bringing Pingry to within a goal. But then,

as Pingry pressed forward with numbers to tie the game, they got caught in a Ridge counterattack for the decisive third goal. Vieira scored in the waning moments of the game, but it wasn't enough.

The same scenario played out in the Parochial A state tournament. Munger's goal gave Pingry a 1-0 opening-round victory over Seton Hall Prep, but against Don Bosco Prep in the semifinals, Don Bosco's Eric Zekiroski broke a 0-0 tie – and Pingry's hearts – when he beat goalkeeper Mark Garcia with just five minutes left in the second overtime.

Defensive leader Spano and Pingry's scoring leader Stamatis (17 goals and 10 assists) were named to the All-County and All-Area First Teams, with Vieira joining them on the All-Conference First Team. Munger, Fechter, Liam Griff, and Garcia were also honored in post-season awards.

Liam Griff was one of the multi-sport athletes who formed the core of the 2003 team. In addition to soccer, he captained the basketball and lacrosse teams. Coach Rohdie jokingly labeled him "Captain America."

"As sophomores," Griff recalls, "we had enjoyed the terrific 2001 season, and struggled with the rest of the team through a difficult 2002 in which nothing seemed to gel for the team. So going into our senior year, our expectations weren't very high. Kenny Spano was the only real 'soccer player' in our class who played club soccer. The rest of us were just good athletes who had speed, size and toughness and just worked really hard. I think we may have given up five or six goals all season.

"What Miller and Coach Rohdie did that made a difference was to simplify the game. I don't want to say 'dumb it down,' but they put us in positions so that our athleticism and skill in other sports could make a difference. I played marking back with Kevin Vieira, who was terrific, and Kenny, at sweeper, was solid as a rock. Mark Garcia was in the first year of a great Pingry career in goal. We'd stop other teams then get the ball to the underclassmen like Munger, Stamatis and Fechter who could actually do something with it. In retrospect, we played a lot better than our ability on paper – this may have been one of the last Pingry teams in which many of the key players were two- and three-sport athletes like me and not full-time soccer players. The other thing that made a big difference was that we all got along really well, on and off the field – from seniors to freshmen. Miller and Coach Rohdie helped us become a family."

Liam Griff '04

Adam Rohdie, *Assistant Coach*
David Fahey, *Assistant Coach*
Mike DeGrande, *Assistant Coach*

Azofra, P.	Gandolfo, J.	Scopelianos, G.
Castle, D.	Garcia, M.	Silbermann, M.
Cipriano, P.	Griff, L.	Spano, K.
Coleman, L.	Griff, M.	Sprenger, E.
Combias, B.	Kimber, K.	Stamatis, J.
DiLeo, M.	Kyle, N.	Tuller, A.
Dwyer, S.	Leibowitz, A.	Vieira, K.
Eboh, O.	Lubetkin, J.	Young, A.
Fechter, B.	Magrane, R.	Zimering, J.
Flowerman, S.	Munger, W.	
Freedman, A.	Schonberg, E.	

Unbeaten Pingry is king of the hill
Stamatis keys victory over Montgomery for SCT title

Stamatis stars, propels undefeated Pingry, 5-1

Munger's goal lifts Pingry by Bernards

2003 Season
Liam Griff, Captain
Kenny Spano, Captain
Seth Flowerman, Captain
Alex Tuller, Captain
15-2-1
Undefeated Regular Season
Conference Champions

The 2004 Season

Against Delbarton in the Non-Public A North semifinal, a makeshift, patched-together Pingry defense conceded two goals before the team settled down and began taking control of the game. Then, as he had been doing since his freshman year, Will Munger came up with a clutch goal cutting Delbarton's lead in half, and with 1:04 left in the game he scored the tying goal – until the referee signaled off sides.

The Pingry players and bench exploded in protest, because the referee had simply not seen Delbarton's sweeper hanging back by the far post, behind the goalkeeper. It didn't matter. The tying goal was disallowed. It was the only loss Pingry suffered in a 19-1-0 season that ended with Pingry ranked the No. 2 team in the state.

The 2004 team was led by senior captains Brad Fechter, Will Munger, John Stamatis, and Kevin Vieira, all four-year varsity players who went on to play Division I college soccer after graduating from Pingry.

As a senior, Stamatis was called on to increase his offensive contribution, and he responded with 31 goals to end his high school career as Pingry's fourth leading scorer with 60 goals. He had a lot of help from Munger and Fechter, as well as senior Rob Magrane, junior Jack Gandolfo, and sophomores Kim Kimber IV and Jeff Zimering. The speed, skill, and game sense of Vieira, one of the top defenders in the state, and juniors Len Coleman and Sam Dwyer, all playing in front of junior goalkeeper Mark Garcia, allowed Pingry to play a 3-5-2, freeing Fechter, Munger, and junior midfielders Tom Strackhouse, Peter Cipriano, and Brian Combias to dominate the midfield.

Pingry was tested only once in the regular season, against a tough Morris Catholic team, with Stamatis' goal in the 67th minute off a pass from Strackhouse providing the margin in a 1-0 victory. Pingry broke open a 1-1 deadlock in the Somerset County quarter-finals against Bound Brook. Against Bridgewater-Raritan, Stamatis collected a perfect 30-yard Munger pass off his chest and one-touched the winning goal in the 60th minute.

In the finals against Montgomery, Kimber's score off a Stamatis cross put Pingry ahead, and Stamatis' solo goal with 6:24 left in the first half gave Pingry what would turn out to be the winning 2-1 edge. Miller summed up the game saying, "This was an excellent victory. The kids played hard and I'm proud of them."

Pingry's second championship opportunity came against Bernards in a game that decided the Colonial Hills Conference title. Munger's two goals gave Pingry a comfortable victory, but at a big price. The deliberate, vicious foul that ended Kevin Vieira's season meant Pingry would have to fight for the Non-Public A title without Vieira's defensive leadership and lock-down play.

After a Stamatis hat trick disposed of Bergen Catholic 3-2, Pingry, now at 19-0-0, entered the Non-Public A North semifinal against Delbarton riding a wave of confidence. That wave was shattered when four players were suspended for the game for a team rules infraction, forcing Pingry to cobble together a defense with players in different positions and reserves in starting roles. It was a hard way for one of the best teams Pingry had fielded to end the season. Stamatis was named the Central New Jersey Player of the Year and was joined by Vieira, Fechter, and Munger on the All-County First Team.

Among decades of Pingry defensive standouts, Kevin Vieira stands out as one of Pingry's very best. In describing his impact, Miller said, "He's marked some of the best players in our area for four years. Shutting down the county's leading scorer, John Perez from Bound Brook, is just one of so many examples. He's got great speed, wonderful balance, and he reacts well. We've played him as sweeper, midfield, and occasionally he'll go up front if we need it. You find a weakness, you move him into it."

John Stamatis came from a strong soccer heritage. His father, Jim Stamatis, received the Hermann Award, emblematic of the top college player in the nation, in his senior year at Penn State. In describing John Stamatis' value to the team, assistant coach David Fahey said, "John provided sparks for us every time we needed them, whether it was scoring a big goal or setting one up. He changed the game for us, time and time again." Heading into his senior year, Stamatis had set a goal of eclipsing Mike DeGrande's 63 goals. He just missed, recording 60 goals and 30 assists in his four-year career. "The fact he was chasing that record all year," added Fahey, "and still had 17 assists just shows you what an unselfish player he was."

Kevin Vieira and John Stamatis '05

David Fahey, *Assistant Coach*
Mike DeGrande, *Assistant Coach*
Alan Donnelly, *Assistant Coach*
Kevin Schmidt, *Assistant Coach*
Kris Bertsch, *Assistant Coach*

Castle, D.	Greene, B.	Schonberg, G.
Cipriano, P.	Griff, M.	Scopelianos, G.
Coleman, L.	Jurist, S.	Smith, P.
Combias, B.	Keil, N.	Sprenger, E.
Devers, N.	Kimber, K.	Stamatis, J.
Donnantuono, A.	Lan, A.	Strackhouse, T.
Dwyer, S.	Lubetkin, J.	Tuller, D.
Eboh, O.	Magrane, R.	Vieira, K.
Fechter, B.	Miicke, K.	Young, A.
Gandolfo, J.	Munger, W.	Zimering, J.
Garcia, M.	Schonberg, E.	

PINGRY 2 BERNARDS 0

BERNARDS — Senior midfielder Will Munger booted in two goals, clinching the Colonial Hills Conference Colonial Division championship for Pingry.

BERNARDS (13-4) .... 0 0—0
PINGRY (17-0) .... 1 1—2
GOALS: Munger 2.
ASSISTS: Stamatis.
SAVES: B—Bruton 7; P—Garcia 5.

Pingry beats Bernards, clinches CHC title

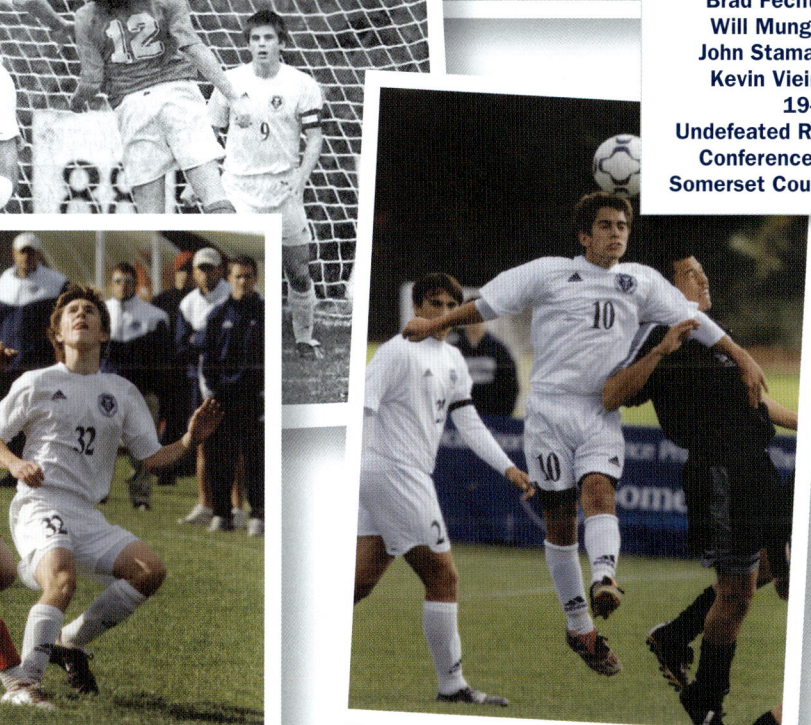

2004 Season
Brad Fechter, Captain
Will Munger, Captain
John Stamatis, Captain
Kevin Vieira, Captain
19-1-0
Undefeated Regular Season
Conference Champions
Somerset County Champions

The 2005 Season

Entering the 2005 season, tri-captain Tom Strackhouse remembers, "We knew we weren't as talented, from front to back, as the 2004 team, but Miller did a great job putting the players we did have in positions to contribute to the team's success." In order to get more scoring punch up front, he moved tri-captain Len Coleman, a star defender for both Pingry and his club team, forward to striker, where his 6'4" size, speed, and athletic ability could make a difference. "Defensively," Strackhouse continues, "that meant we were losing both Lenny and Kevin Vieira from the previous year. The guys who replaced them, seniors Brian Combias and tri-captain Sam Dwyer at sweeper, and juniors Austin Lan, Nick Devers and Rich Bradley, were just tough, hard-working, tenacious players who knew their role and didn't make mistakes." Pingry also had four-year starter Mark Garcia in goal, whose 13 clean sheets in 2005 were a career best.

The team's strength was in the midfield, consisting of seniors Strackhouse, Jack Gandolfo, and Peter Cipriano, and junior Austin Lan. Joining Coleman on the front line were juniors Kim Kimber IV and Jeff Zimering. For an unheralded group, the 2005 team's performance was spectacular. They opened by scoring 51 goals to their opponents' single goal over the first nine games, and finished with an average of five goals per game while yielding just three goals over the entire regular season. The decision to play Coleman up front paid off in his 19 goals, followed by Zimering's 16.

After disposing of Bound Brook 7-0 in the opening round of the county tournament, Pingry faced a strong Hillsborough team in the semifinals. Hillsborough was successful in shutting down Coleman and Zimering, but, as he had several times in key matches, Cipriano came through with the only goal of the game off a header from Combias. Hillsborough had their best chance in the second half when Yannick Smith had a one-on-one with Garcia, who made a diving save to preserve the shutout. "Hillsborough has two of the best forwards in the state," said Garcia. "I thought our marking backs did a great job. They really stepped up."

Heading into the finals of the county tournament, 13th-ranked Pingry was a clear underdog to third-ranked Bridgewater-Raritan, led by its sophomore sensation Matt Kassel, their leading scorer with 20 goals and 12 assists. To counter Kassel, Miller moved Coleman back on defense to blanket Bridgewater-Raritan's offensive threat. He took Kassel completely out of the game, the only time Kassel had been held scoreless all season. With Coleman out of the offensive picture, other players needed to step up, and they did. Midway through the first half, Gandolfo headed a cross to Zimering, who converted for a 1-0 lead. In the second half, Kimber launched one of his spectacular flip throw-ins 30 yards into the box, to Zimering, who set up Gandofolo for the insurance goal.

Against Seton Hall in the opening round of the Non-Public A tournament, Pingry faced a team with defenders able to match Coleman's size and speed. With Coleman and Zimering blanketed, Pingry couldn't crack Seton Hall's defense and went down by a 1-0 score.

Coleman was named to the All-State First Team; Strackhouse, Coleman, and Dwyer were All-County First Team selections; and Garcia, Gandolfo, Zimering, and Combias also earned post-season recognition.

Going into the county championship game, sports writers had made Bridgewater-Raritan the clear favorite. Tom Strackhouse remembers the team got together before the game and vowed, "The hell with that." The game was played at Ridge High School, and as the team, with Strackhouse and Lenny Coleman in the lead, walked onto the field, clapping rhythmically past the Bridgewater-Raritan players, Coleman screamed at the top of his lungs, "Kassel, I'm coming for you!" "That set the tone for the game," says Strackhouse. "For the first 15 minutes we hit everything in sight. There were bodies flying all over the field. I think we picked up six or seven yellow cards, but Bridgewater-Raritan didn't know what hit them." Late in the game, with Pingry ahead 2-0, Kassell's only shot all game long sailed over the crossbar. As he stood with his face in his hands, Coleman came up to him and put his arm around his opponent's shoulder. "I told him that was the best chance he was going to get all night. It was pretty much all over." Coleman summed up the team's second county championship in a row by saying, "We don't really have any completely dominating players, so this win was more of a team effort tonight."

Tom Strackhouse and Lenny Coleman '06

David Fahey, *Assistant Coach*
Kevin Schmidt, *Assistant Coach*
Mike DeGrande, *Assistant Coach*
Alan Donnelly, *Assistant Coach*

Bradley, R.	Gandolfo, J.	Miicke, K.
Buteux, A.	Garcia, M.	Ramirez, C.
Cipriano, P.	Greene, B.	Rybak, M.
Coleman, L.	Griff, M.	Saetre, S.
Combias, B.	Hynes, E.	Schonberg, G.
Constantino, J.	Jurist, S.	Scott-Wittenborn, N.
Devers, N.	Kimber, K.	Smith, P.
Donnantuono, A.	Kudziela, I.	Stamatis, W.
Dwyer, S.	Lan, A.	Strackhouse, T.
Fechter, M.	Layng, E.	Tuller, D.
Freedman, J.	Lee, H.	Zimering, J.

2005 Season
Len Coleman, Captain
Tom Strackhouse, Captain
Sam Dwyer, Captain
15-1-1
Undefeated Regular Season
Conference Champions
Somerset County Champions

Pingry repeats as champs

BOYS SOCCER
SOMERSET COUNTY TOURNAMENT
PINGRY 2
BRIDGEWATER-RARITAN 0

By MINDY DREXEL
Staff Writer

BERNARDS — Pingry School senior Lenny Coleman and Bridgewater-Raritan sophomore Matt Kassel knew each other well.

Although this is the first time this season the two schools have played each other, Coleman and Kassel have faced each other many times over the years while attending soccer camps.

Coleman had the last laugh Saturday when he shut down Kassel as the second-seeded Pingry boys soccer team won the Somerset County Tournament final 2-0 over top-seeded Bridgewater-Raritan at Ridge High School.

"I've known Kassel from outside of school, so I knew he was a good"... Pingry coach Miller Bugliari said. "That's as good of a throw-in as you can see. He's throwing the"...

With fewer than seven minutes left in the game, it was Kassel's turn to experience a close miss. Wide open, Kassel received a cross...

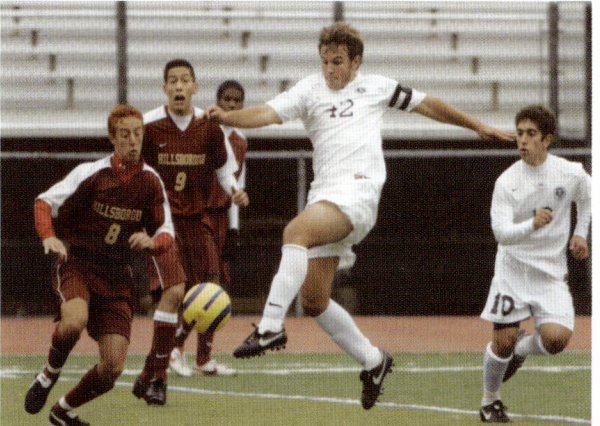

Hall of Fame to induct Pingry coach Bugliari

Staff report

BOYS SOCCER

ONEONTA, N.Y. — Miller Bugliari, who has guided the boys soccer team at The Pingry School for 45 years, has been selected as the 41st member of the Hall of Fame of the National Soccer Coaches Association of America, the nation's largest coaching organization.

"Miller has been an outstanding role model for coaches through his success along the sideline and in the coaches association," said NSCAA President Schellas Hyndman, the coach at Southern Methodist University. "Along with his incredible coaching record, he has been our president, has been a member of the NSCAA Board of Directors and has served as an important guiding light for us."

A Pingry graduate, Bugliari was... That same year, he was inducted into the National High School Federation Hall of Fame.

Bugliari is a 1958 graduate of Springfield College, where he played for legendary coach and fellow NSCAA Hall of Famer Irv Schmid. He also has a master's from New York University.

Bugliari will be inducted at the annual NSCAA Awards Banquet on Jan. 20, 2006, as a part of the association's annual convention in Philadelphia. He will be enshrined in the NSCAA Hall of Fame exhibit at the National Soccer Hall of Fame in Oneonta, N.Y., in August.

The 2006 Season

It's rare for a 20th-ranked team with a 10-2-2 regular season record to win a county title, let alone a state championship. But that's exactly what the young, relatively inexperienced 2006 team managed to do, in spite of injuries to three of its senior leaders, captains Jeff Zimering and Kim Kimber IV and defensive leader Nick Devers.

Other key players included senior captains Austin Lan and Richard Bradley, plus juniors J.P. Patrizio, David Miller, Eric Hynes, and a new starting goalkeeper, Grant Schonberg. A very strong sophomore group included Matt Rybak, Brendan Burgdorf, Eric Oplinger, David Louria, and two players whose last names were all too familiar to Pingry opponents: Matt Fechter and Will Stamatis. Three freshman also started or made important contributions as the season progressed: Tyler Smith, Andrew LaFontaine, and Scott Keogh.

Heading into the post-season, Miller remarked, "I think we've peaked the last few years during the tournament. This is a new, younger team and we don't know how they're going to react." Both Miller and Pingry's opponents found out. Pingry rolled past Montgomery 6-1 in the county quarter-finals and defeated Bernards 2-0 in the semifinals. In spite of being limited by an ankle injury, Zimering, whose 23 goals led the 2006 offense, provided both goals on assists from Fechter.

The county final against Hillsborough was played in a gusting, swirling wind on a fast field that made it hard for both teams to play their game. Hynes scored both of Pingry's goals on assists from Austin Lan and Fechter. Hillsborough's two opportunistic scores, the last coming with two minutes left in regulation, sent the game into two 10-minute overtimes, which were interrupted when the lights on the field, set to a timer, went out, causing a 10-minute delay. After 100 minutes of soccer ended in a deadlock, the teams were declared co-champions – for Pingry, its third consecutive Somerset County championship.

In the Non-Public A North quarter-finals against No. 3-ranked and top-seeded Seton Hall, which had eliminated Pingry the previous year, Zimering scored Pingry's only goal on a direct kick off a Fechter feed in the 12th minute. From then on the story was all Grant Schonberg. The newspaper write-up said, "[Schonberg] stoned a harried Seton Hall attack for the rest of the game." His acrobatic saves turned away 15 Seton Hall shots. "We…needed a great effort from Grant," Zimering said. "He was just phenomenal." In previous years, Delbarton had dealt Pingry some frustrating – and questionable – losses. This year, another strong defensive effort and goals by Zimering and Hynes, on Keogh's assist, took Pingry through the semifinals.

In the Non-Public A North finals, it was Kimber's turn to shine. He had been crippled with injuries much of the season, but against third-seeded Don Bosco Prep, in a hotly contested, physically bruising game that threatened to get out of hand, Miller turned to Kimber and said, "Win the game for us," and he did, with a game-tying goal late in regulation and a clinching penalty kick in the shootout. Once again, Schonberg stood tall in the goal, making back-to-back saves.

That brought Pingry another state championship showdown with Christian Brothers Academy, and another defensive gem for Pingry. This time it was Fechter's turn to provide the game-winner, and his 30-yard blast gave Pingry a 1-0 lead. Kimber deflected CBA's best chance, tracking back to clear what would have been a sure goal, and once again Schonberg turned away CBA's other shots.

Schonberg, Zimering, and Lan were selected for the Somerset County First Team, and Kimber, Hynes, Bradley, and Devers also received post-season recognition.

If you never saw Kim Kimber's acrobatic flip throw-in, you need to look at the movie of the 2006 Hillsborough game on the Pingry Soccer Facebook page. It's not just that the move takes incredible athletic agility just to perform it – mastering the move required long hours of hard work. But in some ways it captures the spirit of Kimber, whose career and life were tragically cut short with his death in 2009. Part of his unique quality as a player and person was his irrepressible spirit and love of the game, and part was just his style and flair. Most important, his flip throw-in was a demonstration of his passion to win. The flip throw-in was a weapon that could turn an out-of-bounds ball in the opponent's end into a corner kick. Going into the Don Bosco game, Kimber had said, "We just keep battling. Why not us?" That's how he played the game.

Kim Kimber IV '07

David Fahey, *Assistant Coach*
Mike DeGrande, *Assistant Coach*
John Rhodes, *Assistant Coach*
Kevin Schmidt, *Assistant Coach*
Andrew Babbit, *Manager*

Babcock, C.	Keogh, S.	Patrizio, J.
Bradley, R.	Kimber, K.	Ramirez, C.
Burchenal, C.	LaFontaine, A.	Rybak, M.
Burgdorf, B.	Lan, A.	Schonberg, G.
Constantino, J.	Louria, D.	Sellinger, R.
Devers, N.	Markoff, S.	Smith, T.
Fechter, M.	Maxwell, R.	Stamatis, W.
Feldman, T.	Miller, D.	Starr, C.
Freedman, J.	Oplinger, E.	Zimering, J.
Hynes, E.	Palmer, G.	

Pingry wins state title on rare goal by Fechter

Pingry gains SCT top seed

2006 Season
Richard Bradley, Captain
Kim Kimber, Captain
Austin Lan, Captain
Jeff Zimering, Captain
16-2-2
Conference Champions
Somerset County Champions
Non-Public A State Champions

The 2007 Season

The 2006 team was a young squad that had to find itself; the 2007 team, despite its youth, was a veteran group set on repeating as county and state champions. Offensively, returning starter and captain Eric Hynes set the pace with 17 goals, with solid contributions from juniors Will Stamatis, Matt Fechter, and Brendan Burgdorf. The team's greatest strength, however, was its defense. The 2007 team had to replace defensive stalwarts Austin Lan, Nick Devers, and Richard Bradley. "It's surprising," Miller noted, "that we lost all that talent and came back with a decent team."

The defense was led by returning goalkeeper captain Grant Schonberg, who capped off a brilliant two-year career by allowing just two goals in the regular season while recording 15 shutouts. Playing in front of him in Pingry's 3-5-2 alignment were returning sophomore starters Scott Keogh at sweeper, and Tyler Smith and junior Conor Starr as marking backs. Senior co-captains David Miller and J.P. Patrizio anchored a highly talented midfield group that included juniors Fechter, Burgdorf, Matt Rybak, David Louria, Eric Oplinger, and Todd Feldman, and returning sophomore starter Andrew LaFontaine. Two freshmen, Matt Sheeleigh and Randy Falk, also made important contributions coming off the bench.

In the county tournament finals, as they had in 2005, Pingry faced Group IV champion Bridgewater-Raritan and Gatorade Player of the Year Matt Kassel. Before the game, Kassel commented, "[The county championship] is the one thing we haven't won since I've been here. It'd be nice to finally get it my senior year." Kassel had scored 103 goals in his high school career. In spite of tight marking by Pingry's defense, he added two more in the championship game to give Bridgewater-Raritan a one-goal lead after Rybak had opened the scoring for Pingry with 33:04 left in the second half. Unfortunately for Kassel and Bridgewater-Raritan, Eric Hynes matched Kassel's output, and his two goals gave Pingry a hard-fought 3-2 win and its fourth straight Somerset County title.

Thinking back to the previous year's tie with Hillsborough, Hynes said, "That left a bad taste with us. We wanted to win it outright. This feels great. To win a county championship is a terrific feeling. We didn't want to settle for anything less this year." But the victory was also a capstone experience for Pingry's defense, especially Rybak, LaFontaine, Smith, and Keogh. "Everybody on this team stepped up tonight," said Keogh. "It wasn't just one person. It was an entire unit. I'm so proud this team has won four straight titles."

After locking down a conference championship by beating eighth-ranked Morris Catholic 3-1, Pingry powered through the county tournament, disposing of Gill St. Bernards in the quarter-finals and defeating a tough Somerville team 2-0 on Fechter's first-half direct kick and Keogh's penalty kick after Fechter had been taken down inside the 18-yard line on a breakaway.

Going into the Non-Public A tournament, fifth-ranked Pingry boasted a glittering 16-0 record. Its quarter-final opponent, 14th-ranked Pope John, came in at 17-1-2. Both teams fought through regulation and two overtimes without scoring, sending the game into penalty kicks. This time, Pope John converted three of their chances while Starr and Keogh were the only scorers for Pingry.

All-County and All-Area First Team awards went to Schonberg, Hynes, and Fechter, and Keogh, Rybak, and Stamatis were also honored. A Second Team All-State selection as a junior, Schonberg was named the top goalkeeper on the 2007 All-State First Team.

Grant Schonberg completed a stellar two-year career by being named the Somerset County Player of the Year. Sitting behind Mark Garcia, Schonberg got little playing time as a freshman and sophomore. "I just watched and soaked in the tradition," he said. "By the time junior year came around, my adrenaline was pumping and I was so ready to play. There's just something about playing for Pingry. I wanted to do my best every time I stepped on the field."

Grant Schonberg '08

THE LIFE & TIMES OF MILLER A. BUGLIARI

David Fahey, *Assistant Coach*
Anthony Trippichio, *Assistant Coach*
Mike DeGrande, *Assistant Coach*
Andrew Babbit, *Manager*

Babcock, C.	Keogh, S.	Patrizio, J.
Burgdorf, B.	LaFontaine, A.	Pinke, W.
Devers, N.	Louria, D.	Rybak, M.
Elkind, D.	Markoff, S.	Sartorius, A.
Falk, R.	Martin, P.	Schonberg, G.
Fechter, M.	McNulty, K.	Sheeleigh, M.
Feldman, T.	Miller, D.	Smith, T.
Hellauer, C.	Oplinger, E.	Stamatis, W.
Hynes, E.	Palmer, G.	Starr, C.

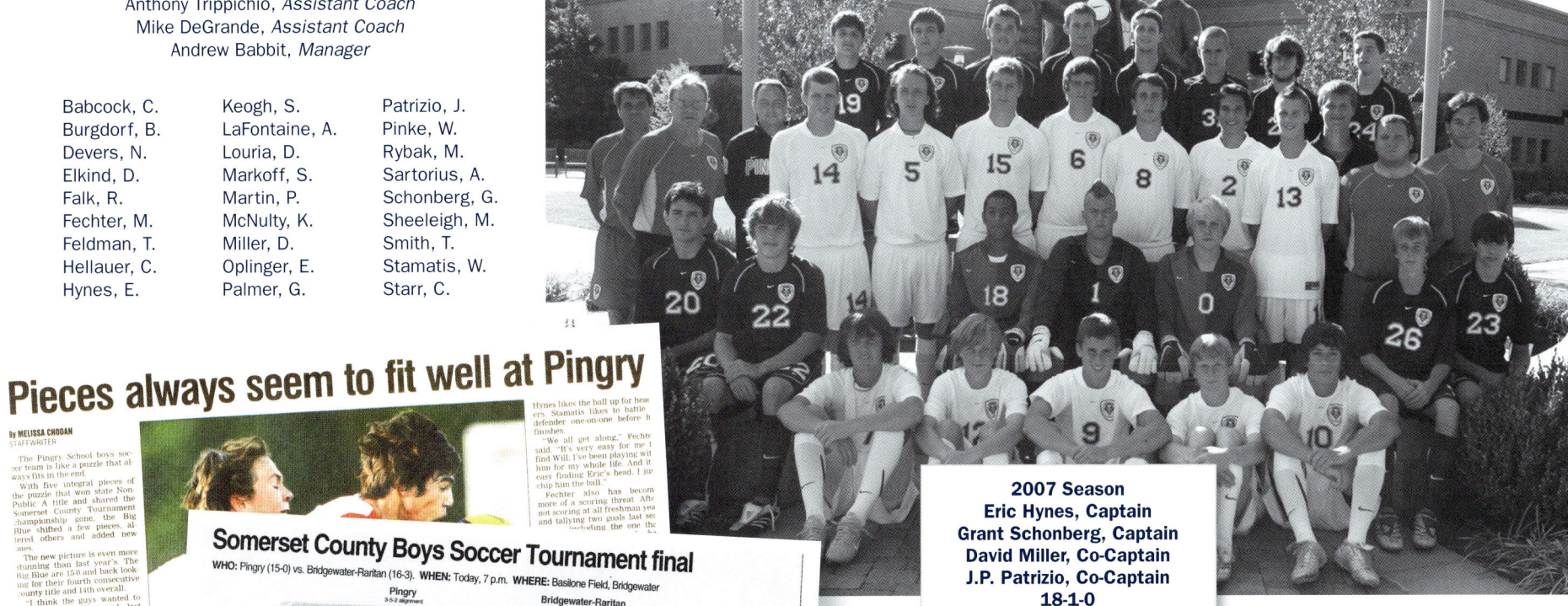

2007 Season
Eric Hynes, Captain
Grant Schonberg, Captain
David Miller, Co-Captain
J.P. Patrizio, Co-Captain
18-1-0
Undefeated Regular Season
Conference Champions
Somerset County Champions

Pieces always seem to fit well at Pingry

By MELISSA CHOGAN
STAFF WRITER

The Pingry School boys soccer team is like a puzzle that always fits in the end.

With five integral pieces of the puzzle that won state Non-Public A title and shared the Somerset County Tournament championship gone, the Big Blue are 15-0 and back looking for their fourth consecutive county title and 14th overall.

"I think the guys wanted to emulate what happened last year," Pingry coach Miller Bugliari said. "It's surprising that we lost all that talent and came back with a decent team."

The Big Blue have been more than decent, allowing only two goals this season while tallying 71.

"I think a lot of kids that didn't get a chance last season that wanted to worked really hard after last season knowing that they have a shot," senior striker Eric Hynes said. "They've done great. It's been tough shoes to fill."

Hynes likes the ball up for headers. Stamatis likes to battle defender one-on-one before he finishes.

"We all get along," Fechte said. "It's very easy for me t find Will. I've been playing wit him for my whole life. And it easy finding Eric's head. I ju chip him the ball."

Fechter also has becom more of a scoring threat Afte not scoring at all freshman yea and tallying two goals last sea

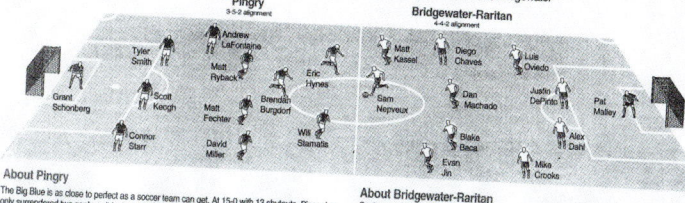

Somerset County Boys Soccer Tournament final

WHO: Pingry (15-0) vs. Bridgewater-Raritan (16-3). WHEN: Today, 7 p.m. WHERE: Basilone Field, Bridgewater

About Pingry
The Big Blue is as close to perfect as a soccer team can get. At 15-0 with 13 shutouts, Pingry has only surrendered two goals as it looks for its fourth straight county title. The strength of the team starts in the back with keeper Grant Schonberg. It works its way up with a solid 3-5-2 formation. Scott Keogh took over at sweeper for Austin Lan this year, with Connor Starr and Tyler Smith as the squad's marking backs. The Big Blue's entire midfield is quick and reads the field well. Matt Fechter, a center-midfielder, leads the team with 14 goals. Most of Fechter's goals were assisted by strikers Eric Hynes and Will Stamatis. Both have 15 goals this season.

About Bridgewater-Raritan
Senior center-midfielder/striker Matt Kassel leads Somerset County in scoring and does not need a good look or touch to find the back of the net. The Big Blue defense should be his toughest match of the season. But with a target on Kassel's back, it frees up a number of other talented players that have proven they can score as the Panthers go for their first title since 2003. Sam Nepveux has tallied a few goals for the Panthers, as have Evan Jin and Dan Machado. Pat Malley will be starting in goal with Alex Dahl and Justin DePinto as the stopper-sweeper combination in front of him.

Superstar Captains Schonberg and Hynes Lead Boys' Soccer to Successful Season

By GIANCARLO RHOTTO (V),
EVAN ROSENMAN (VI), and
MEREDITH SKIBA (V)

The Pingry Varsity Boys' Soccer team has again continued a tradition of winning and success. Last year, the team took home a county co-championship and a Non-Public A State Championship after outplaying Seton Hall Prep, Delbarton, Don Bosco, and Christian Brothers. Even after losing five critical seniors from last year – Jeff Zimering, Austin Lan, Richard Bradley, Kim Kimber, and Nick Devers – the team still won their fourth consecutive Somerset County championship with a 3-2 win over Bridgewater-Raritan with goals by captain Eric Hynes (VI) and Matt Rybak (V).

As the season comes to a close with an impressive current record of 17-1, the team has garnered attention on both a state-wide and national level.

In the conference, the team has managed to improve on last year's terrific season. After losing to Morris Catholic in a close match last year, they defeated them in a 3-1 contest at home earlier in the season. The team also defeated Montclair Kimberly Academy, whom they tied last year, by "sweeping" the season series in 1-0 and 6-0 victories. The first of those games went into overtime, with the team finally emerging triumphant with a goal from Brendan Burgdorf (V).

The offense has been fueled by the strong playing of Hynes, Will Stamatis (V), and Matt Fechter (V), all highly skilled players who put their creativity to use on the field.

The team's stronghold, however, has been its highly praised defense. Anchored by goalie and captain Grant Schonberg (VI), let in only four goals all season – two in conference games versus Morris Catholic and Kinnelon and two shot by Bridgewater-Raritan's Matt Kassel, one of the state's top players, in the county finals. The skillful defense of senior co-captain David Miller has been key, while the playing of juniors Conor Starr, Brendan Burgdorf, Matt Rybak, and Todd Feldman, and sophomores Scott Keough, Tyler Smith, and Andrew LaFontaine frustrated opponents, rarely allowing them to get quality shots on the goal or even to possess the ball.

In the course of the boys' success, they rallied the entire school with team spirit and excitement. Students and faculty turned out in huge numbers to support the team at the County Finals and the State Game.

Despite the team's strength and dedication, they suffered a heart-breaking loss to Pope John during the second round of the state tournament. Although there was a terrific effort from seniors J.P. Patrizio, Hynes, and Miller, the game was still scoreless after double overtime and was ultimately decided in penalty kicks. Despite this outcome, student pride in the soccer players remains palpable, and the entire community celebrates the soccer team as a great source of inspiration and strength. As longtime coach Miller Bugliari says, "Winning the county finals was a wonderful achievement for this year's team. I am so proud of how they played that it was tough to stop one of the best players in the country. The playing of Grant Schonberg, Eric Hynes, and David Miller was extraordinary."

SCT BOYS SOCCER
PINGRY 2,
SOMERVILLE 0

Physical defense propels Big Blue

By JERRY CARINO
STAFF WRITER

BERNARDS — With each passing game, The Pingry School boys soccer team's defense looks more and more like a brick wall.

Just ask Somerville, which ran smack into it in Saturday's Somerset County Tournament semifinals.

Recording its 13th shutout of the season, top-seeded Pingry (14-0) toughed out a 2-0 win and will play for its fourth straight county title against second-seeded Bridgewater-Raritan next Saturday. It promises to be the toughest test yet for Pingry, because Bridgewater-Raritan senior Matt Kassel is the state's most polished goal-scorer.

"This is our tournament," Pingry goalkeeper Grant Schonberg said. "When teams come in here, they're coming

The **2008** Season

Going into his senior year, captain Will Stamatis summed up how he and the other seniors felt about the season. "So many factors were at work. We had a lot of talent coming back; we were very upset at losing in the first round of the states last year; Coach was in his 50th year at the school (and approaching his 700th victory). The stars were aligned for something great to happen." And that's exactly how the season played out.

Pingry put together a 19-0-1 season, ending up as the only undefeated team in New Jersey, tying nationally ranked Chaminade of New York 0-0, winning an unprecedented fifth straight county championship and the NJSIAA Non-Public A state crown, and claiming its second *Star-Ledger* trophy as the No. 1 team in the state and the 11th-ranked team in the nation.

Senior forwards Brendan Burgdorf (20 goals and 15 assists) and Stamatis (20 goals and 13 assists) and "super sub" sophomores Eric Schoenbach (8 goals and 4 assists) and Matt Sheeleigh led an offensive effort that averaged more than four goals a game, with 14 different players scoring at least once during the season. Pingry's midfield, with seniors captain Matt Fechter (6 goals and 12 assists), Eric Oplinger, David Louria, and Matt Rybak, and sophomores Sheeleigh and Randy Falk, controlled the flow of the game. Pingry's two new goalkeepers, seniors Grant Palmer and Cory Babcock, combined for 15 shutouts, but the cast around them was made up of seasoned defenders: returning senior starter Conor Starr, and juniors Scott Keogh, Tyler Smith, and Andrew LaFontaine.

Pingry began the season ranked No. 2 in New Jersey and took over the top spot on October 17. "When we were ranked No.1, that put a target on our back for sure," Miller said. "And we knew from that point we were going to have to earn that ranking every day." His players clearly got the message. "At the beginning of the year," Burgdorf reflected, "all we were thinking about was Chaminade. After that, we just kept focusing on the next milestone: Coach's 700th win, counties, then states."

An undefeated season takes an extraordinary degree of team commitment, individual effort, and a little luck. Against Chaminade, the team was understandably nervous. Chaminade attacked early – and hit the goal posts twice. Then Pingry settled down, Palmer turned away the next eight shots, and both teams fought to a well-earned 0-0 tie. It would be the only game Pingry didn't win in the 2008 season.

The team got the individual effort it needed in critical games. Burgdorf's goal against Morris Catholic earned Pingry its last Colonial Hills title in Pingry's final year in the conference. Oplinger's goal in overtime disposed of Morris Catholic in the Non-Public A semifinals. Schoenbach delivered the game-winner in a 1-0 victory over Pingry's nemesis Delbarton. Smith's header provided the breakthrough goal in the county semifinals against Bridgewater-Raritan, and Stamatis' two goals broke open the state championship game against St. Augustine.

After Pingry's final game of the season, Miller summed up by saying, "Years like this don't come along very often. It truly was a wonderful and magical season." Pingry was named the *Star-Ledger* Team of the Year, Miller was named Coach of the Year, and Burgdorf was named Player of the Year. Stamatis and Burgdorf were named to the All-State First Team; Stamatis, Fechter, Keogh, and Burgdorf were selected for the All-Area and All-County First Teams; and post-season honors were also earned by Palmer, Starr, Smith, and LaFontaine.

As Brendan Burgdorf went to the sideline near the end of Pingry's county championship victory against Gill St. Bernards, the Pingry fans were chanting "MVP! MVP!" Burgdorf remembers thinking "I wasn't so sure. Eric Schoenbach had a great tournament." But based on his two goals to seal the win, the fans turned out to be right. As the post-game honors kept coming in, Burgdorf was quick to praise Miller and his staff: "I wasn't a great soccer player when I came here as a freshman."

Burgdorf started out on the varsity as a defender, but as his knowledge of the game and physical presence on the field improved, Coach Fahey moved him to striker, where he also wound up playing for his club team. "I've learned a lot over the past three years," added Burgdorf. "It's good to be a senior now and be finishing the year with Coach."

Brendan Burgdorf '09

THE LIFE & TIMES OF MILLER A. BUGLIARI

David Fahey, *Assistant Coach*
Kim Kimber III, *Assistant Coach*
Anthony Tripicchio, *Assistant Coach*
Mike DeGrande, *Assistant Coach*
Chad Butler, *Manager*

Babcock, C.	Ju, C.	O'Donnell, C.
Burchenal, W.	Keogh, S.	Palazzolo, S.
Burgdorf, B.	Key, D.	Palmer, G.
Devers, M.	LaFontaine, A.	Pinke, W.
Elkind, D.	Lieberman, A.	Porges, F.
Elliot, F.	Louria, D.	Rybak, M.
Falk, R.	Louria, S.	Sartorius, A.
Fechter, M.	Martin, P.	Schoenbach, E.
Feldman, T.	Meiring, N.	Sheeleigh, M.
Gadsden, H.	Michels, J.	Smith, T.
Hellauer, C.	Miller, S.	Stamatis, W.
Jacob, A.	Oplinger, E.	Starr, C.
Jordan, R.	O'Connell, C.	

2008 Season
Will Stamatis, Captain
Matt Fechter, Captain
19-0-1
Undefeated Season
Conference Champions
Somerset County Champions
Non-Public A State Champions

Big Blue boys earn 5th crown in row

Amazing season for No. 1 Pingry

Stamatis fuels Pingry to crown
His two goals lift No. 1 team past No. 19 St. Augustine

KEY TO SUCCESS
Burgdorf was Big Blue's on-field leader

205

The 2009 Season

The seniors on the 2009 team faced a challenge that the players from the mid-1960s, the mid-1990s, and the 2002 team would have instantly recognized: following up on an undefeated season – with the added pressure of starting the season ranked first in the state and fifth in the country. But in 2009 the stakes were significantly raised. In yet another NJSIAA reshuffling, Pingry was moved from the Colonial Hills Conference to the much tougher Skyland Conference, which meant battling against Group IV teams like Bridgewater-Raritan, Hillsborough, Watchung Hills, Hunterdon Central, Franklin, and Montgomery – opponents that Pingry used to meet only in the county tournament. In addition, while the 2008 team had the milestone of Miller's 700th victory to aim for, the 2009 team would celebrate Miller's 50th year as Pingry's coach. And they had to do it without the eight seniors, including several All-State and All-County players, from the year before.

Captained by four-year lettermen Scott Keogh, Tyler Smith, and Andrew LaFontaine, the 2009 team was a mix of veterans and promising newcomers. The starting forward positions were manned by Smith, junior Eric Schoenbach and sophomore Freddy Elliot. Juniors Matt Sheeleigh, Adam Jacob, and Randy Falk and sophomore Mael Corboz started at midfield, and seniors Keogh, LaFontaine, and Peter Martin formed the wall in front of the team's goalkeepers, senior Fred Porges and sophomore Dylan Key. Throughout the season, senior Will Pinke, junior Andrew Young, and freshmen Brian Costa and Cameron Kirdzik came off the bench to contribute to the team's success.

Against stronger competition, goals were harder to come by. Offensively Pingry was led by Smith (10 goals and 4 assists), Keogh (9 goals and 7 assists), Sheeleigh (9 goals and 6 assists), Schoenbach (9 goals and 3 assists), Elliot (8 goals and 2 assists), and Corboz (12 assists). In its first year in the Skylands Conference the team won its division with a 7-0 record, shutting out Hillsborough, Watchung Hills, and Immaculata.

In the county tournament, Keogh's two goals provided the 3-2 margin over Immaculata. Bernards came into the semifinal match riding an 11-game winning streak. Pingry's 4-1 victory, with two goals from Smith and one apiece from Sheeleigh and Elliot, put an end to that run. In the final against familiar foe Bridgewater-Raritan, played in a steady, drenching rain, Elliot's goal at 17:34 in the first half gave Pingry a 1-0 lead, which Bridgewater-Raritan was able to equalize four minutes into the second half. For the rest of the game, Pingry pressured hard, and thought they had a win when Elliot lined a pass from Corboz, driving Bridgewater-Raritan goalkeeper Travis Ives back across the line. The referee disagreed. The game ended, after two overtimes, in a 1-1 tie, making Pingry co-champions – Pingry's sixth consecutive title. Against Pope John in the opening round of the Non-Public tournament, a goal late in the first overtime left Pingry on the wrong end of a 1-0 score.

The 2009 team worked hard to win their conference and county tournaments, in a 16-1-0 season in which they held on to the top ranking in the state and a Top 10 ranking in the nation until their last game. Keogh was named to the All-State First Team and was joined by Smith on the All-County First Team. Keogh was also named the Somerset County Player of the Year.

Halfway through the season, with Pingry at the 10-0 mark against Skylands Conference competition, captain Scott Keogh said, "It's definitely different, a lot bigger schools, a lot bigger kids, and more athletic kids. It's been pretty good so far. I'm having more fun because the teams are definitely tough. To be able to come here and play for a coach like Miller Bugliari is just incredible. I didn't understand what all the tradition was about when I first came here. I do now. Going to school and being a member of the soccer program makes you not only a better player but a better person. [Coach] has been through so many teams and you forget about it sometimes because he makes you feel like you're the only team he ever had."

Scott Keogh '10

Anthony Tripicchio, *Assistant Coach*
Brad Fechter, *Assistant Coach*
Chad Butler, *Manager*

Branchina, N.	Jacob, A.	Miller, S.
Burchenal, W.	Johnston, L.	O'Connell, C.
Cohen, J.	Jordan, R.	O'Donnell, C.
Corboz, M.	Kenny, E.	Pike, S.
Costa, B.	Keogh, S.	Pinke, W.
Elliot, F.	Key, D.	Porges, F.
English, M.	Kirdzik, C.	Schoenbach, E.
Falk, R.	LaFontaine, A.	Sheeleigh, M.
Fechter, C.	Lieberman, A.	Smith, T.
Flugstad-Clarke, H.	Louria, S.	Stone, M.
Gadsen, H.	Martin, A.	Valente, M.
Hamm, B.	Martin, P.	Young, A.
Homer, W.	Meiring, N.	

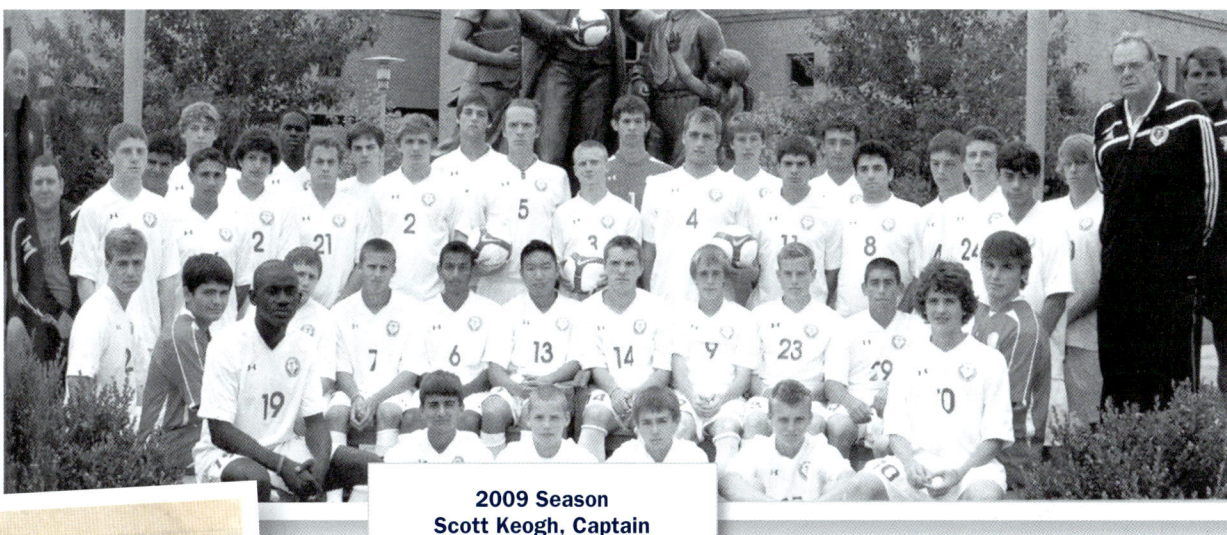

2009 Season
Scott Keogh, Captain
Andrew LaFontaine, Captain
Tyler Smith, Captain
16-1-0
Undefeated Regular Season
Conference Champions
Somerset County Champions

The Pingry Record — SPORTS, Page 8, November 30, 2009

Boys' Varsity Soccer Ends Strong Season as County Co-Champions

Pingry defensive star Keogh also achieved offensive goals

Scott Keogh of Pingry is The Star-Ledger Player of the Year in Somerset County.

Bugliari marking 50th season on the sidelines at Pingry

The 2010s: A Different World

"It still comes down to knowing and caring about the game and the kids, and doing the best you can."

MILLER, 2014

When one looks back over 50 years of Pingry soccer, the differences between 1960 and 2010 are startling. Players from the 1960s and 1970s would certainly admire the technical skill of players today, and the finesse with which they execute a controlled passing game. They would also respect the tough physical play and team defense.

But they'd instantly notice a quieter Pingry sideline. Miller doesn't yell at players the way he used to. And after a game in which Pingry didn't play well, players from previous decades would ask, probably in amazement, "Why aren't they running?"

Ask today's players about "orcas" and they might think you were talking about Sea World; ask them about "The Ring," and they would probably think you were referring to Tolkien.

There have been other changes that were, in fact, long overdue. If you read the histories of the 1964, 1985, or 1990 teams, you realize it was normal practice when a player got hit in the head and required stitches, for him to be bandaged up and come back in, or at least play the next game. Coaches and doctors are far more careful about head injuries now, and should be. No soccer victory is worth potential brain damage.

But there are less obvious cultural differences as well. Matthew Stanmyre in the October 14, 2013, *Star-Ledger* wrote:

> When high school coaches across New Jersey raise their voices at practice or punish players with wind sprints this year, the message might not be the only thing they worry about. They might also fear for their jobs.
>
> With the Anti-Bullying Bill of Rights Act in place and memories of the Mike Rice coaching scandal at Rutgers lingering, the line between motivational coaching and abusive tactics is blurrier than ever in high school sports. Shout at a player in front of teammates, hold a kid after practice for extra work or bark profanity and some parents could say their child is being bullied and prompt an investigation by the state.

Developing "Pingry Toughness"

But Pingry players still need to be able to outwork opponents late in the game and play tough defense. It just happens in different ways now. In *Best Practices for Coaching Soccer in the United States*, Bob Jenkins writes: "In general, most players this age who are playing at a competitive club level are technically good and can solve problems well in slower games or isolated situations. When the demands of the game and the speed of play increase, many have a hard time mastering the ball, staying tuned in, seeing enough, and making sense of their play. By placing players in competitive situations, i.e. faster games, these aspects improve dramatically over time." Pingry players may not run as much after practice as they used to, but in carefully designed drills as Jenkins describes, they run a lot *in* practice. "If you increase the space or tempo of a drill," says David Fahey, "you can get kids to work much harder. Emotion helps, too, in competitive drills and small-sided games where players' pride is on the line." The same holds true for developing mental and physical toughness. Today's defenders have "ritual" drills like the "pressure cooker," in which four defenders stand in the box while coaches and other players rapidly fire shots directly at them at full speed. Defenders have to stop the shot with their body and get right back up on their feet for the next ball coming in. The drill is intense, noisy – there's a lot of enthusiastic yelling going on – and incredibly physical, just like the great defense that has always been the hallmark of Pingry teams.

Looking back, some might say Miller has gone "soft" over the years. A better explanation is that he is still able to understand and adapt to the kids he coaches. Brian O'Donnell '81 explains, "You can't yell at players today. They'll just turn you off. You have to explain what you expect so they understand it." Miller now acknowledges, "I was a little more fiery as a younger coach. I try to be a little more encouraging now."

Finding Opponents to Play

The headline of Melissa Chodan's September 28, 2010, *Courier News* article on high school soccer read: "Power points system creates odd situations." In describing the NJSIAA's revised qualifying system for state tournaments, she wrote, "Skyland Conference teams have another thing to think about when playing the Pingry School boys soccer team."

A loss to Pingry, categorized as a Group I school, would cost a Group IV school three points. A Pingry victory over a Group IV school would earn Pingry eight points, but a Group IV school would only get two points for beating Pingry, a Group I school. "It doesn't make any sense," North Hunterdon coach John Simpson was quoted as saying in the *Courier News* article. "You have a school [Pingry] that's consistently in the top five in the state year in, year out, and it has the same effect as far as the point system as any other Group I school." The point system has put Pingry in a scheduling bind. After years of 7-0 or 10-0 beatings, Group I, II, and III schools are reluctant to play Pingry, and Group IV non-conference opponents are equally unwilling to schedule Pingry because of the point system. So that means Pingry is now forced to fill its schedule with Group IV Skyland Conference teams, often on a home and home basis. Miller used to be able to count on a few "breathers" in the schedule; they rarely exist now. More importantly, in the past, games against lesser opponents allowed Miller and his staff to get younger players into the game. Those development opportunities are far less frequent now.

Changing Player Opportunities

Fifty years ago, most of the best players were still learning the game in high school and preparing for professional careers in college. The 1994 USMT featured players who had developed at University of Virginia, North Carolina, UCLA, San Diego State, and Rutgers. Now the best players compete in Academy Programs and are affiliated with professional clubs instead of attending college. And the dividing line has gotten even sharper recently. The new official United States Soccer Federation's position is that high school age players may compete for their club, or their high school, but not both.

Alison Casey is the mother of Jack Casey '16. She has loved watching her son develop a passion for soccer from early childhood, and treasures the experience he is getting playing soccer for Pingry. As a parent, however, she views the USSF's requirement that players must choose between playing for their PDA club or high school soccer with dismay. "I think it's a terribly unfortunate decision for children. Jack has benefited greatly from his PDA development under coaches like Gerry McKeown. But playing for your high school team, especially Pingry, is about much more than improving your soccer skills.

"If teenage kids have to forgo high school soccer to become really skilled players, they lose out on all the other benefits I see Jack getting as a Pingry player. Coaches like Miller and David Fahey care about kids not just as soccer players, but as students developing academically and young men learning the meaning of values. You watch the camaraderie of Pingry kids working together on the team. They are developing lifelong friendships. It's hard to imagine grown men getting excited about attending the 25th reunion of their PDA team. It's the same for the soccer team parents; we become friends. And the other thing this decision takes away is kids' opportunity to experience and excel at other sports. Young people specialize early in Europe. We're a different culture; America isn't France or Germany or Spain. Jack loved basketball and had a real talent for track. He had to give all that up because of his PDA commitments. That's a loss for Jack and a loss for Pingry."

Pingry's best players, with rare exceptions, have continued to follow the more traditional path of college soccer, such as, most recently, All-American Matt Fechter '09 (Colorado College), All-Ivy selections Will Stamatis '09 (Columbia), Brian Costa '13 (Princeton), and Cameron Kirdzik '13 (Yale), Brendan Burgdorf '09 (Bucknell), Freddy Porges '10 (Hamilton College), Tyler Smith '10 (Middlebury), Scott Keough '10 (Villanova), Randy Falk '11 (Penn State), Matt Sheeleigh '11 (Harvard), Andrew Young '11 (MIT), Freddy Elliot '12 (Columbia), Mael Corboz '12 (Maryland), Henry Flugstad-Clarke '13 (Yale), and Christian Fechter '13 (Davidson). If the route to college soccer changes from high school to PDA performance, players who want to continue playing the game they love in college will be forced to concentrate on PDA soccer. Alison Casey watched Jack play in a PDA tournament this spring. "The stands were packed with college coaches," she says.

As soccer continues to evolve, one hopes that the combination of academic excellence, a deeply nurturing social and emotional team culture, superb coaching, and the chance to experience the thrill of championships will continue to draw the kinds of players who will sustain Pingry soccer's proud tradition. As for Miller, Kris Bertsch '99 said it best after Miller's 800th victory: "The reason he's been able to do it for so long is he loves interacting with kids – coaching and teaching. I think he can do it 15 more years."

Signature Victories

800th - 2014

Jamie Cook's curling direct kick into the far corner from outside the box gave Pingry a well-played, hard-fought 1-0 victory over Watchung Hills and Miller his 800th victory. "This is easily the greatest goal of my life," said Cook. "I'm glad I was able to contribute and get the 800th and do what I can to help the team." After the game, the team joined with alumni from the '60s, '70s, '80s, '90s and 2000s to celebrate with Miller.

"It's great for New Jersey coaches, it's great for Pingry, and it's great for me," said Miller. "Let's face it, the guys I coach against weren't born when I started… that's a scary thought sometimes. I know this was exciting for the coaching staff and the kids. I've got a folder full of congratulatory notes from former students, players, colleagues, and other coaches which I'll always treasure. Personally, not that it had to be this game, but you want to get it over with. I didn't want it to keep dragging on game after game, so I'm happy about that. At this point, a milestone isn't something you aim for, it's a marker along the way toward what really matters: helping my coaches and kids continue to improve this season so they achieve the best they're capable of."

The Legacy

Because Miller is so inextricably linked with Pingry soccer and the school as an institution, it might be easy to overlook the fact that for over 50 years he has played a powerful role in the growth of soccer in New Jersey – and in the United States. Perhaps Miller's strongest and farthest-reaching legacy to soccer may be the impact of his former players now making their mark in college, professional, and world soccer as coaches and executives.

Kris Bertsch '99

After helping develop the soccer programs as an assistant coach at Syracuse University and NCAA No. 1 ranked UConn, Kris was named assistant coach at Xavier University in 2011 where, in his first year, he played a crucial role in helping lead Xavier to an Atlantic 10 Championship and NCAA tournament berth, and was named NSCAA Mid-Atlantic Assistant Coach of the Year.

Bob Jenkins '80

Bob returned to coach at Pingry before embarking on a career that led to his appointment as the USSF's Director of Youth Development in the early 2000s. After a stint as Director of Coaching for the Richmond, Virginia Strikers beginning in 2008, he returned to the Federation as coach of the U.S. Under-18 Men's Team. In 2006 he wrote the U.S. Soccer Federation's highly acclaimed *Best Practices for Soccer Coaching in the United States*.

Brian O'Donnell '81

Brian established himself as one of the most successful youth coaches in the country, winning over 20 state cups and three regional championships. He joined the staff of the Sereno, Arizona Soccer Club in 2004, and now serves as its Boys Director of Coaching. In 2014 he was appointed fitness coach for the United States Under-21 Men's Team, working under head coach Tab Ramos.

Jon Pascale '93

Jon's coaching career began at the University of Pennsylvania, Georgetown, and Stanford before he became head coach at the University of California San Diego in 2008. In 2012 and 2013, he was named California Collegiate Athletic Association Coach of the Year. Since 2010, Pascale has also served as a scout for the USSF, concentrating on the Southern California region to identify potential prospects for selection to youth-level national teams.

Charlie Stillitano '77

Charlie began his career in international soccer in 1992 as the New York/New Jersey Venue Executive Director for the 1994 FIFA World Cup. Following the World Cup, he served as Vice President and General Manager of the New York/New Jersey MetroStars of Major League Soccer. He served as an inaugural board member of the U.S. Soccer Foundation from 1993 to 2007 and as its Vice Chairman for 11 years, during which time he was the principal founder and Chief Executive Officer of ChampionsWorld LLC, promoting games featuring the world's top soccer clubs, a role he now continues in as CEO of the Soccer Division at RSE Ventures, Inc.

The 2013 Rededication of the Miller A. Bugliari World Cup Soccer Field

By 2013, the Miller A. Bugliari World Cup Soccer Field had witnessed 20 championship teams and two decades of hard use and needed to be completely restored. Thanks to the leadership of another of Pingry's "First Soccer Families," the Warren Kimbers, and the additional support of the Casey, Jacob, and Mullett families, the World Cup Field received a dramatic renovation, including the entire reconstruction of the subsurface and drainage, the laying of new sod, and – for the first time – new permanent seating built right into the terraced hillside. The refurbished field was dedicated in 2013 to the late Warren "Kimmy" Kimber IV '07, whose life tragically ended in 2009.

"Kimmy" Kimber was one of those rare people who brighten the lives of everyone they meet. Like his father, Kim Kimber III '76, he was a superbly gifted natural athlete who excelled at all sports. He was an intense competitor, but even more than that, he had an irrepressible love simply of playing the game with infectious joy. "He was a game changer," remembers Miller. "Whenever he entered a game, the excitement level instantly jumped to a high level."

Lots of athletes, even good ones, second-guess themselves and hold back – almost as if they are afraid of their own greatness in big moments. That was never a problem for Kimmy. He lived exuberantly in the moment. At the October 5, 2013, rededication of the World Cup Field in Kim Kimber IV's memory, Miller became deeply emotional in paying tribute to the player he loved. "What a great teacher and coach he would have been. What an outstanding player and athlete he was. In my mind, he is always on this field, and this dedication recognizes and acknowledges all that he meant to us, his family and friends."

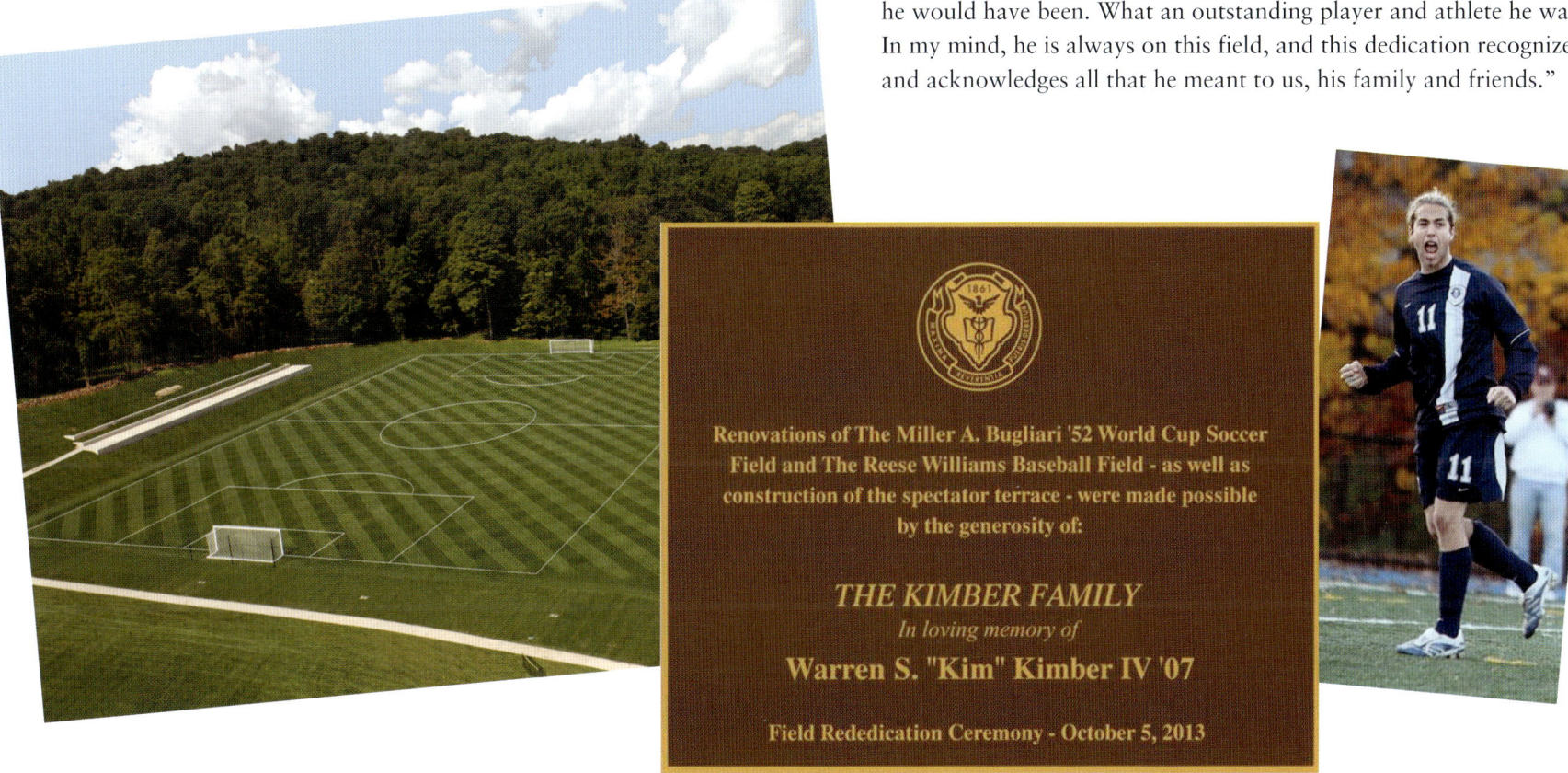

Renovations of The Miller A. Bugliari '52 World Cup Soccer Field and The Reese Williams Baseball Field - as well as construction of the spectator terrace - were made possible by the generosity of:

THE KIMBER FAMILY
In loving memory of
Warren S. "Kim" Kimber IV '07

Field Rededication Ceremony - October 5, 2013

The 2010 Season

Because Pingry had graduated so many top players, sports writers wrote off the 2010 team at the start of the season as a championship contender. Senior Randy Falk, speaking for the team, had a different perspective. "I know that we can accomplish anything we can set our minds to. We've got a really talented group of underclassmen that will help the seniors do great things this season."

Pingry was led by four senior captains: Falk and Eric Schoenbach as strikers, midfielder Adam Jacob, and defender Matt Sheeleigh. Joining them as starters were junior midfielders Mael Corboz and Freddy Elliot, senior defenders Andrew Young and Henry Gadsden, sophomores Christian Fechter, Cameron Kirdzik, Henry Flugstad-Clarke, and Brian Costa, and freshman Matt Mangini in Pingry's 4-4-2 alignment. Junior Dylan Key returned in goal.

Pingry powered through its regular season, defeating its Group IV Delaware Division Skylands Conference opponents Hunterdon Central, Franklin, North Hunterdon, and Watchung Hills by identical 2-0 scores. Over the season the defense recorded 10 shutouts and limited their powerful opposition to just nine goals in an 18-2-1 season.

Entering the Somerset County Tournament as the top seed, 13-0 Pingry polished off Bernards 4-1 on sophomore striker Cameron Kirdzik's hat trick. In the finals, Pingry faced a familiar foe, Bridgewater-Raritan, which had tied Pingry in the previous year's championship game 1-1. Pingry scored first on Falk's penalty kick. Bridgewater-Raritan equalized 11 minutes into the second half, also on a penalty kick. Then Falk took over the game. After Schoenbach dribbled by two defenders, he passed the ball to an unmarked Falk, who blasted a 35-yard rocket past Bridgewater-Raritan's startled goalkeeper. Falk's third goal of the game gave Pingry the win and its record-breaking seventh consecutive Somerset County title.

In the opening round of the state tournament, Pingry blistered DePaul 5-0 on Falk's hat trick. Key only needed to make three saves. That brought a sectional semifinal Non-Public A match against another familiar opponent, undefeated Seton Hall, the No. 1-ranked team in the state. The headline read "No. 4 Pingry jars No. 1 Seton Hall."

The two teams fought for 100 minutes without either team being able to score against the other's tenacious defense. In the resulting shootout, goalkeeper Key came up huge, turning away three of Seton Hall's penalty kicks, while Jacob, Corboz, and Falk each connected to give Pingry the win.

For the North sectional championship, Pingry met yet another familiar nemesis, Delbarton, the first-seeded team in the tournament. This time there was no chance for a missed call. Pingry's 3-1 victory made them North sectional champions. The only team that remained to beat was St. Augustine, which Pingry had lost to in 1991 and beaten in 2008.

St. Augustine shocked Pingry in the third minute when Connor Hurff slipped a shot past Key in the right corner. Falk had entered the game with a team-high 15 goals. Against St. Augustine he was limited to just two shots. Thirty seconds into the second half Pingry conceded another goal, and while the team responded in the second half with much greater intensity, Pingry still was shut out 2-0.

The loss in the state tournament didn't dim the luster of a season in which Pingry wound up rated the No. 2 team in the state by the *Star-Ledger*.

Falk, Sheeleigh, Schoenbach, and Key were selected for the All-County First Team, with Elliot and Corboz also being honored.

Matt Sheeleigh's soccer background was like that of most outstanding Pingry players. While his speed on the ball and effortless skill might lead an observer to think he was just a naturally gifted athlete, the reality is that he had been playing for a top club, the Players' Development Academy, since he was nine years old. With PDA he had competed in most states in the country and in Mexico, Holland, Germany, Italy, Scotland, England, Ireland, and Spain. But for Sheeleigh, as for so many other Pingry players with years of club soccer competition, the team experience that mattered was his time playing for Pingry. "The thing I will miss most about high school soccer," the Harvard-bound Sheeleigh said at the end of the season, "is the brotherhood. The amount of pride, confidence, tradition, history, and support behind the men's program at our school is unmatched."

Matt Sheeleigh '11

THE LIFE & TIMES OF MILLER A. BUGLIARI

Anthony Tripicchio, *Assistant Coach*
Brad Fechter, *Assistant Coach*
Tom Strackhouse, *Assistant Coach*

Bianco, S.	Gadsden, H.	Mangini, M.
Chan, M.	Green, J.	Martin, A.
Cohen, J.	Homer, W.	Pike, S.
Corboz, M.	Hugin, J.	Schoenbach, E.
Costa, B.	Jacob, A.	Sheeleigh, M.
Eboh, K.	Johnston, L.	Skinner, H.
Elliot, F.	Kenny, E.	Sullivan, N.
English, M.	Key, D.	Wright, T.
Falk, R.	Kirdzik, C.	Young, A.
Fechter, C.	Lipper, M.	
Flugstad-Clarke, H.	Louria, S.	

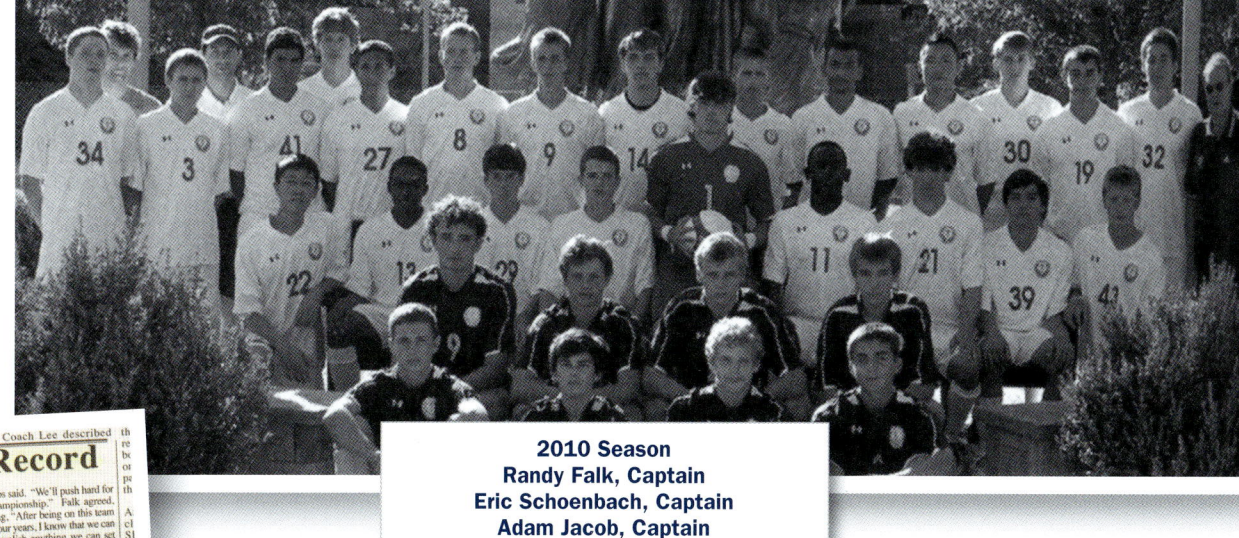

2010 Season
Randy Falk, Captain
Eric Schoenbach, Captain
Adam Jacob, Captain
Matt Sheeleigh, Captain
18-2-1
Conference Champions
Somerset County Champions
Non-Public A Sectional State Champions

Varsity Boys' Soccer Has Undefeated Record

By ANDREW ADLER (III)

This season, boys' Varsity Soccer has bolted forward with hopes of reaching the state championship. So far, the team is undefeated with a record of 7-0.

Coach Miller Bugliari has been coaching boys' Varsity Soccer for 51 years, and this year, like so many others, is shaping up to be a promising one.

Despite these setbacks, captains Adam Jacobs (VI), Matt Sheeleigh (VI), Randy Falk (VI), and Eric Schoenbach (VI), who have each played on Varsity for four years, are leading the team to another successful season. Even after losing valuable players from the schools they play are much larger than Pingry.

Jacobs said, "We'll push hard for a championship." Falk agreed, saying, "After being on this team for four years, I know that we can accomplish anything we can set our minds to. We've got a really talented group of underclassmen that will helps the seniors do great things this season."

Although the team may have

Boys' Soccer Wins County and Sectional Championships

overtime. Goalkeeper Dylan Key (V) stopped the three penalties he faced, and Pingry prevailed. "Dylan was huge for us in that game," said junior Mael Corboz. "To stop that many penalty kicks is really rare, and he did a fantastic job."

The sectional state finals took place on November 11th at Passaic Valley Tech, the same location as the state game against Delbarton in 2008. Even though Delbarton scored within the first minute, Pingry roared back and held them to just that goal. The final score was 3-1, and Pingry came away with

Freddy Elliot (V) stealing the ball.   B. Morrison '64

By ANDREW ADLER (III)

Falk (three goals) helps Pingry secure SCT title

BOYS SOCCER
By Carolyn Freundlich
FOR THE STAR-LEDGER

Senior Randy Falk decided to take a risk when Pingry lost its edge.

"I had my eye on the goal after they scored on the PK," the forward said, referring to the game-tying penalty kick. "I knew it would take something special to make it happen, so I went for it and it happened to go in. If I didn't take that risk,

lead with nine on the season, opened the scoring with a safer shot. After getting tripped up in the penalty box at the 20-minute mark, Falk converted the penalty kick to give Pingry a 1-0 advantage at intermission.

After the break, Bridgewater made an offensive push, firing five shots on net before connecting.

Derek Luke scored on a penalty kick 11 minutes into the second half to knot the

No. 4 Pingry jars No. 1 Seton Hall

Adam Jacob, Mael Corboz and Randy Falk each connected on a penalty kick and goalie Dylan Key came up big in goal as Pingry, No. 4 in The Star-Ledger Top 20, earned a shootout victory over No. 1 Seton Hall Prep

The 2011 Season

By 2011 Pingry's returning players knew what they were facing: they had to get through the meat grinder of a Skylands Conference schedule and then have enough left in the tank to battle through the county and state tournaments. Getting a top seed in Somerset County was also critical, since the top team got a double bye in the tournament and had to play three games, not five.

Returning starters included the team's four senior captains, returning All-County goalkeeper Dylan Key, midfielder Mael Corboz, defender Andrew Martin, and striker Freddy Elliot. "We're going to have to work hard to win our conference, counties, and states," acknowledged Elliot at the midpoint of the season, with Pingry's record still a perfect 11-0. "Each game gives us a chance to play together and gain more chemistry," added Key. "From freshmen to seniors, we all have each other's backs."

The team's chemistry was evident in its offensive production. Through the season, seven different players – Elliot, Corboz, Cameron Kirdzik, Henry Flugstad-Clarke, Brian Costa, Matt Mangini, and Christian Fechter – provided the scoring punch that resulted in another undefeated regular season. For the team, the most rewarding of these victories was Miller's 750th career victory, 2-1 over Bridgewater-Raritan on Elliot's goal off a Costa assist with one minute left in regulation. Defensively, Key recorded 12 clean sheets and the defense yielded just eight goals in the season.

In the county tournament, Corboz's hat trick triggered a 9-0 romp over Bound Brook, and Kirdzik's clutch goal in overtime gave Pingry a 1-0 victory over Montgomery, which Pingry had beaten 3-1 in the regular season. Whether the schedule was taking a toll, or teams were learning how to exploit Pingry's weaknesses, return engagements weren't easy against Skylands Conference opponents. In the county championship, Bridgewater-Raritan, which had run off a string of 17 victories since losing to Pingry on September 15, gave Pingry its first loss of the season, 3-1. Pingry held an 18-4 advantage in shots, but Bridgewater's goalkeeper Alex Kaminetzky had a career day with nine saves. Bridgewater went out in front 1-0 in the 16th minute, then bunkered in, and as Pingry pushed forward in numbers to equalize, Bridgewater scored twice more on counter-attacks.

More misfortune awaited in the state tournament. Pingry beat Marist 10-0 and then fought past Bergen Catholic 1-0, when Elliot converted on Mangini's pass. That brought Pingry head-to-head against a team that had given Pingry more than its share of heartbreaks, Delbarton.

After a tense but scoreless first half, Delbarton went on top on Matt Clausen's goal off an assist by Greg Seifert. Getting a lead against Pingry, however, has never been any guarantee of victory. Mael Corboz added his name to the long list of heroic Pingry efforts when he converted on a penalty kick in the last minute to tie the game, to the joyful celebration of the Pingry home crowd. The teams battled through two overtime periods to send the 1-1 game into penalty kicks. Then what had been a fiercely contested battle between two well-matched teams turned into a guessing game. Delbarton's final 4-3 edge stilled the jubilant Pingry crowd and brought a disappointing end to what had been a glorious season.

Corboz was selected to the All-State First Team and was named, with Key, Elliot and Martin, to All-County and All-Conference First Teams. Flugstad-Clarke and Kirdzik also received post-season honors.

"What was it like playing for Miller? He was terrific in the way he'd understand what you needed to work on as a player, even if you were already pretty skilled and experienced as I was. In my case it was developing the strength to shoot more accurately from a distance. But he gave every player that kind of constant guidance and support. The other thing is his extraordinary kindness, generosity and concern. I remember him getting mad at the starters when we didn't put teams away we should have beaten easily, because he wanted to use those games to get game time for the kids who weren't starters, or who might not otherwise even get into a game. Another thing that stands out is his steadiness. He was always calm with us before a game, whether it was a weaker team or a championship final. The message you got is that he believed in you and trusted you.

"And finally, his concern doesn't stop when you leave Pingry. I talk with him every two weeks or so just to stay in touch and get the value of his insight."

Mael Corboz '12

David Fahey, *Assistant Coach*
Brad Fechter, *Assistant Coach*
Kim Kimber III, *Assistant Coach*
Mike Coughlin, *Assistant Coach*

Bianco, S.	Green, J.	Martin, A.
Chan, M.	Haltmaier, B.	Monteagudo, L.
Corboz, M.	Helfman, M.	Moore-Gillon, C.
Costa, B.	Hugin, J.	Patrizio, M.
DeAlmeida, R.	Key, D.	Rakhit, R.
Eboh, K.	Kirdzik, C.	Skinner, H.
Elliot, F.	Lipper, M.	Sullivan, N.
Fechter, C.	Lurie, M.	Thompson, H.
Flugstad-Clarke, H.	Mangini, M.	Wright, T.

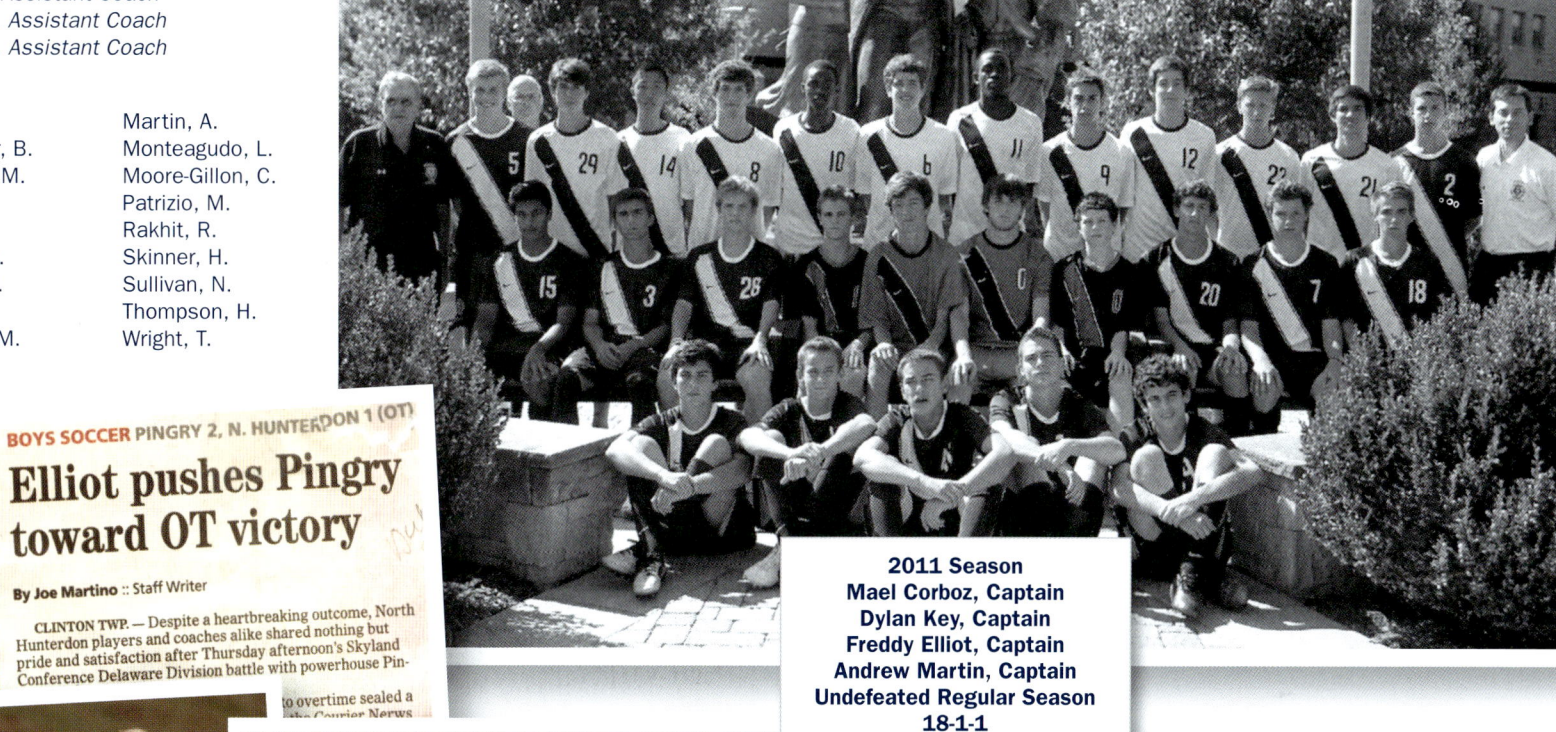

2011 Season
Mael Corboz, Captain
Dylan Key, Captain
Freddy Elliot, Captain
Andrew Martin, Captain
Undefeated Regular Season
18-1-1
Conference Champions

BOYS SOCCER PINGRY 2, N. HUNTERDON 1 (OT)

Elliot pushes Pingry toward OT victory

By Joe Martino :: Staff Writer

CLINTON TWP. — Despite a heartbreaking outcome, North Hunterdon players and coaches alike shared nothing but pride and satisfaction after Thursday afternoon's Skyland Conference Delaware Division battle with powerhouse Pin-

12-0 Pingry prevails in OT, 2-1

BOYS SOCCER

Freddy Elliot scored six minutes into the first overtime to lead Pingry, ranked No. 2 in The Star-Ledger Top 20, to a 2-1 victory over North Hunterdon yesterday in Martinsville.
Christian Fechter scored in the first half to give Pingry a 1-0 lead and Mael Corboz had an assist for Pingry (12-0). Dylan Key finished with six saves.
North Hunterdon (8-4) tied the game in the second half when Brian Fokken scored off a pass from Connor Ventura. Jon Scott stopped nine shots.
North Hunterdon had a chance to take the lead with two minutes

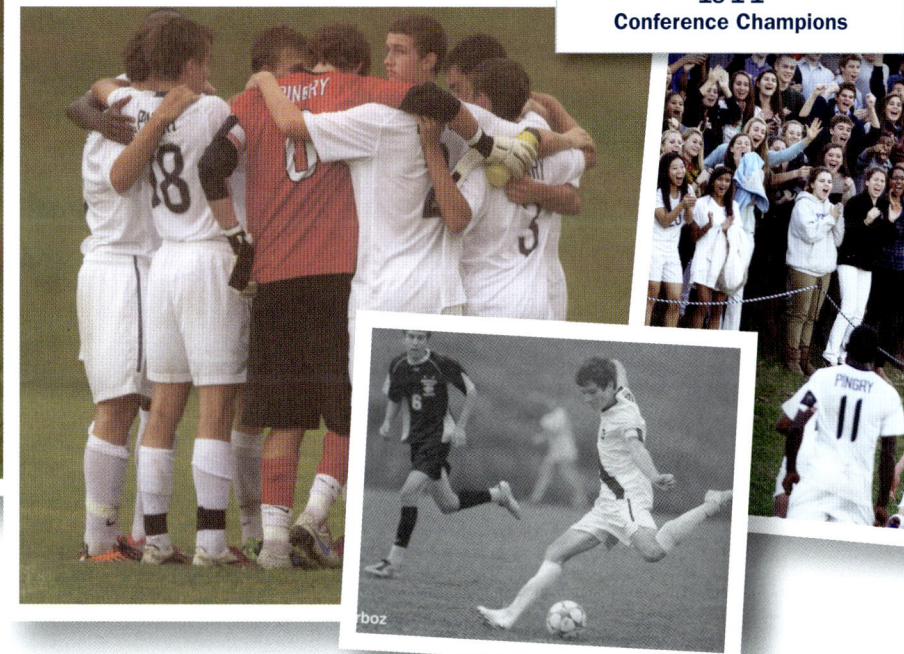

The 2012 Season

The 2012 team liked to keep things interesting. In compiling a 16-2-6 season, sharing the county title with Hillsborough, and winning the state sectional title, they came from behind to win or tie seven times, won two tournament games in overtime, and won two more in penalty shootouts. "I don't know whether they think everything is going to end and it makes them focus on the realization that they had better score," remarked Miller. "They do seem to really concentrate in overtime."

Captain Cameron Kirdzik had been Pingry's leading scorer since his sophomore year. He continued that strong leadership his senior year with 12 goals and 4 assists. His supporting cast included captains Christian Fechter's 8 goals and 10 assists, and Henry Flugstad-Clarke's 8 goals and 3 assists. Reeve Carver '14, Chris Lucciola '15, Roberto DeAlmeida '15, captain Brian Costa '13, Spencer Bianco '13, Matt Mangini '14, Jack Casey '16, Louis Monteagudo '14, and Jamie Cook '14 also contributed key goals and assists throughout the season. Defenders Mac Hugin '13, Rahul Rakhit '13 and goalkeepers Charlie Moore-Gillon '14 and Max Lurie '15 also buttressed a defense that shut out nine opponents and yielded just 10 goals in 22 games.

At the start of the season, Pingry was invited to participate in the Gateway Classic Invitational Tournament of nationally ranked teams in St. Louis, beating the eighth-ranked team, Peoria Notre Dame, 2-1 and losing to second-ranked Sacramento Jesuit 1-0. Pingry's showing raised them to the 10th-ranked school in the country. They battled through the Skylands Conference schedule with only a 1-1 tie against Watchung Hills marring their record, and they fought back from a 2-0 deficit to ultimately beat Bridgewater-Raritan on penalty kicks.

The county championship game against Hillsborough was another nail-biter. Hillsborough scored first, and not until the 60th minute was Pingry able to equalize for the tie, on DeAlmeida's long throw-in which Fechter centered for Kirdzik's header. Then an apparent game-winner by Kirdzik was called back for off sides.

The Non-Public tournament featured the same kind of last-minute heroics. Pingry won the quarter-final against Saint John Vianney in another shootout after 100 minutes of scoreless play, with Lurie making critical saves on two penalty kicks. They came from behind in the sectional semifinal to best Notre Dame 4-2, and beat Bishop Eustace in overtime on Fechter's golden goal.

And once again, they met Delbarton for the Non-Public A state title. After dominating the run of play, with Mac Hugin stifling Delbarton's top scorer, 6'4" Matt Clausen, Pingry had Delbarton right where they wanted them – in a scoreless tie headed for "Pingry time." Delbarton had a last-gasp corner kick – the kind of play Pingry had successfully defended against all season long. But Clausen elevated just enough over the Pingry defenders to head in the crushing winner with 16 seconds left in the game.

Pingry still finished as winners in Somerset County and the Delaware division of the Skylands Conference and were crowned Non-Public South A state champions. Pingry was named the *Star-Ledger* team of the year, Fechter was named *Star-Ledger* All-Area Player of the Year, Flugstad-Clarke the Somerset County Player of the Year, and Costa was named the Gatorade New Jersey Player of the Year, the first Pingry player to be so honored. Costa, Fechter, Flugstad-Clarke, and Kirdzik were named to the All-County, All-Area, and All-State First Teams, and post-season recognition was also given to Bianco, Hugin, Mangini, and Rakhit.

Pingry has had more than its share of Player of the Year awards. In 2012, three players were so honored, Brian Costa, Henry Flugstad-Clarke, and Christian Fechter. Costa, a three-year starter, was a classic box-to-box midfielder who controlled the run of play and catalyzed Pingry's possession-style play. Rick Szeles, coach of Bridgewater-Raritan, said, "He's the type of player that after the game you ask, 'Who was that kid?' He has great skills and field presence and demonstrates great sportsmanship and work ethic."

For two years Flugstad-Clarke anchored one of the best defensive units in the state. He displayed what was described as "an uncanny knack for always being in the perfect position" as a defender and offensive player, scoring seven goals and three assists his senior year.

Miller described Fechter, the youngest of three brothers to star at Pingry, as "our most versatile player. We played him at defense, midfield and up top. He got some big goals for us and was someone we could always count on. He's just a wonderful player and a wonderful person."

Brian Costa, Henry Flugstad-Clarke, and Christian Fechter '13

THE LIFE & TIMES OF MILLER A. BUGLIARI

David Fahey, *Assistant Coach*
Kim Kimber III, *Assistant Coach*
Mike Coughlin, *Assistant Coach*
Eric Hynes, *Assistant Coach*
Julian Greer, *Manager*

Bianco, S.	Haltmaier, B.	Monteagudo, L.
Carver, R.	Helfman, M.	Moore-Gillon, C.
Carver, S.	Ho, C.	Nair, R.
Casey, J.	Hugin, M.	Patrizio, M.
Cook, J.	Kaisand, A.	Rakhit, R.
Costa, B.	Kirdzik, C.	Rao, A.
DeAlmeida, R.	Klawitter, E.	Thompson, H.
Fechter, C.	Lucciola, C.	Tulloch, A.
Flugstad-Clarke, H.	Lurie, M.	Werner, M.
Foster, K.	Mangini, M.	Zachary, G.

BOYS SOCCER
Bugliari's Big Blue starts 2-0

NJSIAA BOYS SOCCER
Pingry works OT again for title

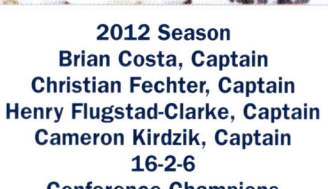

2012 Season
Brian Costa, Captain
Christian Fechter, Captain
Henry Flugstad-Clarke, Captain
Cameron Kirdzik, Captain
16-2-6
Conference Champions
Somerset County Champions
Non-Public A Sectional State Champions

217

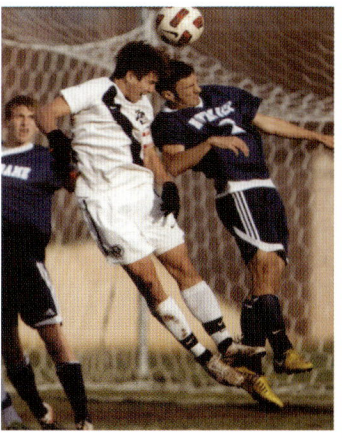

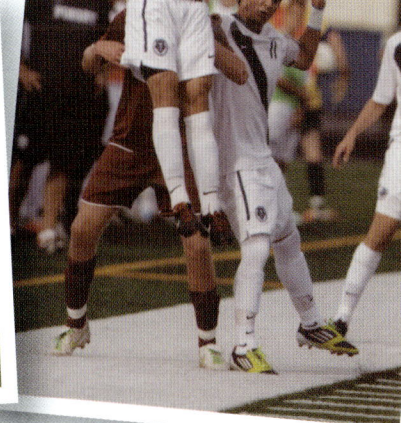

The 2013 Season

One pre-season assessment said: "The Big Blue never rebuild; they reload. But this might not be your father's Pingry we've gotten used to. The 2013 Big Blue are about as inexperienced a team as you'll ever see them field." Just four starters from 2012 returned, senior captains Matt Mangini and Lou Monteagudo plus junior goalkeeper Max Lurie (61 saves) and forward Roberto DeAlmeida. Unlike other Pingry teams with a solid core of PDA and club soccer players, the 2013 team would need to rely on athletes with expertise in other sports like basketball and lacrosse, such as seniors Max Helfman, Reeve and Sean Carver, and juniors Clayton Wright and Jamie Smith. And again, unlike previous teams, the 2013 squad had no pure strikers to count on for offense; goals had to come from Mangini (16 goals, 11 assists), senior Akshay Rao (5 assists), junior Chris Lucciola, and sophomores Jack Casey (4 goals, 5 assists) and Jack DeLaney (5 goals, 1 assist).

Pingry's defense lost its complete core to graduation, requiring newcomers like senior George Zachary and juniors Jamie Cook, Joey Padula, Smith, and Wright to raise the level of their game individually and collectively to meet the rigors of Pingry's Skylands Conference schedule and the county and state tournament gauntlets.

Mangini remembers looking at the team his senior year and wondering if it could come even close to the success of the teams he'd played on in his sophomore and junior years. But almost predictably, during the pre-season trip to Portugal, the team started to come together, and the 2013 squad entered the season with newfound confidence in themselves. Then it all started to unravel. A young, inexperienced team can handle a couple of injuries to key players; losing four starters was too great a handicap. For long stretches of the season Zachary, DeAlmeida, Helfman, and Wright had to sit on the bench, as role players and freshmen like Obi Ikoro and Henry Kraham were forced to take on greater responsibility and adapt to new positions.

The team saw the Skylands Conference championship slip away from them in a 1-0 loss to Hunterdon Central, and struggled through a heartbreaking loss in the county tournament to Montgomery, their first victory over Pingry in the school's history. Pingry controlled the run of play, but Montgomery's speed and athleticism triggered two counterattacks that left Pingry down two goals in the final period. Ikoro brought Pingry within a goal when he headed in Monteagudo's cross, and in the final two minutes Pingry mounted a blistering attack on Montgomery's net only to see the tying shot, at point blank range, sail futilely over the crossbar in the final seconds.

That left the Non-Public A championship. After beating St. Joseph 4-0 and Christian Brothers 1-0 on Monteagudo's first half goal off Rao's assist, Pingry met 17-1-3 Notre Dame in the sectional finals. Pingry trailed 0-1 at intermission but took over the game in the second half. DeLaney's conversion of a Casey pass in the 60th minute tied the score. Mangini made sure of the victory in the 74th minute when he collected the ball at the right corner, drove up the dead ball line, and played a picture-book cross that DeLaney clinically finished from five feet out. Against Delbarton in the state championship, Pingry couldn't dent their tough defense and went down in a 2-0 loss, but could take pride in repeating as Non-Public A sectional champions.

At the beginning of the season, the coaches had given the team practice pinnies listing all the championship years of Pingry teams to remind the team: "This is who we are. This is what we do." By looking at the years that weren't listed, you could also tell the teams that had fallen short of the goal that defines a truly successful Pingry team: winning a championship. As his team struggled through an injury-plagued season, co-captain Matt Mangini worried, "Will we be another of those teams that failed to get it done?" The answer, and the turning point for the team, came late in the season after the bad loss to Montgomery. On their run by themselves, without the coaches, the captains called a meeting in the woods. The team circled around, and one by one, the seniors – starters and bench-sitters – talked about what Pingry soccer and the season meant to them. "Something changed for us then," says Mangini. "It helped that we got our injured guys back, but there was just a different intensity and confidence." It translated into the game against Notre Dame in the Non-Public state sectional final. "We were behind at halftime, but nobody panicked. I remember Coach Fahey telling us, 'I'm not worried. You're better than them. Play your game.' And we did – for the title."

Matt Mangini '14

David Fahey, *Assistant Coach*
Mike Coughlin, *Assistant Coach*
Kim Kimber III, *Assistant Coach*
Jake Ross, *Assistant Coach*
Julian Greer, *Manager*

Carver, R.	Kaneko, G.	Nair, R.
Carver, S.	Klawitter, E.	Padula, J.
Casey, J.	Kraham, H.	Rao, A.
Cook, J.	Kwan, Je.	Rothpletz, P.
DeAlmeida, R.	Kwan, Jo.	Smith, J.
DeLaney, J.	Lucciola, C.	Sorenson, J.
Foster, K.	Lurie, M.	Tulloch, A.
Green, Z.	Mangini, M.	Werner, M.
Gupta, T.	McGregor, G.	Wright, C.
Helfman, M.	Monteagudo, L.	Zachary, G.
Ho, C.	Moore-Gillon, C.	Zachary, P.
Ikoro, O.	Mullett, G.	Zhu, C.

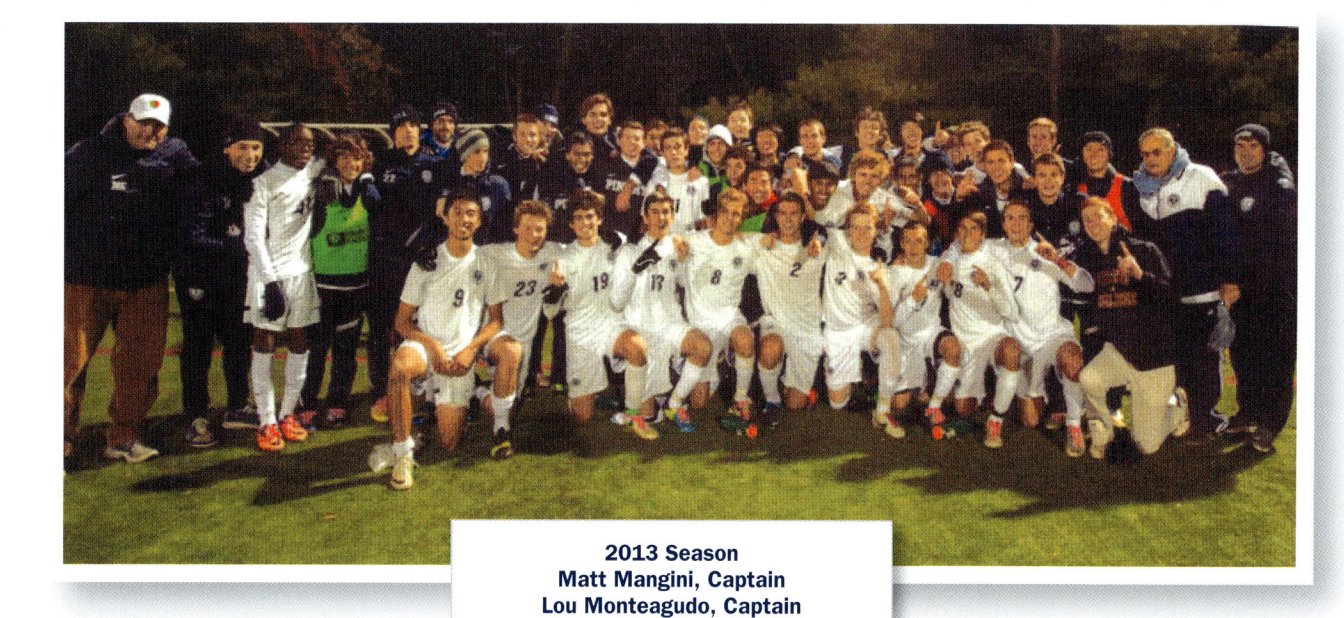

2013 Season
Matt Mangini, Captain
Lou Monteagudo, Captain
15-5-1
Non-Public A Sectional State Champions

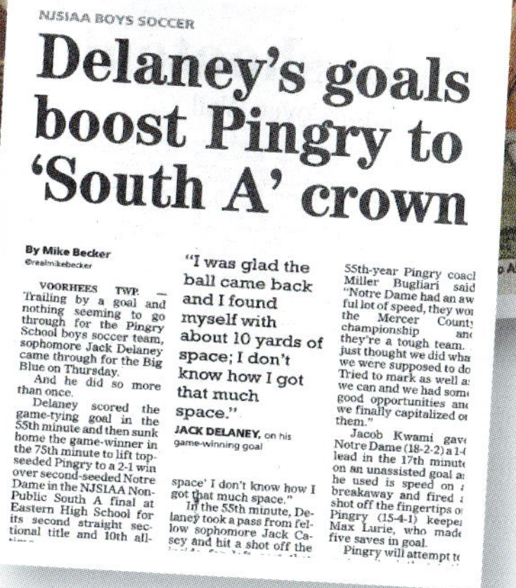

Boys' Soccer Enjoying Terrific Fall Season

Pingry shakes jitters, tops North Hunterdon

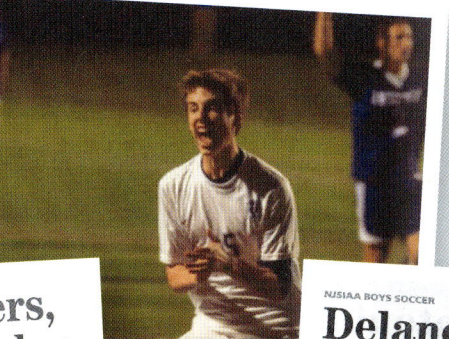

Delaney's goals boost Pingry to 'South A' crown

The 2014 Season

On some days you forget to set the alarm – or just sleep through it. The 2014 team didn't really wake up to its potential until the playoffs, but when they did, the result was a dominating sweep of conference, county, sectional and state championships.

Starting the season, with the return of six starters, led by senior captains Max Lurie, Jamie Cook, Clayton Wright, and Roberto DeAlmeida, the 2014 team was poised to be great. "This team was unusual," remarked Coach Fahey, "because there was so much competition for playing minutes in games. This year we had so much depth it made training better, and more fun, even if picking a starting team was more difficult." But potential and performance are two different things. Impressive hard-fought victories – over Bridgewater-Raritan, Franklin, Hunterdon Central, Watchung Hills, and Hillsborough – were followed by frustrating losses to Montgomery, Phillipsburg, and Hunterdon Central in the rematch of Pingry's earlier 2-0 victory.

Pingry's all-senior defense, with returning starting goalkeeper Lurie (13 shutouts) and veterans Cook, Wright, Rob Diaz, and Joey Padula, was a tough, seasoned group. And when Wright was lost to injury, junior Brendan Kelly and sophomore Ollie Martin stepped up their level of play. The midfield, however, with senior Chris Lucciola, juniors Jack DeLaney, Jack Casey, Yanni Angelides, and Phillip Zachary, sophomores Obi Ikoro and assist leader Henry Kraham, along with freshmen Alexy Alin-Hvidsten and Vineil Reddy, took longer to gel. When strikers DeAlmeida (13 goals), Jamie Smith, and midfielder Casey (7 goals) were injured early in the season, fourteen other players scored in critical wins, led by Cook, DeLaney, and Alex Ramos.

Championship teams peak at the right time. In the county tournament, Pingry disposed of Immaculata 4-0 and held off Bernards High in the county semifinals 3-2, with Lurie preserving the victory by stuffing a Bernards penalty kick. In the finals against high-scoring Gill St. Bernards, DeAlmeida took over the game. After a penetrating run, he was pulled down in the penalty area. He blasted the ensuing penalty kick into the left corner for the lead. His second goal iced Pingry's 2-0 victory and 23rd county championship.

In the state sectional tournament, Pingry demolished Wildwood Catholic and St. Rose by identical 5-0 scores to meet Gill St. Bernards again in the South finals. In a thrilling rematch of the county finals, Gill jumped out to a 1-0 lead four minutes into the game. Seconds later, DeAlmeida wove through two defenders to curl in the equalizer. Gill took the lead again, but Ramos's clutch goal tied the game near the end of the first half. Ikoro's golden game-winner, with two minutes left in the second overtime, gave Pingry its fourth state sectional championship in the decade.

That left 18-4-3 Hawthorne Catholic in the Non-Public B State Championship. The game was played at Kean College, and before the game, Miller took the team to the nearby old Hillside field where he and Coach Kimber had shared so many victories. It must have rubbed off. Pingry blistered Hawthorne Catholic 3-1 on Smith's two goals in the first 10 minutes and Casey's insurance goal three minutes later. Players from the Hillside days would have been proud.

DeAlmeida, named Somerset County Player of the Year and a Regional All-American, was selected to the All-State Second Team. He was joined on the All-State Non-Public First Team by Casey, and on the All-County and All-Area First Teams by Casey and Cook, with Lurie and DeLaney also being honored.

When Roberto DeAlmeida showed up on the varsity as a freshman, his coaches and teammates immediately recognized he was a special player. But in the 2012 Non-Public finals against Delbarton his sophomore year, he went down with his third concussion and was sidelined the rest of the year. He wound up missing most of his junior Pingry season and entire club season as well. A lot of players would have folded under that adversity; Roberto's deep faith and courage wouldn't allow that. For long, painful months he worked to strengthen his neck, back, shoulders and core. Told he could never head a soccer ball again, he learned to redirect high balls with his shoulders.

The payoff for all that work came late in the season, with his dominant play against Gill during Pingry's championship run. "I don't really have any emotions right now, this is such a surreal feeling," he said after the game. "I just have to thank God for giving me this opportunity tonight."

Roberto DeAlmeida '15

David Fahey, *Assistant Coach*
Kim Kimber III, *Assistant Coach*
Jake Ross, *Assistant Coach*
Mike Coughlin, *Assistant Coach*
Tan Tan Wang, *Manager*

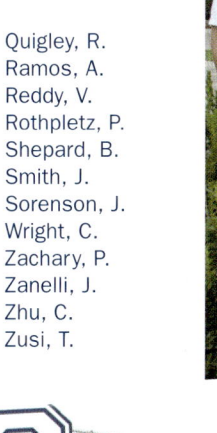

Acosta, E.	Ikoro, O.	Quigley, R.
Alin-Hvidsten, A.	Kaneko, G.	Ramos, A.
Angelides, Y.	Kecici, S.	Reddy, V.
Casey, J.	Kelly, B.	Rothpletz, P.
Cook, J.	Korth, P.	Shepard, B.
Cummings, M.	Kraham, H.	Smith, J.
DeAlmeida, R.	Lucciola, C.	Sorenson, J.
DeLaney, J.	Lurie, M.	Wright, C.
Diaz, R.	Martin, O.	Zachary, P.
Dugan, C.	McGregor, G.	Zanelli, J.
Flugstad-Clarke, M.	Mullett, G.	Zhu, C.
Gully, J.	Padula, J.	Zusi, T.

2014 Season
Roberto DeAlmeida, Captain
Jamie Cook, Captain
Max Lurie, Captain
Clayton Wright, Captain
18-3-2
Conference Champions
Somerset County Champions
Non-Public B Sectional State Champions
Non-Public B State Champions

799 — THE CHASE FOR 800 CAREER WINS CONTINUES ON TUESDAY SEPTEMBER 16 PINGRY VS WATCHUNG HILLS

Pingry sets tone with early goals
BOYS SOCCER: NON-PUBLIC B
By Rob Edwards, NJ Advance Media for The Star-Ledger

Pingry wins on Ikoro's OT goal
MATT SILVA

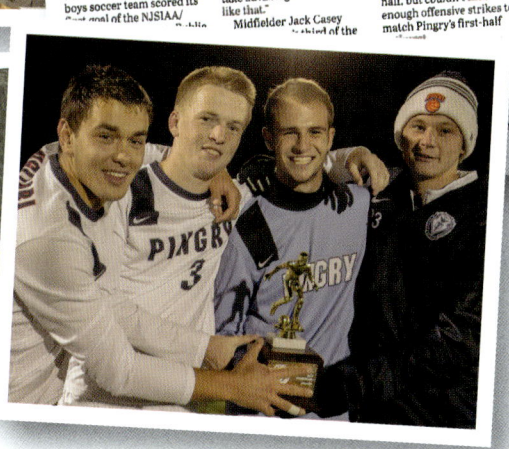

Miller the Coach

I hope I have provided all my players with lessons in leadership and taught them how to compete hard and win… or lose… with grace. Of the two, I much prefer the first.

— MILLER BUGLIARI

If you're a serious soccer fan, the first thing you might notice when you step on the Miller A. Bugliari Field in Basking Ridge is the field itself. Thanks to the Italian National Team, which trained here for the 1994 World Cup, and the field's recent restoration in memory of Kim Kimber IV '07, it's beautiful – a perfect pitch for playing championship-quality soccer. And that's appropriate, because the next thing that probably jumps out at you are the banners ringing the field, like World Series pennants flying over Yankee Stadium. The first one dates back to 1962. There's a message here: "This is what we do. This is who we are." And the message doesn't just exist as a symbol on banners; it lives inside the hearts of generations of Pingry soccer players, including some of the sons of Miller's first players. So the question is: how did those banners get there?

Core Principles

Mike Chernoff '99 was the starting goalkeeper his senior year, but his main sport was baseball, not soccer. "Coach loved that I was a 'baseball player' playing soccer and never judged me for not making soccer my No. 1 sport or priority. In fact, after high school he would actually come down to Princeton and visit me each year in college to watch me play baseball. Pretty amazing."

Chernoff's love of baseball translated into a career. He now is the Assistant General Manager of the Cleveland Indians. "How do I sum up what I think I learned in four years of playing for Miller? That's difficult. But as I reflect on things, I think it comes down to a few things:

"*Expectations:* Miller believed in everyone but had incredibly high expectations. It was a given that we were going to succeed, but more importantly, he gave us the tools and instilled the work ethic to help us understand how to succeed. There's not much more you could ask of a coach. We always believed that he had a plan and that if we did the things he was asking, we would be great.

The Bugliari Way

As Bronson Van Wyck '63 sees it, "The Bugliari Way" includes three vital essentials of life.

Commitment to Excellence: This means much more than winning the game. It is being resourceful; it is stretching one's self. It is not just using one's talent to the fullest or "trying one's best"; it is continuously adapting, adjusting and integrating one's self to meet higher standards.

Commitment to Others: Individuals lose; teams win. From one's first day with Miller you learn it is OK for you to be who and where you are as part of the team – the school – the community; and with that comes an immense amount of love and nurturing. No matter whether you are the smartest or the most talented, it is first and foremost "you" becoming a meaningful team member by helping the whole do better and be better – not just developing yourself. It is being open and accepting others' different opinions and ideas – there is no place for insisting only on one's own way. It is striving for togetherness within our differences so that winning as a team becomes far bigger than any individual achievement.

Commitment to Personal Growth: Every day "it is your turn." All of us have good and bad days; most of us know at every moment whether we are putting out or not. Therefore: every day, think of yourself as working on your game to better the whole; every day, work on getting to the "sweet spot" and not being satisfied with the status quo.

In total, each day go farther, recognizing that life is a continual striving for the "whole around us" in order to benefit from our efforts, our love and nurturing of each other. The key – Miller's creative way of implementing a way for us to be "meaningful" as part of his team and his life of love.

Bronson Van Wyck '63

"*Preparation:* From early on in our Pingry careers, he exposed us to opportunities to learn from older kids and experience what it was like to be on the varsity. You looked up to the leaders of the varsity team and learned to keep your mouth shut and watch their example. But he found times to expose everyone to that environment before plunging them into it. At the game level, I can't imagine that any high school team was as prepared as we were.

"*Work Ethic:* Coach liked players that cared and worked hard, regardless of their 'talent.' He respected you if you gave everything you had.

"*Teamwork and Leadership:* Coach taught us how to be leaders and how to inspire and motivate the players around us, both by example and with our words and actions. He relied on seniors and captains and gave players the freedom to lead. Everything revolved around teamwork and ultimately the team. It was not about individuals. There was a clear sense of the history of Pingry soccer, and we didn't want to let down our past Pingry soccer generations by not living up to the expectations of the program.

"Coach had incredible ability to coach, mentor, and connect with each player, but he also instilled self-discipline and leadership in his players."

By the 1970s, following the undefeated streaks of the 1960s and the first championships, the team's history of success had come to define its identity: a tradition of excellence each succeeding team needed to live up to – a torch that had been passed and must be kept burning brightly.

The Office

"There are so many aspects to Miller's extraordinary success and influence as a coach," Jon Pascale '93 reflects, "notably the incredible tradition of Pingry soccer he has created. As a new kid, transferring to Pingry my junior year, I'd sit in his office and marvel at the history around me on the walls and the legacy of success it represented. And then I wound up playing college soccer for Bob Jenkins, whose achievements I'd read about as a high school kid. It was like being part of a huge family."

Jon Pascale '93

Creating a Team Identity

Ask Miller about his goals when he started the soccer program and he says, "I wanted to build an attractive program, one that kids would want to be a part of." Part of that attractiveness had to do with how the team looked on the field. In the 1959 soccer

---

The Tradition

"When I put on the Pingry jersey the first day, it felt strange. But I realize now that the reason for that feeling was the result of representing something bigger than myself. A Pingry soccer player doesn't play for himself, he plays for all those who came before him."

Matt Sheeleigh '11

---

team photo, the team's uniforms are shirts in different shades of blue and a mix of different stockings. Their shoes are unshined (and in an interesting detail, the toes of most of them are scuffed). In the mid-1960s, Pingry football teams were still wearing 1930s-style pants with tattered old jerseys modeled after Princeton football uniforms and providing their own helmets – in whatever style, and sometimes color, they chose. Miller, by then, had abandoned the equally tired, old-fashioned soccer shirts of the 1950s and started to dress his teams in crisp, professional-looking uniforms. And the players' shoes are shined.

The sharpness in appearance shaped the team's essential character. There's a reason why Pingry teams over the decades have put together incredible unbeaten streaks at home, spanning multiple seasons, the most astounding being a 14-year unblemished record from 1960 to 1974. Tom Trynin '78 remembers how Pingry teams in the 1970s made their appearance on the field. "We'd walk through the woods to the left of the playing fields in silence and then suddenly emerge as a team onto the Miller A. Bugliari Soccer Field. 'Here we are. This isn't just another game; you're going up against the Pingry soccer team.' It was pretty impressive."

"Tough Love" on the Soccer Field

Bill Maass '70, captain of the 1969 team, captured Miller's complex coaching approach in his contribution to Miller's 50th Anniversary Celebration: "It's difficult to explain Miller's coaching style, but it definitely includes both 'soft' and 'hard' elements. The 'soft' element is the clear understanding he gives all his players that he cares deeply for each of them – whether they are a three-year starter or a one-year bench-warmer. This understanding enables the 'hard' elements to work. By 'hard' I mean the discipline. In our years this meant during the cooler days of late fall being required to wear a ski hat after taking a shower so you wouldn't catch a cold – and then being fined a quarter if you nevertheless did catch a cold; weekend curfews (which he checked on); wearing the lead-weighted vest or spats; practicing for an hour or so directly after any game in which the team didn't work as hard or play as well as it should have; and knowing that if you didn't hustle, you didn't play. I've played on numerous soccer teams during the years since I left Pingry, but the only team on which I have immediately and perennially felt comfortable is the Pingry Alumni Team."

The Pursuit of Excellence

Phil Lovett '79 remembers: "Coach always had very large teams. He never cut anyone. Provided you were the correct age (seniors and juniors) and you followed the rules, you were on the team. This meant we had a lot of not very good players who didn't play very many minutes in games. A few years after I graduated from Pingry, I asked Coach why he took on so many players when a smaller team would be easier for him to manage. He responded that Pingry soccer is about pursuing excellence – meeting high standards without excuses. Because many people never get the chance to have that experience in life, he felt just being part of the team should be a learning opportunity available to all."

Phil Lovett '79

Miller's Managers

Miller treated his soccer managers like his players: as important, valuable members of the team. He treated them with respect and insisted players do the same. They were, in effect, assistant coaches responsible for the many logistical details of managing a complex season.

Peter Blanchard '70 speaks for generations of Miller's managers: "I was one of the soccer managers in 1969, and how I came to be a soccer manager and what that experience was like says everything about the kind of person Miller is. At Pingry, I was the kind of shy, withdrawn student that easily gets completely ignored by everyone – except Miller. He 'found' me as a 9th grade biology student who was just drifting along, and gave me a special project to get me engaged – I recall it was something really preposterous like an illustrated journal of chicken behavior.

"I would never have imagined that project would turn into a 10-year career as a biology teacher, or my lifelong commitment as an environmental activist, founder of a conservation non-profit, and an author. Miller couldn't have seen that either, but what he did see was someone who needed, if you'll forgive the chicken analogy, to be brought out of his shell. But that's Miller. I was a terrible athlete, unlike my son, but Miller recognized that I had a lot of unfocused positive energy, so he made me a soccer manager.

"Without being overly dramatic, Miller not only influenced my life, he might have saved it. At Pingry and for some years after, I suffered from bouts of depression. So Miller constantly invited me to visit with him and Elizabeth, first in Summit and then in Tewksbury, to just talk about what I could do with my life.

"Through hours of conversation and countless cups of hot cocoa (made by Elizabeth, of course), his deep, unfeigned interest, gentle guidance, and total acceptance helped me discover the confidence and passion to make something really meaningful out of my life. He is the teacher of a lifetime."

Chris "T-Bone" Colford '72, a Soccer Manager from 1969 through 1971.

Attracting Talent

We can't recruit, because it's both illegal and unethical. Luckily we can attract some good kids because we have a pretty good program. Kids come to Pingry for a good education, and thank God some of them are soccer players.

Miller Bugliari

Over the years dozens of parents of promising high school players, interested in having their sons play for Pingry, have invited Miller to talk with them about the school and the soccer program. Lots of coaches would attempt to "sell" their program or even engage in aggressive recruiting. What Miller has always talked about is not Pingry soccer but their children's future – the opportunities and doors that would be opened as the result of a Pingry education.

> ### "Selling" Pingry
>
> Charlie Stillitano '77 vividly remembers when Miller showed up at his house to talk with his parents about Pingry Soccer. "My dad was concerned that my older brother Leo wasn't being challenged academically at high school. As a top high school soccer official, my dad knew all about Miller and Pingry, so he invited Miller to come by one night.
>
> "Miller walked in wearing a seersucker suit. I thought that was pretty amazing. We lived in a blue-collar neighborhood. None of the men we knew would have been caught dead wearing something like that. I was at Roselle Catholic, and doing OK academically, but I decided to listen to what somebody in so weird an outfit might have to say about soccer. Miller talked, instead, about what a Pingry education might do for Leo in terms of preparation for success in a competitive, well-respected college and the opportunities in life that could offer him. My parents were impressed, Leo was convinced, and so was I. It was the best move both of us could have made in our lives."
>
> Leo went on to star at Columbia – fittingly, they called him "The Lion." Charley did the same at Princeton.
>
> **Charlie Stillitano '77**

Leo Stillitano '76

Miller was just as far-sighted and committed when it came to getting Pingry kids – regardless of whether they played soccer – into the right college environment. One example out of hundreds typifies Miller's approach. One year, when Miller helped another of his players get accepted into Princeton, some faculty members and administrators objected: "He isn't the type of student Pingry should send to Princeton." "Of course he is," said Miller. "He won't be an A student; lots of Princeton students aren't. But he can handle the academic work, have a great college soccer experience, and make social contacts who will be invaluable friends the rest of his life."

Bob Jenkins '80 could speak for all the new players who have come to Pingry over the decades. "It was a great learning environment; I got exposed to other aspects of life like the arts I never would have experienced in high school. But what struck me was the extraordinary support I received from the whole Pingry community. It was a turning point in my life. At Chatham Township High School, I was on my own. At Pingry, besides his own support and help, Miller put me in touch with teachers and mentors like Manny Tramontana, Frank Romano, and Tom Johnson who I knew had my best interests at heart. When I got to Duke, I could write, think critically, and I knew how to learn."

The Psychology of Winning

Nate Zinsser Ph.D. '73 is a certified sports psychology consultant who directs a program of mental toughness training at the United States Military Academy (West Point) that is also taught to thousands of U.S. Army soldiers and officers at military posts throughout the United States. Nate also consults to professional football and hockey players, U.S. Olympic team members, surgeons, and other "white-collar athletes."

"I never played soccer for Miller," Nate recalls. "My sports were football, wrestling, and lacrosse. In January of my ninth grade year I was talking enthusiastically at lunch about the prospects for the Pingry wrestling team. A classmate matter-of-factly replied, 'Nate, shut up. You're NEVER going to be any good. Guys at this school don't wrestle well. We're good in soccer, sometimes we're good in swimming and tennis, but we've never been good at wrestling and we never will be.' I heard in my classmate's statement something that I would carefully study years later in graduate school – the crucial but usually unconscious connection between expectation, effort, and achievement. I heard the key to Pingry soccer's success, the key to Miller's success as a coach of young athletes, and the reason why Coach Bugliari ranks as one of the greatest sport 'psychologists' ever.

"That key was Coach's ability to communicate to young players (often seventh and eighth graders) that if they worked on their skills every year, spent time in the off-seasons getting touches on a ball, played winter soccer and attended a soccer camp in the summer, they would, by the time they were juniors and seniors, be very good players competing each year for championships. By getting this *expectation* across, by getting them to believe in a possibility, Coach got these players to invest *effort* over a period of years, which in turn made the *achievement* of winning seasons and championships possible.

"I don't know if Miller ever studied the psychology of expectation: that a person has to believe in personal and team success BEFORE that success can be achieved. But I do know that he understood this process on a deep, personal level; that he communicated it every team meeting and every practice; and that every athlete he coached felt it and benefited from it. I know I sure did. Seeing all around me the success of Pingry soccer for all those years, I knew that I could either believe what my classmate at the lunch table believed, or I could harness a little of what Coach Bugliari was using and create a positive expectation for myself and those around me. In my junior year, after the wrestlers in my class did get some experience, the Pingry wrestling team had its first winning season in over a decade, and we did it again the next year. That experience led to my career as a sports psychologist and the ability to share what Miller taught me with thousands of other athletes. We all have Miller Bugliari – a great 'psychologist' – to thank for that."

Coaching is teaching, and that's what I try to do, teach the game of soccer… every day on the field, during practice and during games. Our practices are light on scrimmages and heavy on technique and instruction, especially concerning the team's weak spots. I'm a teacher. We continually work on the basics of dribbling, passing, shooting, and heading, and we stress the importance of everyone using their skills to the advantage of the team. But it's just as important to make soccer fun and to reward players when they deserve it.

MILLER BUGLIARI

Creative Coaching

Miller has always been as creative as a coach as he was as a teacher in looking for ways to help kids learn. Alan Gibby '66 recalls one unusual Miller early innovation. "My sophomore year, we beat Linden at home 5-0 in late October. Miller was upset that regardless of the score, we hadn't 'left it all on the field.' More practice was called for, but by now, it was actually nighttime. No problem. Miller had thought about that. 'Ziggy, go get the ball,' he said to captain Bob Ziegenhagen. We practiced in the dark with an illuminated ball that glowed as if it were radioactive." Bob Dwyer '65 was also part of that experiment. "It was a great idea, until we had to stop after 15 minutes – we could see the ball, but not each other. Players were colliding at full speed all over the field."

David Bugliari '97 remembers one of Miller's equally unusual, but more effective, creative teaching strategies. "My junior year, the team was having a hard time visualizing how to move in space to create passing opportunities for each other. With our attention on the ball at our feet, we simply weren't seeing what we needed to see. So my dad switched the drill and had us practice 'handball,' throwing the ball as if we were a basketball team: take two steps and pass it to a teammate. Simple. It worked." Pingry players today play handball in practice. It still works.

Making a Complex Game Simple

Charlie Stillitano '77 has passionately lived and loved soccer all his life. What stands out for him is Miller's ability to simplify and focus the game for his players. "Anyone can tell you what a player *can't* do," Charlie says, "but Miller uniquely understands what each of his players *can* do. He designs roles to leverage each player's strengths as individuals – and as part of the team. Then he gets them to trust him and carry out their roles and responsibilities with maximum effort – and trust their teammates to do the same. You saw the same quality in Sir Alex Ferguson, who was able to take decent players at Manchester United and turn them into champions. The individual pieces all work together. Players realize that every day, in training and games, they need to work with each other and help each other out. That's how Miller has been able to get high school kids to play what are often really complicated schemes and consistently beat better teams. The sum turns out to be much greater than the parts.

"The final part of simplifying the game is Miller's unrelenting focus on fundamentals. It's what sets the great coaches apart. I remember Sacchi, after Italy's 1994 World Cup loss to Ireland, telling his defenders, even Maldini, 'We're working on heading the ball today.' It's the same with Miller. He knows the importance of repeatedly drilling on basic skills until they become ingrained."

Assistant Coach David Fahey points out the attention to detail that goes into Pingry skills development: "We constantly emphasize doing things right – in pressure shooting drills, taking small steps, turning square to the goal, striking the ball in the middle so it doesn't fly over the goal post, and aiming for the far corner. I know players find it frustrating at times, but we're teaching muscle memory. You want technique to become so instinctive that players are now free to just read the game and seize opportunities."

That same attention to detail characterizes how players learn the essential principles of the game. *"Clear the ball at its highest point!" "Never let a ball bounce in front of the goal!"* For defenders, these phrases become almost like mantras; by season's end players might be reciting them in their sleep. But in critical moments near the end of a game, when players are beyond exhaustion, continuing to anchor to principles like these in spite of fatigue can spell the difference between victory and heartbreaking defeat.

Getting Back at "Coach"

Given the pressure Miller put on his players, and the kind of smart, quick-witted, and aggressive kids who played for him, it was inevitable that players would try to retaliate. Of the dozens of examples, Charlie Cox '70's experience in 1969 captures how hard it actually was to get "one up" on Miller. "I was a senior and on the varsity soccer team. Of course, this was a time when Pingry was all male and we were still required to wear sports jackets and ties. It was also a time of revolutionary change, and our class was particularly vocal and challenging to authority. We were constantly pushing the envelope on what we could do to make a statement. Well, one day I decided to make my statement by following the letter of the law for the dress code, but obviously not the spirit. Instead of the typical tweed jacket or blue blazer, I wore an elaborately trimmed bellman's jacket from the famous Willard Hotel in Washington, D.C., that had come into my possession (that's another story). I ran the gauntlet of administrative scorn that day, but somehow was able to continue wearing it throughout the day.

"We had an away game that day at Peddie and, as usual, all team members reported to the front of the school with our athletic bags to load on the bus. Of course, I'm standing there smirking, fully expecting to get some sort of rise from Miller regarding my bellman's jacket. Assistant Coach Dan Phillips walked by me and just shook his head in disgust, but Miller didn't even acknowledge me. However, when it came time for us to load our gear and get on the bus, Miller had the entire team get on the bus before me and then turned to me and said, 'Hey bellman, load all of these bags and gear on the bus for me.' So, all of my teammates stared out the window at me from the bus, as did the coaches, while I proceeded to load all of the athletic and equipment bags on the bus. I was both embarrassed and mad at the same time, probably because Miller had clearly outwitted me. In hindsight, it was brilliant on his part and just one of the many laughs we continue to share today."

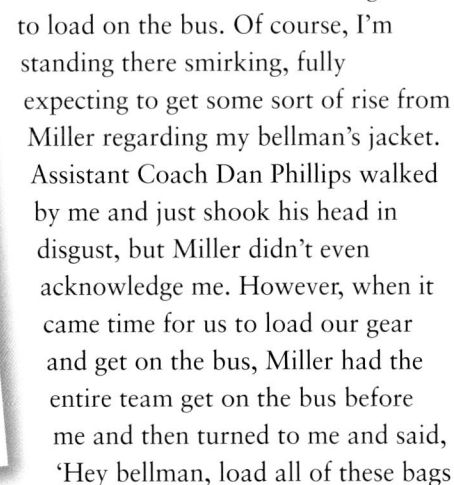

Miller's Superstitions

Miller's superstitions and unusual behavior are themselves the stuff of legend. Peter Mindnich '71 says, "The favorite Millerism for me is the palm rubbing. He would do it to let off some of the tremendous energy that flowed within him at all times. I will do that hand rubbing when I am feeling excited, and it has such a powerful effect – you just want to get out there and make something great happen. Pure excitement and energy."

Among the legends:

The old blazer that finally rotted away so completely that even a starving moth would pass it up.

The "Elephant Coat," actually a 1950s Pingry football sideline parka, by the 1980s completely threadbare, carried to games like a sacred talisman.

The "lucky socks," "lucky warm-up pants," or "lucky towel" he would continue to wear (unwashed) during winning streaks.

Miller's Medicine Chest, containing salt tablets to ward off cramps and heat exhaustion, Life Savers as an all-purpose treatment for everything from stress to headaches to an upset stomach, and several rolls of almost-finished athletic tape to chew on like a pacifier.

Never letting anyone stand to his right on the sideline during a game.

Having to immediately shut the door to his Basking Ridge Office/Museum on entering "so the luck doesn't get out."

Instantaneously tapping the wall in the same motion as turning on a light switch to see if he still was quicker than the flow of electricity to the light.

Not putting anything in the wastebasket in his office in order to keep the cleaning crew from touching anything.

Not stepping on the floor mat with the "Giants" logo at the entrance to Miller's office.

"Millerese"

Pingry students who played soccer have studied, if not mastered, two foreign languages: whatever they took academically, such as French, Spanish, or German, and "Millerese." Of these, "Millerese" has proven by far to be the most difficult, in part because like Etruscan, no dictionary or written grammar exists. The study of "Millerese" is different, too. No textbook, of course, but no classes or assignments either. One just experiences it, as if having been dropped by helicopter into the Brazilian jungle and being forced to communicate with a lost tribe that is meeting someone from the outside world for the first time. Learning "Millerese" requires a lot of footwork, too. Tom Trynin '79 describes a typical lesson. Miller would spot him in the hall between classes:

"Tommy. Come here. Walk with me."

"Sure, Coach. What's up?" Miller wouldn't answer, of course.

What followed was a tour of the building, Miller stopping to chat with this student or that faculty member, Tom dutifully following along, until they made the long return to Miller's office.

Once inside, Miller would sit down.

Tom would sit down.

Miller would ask: "How are you doing?"

"Fine, Coach. I'm fine."

"Lawrenceville's up. Gotta be ready."

"I'm ready, Coach. I'm ready."

"Good."

That ended the lesson, and Tom would be free to leave, 10 minutes late for his next class, trying to work up a plausible excuse that didn't involve saying "I was walking around the building with Mr. Bugliari saying nothing."

Miller's meaning often lies hidden in the silences, like lacunae in an ancient manuscript or the lost portions of a Dead Sea scroll. But it has, as well, its own unique vocabulary. Some examples:

"You guys are incredible!"

"Let me explain your priorities: Studies, Sports, Social."

"Get the ball out of the middle!"

"Don't diddle with the ball so much!"

"Frank! Phone call."

"Stop talking to the trees."

"It costs me money to keep you here at Camp Waganaki!" (The inevitable response when players complained about their meager kitchen crew salaries.)

"Move your two feets!"

"Tired? You're tired? I'll tell you when you're tired!"

"The time for you to start worrying is when I DON'T yell at you!"

"Please go baseline! Rohdie, tell them that when we go baseline we win, Baseline-win!"

"Fahey, get him out of there, he's killing me!"

"Bachagaloop!" (A reference to the great 1990s Italian goalkeeper Valerio Bacigalupo.)

Nick Sarro-Waite '99 remembers when Miller had the team line up after a game to walk the field looking for a tooth an opposing player had lost when he collided with a Pingry player during the game. "We were laughing and joking around until Miller yelled, 'Stop yapping and look for that tooth!' Then we really broke up. But we found the tooth."

The ultimate Millerism, however, may be the one Kris Bertsch '99 has been puzzling over for decades, heard when the team was going through an especially bad practice: "Will you guys stop playing balloon tag and pop the counselor!"

Miller's Assistant Coaches

With a new assistant, you first figure out how their strengths can help the program. The other part is trust – giving them a specific role in games, such as handling substitutions. It's not easy. For them to own the role, you have to relinquish it yourself, while still making sure they understand "this is what I want." But then you have to let them do it.

MILLER BUGLIARI

You can't build championship teams unless players continuously strengthen their skills and knowledge of the game through practice, coaching, and feedback. The more individual attention players get, the faster they improve. So for Miller, from the very beginning, creating the soccer program he wanted meant developing a coaching staff, first at the freshman and JV level, then into the Middle School, and finding assistant coaches for the varsity team.

Miller's first full-time assistant was Frank Romano. "He was such a terrific basketball coach that he took naturally to the job of goalkeeper coach, freeing me to work with the field players," Miller says. "After two years, Fred Walters got involved. He wasn't a soccer guy, but he was a good disciplinarian and took a lot of the increasing administrative work off my hands. Fred and I would go into New York and catch play openings off-Broadway to relax before big games."

Manny Tramontana was Miller's JV soccer coach for 45 years. "As with all his assistants, he brought me along, and I'm grateful for that," Manny says. "But in fact, no other assistant coach could possibly have put up with Miller for that long. Through the 1980s, I developed the players that would eventually become varsity starters. Even when Miller started calling up talented sophomores and freshmen to the varsity, he was always gracious in 'lending' me varsity underclassmen on the 'taxi squad' to play in JV games against tough opponents. Shortly after Miller established the varsity Union County tournament, I started a county JV tournament. We won the title a whole bunch of times and in many years could have beaten most of the varsity teams on Miller's schedule."

"Dan Phillips '59, who coached from 1967 to 1976, was my first long-term assistant," Miller recalls. "He'd played the game, had a real passion for it, and was great with the kids. I appreciated how hard he worked at constantly improving his knowledge of the game and coaching skills. He also had the task of trying to calm me down during games. That was more of a challenge for him."

Dan Phillips '59

"When I was assigned to coach third team soccer in the early 1960s, Miller immediately offered to help. And did he ever help! He taught me the necessary drills, passing strategy, and how to use the manager effectively. In addition, he brought the big varsity guys down to my little guys to demonstrate and teach. We both knew the powerful effect of that experience on the younger boys. They knew that when I told them something, the basic instruction was coming from The Coach Himself. My final season of coaching, in the fall of 1964, when I coached the JV, we were undefeated, thanks to his teaching me and his inspiration to all soccer coaches and players."

Dave Koth '47

"I think Assistant Coach Dan Phillips deserves some special mention about the Lawrenceville game. Miller had out-of-state obligations for a couple of the days prior to the game, and while in close contact with Miller, Dan really helped get us ready for that game. Of course, he was a valuable coach all year, but he really stepped up for that championship game… something I think we all remember and appreciate."

Paul Ciszak '72

"I was deeply grateful," Miller acknowledges, "to the following faculty members who coached junior teams, starting, of course, with my 'right hand man,' Manny Tramontana, and my long-time Middle School coach Jack Lewis, along with Rick Bosland, Fred Fayen, and Graham Touhey, and now Jeff Patten, Wayne Pagliari, and Tony Garcia.

"Gerry McKeown is a good friend who grew up playing and later coaching in Kearny and now coaches for the Players' Development Academy. He's always been a great resource I could talk with and gain insight from.

"Six other men who came into the program for a while and helped a lot were August Wooter, a really good player Art Kurz's dad found for us, Steve Samson from Kean College and his brother Bucky, and Ken Thibault from Morristown High. Rich Thomas '62 returned to Pingry to coach lacrosse and helped me out in the soccer program in 1972, as did Pingry teacher John Hutchinson in the late 1970s.

"Charlie Stillitano, Sr., 'Big Charlie,' was an invaluable resource as my 'Technical Director' for over a dozen years until his tragic and sudden passing in 1991."

Don Burt '69

"When Miller talks to you, you feel as if you are the most important person in the world to him at that moment – and amazingly, at that moment you are. He was that way with me as a first-year assistant coach. Miller was the top guy and I was a rookie; no question there. But he respected me, asked me for input, and made me feel as if my contributions to the team mattered."

Bob Jenkins '80

In 1965, Miller started what would become one of the greatest strengths of the Pingry soccer program: former players who served for a few years as assistant coaches. Steve Hart '61, the outstanding goalkeeper of the 1960 team, was the first, followed by former All-State or All-County players Don Burt '69 and Leo Stillitano '76 in the 1970s and Bob Jenkins '80, Brian O'Donnell '81, Jimmy Gensch '83, and Sander Friedman '83 in the 1980s, and from the 1990s teams, Mike Coughlin '90, Mike DeGrande '94, Kevin Schmidt '98, and Kris Bertsch '99. More recently, former players Gianfranco Tripicchio '00, Anthony Tripicchio '02, Brad Fechter '05, and Eric Hynes '08 have played important roles in the ongoing success of Pingry soccer.

From the late 1980s through 2005, two men were inseparably part of Pingry soccer: Rob Macrae '82 and his Wesleyan University buddy Adam Rohdie. Macrae, captain of the 1981 team, had been working on Wall Street after college, but realized he wanted to teach and coach "to repay the debt I felt I owed to Miller."

In 1997, Macrae talked Rohdie into joining Miller's staff. Players describe Macrae as a thoroughly buttoned-up, squared-away guy; Rohdie was the kind of big, explosive spirit who pushes boundaries – like the time he lost a bet and showed up at school wearing a dead fish for a necktie. Rohdie quickly became Miller's alter ego. Miller still yelled at kids in the 1990s and 2000s, with no loss of passion. In almost a "bad cop/good cop" synergy, Rohdie was the balancing presence who could help a player understand that Miller's temper was his way of saying "I care about you." Rohdie also personalized the same kind of hard-nosed toughness and joy in physical competition that had marked Miller as a player. When Rohdie yelled out to the team, "OK! Who wants to take a shot at the title?" players knew they were in for an uncompromising test of their physical strength and personal character.

Miller, Rob Macrae '82, and Adam Rohdie

Rohdie left Pingry in 2005 to serve as headmaster of the Greenwich Country Day School, as his friend Macrae had left to become headmaster of Cincinnati Country Day School. But the two of them made an indelible mark on the proud history of Pingry soccer and made an equally important contribution to Miller's ongoing evolution as a coach.

First Assistant Varsity Coach David Fahey '99 captures what brings former players back to coach with Miller. "I was so fond of Miller when I was a player, and learned so much about soccer, that I knew working for him and coaching with him would be an opportunity for me to learn other life lessons. When I was a student, I loved the connections that coaches made with players and I wanted to experience that from the other side of the coin.

"One of those connections was the bond I felt with former faculty member and coach Adam Rohdie. Adam was a mentor. He was a mix between a brother and a boss. We loved him, because it was so clear that he cared about us as people as well as student athletes, and we feared disappointing him because we all wanted to keep and maintain his respect."

Miller's current staff includes four men who followed up illustrious playing careers to contribute even more strongly to Pingry's tradition of championship soccer: Kim Kimber III '76, Mike Coughlin '90, Jake Ross '96, and Fahey. These alumni coaches are more than just skilled former players; they represent the living tradition of Pingry soccer that has shaped individual players' and teams' expectations and defines the standard of excellence Pingry teams aspire to achieve.

Championship Coaching

So how did all those championship banners get there on the fence lining the Miller A. Bugliari Soccer Field? Miller will be the first to tell you the players won them, he didn't. But coaches do develop championship teams, and the final, most profound, most important, and yet most startling aspect of Miller's coaching is that all of it is centered, all of a piece – the all-embracing context: school, soccer, social; the values: hard work and commitment to the team; the living legacy: championship play; the measure of success: winning and losing with grace; the synthesis of intensity and laughter; the love of it all.

Perhaps the best summary of Miller as a coach comes from Elizabeth, mother to three Pingry players: "Without necessarily knowing it or doing so intentionally, Miller's coaching and teaching have always been about life lessons. His ability to concentrate in the moment, so fiercely that he is hardly aware of the extraneous, translates into the way his teams play. Hard work, the importance of the team, the shared goal and a sense of humor that makes everything OK, have taught his players about leadership. It is not about being a 'star' – it's about honor and loyalty. He turns boys into men."

Anthony Tripicchio '02, Miller, David Fahey '99 and Kim Kimber '76.

Parents' Perspective

Jerry Pascale, father of Jon '93, recalls meeting Miller for the first time to discuss the possibility of Jon's attending Pingry. "Mike DeGrande and Andy Lewis played club soccer with Jon and were constantly talking up Miller and Pingry. But when I went for my interview with Miller, I had my best suit on and was really nervous. By the time our conversation was over, I was convinced that the very best thing I could do for my son was to put him in Miller's hands – and that turned out to be the wisest decision I could have made. At the time, Jon was enrolled at Immaculata. Father Kennedy, the headmaster, was passionate about the football team, and didn't want to hear about soccer. So I knew Jon's soccer experience would be better at Pingry – I just didn't know how much better. He wound up playing for another great coach, Bobby Jenkins '80, at American University, and that launched Jon on his own wonderful coaching career. Of course, there is so much more to the experience of having Miller coach and mentor your child than just the soccer. While Jon was a standout in club soccer, in those years, high school soccer and academics were still the normal path to college. I felt a huge degree of comfort in knowing Miller would help Jon all along the way, and that Jon would rise to the challenge. Miller's a good friend, and we enjoy our time together now, but I can barely find words to say how grateful I am for what he did for Jon."

Thomas Boova spent a year coaching football at Pingry and is a parent of two Pingry graduates. "Both adore the school," he says. "My daughter Laura '04 puts it best, 'I'm all about Pingry.'"

"My daughter played at Pingry and Georgetown. Miller was as interested in her soccer as any of the boys. His interest in her academics goes without saying. As a parent, there are no words sufficient to express how grateful we were for his concern for her as well as my son.

"My son Kevin '02 played football, basketball and lacrosse at Pingry. In the 7th grade he was badly hurt playing football. Although he was ultimately cleared to resume playing, I kept him out. Most felt his future was in lacrosse. It was. He was one of the four Pingry captains in six years who went on to captain Amherst College. Miller knew what had happened to Kevin. He seems remarkably in tune with kids like him. Kevin played soccer until he was old enough to play football and Coach knew it. He suggested Kevin come back to soccer. Coach's remarkable capacity to comfort, but most important instill confidence, was instantly on display. As the college process began I was asked to come visit with Coach. I told Kev his mother and I were going to see Coach Bugliari. 'Why?' he asked with this look of horror. 'Not really sure, Bud, but he called, so we're going.' A few minutes went by and he said, 'Do you have to go?' 'Yes,' was my reply, 'I would have no reason not to go.' 'OK, then, just remember one thing. When you go in Coach's office make sure you close the door so you don't let the magic out!'

"I've spent a lifetime in athletics. There are four bowl rings in my family. My children were blessed to have had wonderful careers and I was blessed to have been able to watch it all. However, perhaps one of my greatest pleasures and honors was to have been invited as a chaperone for the Italy Trip my son's senior year. Only Coach could have made you think going on that trip was the equivalent of the presidential service award!"

Conor Mullett '84 played for Miller and is now a Pingry Trustee. His son Griffin '16 is now on the varsity soccer team. Watching his son play for his old coach is a wonderful and poignant experience for Conor. "If I were asked," he says, "about how Miller has changed over the years, on reflection I'd say 'Not very much.' His unchanging essence has always been his ability to gain both his players' respect and their admiration. There are a lot of 'tough' coaches who are just tyrants, and their players hate them, even if they win. There are also coaches who want their players to like them. Miller manages to achieve both those goals seamlessly. Perhaps he's a little less 'hands-on' in practice – he has terrific assistant coaches to help him – but his presence and impact is still what holds everything together. And his energy level is still remarkable. I've had the pleasure of chaperoning pre-season trips to Europe, and in the evening, when many of the adult chaperones are relaxing by the hotel bar, there's Miller, after a full day of working with the kids, still holding court and entertaining us with his stories."

Miller's Friendship with Other Coaches

"I was President of the National Soccer Coaches Association of America and had only half-heartedly complained that they sent me to places like Harrisburg, Pennsylvania, while other Board members represented the Association in soccer-oriented places like Brazil and the European countries," Miller recalls. "One year they sent me to Trier, Germany for the annual Bundesliga meeting. Hundreds of coaches attended the conference to renew their coaching licenses, or in my case, earn German qualification.

"I flew into Berlin and visited Elizabeth's cousin, Susan McKinley. I was fascinated by the Berlin Wall and how the divided country worked. In Trier, I was met by my wonderfully gracious host Horst Richardson, the coach of Colorado College, who served as my interpreter. The Germans were very organized, as you might expect. In fact, when I was late for one meeting, I was told my beer ration would be cut if I ever let it happen again. I didn't. It was a wonderful experience, and gave me the pleasure of meeting other international coaches from Luxembourg, Iceland, and Belgium, in addition to the Germans.

"Over the years, my work with the NSCAA and Pingry soccer trips to Europe have simply expanded those great associations."

> "I first met Miller Bugliari many years ago when I was asked to run the coaching side of Hubert Vogelsinger's camp at the Lawrenceville School in New Jersey. That was one of the best days in my life, as Miller was on staff to coordinate all the facets of the camp – the coaches, the meals, the fields, and the school. Running a camp is never easy, but when you are a guest camp in a school there are so many people you have to work with, and there was nobody better than Coach Bugliari at bringing everyone together. He is a master at human relationships. He never got rattled or angry and always had a very calm demeanor. I think I learned more that week about how to deal with people than any other time in my life. Since that week we have been constant friends, and I can't think of anyone's company I enjoy more to talk about soccer than Miller Bugliari."
>
> **Bobby Clark, Head Coach, University of Notre Dame**

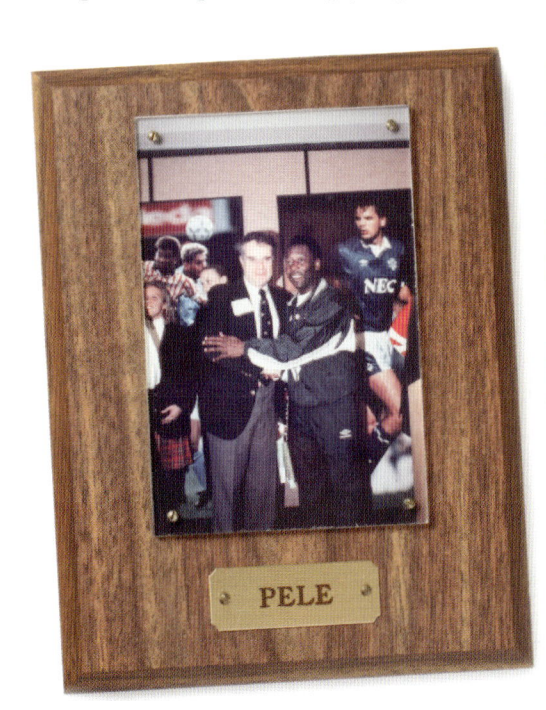

(Left): Miller, Real Madrid Coach Carlo Ancelotti and Charlie Stillitano '77.

Miller with USMT Coach Bruce Arena (right) and his staff.

(Right): Charlie Stillitano '77, Brazil Coaches Carlos Alberto Parreira and Jeff Tipping, and Miller.

THE LIFE & TIMES of MILLER A. BUGLIARI

Looking back on more than a half-century of spirited competition, Miller says, "I've really enjoyed and benefited from my friendships with other high school coaches like Al Czaya, Frank Severage, Frank Chirichillo, Herb Kassel, Tom Breznitsky, Jim Jesky, Rick Hildebrand, Ken Cherry, Rick Szeles, Evan Baumgartner, Joe LaSpada, Dave Donovan, Marty Berman, and Columbia's famous coach Gene Chyzowych, with whom I had a decades-long friendly competition for cumulative victories until his sad passing last year. They're all great coaches in their own right who have challenged me to grow professionally. I've also had the pleasure of working with and learning from terrific professional and college coaches in soccer camps, including Manfred Schellscheidt, Bob Bradley, Jeff Tipping, Nelson Rodriguez, Tab Ramos, Bobby Clark, Rick Meana, Jim Harrison, Gerson Echeverry, Jim Barlow, Kevin Anderson, and Ian Hennessey.

"Thanks in large measure to Charlie Stillitano and Martin O'Connor, over the years I've met and established enjoyable relationships with many famous international soccer coaches as well. In 1982, I spent time with Enzo Bearzot, coach of Italy's World Cup Champions. In 1992, I spent a week with Steve Heighway's coaching staff at Liverpool in the English Premier League, observing how they developed the players on their Under-19 team and how the senior team practiced and worked together as a team. The arrival of the Italian National Team under coach Arrigo Sacchi at Pingry was, of course, an incredible experience. In 1999 I spent a week in Montecatini, Italy, with the New York MetroStars' coaches Bora Milutinovic and Nelson Rodriguez, and players including Tim Howard, Tony Meola, Roberto Donaldini, and Tab Ramos, watching what a professional team does to get ready for the season. I've also had the great pleasure of getting to know Sir Alex Ferguson of Manchester United, and the other professional coaches our team has met on our many trips to Europe."

Miller with (l) Carlo Tramontozzi, and (center) Italian National Team Coach Marcello Lippi.

Miller with Italian Coach Enzo Bearzot.

(Left to right): Martin O'Connor '77, Charlie Stillitano '77, Manchester United Coach Sir Alex Ferguson, Miller, Sean O'Donnell '75.

"I've worked Miller's camps for 15 years. There is nobody I admire more or respect in this game. When I pack it up someday, if I had anything like the career he's had, I'll be able to die a happy man."

Marty Berman, Head Coach, Seton Hall Prep

"I have hosted Miller at Old Trafford, Carrington, the Champions League finals, and on our U.S. tours, and have enjoyed my personal time with both him and his wife Elizabeth.

"Miller's 55 years of coaching success speaks for itself. The foundation of this success rests on his great personal respect for his players and everyone he comes in contact with. Another key element is his consistency. His discipline, work ethic, and determination have been essential to his longevity of success. Equally important is Miller's sense of honor. My time with him revealed a man of great character and responsibility to not only his family, but his players and friends – a man who could always be counted on when needed.

"One of the greatest assets of a leader is his ability to reach out to people, to recognize them and show he appreciates them. Miller is able to do this through the warmth of his personality. It has been a real pleasure for Cathy and me to get to know Miller and Elizabeth."

Sir Alex Ferguson, Former Head Coach, Manchester United

Connecting with Alumni

Miller's connection to former students and players is one of the strongest components of Pingry's outreach to its alumni. And one centerpiece in this outreach is the annual alumni soccer game.

Miller says, "Early on, I thought an alumni game was a classic way to keep former players involved in the program and connected to the school." As it evolved over time and successful players who had competed in college returned, it became a way to help current players, especially the younger ones, get a sense of what they could aspire to achieve if they worked hard enough. It's impressive to hear the roll call of former All-State and All-American players. And the most impressive part of the ritual is Miller's introduction of each player done completely from memory, without any more notes than a list of the attendees.

Martin O'Connor '77 captained the basketball team; he wasn't really a soccer player. Miller made him part of the soccer squad for his leadership qualities. He still attends alumni games not to play but just to be part of the experience. "The thing that stands out for me about Miller's introductions is what he's doing for his former players. He's making them special, and giving them dignity. That's a great gift, and so typical of Miller."

Stuart Lederman '78 played soccer until he wrecked his knee, then spent his junior and senior years as the soccer team's athletic trainer. For years since graduation, he has been the "coach" of the Alumni team, although his demeanor on the sideline is significantly calmer than Miller's. "You can see the varsity players listening to these introductions," Lederman says, "and thinking to themselves, 'What will Coach be saying about me in future years when I come back? What is the mark I want to make?' But it goes way beyond that. Long before the word 'networking' existed, Miller understood the value of connections for the kids he taught and coached. He's enabling each group of seniors to join a wonderful, supportive, collective family."

In the early years, Miller used the alumni game as pre-season preparation. They were highly contested games that the Alumni typically won. "Because of the chance of injuries," Miller remarks, "we don't go full out against the Alumni any more. You'd be putting freshmen and sophomores against grown men, playing with a high level of intensity and pride.

"But it's also now a terrific reunion. Not only do we get regulars coming back each year, but each year a couple of players show up for the first time to reconnect with the program and renew old friendships."

David Fahey '99 can relate to the alumni game as a player and now a coach. "The alumni game is a special day in our season because it creates a timeless link between today's boys and yesterday's alums. You introduce the current team to a group of 50, sometimes 60 former players that they've heard stories about, looked at pictures of, stacked themselves up in the record books against, and you help them bond around a shared identity. You remind the alums that they built a program, and you remind the players that they are working to keep it at the level where it belongs.

"You celebrate what Miller has done for this school. When Miller speaks, it's not just a recount of county championships and individual accolades, though a lot of it is. But instead, it includes mention of an alum's career prominence, civic engagement or parenting. You get a reminder that there's something more to this than just wins and losses. That only makes the program stronger."

Playing the Pingry Alumni

"My sophomore year, Coach Bugliari loaned me to the Alumni because they didn't have a goalkeeper. The game started and big Artie Kurz '65, whom I knew from playing at Farcher's Grove, was the sweeper. He was maybe 28 years old and a killer. In about the 30th minute, Jimmy Betteridge '72 came down the left wing, I came out to narrow the angle, and he hit a rocket from about 12 yards which was so hard I was handcuffed. It hit me in the neck and knocked me completely unconscious, and the shot went over the crossbar of the goal for a corner kick. When I came to, Coach and Artie Kurz were standing over me. Artie picked me up with one hand, smacked me in the face to wake me up, and growled, 'Nice save, Kid.' Then he added, 'Nobody scores against the Alumni – ever. Especially when I play."

Guy Cipriano '74

THE LIFE & TIMES *of* MILLER A. BUGLIARI

Miller's Records

- *Star-Ledger*/NJ.com Trophy: 1996, 2008

- NJSIAA Non-Public "A" State Champions: 2001, 2006, 2008

- NJSIAA Non-Public "B" State Champions: 1991, 1995, 1996, 2014

- NJSIAA Non-Public Sectional State Champions: 2000, 2001, 2006, 2008, 2010, 2012, 2013, 2014

- NJSIAA "Prep" State Champions: 1962, 1964, 1965, 1966, 1968, 1970, 1971, 1972, 1973, 1974, 1981, 1982, 1983, 1985, 1987

- Union County Champions: 1964, 1970, 1974, 1975, 1976, 1977, 1983

- Somerset County Champions: 1985, 1988, 1991, 1992, 1994, 1995, 1996, 1997, 2000, 2001, 2004, 2005, 2006, 2007, 2008, 2009, 2010, 2012, 2014

- Undefeated Regular Seasons: 1962, 1964, 1965, 1966, 1970, 1971, 1972, 1978, 1988, 1991, 1994, 1995, 1996, 2000, 2001, 2003, 2004, 2005, 2007, 2008, 2009, 2011

- Conference Champions: 1995, 1996, 2000, 2001, 2003, 2004, 2005, 2006, 2007, 2008, 2009, 2010, 2011, 2012, 2014

- Miller was inducted into the National Soccer Coaches Association of America (NSCAA) Hall of Fame in January 2006 and was enshrined in the National Soccer Hall of Fame (NSHOF) in August 2006.

- He is a former President of the National Soccer Coaches Association, and continues to work with the New Jersey State Coaching Association as a clinician.

- He has been named "New Jersey State Coach of the Year" seven times and "National Coach of the Year" four times. He is a member of the New Jersey Governor's Fitness Council, the New Jersey Youth Hall of Fame, the New Jersey State High School Hall of Fame, and the Springfield College Hall of Fame.

- In 1995, Miller received Pingry's highest alumni award, the Letter-in-Life. He was also inducted into the Pingry Athletics Hall of Fame.

THE LIFE & TIMES *of* MILLER A. BUGLIARI

242

2002 PINGRY SOCCER
National High School Soccer All-Star Game
1975
UNION COUNTY CHAMPIONS

Miller's Office

I round the corner in my school and stop outside an office. Inside sits my soccer coach, calmly talking on his phone and looking at a pile of scattered, unorganized papers on his desk. I hesitate, not sure whether to knock lightly or continue standing outside the door. Fortunately, Coach lifts his head and notices me standing outside. He smiles and waves his hand, motioning for me to come in. I quietly open the door, and close it quickly (keeping the "magic" inside the room). It is my senior year at The Pingry School and my 100th time inside Coach Miller Bugliari's office. Yet, my eyes still gravitate toward the mementos, plaques, pictures, and newspaper clippings that line the walls of his office, all celebrating his last 50 years as a Pingry soccer coach. After glancing around the room for half a minute, I sit down in a Pingry armchair next to his desk. I turn my head to the left and take a good, hard look at Coach, beginning to realize just how many people he has influenced. Most importantly, I become aware of how much he means to me, and how fortunate I am to have grown close to him.

Coach turns, looks me in the eyes, and raises his pointer finger, indicating that he'll be off the phone in a minute. Consistently spending time on the phone has become a trademark of Coach's personality; he is always reaching out to connect with past Pingry soccer players, coaches, parents, and old friends. He has a phenomenal ability to remember people from many years back, and cherishes each and every one of the connections he has made. Coach hangs up the phone and turns toward me.

"Who were you talking to? The president?" I asked jokingly.

Laughing, Coach replies, "No, that was the coach from Columbia High School. We go way back." He pauses for a second then asks, "Are you preparing for the game on Saturday? It's a big day for you; it's your last county final as a Pingry soccer player."

"I've been preparing for Saturday all week, Coach. I'll be ready," I respond.

Over the last four years, he has gradually instilled in me confidence and leadership qualities through his subtle actions. When I pass Coach in the hall, he always stops to ask how school, family, and soccer are going. Occasionally, he will introduce me to one of the thousand alumni that have returned to Pingry just to catch up with him. He has taught me the ability to communicate constructively with my peers, coaches, family members, friends, and teachers. As a leader, he has taught me to become someone who is easy to approach with problems concerning soccer, school, or just life. Just recently, a few teachers approached me about one of my younger teammates who was struggling in school both academically and socially. They asked me to watch out for him and make sure he felt comfortable in all situations. With this conversation in mind, I made sure to go out of my way to greet him in the hallways and ask him how his day was going. I told my friends on the soccer team to watch out for him as well, and every so often, I pull him aside and talk more in depth about his ongoing experiences with both school and soccer. I've always been an approachable and communicable person, but after spending four years under Coach and observing how dedicated he is to his players, both past and present, I have realized how truly important it is to be unconditionally there for others.

Off and on the field, Coach demands excellence from all his players in a kind and sensitive way. He has a unique talent of bringing out the best in everyone around him. I am lucky to have the experience and the memories, both as a player and friend of Coach. He has taught me so many different aspects of life through his actions and words. The lessons I have learned from Coach Miller Bugliari will be put to good use in the next four years of college and for the rest of my life.

BRAD FECHTER '05

THE LIFE & TIMES *of* MILLER A. BUGLIARI

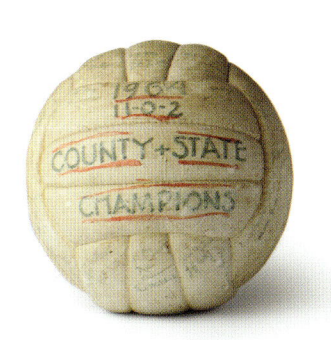

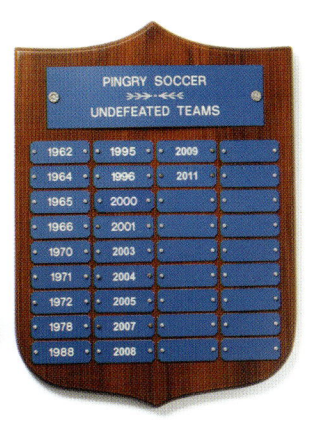

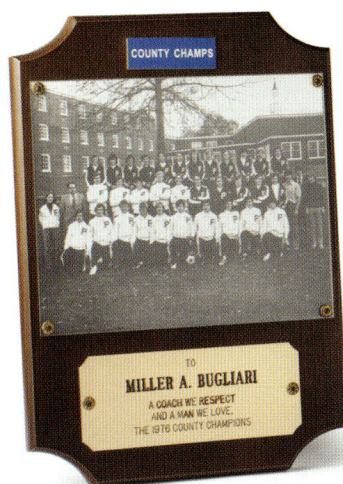

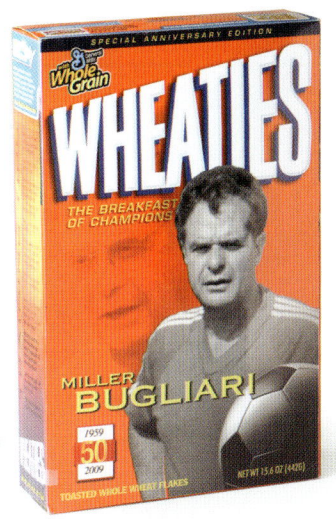

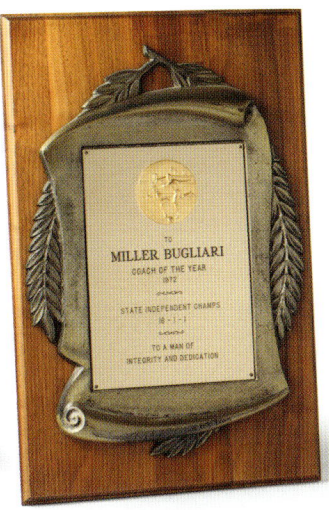

A sampling of the many awards of achievement and memorabilia displayed on the walls of Miller's office (see gatefold).

245

244

243

Miller Miscellany

Miller in the NFL

"My NFL experience officiating started in 1974. Charley Baxley, a dear friend and parent of five Pingry children, Jim '75, Andrew '78, Kathy '79, John '80, and Maureen '82, asked me if I would like to be an alternate on the New York Giants chain gang. Of course I said 'yes.' What a thrill to see athletes that close and experience the game at that level."

It's hard for fans today to imagine how primitive the league was in those days. In 1970, the newly formed Players' Association managed to get owners to agree to minimum salaries: $9,000 a year for rookies and $10,000 a year for veterans. Miller remembers a pre-season game against the Penn freshmen in the late 1960s at Franklin Field. Somehow there had been a scheduling mishap and the Cleveland Browns football team showed up at the same time as the game to practice on the field before playing the Philadelphia Eagles the next day. They were told they'd have to wait until the Pingry game was finished! Miller recalls some of the NFL players hung around to watch the game, including the Browns' famous place kicker Lou Groza, a toe-kicker in the years before the Gogalak brothers revolutionized place kicking with their soccer-style approach.

"My first game," Miller recalls, "was in the old Palmer Stadium in Princeton, for a Giants vs. Eagles pre-season game. Things were much simpler and more relaxed then. No video replay or megatron TV screens. The fans were having a great time and seemed to be in a party mood. The guys on the chain gang were alternately booed or cheered along with the referees.

"After the game, as I was leaving, someone thought I was a player (players were a lot smaller then) and asked for an autograph. I was happy to sign his program. There are so many great memories, like doing a game at the Yale Bowl between the Giants and the Jets and watching Joe Namath, whose knees then were so bad he could barely run, hobble for a touchdown on a bootleg right in front of me. I was in Giants Stadium for the "Miracle of the Meadowlands" when the Giants fumbled the ball in the last seconds and the Eagles' Herm Edwards returned it for the winning touchdown.

"In the early days, one of my jobs was to get the bean bag the referee would drop to mark where the ball had been caught. I remember one time, against the St. Louis Cardinals, I was late getting onto the field to retrieve the bag and found myself in the middle of the play. Needless to say, I got off the field in a hurry.

"I was also there for the famous 'Snowball' game against the San Diego Chargers on December 23, 1995. It had snowed a day or so before, and there hadn't been time to clear the snow from the seats. It was a bad season for the Giants, and the home fans were pretty disgusted. They showed their displeasure by pelting the players on the field with snowballs. I was near the sidelines when someone yelled, 'Hey Miller!' from the stands. That's happened a lot over the years – a lot of Pingry families have season tickets, and always like to get my attention in a game. So I turned around to see who was yelling at me and got hit in the face with a snowball. By the end of the game, as the temperature dropped, the snowballs turned to ice balls, and the players and officials were running for cover."

"Every once in a while I would get hit on the sidelines. The more experience you get, the sharper you watch the play on the field and the faster you move backwards. Sometimes a player would try to help me right before the collision, but that usually resulted in getting hit even harder. The worst hit I may have taken was from Lawrence Taylor, but a lot of NFL quarterbacks had that experience, too. I remember the 1986 playoff game against the San Francisco 49ers in which Jim Burt knocked quarterback Joe Montana out of the game – an overwhelming 49-3 victory for the Giants. We came in after the game to our dressing room attached to the visiting team locker room, and there was Montana, sitting in a chair, still barely conscious from the blow he had taken from Burt.

"I've attended several Super Bowls, but officiating one was a terrific experience. It was unlike any other game I ever worked because of the elaborate entertainment and the horde of celebrities on the sidelines. We could barely move through the crowd of people to do our job, and had to watch to keep from tripping over all the TV and lighting cables. I did enjoy getting my picture taken with Phil Simms and Joe Namath, however.

"Over the years, my experiences have allowed me to meet other famous celebrities. It's all great fun."

Miller taking a hit from Seattle's Marshawn Lynch in 2013.

Miller the Historian

Miller's love of history has been a lifelong passion. On his 1958 trip to Europe, Miller decided he wanted to see the Rosetta Stone in the British Museum. But it was locked up, viewable only by credentialed researchers. That obstacle didn't deter Miller. He caught the name of the museum official who politely told him viewing the Rosetta Stone was out of the question, went to the guard at the door of the room containing the stone and said, with utter confidence and authority, "Dr. XXX has given me permission to view the Rosetta Stone. Would you let me in, please?" As the Brits might say: "It was as easy as Bob's Your Uncle."

Perhaps because Miller grew up during the Second World War, he's been particularly drawn to historic places like London, Bletchley Park in Buckinghamshire, where the Germans' Enigma code was cracked, and battle sites like Normandy, El Alamein, and Monte Cassino. He's traced the path of the American 5th and British 8th armies up into Italy from Sicily, and visited Berlin and Hitler's Eagle's Nest retreat at Obersalzberg in Berchtesgaden.

John McLaughlin, father of John '78, is a historian who shares Miller's fascination with World War II. He recalls a trip to Europe with Miller in 2013. "Miller and I were part of a World War II battlefield tour of Sicily and Italy. After the first two days in Rome on our own to see the Roman sites, Richard Schonberg joined us and six others on the tour. Richard is another longtime friend of Miller, and his sons, Eric '05 and Grant '08, also played for Miller. Needless to say, we had a wonderful time on the trip.

"Every evening the eight persons on the tour would have dinner, usually at a round table, and conversation was lively, much aided by the usual beverage of choice, the local wine, which flowed freely. Not surprisingly, Miller tended to dominate the discussions. No one objected, because he is always interesting and informative. On this particular evening Miller and Richard got into a long and lively argument about philosophy, mathematics, and many other obscure subjects. No one ventured into the discussion to interrupt Miller or Richard. It was one on one, and we were enjoying the bout. The arguments sometimes became quite animated, especially when the subject was advanced math and science, subjects on which Richard is really well informed.

"It seemed to me and the rest of the group that Richard was winning more points, and to me this was quite amusing, because Miller has about the same ratio of winning arguments as he has wins in soccer. But on this evening he was definitely falling behind. After a particularly telling point made by Richard, Miller seemed to be stumped. We awaited his response. It took a few seconds for Miller to gather himself, but finally, after pausing dramatically to pour another glass of wine and slowly take a sip, he raised his hand and solemnly but emphatically announced: 'Richard, what you say did have currency for a time in scientific circles, until June 1943 when the world renowned physicist Zingrelli, in his Nobel Prize-winning book, totally refuted just about everything that you just said.' There was total silence. Even Richard looked stunned. This clinching point seemed to conclude the argument. Then I, half out of ignorance but curious to know more, spoke up and said that I had never heard of Zingrelli. 'Please tell us more about him.' I said.

"Miller paused, started to grin, and then, half sheepishly, quietly said: 'I made it up.' Well, we broke up in laughter. It was a stunning end to the evening.

"Richard and I thought we would have some fun. Richard went on the Internet and obtained some pictures of Miller, and we drafted a 'Wanted for Questioning' poster in connection with the disappearance of the renowned physicist Zingrelli. Posters with Miller's picture were posted throughout the hotel before Miller came down for breakfast. When he saw them he got a great kick out of it."

Schonberg and McLaughlin can't be blamed for wanting to get back at Miller. On their trips to Europe, Schonberg liked to take videos of the places they visited. He intended these to be serious historical records; Miller had other ideas. So Schonberg's video of Bletchley Park has a sound track of the high-pitched squeal of Morse Code dot-and-dash transmission provided by Miller. Since Miller learned code in the Army, he might have actually been sending a message!

Wanted for Questioning

Miller Bugliari alias "Bugsy" wanted in connection with an investigation into the missing physicist Zingrelli. Bugliari believed to be a soccer coach traveling incognito with WWII tourists in Sicily.
REWARD
contact the Avventura Polizia.

THE LIFE & TIMES of MILLER A. BUGLIARI

The Bugliari Family in Italy

In 2002 Miller traveled with Aldo Tripicchio to Calabria, Italy, to discover his family's roots and the town from where his grandparents emigrated to America, Santa Sofia d'Epiro. Like all of Italy, Calabria, in the southern part of the Italian "Boot," was eventually conquered by the Romans after fierce resistance in the 3rd century B.C.E. In the succeeding century it was repeatedly invaded and occupied by different peoples. Miller's ancestors were Albanians who fled to Italy to escape the Turkish conquest of Greece in the 1500s.

The Bugliaris were prosperous landowners. In addition to excelling as a teacher who founded the College of Sant'Adriano, Archbishop Francesco Bugliari (1742-1806) was a passionate supporter of the rights of his people, which led to his assassination in 1806 by brigands hired by his political opponents. Archbishop Giuseppe Bugliari (1813-1888) is reputed to have constructed the Palazzo Bugliari in Santa Sofia d'Epiro, which now serves as a museum for Albanian-Italian culture.

Aldo Tripicchio adds, "I remember our very special trip to Santa Sofia d'Epiro in Calabria, where we visited the Piazza Bugliari, Palazzo Bugliari (yes folks, there are squares and buildings named after Miller!), the Byzantine church built by the Albanians in the 1800s, the official Town Hall, and our welcome and tour by Giovanni the Historian. The day was capped by the roasted pork lunch and a stop in Cosenza. The San Michele Hotel (a Five-Star hotel) in my home town of Cetraro was all Miller's for three days... and my mom's dinners. Miller did upset her because he didn't eat enough!!!"

Miller's Museum

The best insight into Miller as a historian comes, naturally, from Elizabeth. "Miller is a passionate historian. Some people read books; Miller devours them, and naturally, he remembers everything he reads! Our basement now holds Miller's archives: among other things, museum-quality sports memorabilia, books on the great hotels of the world, and Miller's first love, his World War II collection. Besides books, research materials and rare photographs a library might envy, over the years Miller has built an amazing display of historic helmets, swords and uniforms. I can't remember a trip to Europe when we didn't come back with an additional suitcase filled with Miller's latest acquisitions.

"So of course, antique dealers in military artifacts love him – with them he's like a kid in a candy store with a fistful of money. Since it's our money, I've tried, without much success, I'm afraid, to exercise some reasonable limits. Anthony and Boyce love to tell the story of the time they opened the trunk of Miller's car to find a samurai sword and war helmet sitting inside. 'What's this,' they asked Miller. 'Don't worry about that,' he said. 'Don't tell your mother.' Later that day, the phone rang and I answered it. 'This is Bob's Memorabilia,' the caller said. 'I'm checking to see if he still wants the two new pieces he picked up.' 'How much are they?' I asked. '$2,500 each,' he answered. 'That's all right,' I told him. 'Thank you very much, but he's decided he doesn't really want them after all.'"

Miller in Africa

In 1974, Miller was asked to accompany a group of retired scientists from Bell Labs on a tour of Africa, serving as their guide to African flora and fauna. They traveled 3,200 miles from the lush wine country of South Africa to the vast Serengeti plains by plane and Land Rover. As Pingry's reigning expert in class/order/family/genus/species/variety, Miller was in his element, spouting out the Latin names of plants and animals, thirteen to the dozen, with a facility that would have made his old Latin teacher, Albie Booth, proud.

And, being Miller, if he didn't know the right name, he just made it up. One can imagine him confidently saying: "That's a particularly fine example of *Tramontana irascibilis*." "We've seen examples of the stinkwood *(Ocotea bullata)* and sneezewood *(Ptaeroxylon obliquuum)*. This tree is the burpwood *(Eructatea flatulensis)*." "There, hiding behind the acacia plant on the hillside to our right, is the very rare *Okapi Genia makhlinisis*." They saw the "Big Five," lions, elephants, Cape buffalo, rhinos, and leopards, as well as clusters of antelope, troops of chimpanzees, towers of giraffes, implausibilities of gnus, and cackles of hyenas. The wonderful part for Miller was a continent with such astounding diversity of wildlife and natural features.

Miller in Cape Town, South Africa.

Miller in Hollywood

When Miller's sons Boyce and David wound up working in the entertainment industry, Boyce as a TV writer/executive producer and David as an agent, it was really a case of acorns falling near the tree.

"It's been wonderful," Miller says, "for me to be graciously invited to share a little of their world from time to time by attending events and being on the set during shooting. I know the kids at Pingry get a kick out of the photo of me with Ken Jeong from the movie *Hangover III*. And it's been a great thrill for me to meet people whose work I admire, like Clint Eastwood and Bradley Cooper."

Miller also met Robert De Niro during the production of *Silver Linings Playbook*, a movie Miller really enjoyed, but that experience was a little different. De Niro was grappling with the character of Pat Solatano Sr., a rabidly obsessive-compulsive Philadelphia Eagles fan (that's probably repetitious). David described Miller's superstitions and mannerisms to De Niro, who apparently took a lot of notes. When Miller saw the movie, De Niro's character looked a little familiar.

At the preview, Miller got to meet many of the actors and crew, which he loved, but when David introduced Miller to De Niro, saying "This is my dad," Miller remembers De Niro giving him a very strange look. At least De Niro didn't rub his hands together with nervous energy.

From left: Clint Eastwood, David Bugliari, Bradley Cooper, and Miller, on location in Morocco for shooting "American Sniper."

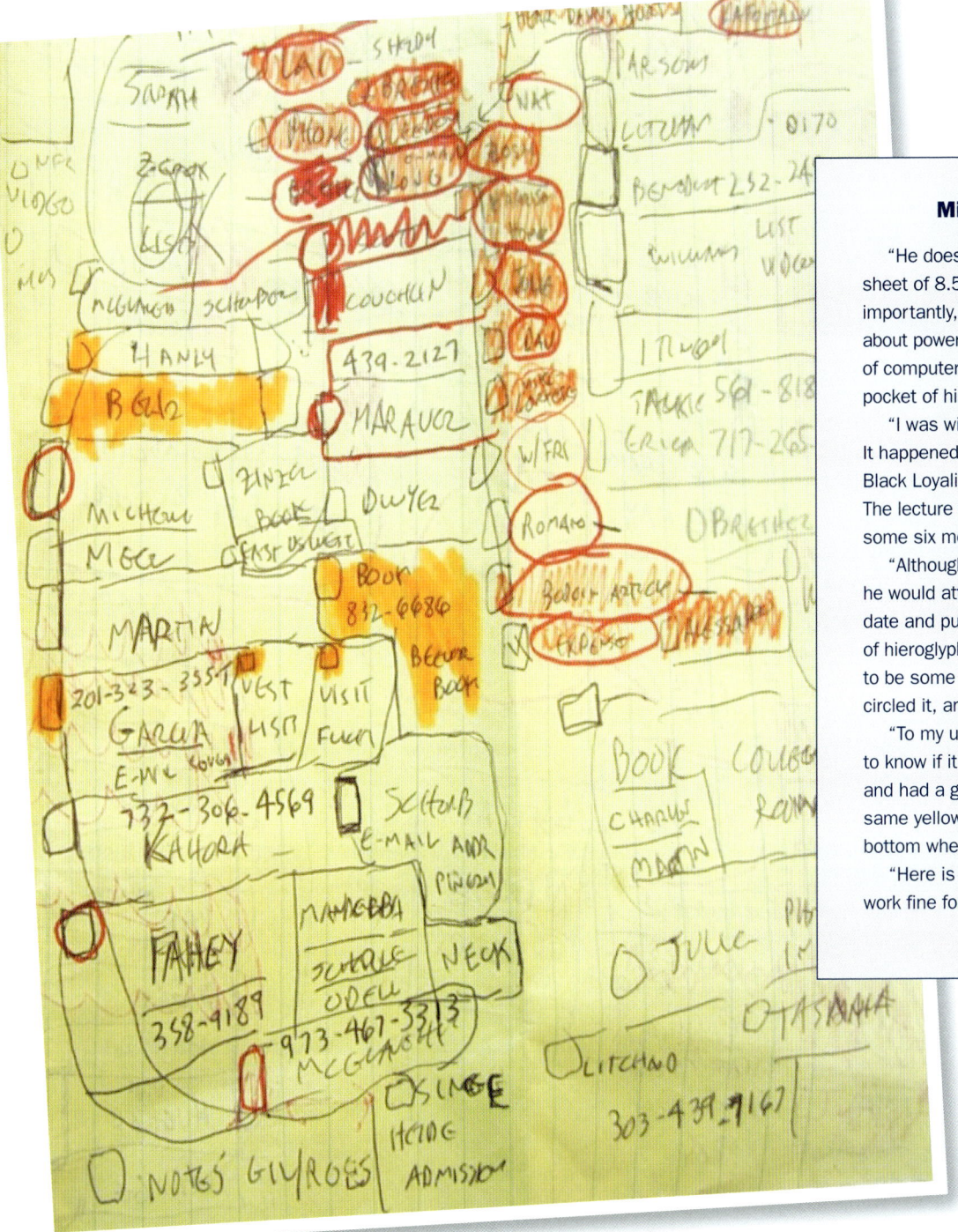

Miller Bugliari's Very "Personal Computer"

"He does not need computers. He can compute perfectly well, on a single sheet of 8.5 by 11 inch paper, folded over twice lengthwise. And, more importantly, he can retrieve it quicker. Further, he does not have to worry about power shortage, low batteries, wi-fi or any other of the modern marvels of computers. He carries this paper with him constantly in the inside breast pocket of his sport coat, and can retrieve it on a moment's notice.

"I was witness to the efficacy of Miller's system several years ago. It happened that I mentioned to Miller that I was giving a lecture on the Black Loyalists who served with the British Army in the Revolutionary War. The lecture was scheduled to be given at Fraunces Tavern, in New York City, some six months or so in the future.

"Although the lecture was at least six months in advance, Miller told me he would attend and travel into the city with me. He asked me the exact date and pulled out this yellow, crumpled sheet of paper with hundreds of hieroglyphic-like chicken scratchings on it and made what appeared to be some kind of an entry on a small corner at the bottom, in red ink, circled it, and said 'I got it,' and will be in touch prior to the lecture.

"To my utter surprise, a day before the lecture he called and wanted to know if it was still on. He met me at the train and we went in together and had a great time. I asked to see his 'note' and he pulled out the same yellow sheet and pointed to some chicken scratching on the bottom where he had marked his note.

"Here is a picture of Miller's 'computer.' I must say it seems to work fine for him."

John J. McLaughlin

The Bugliari Family

Elizabeth's Story

Meeting Miller

I met Miller when I was still at college and he was already a young teacher and coach at Pingry. He had taken a liking to and an interest in my brother, David Budd, Class of 1966 at Pingry. I had come home for the weekend, and in walked this very handsome young man with David. They had gone bowling with several of David's classmates.

Although I never saw Miller again (or thought of him) until after my graduation from college, he never loses an opportunity to say that I wrote him constantly from school…which is completely untrue!

Suffice to say that my first job (who knew???) was to teach Geography at Pingry in the 5th and 6th grade, which I absolutely loved. Pingry was all boys then, but since I had grown up between two brothers, Boyce and David, and we were all competitors, boys were no mystery to me. My older brother, Boyce, rowed at Yale, then Cambridge in England, and ultimately for the Vesper Club in Philadelphia. The Vesper Club "eight," a ragtag group of young men from all over the United States, went to the Olympics in Tokyo and won the gold medal against the two top teams in the world at that time, East Germany and Russia, teams that had trained with each other from their early teens. I asked my brother to come to Pingry to meet my 5th and 6th grade students and show them his gold medal. Quite a sight, little 10- and 11-year-old boys gazing up at this enormous man and listening to his tales of the USA victory! Those little boys who called me "Miss Budd" are all grown now, many with children of their own, and now tower over me when we see each other at Pingry events.

Elizabeth Budd teaching Geography in the Lower School at Pingry.

My younger brother, David, played football at Pingry. He was a halfback and high scorer on the team – with 9 points. Three of the points were earned by kicking a field goal, so that should give you an idea of football at Pingry that year. I went to all of his games, but kept hearing about the soccer team and their phenomenal coach. Intrigued to see a Pingry team actually win something, I went to a soccer game one beautiful afternoon. I sat down in the bleachers next to a mom in the stands just in time to hear the coach rage, "You look like a wet dish rag!!!" "He's talking about my son," she said, proudly. (My habit of standing at the far end of the field away from all family members began early, and Miller and I hadn't even had a date yet!)

Prepping for my class one day, I looked up to see Miller standing in my doorway in a white lab coat. "Everything OK down here?" he asked. "Fine," I stammered, wondering who this guy was. He then asked if I was going to David's next game, at the Peddie School, and so it all began. By the New Year, we were engaged.

And boy was he fun! I never knew from one date to another what he would think up next, a picnic on the beach or a trip to the opera. And what a fund of knowledge. His love of history and travel were amazing, and he loved to argue with my very well-read mother about the meaning of certain words. An example was the word "poignant." He was right and she was sort of right. His definition was #1 in Webster's, hers was #2, but the more well-used meaning was #2, so they would argue about that! They adored each other. My mother's advice to me on finding the right man was, "Find a man who is an honorable man, like your father." I think I did that.

Marrying Miller

Our wedding, at the Church of the Redeemer Episcopal Church in Morristown, New Jersey, was "standing room only." I think almost every boy at Pingry came and a few made it into our reception at Morris County Golf Club. I was 24 years old and had never met anyone quite like Miller. A new bride has to get used to adopting a new name, in my case an Italian name that most people (including me, at first) couldn't pronounce correctly. But nothing prepared me for the letter I received addressed to "Mrs. Millie Bughouse." Looking back over all the years with Miller, they got the first name wrong, but the last name has turned out to be pretty much accurate.

Don't Get Married, Coach!

When Alan Gibby '66 was chosen as co-captain for his senior year, the tension he felt was enormous. His coach had announced that spring that he was getting married to Pingry's 4th grade teacher Elizabeth Budd. "This is the end. It will ruin everything," Alan remembers thinking. "Once he's married, he won't care about us as a team. How could he have chosen to get married my senior year? Why couldn't he have waited until after I graduated!"

After a week of Alan passing her in the hall with his head down, looking totally despondent, Elizabeth called him into her room for a chat. When he came into her classroom and squeezed his 6'2" frame under a primary-school-size-desk, he could barely speak, he was so nervous.

Elizabeth waited with patient calm until Alan, after several false starts, blurted out his message: "I don't think you should marry Coach. He's really mean. He makes us wear lead vests and spats, run until our legs fall off, and practice in the dark. And he yells at us all the time."

Realizing he might have just blown it, Alan tried again: "Well…uh…I mean…if you're going to get married, could you please wait until January after our season's over?"

Elizabeth just smiled, then, with the same reassuring calm, said: "Alan, thank you for coming to tell me this. But you need to realize something important. I don't want to change Miller – I love who he is. I am going to support him. And if that means dinner will be late because he practices until after dark, then dinner will be late." Alan left the meeting with the weight lifted off him.

I loved watching and hearing him coach. It was obvious that the boys idolized him and he was fiercely loyal to them. What was quickly obvious is that he was honest and he was fair. He never cut a player, even one with little athleticism, but he would tell them that if they worked hard and came to practice, he would get them in a game. What also struck me was his interest in all the students, especially those who needed someone to help build their confidence. His ability to make everyone feel that they belonged and were valued was – and still is – an outstanding character trait. He was, quite simply, born to be a teacher and a coach, one who would make a difference in a child's life.

The boys knew that he would have their backs, that they could trust him and his judgment. To this day, he will get phone calls, "Coach, I need to talk to you…," and he never says no, or that he doesn't have time. He finds the time and has been privy to all of life's problems, from trouble with parents, marital issues, illness, to child rearing. His advice is sound and comes from a wealth of knowledge and a caring, loving man.

We were married for three years before we started a family, years that were filled with travel all over the world. And we went to the movies! Before every game! Miller's way of staying calm.

The Pingry "Soccer Mom"

When we were first married, we lived in a wonderful garage apartment at 50 Western Drive in Short Hills. Pasta parties began there! The team would arrive on a Friday night and would spread out in the apartment, many of them having to sit on the stairs when room ran out in our tiny living room. I would serve baked lasagna, Italian bread, a salad, cider, and chocolate chip cookies! It wasn't unusual for some of my 5th and 6th grade students to come by in the afternoon and we would bake those cookies together.

I loved hearing the repartee between Miller and the players – always coaching, always teaching. I know I felt the pressure that first year about the soccer season, and every year since, and I knew not to complain about the time Miller spent with his teams.

And did you know that I threw out his "special" sport jacket? The one in which he had an unbroken winning streak of 57 games? I was cleaning out closets and found the jacket with its shredded lining hanging out of it and thought it wasn't dignified for a Pingry teacher to coach in such an awful outfit. Miller was in disbelief. I felt terrible, but he never got angry.

Many years later, when David brought Alyssa's parents home to meet us, Miller greeted them wearing his "lucky loafers," with duct tape holding the tops to the soles. I was horrified. I'd kept throwing those shoes out and Miller kept finding them. I shouldn't have worried. Alyssa loved them, and insisted Miller keep them on for her parents. They thought they were cute, too. Since David is like Miller in many ways, I guess that was a good sign. And maybe it was Miller's way of ensuring the marriage was blessed with good fortune!

Wee Geordie

When Miller took me on, he also inherited my Basset Hound, "Wee Geordie," named for a movie character who went to the Olympics for Scotland to throw the hammer. I had been correcting five sections of Geography papers, so when we left my apartment for dinner, Geordie let us know in no uncertain terms what he thought of the new man in my life. In amongst all those papers were just two photographs of Miller. Not one paper was harmed. The two photos – chewed to bits. The stage was set, but Miller eventually won Geordie's undying love by rescuing him from an "attack cat" who came to Waganaki, our summer camp, courtesy of one of the counselors.

Geordie later proved his loyalty to Miller at a game at Pingry's North Avenue campus. It was brutally cold, and Mr. Les insisted that I get into his car, parked near the edge of the field. He handed Geordie's leash to a Pingry senior, Don Blasius '68. Don paid no attention to the dog until the referee came over to pick up his jacket and discovered that Geordie had lifted his leg all over it. The ref began berating Don and he replied, "Given the way you called the game, if I were a dog, I'd pee on your jacket, too!" Just about that time a Pingry teacher stepped in, took the dog, and separated the two. I thought Geordie and I should keep a safe distance from the field, since he accompanied me to every game, and you never knew who the refs would be on a given day. The following week, I walked into a game at Scotch Plains – same ref. Geordie and I stayed out of sight.

Elizabeth with newborn Boyce at 67 Oak Ridge Ave. in Summit.

Get Your Own Donkey

On one of their trips to the Budd family's home in Ireland, Elizabeth thought it would be fun to get the donkey from the pasture where it was sequestered with "Molly," their enormous Clydesdale draft horse. Elizabeth planned to take Boyce, age one and a half, for a ride in the donkey cart, so she sent Miller to bring back the donkey. Miller's only prior experience with equine animals, ever, had been at the racetrack. But it seemed like a reasonable request. Surely Miller could manage a small, docile donkey.

Unfortunately, they didn't realize Molly had "adopted" the donkey and was fiercely protective of "her foal." When Miller entered the paddock, Molly, her ears laid back flat on her head, charged like a chestnut locomotive.

On seeing this wild-eyed, four-legged earthquake approaching at a dead run, her huge hooves scattering clumps of sod into the air, Miller turned and ran for his life. He made the paddock gate a few steps ahead of Molly and cleared it in a vault that might have qualified him for the Olympics.

"Where's the donkey?" Elizabeth asked, innocently, when he returned.

"From now on, get your own donkey!" Miller retorted.

Late Night with Miller Bugliari

Miller could have had a show on TV, "Late Night With Miller Bugliari." His uncanny ability to find your vulnerable spot and work from there would have his "audience" helpless with laughter. He gave a surprise party for me one time (in our own home!). He did "stand-up" relentlessly, and no one was spared. My whole body hurt from smiling and laughing. One woman, Gail Williams, met me in the kitchen and gasped, "He is the funniest man I ever knew! I can't take any more, I have to stay in here for a while or my face is going to fall off!"

Competing Against Miller

No one told me that Miller was ambidextrous. I was a pretty good tennis player – I'd played at Morris County Golf Club and at Kent Place and had had a great deal of instruction all my life. On the other hand, Miller had never had a lesson. Frustrating!!!!? He could figure out a way to win – he could raise the level of his game, or make me giddy with laughter, then just as I sent a passing shot past his backhand, he would shift his racquet to his *left hand* and send a forehand back across the net. I wanted to brain him with my racquet! The boys and I guess that Miller, like Boyce, was born naturally left-handed, but his early teachers, as they did in those days, forced him to learn to write with his right hand. They obviously weren't able to stifle his quick wit and sense of humor.

Starting a Family

When Boyce, our oldest, was born, Miller was ecstatic, but terrified to hold the baby. He held him as if he were a time bomb about to go off. But once Boyce could walk and run and showed an interest in any kind of ball, there was no one better as a father. Anthony arrived four and a half years later and David came six years after Anthony. What was so wonderful to me was Miller's emotional attachment to his boys. Here was a man who LOVED his children, who kissed them and hugged them and regularly fell asleep with them while reading a nighttime story. And they, in turn, adore and honor him and are wonderful husbands and fathers unafraid to show affection to their children.

Boyce (top), Anthony (middle), and David (bottom).

"While Dad was in many ways a wonderful father, he had a few limitations. One of those limitations concerned anything that might take place in the kitchen. On the very rare occasions when he had to get us breakfast by himself, typically the best he could manage was taking a rock-hard English muffin out of the freezer or burning toast to cinders, putting it on a plate, and spooning a glob of cream cheese or peanut butter next to it. 'What *IS* this, Dad?' we would ask. 'Breakfast,' he said."

David Bugliari '97

"In April of 1968, my first son, Boyce, was born. In retrospect, I was a bit naïve about the changes that would come as a result of the birth of a child.

"I was at the very top of my golf game in those years, regularly shooting between 75 and 85 on most courses, so when I received an invitation to play in the 'Keynote Open' on the old Homestead Golf Course, I was overjoyed! Of course, I would play!

"In my excitement, it never occurred to me that I would be off having the time of my life, while my wife would be home with a newborn who did not understand the concept of sleep. Elizabeth was cross-eyed with exhaustion. As she likes to say now, 'It was a toss-up who cried more, the baby or me!'

"Well, I won the tournament and like any 12-year-old, I couldn't wait to show off my trophy! I rushed into our garage apartment and woke my poor wife up from the first real sleep she had had in many days to tell her of my triumph. To say that my announcement was met with a chilly silence from my wonderful wife, Elizabeth, would again be an understatement of the situation. I think I got a little better with Anthony and David."

Miller Bugliari

Moving to Tewksbury

We moved from the garage apartment in Short Hills to Oak Ridge Avenue in Summit and lived there for 10 wonderful years. I'm a country girl at heart, however, and by 1978 it was time to move to the property Miller had bought in Tewksbury. So we began the odyssey of building a home. In the middle of everything else I was pregnant with David, our youngest son. When I think back, I do not know how we did it, but I do know that Miller and Boyce, our oldest son, were safely in Maine on moving day when all the frantic effort of moving to a new home took place. (That may not surprise you.) David was seven months old, the dog nearly died from some malady or other, and so in the midst of it all I had to run the dog to the vet while the movers were packing the van.

Suffice to say we all survived, although the moving crew were reluctant to leave me there in the wilderness – there wasn't a light or another house for miles – with two young children and an Irish Setter named Blitzen (Miller called her Blitzkrieg). At least we didn't get hit by a hurricane. That would come later.

Living in the Country

Living in the country in Tewksbury offered a different set of challenges. Walking out one morning with my cup of coffee, I all but stepped on a snake. I will face down a mountain lion, but a snake renders me weak at the knees and nauseous. "MILLER!" I screamed. "There's a snake next to my foot!" I expected him to come rushing to my aid. Instead, he just said, "Move your foot." I could have killed him.

I would never harm a snake in the woods or far from the house, but near the house or in my garden, all bets are off. I asked my brother David if he still had our old .22. His instructions? "The sight is off, aim low left." I never miss, that is how much I am disgusted by and dread snakes. More than one friend of my sons has been suitably chastened and impressed by my marksmanship when witness to "oh, it's just my mom, shooting a snake!"

Similarly, when you live in the country, you cannot just call someone every time a tree falls down. So I learned to use a chainsaw. While I am very respectful of the power of a saw (it does not know your leg from a branch), the ability to use one has come in handy many times. After the storm of the century, Hurricane Sandy, Miller and I could not get down our very long driveway. At least five enormous trees had come down and brought the power lines down with them. I lay in bed one night trying to come up with a way to get us out. What if we had an emergency of some sort?

The next morning, Miller and I took down a section of pasture fence, drove the Jeep down a rather steep incline, took down a tree that was in the way, opened another section of fence and hopped the Jeep down onto the driveway. From there, we could drive down the power line to a neighbor's driveway and we had access to the outside world. As I was taking down the tree, unbeknownst to me, Jake Ross '96 appeared – our son, David, had called him from California and asked him to check on us. Jake took a picture: there I am, in work clothes and goggles, wielding the chainsaw, and there's Miller in his yellow parka looking like, well, a supervisor. We went for two weeks without power, but thanks to Miller's foresight we were in much better shape than so many because we have an enormous generator that operates on propane.

Getting the Boys to Help

Elizabeth was so competent with everything having to do with taking care of an estate it was natural that the boys and Miller respected her expertise. One Sunday, they were deep into that respect, watching a Giants football game while Elizabeth was outside clearing brush. Elizabeth's Mom, who was living with them, came downstairs and saw the four men in full couch potato sloth. She stood behind them for a moment or two to gather an appropriate level of indignation, then proclaimed, "I think it is absolutely REPREHENSIBLE that the lady of the house is slaving by herself outdoors while four grown men are sitting here watching television!" Miller turned around to her with a smile. "Hi Helen. How are you doin'?"

Miller the Communicator

After Miller's version of a power nap (an hour or two) he will often come downstairs and say to me: "How about a soup and a sandwich?" which in "Millerese" means: "Elizabeth, would you please make me a sandwich and a bowl of soup?" It's not that Miller is lazy, he's just, well, somewhat inexperienced in the kitchen.

So I was completely taken off guard when one afternoon at our farm in Ireland, Miller asked me, "Would you like a cup of tea?" Our oldest son Boyce and his family were visiting and Miller's offer got everyone's attention… "Dad? Doing something in the kitchen? Impossible!" Few things are better on a cold, damp day in Ireland, however, than a piping hot cup of tea, so I gratefully said: "Thank you. That would be wonderful."

Miller disappeared into the kitchen and returned minutes later – with a tea bag floating soggily in a cup of barely lukewarm tap water. I was amazed, and asked him, "Miller! What IS this?"

Nonplussed, Miller replied, "It's a special tea for a special lady."

In another example, I was watching Pingry in a Somerset County championship game one year at Pingry that ended tied after overtime, requiring the winner to be decided by penalty kicks. The chosen spot was at the opposite goal. As the referees gathered the players to set up for the penalty kicks, unaccountably, Miller started walking across the field toward me, away from the action.

"Is he OK?" I wondered.

"Water fountain!" Miller called out. "Water fountain!"

The water fountain (right) which Miller wanted to keep in his sightline during penalty kicks.

At the Basking Ridge field, the water fountain was right next to where I always stood, next to parents from the opposing team.

"Does he want me to take a drink of water?" I wondered. By now I was well used to the fact that Miller typically communicates in riddles, but this was *really* confusing. I bent over the fountain, pressed the handle, and instantly got drenched by the explosion of water that came out.

By now, Miller was closer to me.

"Water fountain!" he called out again. Then "Sightline! Sightline!" As this intense man kept walking toward me yelling incomprehensibly, the reaction of the other team's parents had changed from curiosity, to amusement, to anxiety.

"He wants to see the water fountain during the penalty kicks," I guessed, and I moved the spectators away so Miller could see the fountain while the two teams exchanged penalty kicks.

Pingry won the game. As I met Miller amidst the post-game celebration, I asked him: "What was THAT about?"

Miller just laughed. "Heh. Heh. It worked, didn't it?"

"Dad often speaks in fragments. Many times these fragments are hard to decipher. Oftentimes, in our family, we help translate for each other. For example, Dad will say things like: 'Put the thing in the thing.' 'What, Dad?' 'The thing! Put the thing in the thing!' 'Dad, I have no idea what you're talking about.' Using a combination of guesswork and help from visual cues, my brothers and my Mom, we figure out he means to put a picture back in a photo album. Most of you may not know this, but my Dad once thought about being a doctor. I wonder what it would have been like to have Dr. Bugliari tell you, 'Well, we need to run some more tests because you have a thing on your thing.'

"His syntax can be confusing, too. We all still laugh about the time he was telling us about a conversation with a friend and said, 'Bob's in lettuce.' We asked, 'He's WHAT?' 'In lettuce,' Dad answered, like someone explaining something obvious to small children. We were picturing some guy trapped in a field of radicchio that had grown the size of a cornfield. It took a while to figure out Dad meant the guy owned a lettuce farm."

Anthony Bugliari '79

Coaching the Boys

Fast forward to when the boys began to play soccer. We were so careful to never put any pressure on them. The boys loved football as well, but when the choice had to be made all three chose soccer and all three were captains of their teams. Those were interesting days, and probably hard on the boys as well as on Miller, but because of the age difference, they never played on the same team and each of them rode to school with Miller every day, giving each of them such a special relationship and time to share whatever was going on in their lives, including the season.

(From left): David, Miller, Anthony, and Boyce.

> "When Beatrice and I started a family, like most young fathers, I didn't have much of an idea how to go about it. My Mom had died, so Miller and Elizabeth were wonderful mentors. After our first child Charlie was born, I asked Miller and Elizabeth, 'What's the secret to being a good parent?' Elizabeth answered first. 'You have to be willing to be miserable yourself.' She went on to describe a vacation in Vermont they'd planned for months. On the trip, the boys were being so impossible in the car that Miller and Elizabeth told them, 'Stop it, or we're going home.' Boys being boys, they didn't stop, so Miller and Elizabeth turned the car around, and that was the end of their vacation, one that Miller and Elizabeth had really been looking forward to. The lesson about self-control they wanted their sons to learn was more important. It was a good lesson for us, too. Sometimes you have to sacrifice your own pleasure to help your kids develop the values they will need in life."
>
> **Phil Lovett '79**

> "Dad has always had a love affair with magic. So for decades, every trip to Los Angeles to visit friends like Bob Thurston also included an obligatory visit to the *Magic Castle*, a private club devoted to magic, and a showcase for performances by some of the greatest magicians in the world.
>
> "After decades of visits, Dad had to put some effort into getting us to go yet one more time. He'd call me first, and say that David was enthusiastically looking forward to a return trip. 'Really?' I'd say, still somewhat skeptical. Then he'd call David and say that I was really interested in going. It's one of the oldest tricks in the book, but Dad could somehow make it work.
>
> "One time, I remember, we went to one of the side rooms where a magician was doing audience participation acts. He called for volunteers from the crowd, and had them write information on a card like a favorite color and a number, which he then promised to guess by reading their minds. Of course my Dad volunteered. The magician correctly guessed what three of the volunteers had written on their cards. It was pretty impressive. Then he dismissed the participants and ended his act without calling on Dad. So of course I had to ask him, as we were leaving, 'Why didn't you try him?' He answered, 'His mind? I couldn't tell WHAT was going on in there.'"
>
> **Boyce Bugliari '86**

Miller always made a point, especially when Pingry was way ahead, which it usually was, of benching his starters for most of the second half. My boys loved to play and would get furious at having to sit out the game.

(From left): Anthony, David, Miller, and Boyce.

So after a game in which one of the boys hadn't played as much as they wanted to, they would walk to our cars, glare at Miller, and say, "Mom, I'm going home with *you*!" It was even worse when they hadn't played well. I knew to keep quiet and managed never to say the equivalent of "Why on earth weren't you able to score? It was an open goal!"

Boyce's Story
"Among my earliest memories are the summers we spent in Maine at Camp Waganaki. When I was five, I was finally allowed to go 'down the hill' for the day, but each evening I was sent back 'up the hill' to Mommy's cabin. David was too young, but Anthony and I took a lot of heat for that. The other kids were pretty rough on us, a bit like *Lord of the Flies*!

"I grew up in New Jersey and have vivid memories of playing soccer on the beautiful Hillside field at a very young age. At halftime, a few of us would storm the field shooting on the goal until the refs chased us off. Dad really liked the fact that I was naturally left-footed and felt that I had an ability to 'see the field' and had a 'feel for the game.' I remember him telling me that 'This is a simple game. Don't overcomplicate it.' That's a good lesson for life, too.

"I'm amazed at how hard Dad works at continuously deepening his knowledge of the game. I can't imagine the number of college and professional games he's watched, and I've seen him studying soccer books, coaching videos, and tapes for years. He's always learning."

> "Because I had to make the drive to the Hillside campus from Tewksbury, my trips were more torture than anything else. It was a one-and-a-half-hour trip each way, on 78 to Berkeley Heights, where the highway ended in those days, then back roads to Route 24 through Union to the school. One time as we got ready to get off 78 behind a really long line of cars at the exit ramp, I noticed there was no traffic exiting the other way. 'Dad, do a U-turn and get off on the other lane,' I said. 'We can save at least ten minutes.' Of course he didn't want to do it; somehow I talked him into it, and we got off the highway. My guess worked, but all he said was, 'You're unbelievable!'"
>
> **Boyce Bugliari '79**

"Another thing that stands out in my memory was how he handled the guys on the bench who might not get into a game unless we had a substantial lead. Other coaches might lose interest in the game and not pay attention if that were the case. Not Dad. He was intensely coaching these kids as if they were the most important players on the team and their play was the difference between winning and losing the game. That is the kind of respect he showed all of his players and that is why so many of them have such strong affection for him and the program long after their playing years are over.

"Once in a while, though, there were kids that not even Dad had an answer for. During one practice after a particularly bad game, a player on the squad announced to Dad that he had to leave practice early. My father asked why. The player blurted out, 'I have mime practice.' Every jaw on the field dropped. In coaching mode, I had never seen my father speechless. I did that day. Needless to say, the rest of the team got some extra running during that practice."

Anthony's Story
Because he lost his father at such a young age, Miller has always treasured his memories of his dad. One of those was his father's love of fishing, so Miller always hoped one of his boys might take up that sport. The family fisherman turned out to be Anthony. There are two kinds of fishermen – fly fishermen and amateurs; it's the same difference as between professional golfers and weekend hackers. Fly fishing, if it hooks you, turns into an art form, a metaphor for life, and an obsessive compulsion. Anthony's obsession began early, on a trip to Ireland, when Miller took him out fishing.

"I was extremely excited to go fishing with Dad. I was still learning many of the skills necessary to actually get a fish to rise to my fly, but I was determined to try everything I knew: different flies, different sizes, some below the water's surface and some on top. At one point I looked upstream at my father sitting quietly on the bank holding his rod (he had a spin rod and a hook with a worm) with the line drooping down next to him and the hook on the dry bank. I said, 'Dad, what are you doing? You'll never catch anything, you don't even have your line in the water.' He said, 'Ant, I'm enjoying myself… just let me fish the way I want to.' 'But Dad, that makes no sense! At least let the hook be in the river and give yourself a chance!' 'You're unbelievable!' he said.

'I'm unbelievable? How am I the weird one here?' I replied. He laughed and then we both laughed. Even then I knew that I wasn't going to change him. He just wanted to relax and spend time with me."

After graduating from college, Anthony played professional soccer for one year in New Zealand with Scott Aimetti '87. Miller came out to visit him and suggested they go fishing together. As Anthony loaded up the rods, reels, fly boxes, and waders, remembering the Ireland experience, he asked, "Are you sure?" Miller said, "Yes."

They drove for two hours to one of the great New Zealand trout streams, unpacked their gear, and hiked for another hour to the river. Anthony completed the ritual of preparing to fly fish, and waded into the stream. It was a scene right out of the old Brad Pitt movie *A River Runs Through It*. Miller sat down on the bank to watch. Anthony hadn't been fishing for more than 15 minutes when Miller called out, "Isn't it about time we should get going now?" Anthony was dumbstruck. "What! We've only just gotten here." Miller replied, "Well, we aren't going to stay here all day, are we?" Miller was delighted to spend time with Anthony; he just wasn't as thrilled spending time with fish.

"Growing up," Anthony says, "we always accepted that we had to share our father with a thousand other kids. Now, as an adult with five children of my own, I can only hope that they will someday have a coach, a teacher, or a mentor who is as important to them as my father has been to so many. 'Coach' always has time for everyone, whether you played for him in 1960 or 2013, or even if you never played for him. He will listen, he will advise, he will give you options, and he is always fair. I have asked my Dad over recent years if he has ever thought about retiring. He has laughed and said, 'Sure, there are things I'd love to do… travel more, spend more time with your mother and my grandchildren… but I love coaching, and as long as I feel like I'm still connecting with the kids…' My Dad often doesn't finish sentences, and in this case he didn't need to."

> "I remember one time coming home from school we were stuck behind a car that was just crawling ahead of us. Anthony started yelling at Dad, 'Pull around this guy! The left lane is open!' Dad told him to be quiet. Anthony just kept it up. 'Dad, you're killing me! Pass him! We'll never get home!' So finally Dad hit a stretch of open road and floored it by the car in front. As we went by, Anthony leaned out the window and yelled at the driver, 'What's your problem?!'
>
> "At that point the cop in the unmarked police car we'd just passed turned on his strobe lights and pulled us over. We stopped, and the cop came up to Dad's window. 'What's *YOUR* problem?' he asked, none too politely. Dad pointed at Anthony, now slumped down into the passenger seat. '*HE's* my problem. Arrest him!' The cop started laughing, and once again, Dad got away with it."
>
> **Boyce Bugliari '79**

David's Story

"As kids we loved sports, and Dad would always play with us. I can't remember a time when he said 'Maybe later, I'm busy now.' He'd immediately drop whatever he was doing to spend time with us, teaching us skills or just having fun.

"Dad would sometimes have to drive Nick Ross and me to hockey games early in the morning. We'd get dressed in our hockey gear at 6:00 a.m. and head out with Dad. These were the days before GPS, and Dad was in a hurry, so of course we'd get lost. Dad would try to find the rink by trial and error until his patience had completely evaporated. 'That's it!' he'd yell. 'We're going home!' As 10-year-old kids, we'd have to talk him down from his road rage and make sure we got where we were going.

"Trips to school with Dad were an adventure for all of us. Each of us in turn had to develop high-level negotiating skills at an early age in the constant debates over what to listen to on the radio. We wanted to listen to music – our kind of music. Dad wanted to listen to the news – his kind of news. It was a constant battle. As it turns out, Dad loved Eric Clapton's album *Slowhand*, especially the song 'Lay Down Sally,' which Dad insisted on calling 'Long Tall Sally.' (Eric Clapton – Little Richard – anybody could get them confused.) If you could find that song or album on the radio, you were good for music the rest of the trip – with Dad singing along.

"His eccentricities aside, he was extraordinarily patient with us. I've never met anyone else who listens as deeply, or has greater insight in solving personal problems, as Dad. So naturally, I had to test that legendary patience. I remember getting kicked out of class one day and sent to the assistant headmaster's office. He was teaching a class, so I waited in his office. We all knew he liked to lean his chair way back and put his feet up on the desk, so I adjusted the springs on the chair so that when he leaned back, the chair would tip over backwards. He returned just as I had to leave for the next class, but I hadn't gotten 10 feet from his door when I heard a crash followed by an angry yell, 'BUGLIARI!' I headed at a dead run for Dad's office. The assistant headmaster's call to Dad beat me by a few seconds. I walked into the office and Dad bellowed, 'That's it! THAT'S IT! You're going to military school!'

"I obviously got out of that scrape, too. When your Dad is the master of one-upsmanship, you're bound to pick up a few skills along the way."

"What an incredible man he is! He is my father and has always been my mentor, my teacher and my coach. His impact on my life and on my two brothers' lives is immeasurable. He is an extremely honorable man with a code of ethics that is unshakable. He is a true role model for me and so many others. And none of this would be possible without 'Mom.' The two of them are quite a team!"

Anthony Bugliari '79

"Miller and I were blessed with three wonderful sons, and at the moment ten grandchildren. Our philosophy on raising children has been to teach them loyalty, honor, responsibility, and truthfulness. We had great role models in our own parents. We knew that our role was that of parents, not best friends. We had to make some tough disciplinary calls, but they were made out of love. The prize at the end? A close loving family and the joy of watching our own sons and remarkable daughters-in-law as they take on their roles as parents."

Elizabeth Bugliari

The Miller and Elizabeth Bugliari Family

(Left to right): Dorothy, Boyce, Mary Helen, Alice, Delia, and Murphy.

(Left to right): Alyssa, Milo, and David.

(Left to right): Claire, Annie, Katie, George, Anthony, Anthony, William, and Finley (dog).

Miller and Elizabeth in David's new car.

Index

The following names appear in text, captions and/or team rosters on pages 6 through 262:

A

Abbott, C. 143, 145, 146
Ackerman, J. 161, 164, 165
Ackerman, P. 153, 154, 155, 156, 157
Ackley, G. 97
Acosta, E. 221
Adams, Bill 147, 149
Adams, Bruce 99, 100, 102, 103
Adams, Randy 91
Adams, Robbie 107, 108, 109
Aibel, B. 121
Aibel, J. 101, 103
Aimetti, S. 150, 151, 152, 153, 154, 155, 170, 174, 261
Akins, J. 127, 128, 129
Alam, Z. 189, 191
Alchus, D. 66, 178, 179, 180, 181, 182, 183
Alenick, S. 123, 125, 127
Alexander, I. 40, 108, 109, 113, 114, 115, 116, 117
Alexanderson, R. 59
Alfano, J. 147
Alfano, T. 149, 151
Alin-Hvidsten, A. 220, 221
Alford, S. 169, 170, 171, 172, 173
Allan, Chris 54, 129, 130, 131
Allan, Chuck 54, 124, 125, 126, 127
Allan, Dave 54, 121, 122, 123
Allan, David 54, 55, 67
Allen, M. 133
Alley, R. 9
Amabile, J. 125, 127, 129
Ambrose, W. 117, 119
Ancelotti, C. 234
Anderson, K. 235
Anderson, P. 178, 179, 180, 181
Angelides, Y. 220, 221
Angell, J. 154, 155, 156, 157
Antonelli, F. 67
Appelbaum, M. 179, 181, 183, 188, 189
Appruseze, B. 49
Apu 68
Aquino, M. 191, 193
Arace, B. 12
Archer, G. 103
Archer, S. 148
Archibald, M. 7
Arena, B. 234
Arlen, G. 150, 151
Askin, S. 179, 181, 182, 183
Atwater, C. 12, 67
Atwater, E. 91, 93, 95
Auerbach, B. 99
Avila, J. 120

B

Babbit, A. 201, 203
Babcock, C. 201, 203, 204, 205
Badami, C. 64
Baekey, B. 12
Baggio, R. 162
Baird, D. 165, 166, 167
Baker, B. 123
Baker, J. 67
Bald, M. 125
Baldwin, Dave 121
Baldwin, David 9
Baldwin, Dick 12
Barber, T. 94, 95, 96, 97
Baresi, F. 162
Barg, S. 131, 133
Barlow, J. 235
Barnard, L. 86, 87
Barnasse, G. 67
Barrett, B. 97, 98, 99
Barsamian, C. 183
Bartenstein, J. 115, 116, 117
Bartenstein, T. 121, 123
Bartlett, C. 21, 129, 130, 131
Bartlett, P. 21
Baum, G. 90, 91, 93, 94, 95, 98
Baumgartner, E. 235
Baxley, A. 246
Baxley, C. 246
Baxley, Jim 246
Baxley, John 121, 123, 246
Baxley, K. 131, 246
Baxley, M. 246
Bearzot, E. 235
Beckenbauer, F. 111
Becker, D. 145, 146, 147
Becker, M. 149, 150, 151, 152, 153
Bednarsky, T. 168
Behr, T. 40, 41, 43, 67, 78, 79, 80
Beinecke, R. 87
Benedict, G. 23
Benedict, P. 90, 91
Benjamin, T. 169, 171
Bennett, C. 170, 171, 172, 173, 174, 175
Bent, D. 138, 139, 141
Bent, J. 133
Bent, S. 143, 145, 146
Berger, A. 103, 104, 105
Berman, M. 235
Berry, S. 165
Bertsch, K. 66, 159, 161, 170, 174, 175, 176, 177, 178, 179, 180, 181, 197, 210, 229, 231
Bethune, W. 93
Betteridge, D. 121
Betteridge, J. 108, 109, 114, 115, 116, 117, 236
Bevan, D. 22
Bevill, S. 165
Bianchi, R. 120
Bianco, S. 213, 215, 216, 217
Biedron, M. 107, 109
Biedron, S. 41
Birkhold, J. 101, 103
Birotte, A. 141, 143
Blair, J. 101, 103, 104, 105
Blanchard, M. 173, 175
Blanchard, Pete 170, 171, 172, 173
Blanchard, Peter 107, 109, 224
Blasius, D. 254
Blumenstyk, M. 177, 178, 179, 180, 181, 182, 183
Bockskopf, L. 143, 145
Boehm, B. 114
Boffa, J. 44
Boisvert, S. 67
Bolan, J. 72, 75
Bonn, B. 103, 104
Bonn, H. 103, 104, 105
Boocock, B. 67
Booth, A. 8, 12, 67, 250
Boova, K. 188, 189, 191, 233
Boova, L. 233
Boova, T. 233
Boozan, J. 121, 123, 125, 126, 127
Borden, P. 97, 98, 99, 108, 110
Borden, T. 55
Borden, W. 37
Boskey, J. 87
Bosland, J. 131, 133
Bosland, R. 231
Bourne, B. 68
Bourne, M. 151, 153, 155
Boyer, B. 93
Boyer, G. 177
Boyer, J. 170, 171, 172, 173, 174, 175
Boyer, P. 87
Boylan, T. 177, 178, 179
Bradford, B. 124
Bradley, B. 162, 235
Bradley, R. 198, 199, 200, 201, 202
Bragg, N. 182, 183, 188, 189
Brainin, J. 129, 131
Branchina, N. 207
Brauman, J. 175, 177
Braun, M. 149
Breheney, C. 61
Brenner, A. 123, 124, 125
Breznitsky, T. 128, 235
Brewer, F. 99
Briody, B. 122, 123, 124, 125
Briody, K. 116, 117, 118, 119
Briody, T. 118, 119, 120, 121
Brisgel, S. 133
Bristol, B. 105
Bristol, T. 55, 68
Brody, M. 129, 130, 131
Brown, J. 93
Brown-Allen, D. 68
Bruce, R. 110
Brunhouse, A. 68
Bryan, J. 12
Bucci, D. 135
Buchanan, P. 12
Buchner, L. 105
Buck, L. 88, 94, 95, 96, 97
Budd, B. 76, 252
Budd, D. 252, 257
Budd, E. 36, 49, 54, 64, 68, 71, 74, 75, 224, 232, 234, 252, 253, 254, 255, 256, 257, 258, 259, 260, 262
Budd, H. 257
Buffum, D. 8
Bugliari, A. 153, 154, 155, 156, 157, 249, 256, 258, 260, 261, 262
Bugliari, B. 146, 147, 148, 149, 249, 255, 256, 258, 259, 260, 261
Bugliari, D. 74, 83, 173, 174, 175, 176, 177, 254, 256, 257, 259, 260, 262
Bugliari, E. 36, 49, 64, 68, 71, 74, 75, 224, 232, 234, 253, 255, 257, 258, 259, 260, 262
Bugliari, F. 249
Bugliari, G. 249
Bugliari, J. 6, 7
Bugliari, J.V. 6, 7, 54
Bugliari, M.M. 6, 7, 9
Bunn, C. 129
Burani, M. 167, 169
Burchenal, C. 201
Burchenal, W. 205, 207
Burgdorf, B. 186, 200, 201, 202, 203, 204, 205
Burgess, J. 191, 193
Burks, B. 9
Burrows, P. 12, 15, 17, 27, 30, 35, 75
Burt, D. 49, 53, 72, 74, 103, 104, 105, 106, 107, 114, 129, 131, 231
Burt, J. 247
Busch, H. 12, 15, 17, 55
Bushell, D. 91
Bustamante, B. 135, 154
Buteux, A. 199
Butler, C. 205, 207
Butt, C. 24
Bye, R. 101

C

Caiella, N. 178, 179, 180, 181, 182, 183, 188
Cali, J. 97, 98, 99
Callaghan, M. 191, 193
Cameron, C. 157
Campbell, A. 139
Campbell, J. 147
Canavan, M. 142, 143, 144, 145, 146, 147
Carragher, J. 9
Carragher, P. 120
Carro, P. 127, 128, 129
Carson, H. 161
Carter, F. 67
Carter, T. 90, 91, 92, 93
Carter, W. 99, 101
Caruso, J. 90, 91
Carver, R. 216, 217, 218, 219
Carver, S. 217, 218, 219
Cascaldo, G. 67
Casey Family 211
Casey, A. 209
Casey, J. 209, 216, 217, 218, 219, 220, 221
Cassidy, D. 97
Castle, D. 195, 197
Chalmers, J. 91
Chan, M. 213, 215
Chatterji, A. 68
Chernoff, M. 179, 180, 181, 222
Cherry, K. 235
Chiaramonte, J. 149
Chirichillo, F. 89, 235
Chodan, M. 209
Choe, C. 151, 153
Christensen, D. 95
Christow, G. 36, 55, 67, 72, 113
Chwazik, G. 121, 122, 123

264

Chyzowych, G. 235
Cipriano, G. 24, 39, 119, 120, 121, 225, 236
Cipriano, P. 24, 194, 195, 196, 197, 198, 199
Cirovski, S. 178
Cissel, E. 12, 56, 67
Ciszak, P. 43, 48, 108, 109, 113, 114, 115, 116, 117, 230
Clapcich, A. 137, 140, 141, 142, 143, 144, 145, 146
Clark, B. 234, 235
Clarick, G. 139, 141
Clausen, M. 216
Clayton, L. 86, 87
Coe, C. 68
Coerver, W. 112
Coffey, B. 143
Cohen, A. 143
Cohen, D. 139, 141
Cohen, J. 207, 213
Coleman, L. 194, 195, 196, 197, 198, 199
Coletti, J. 180
Colford, B. 101, 103
Colford, C. 44, 45, 109, 115, 117, 224
Colter, C. 117
Combias, B. 195, 196, 197, 198, 199
Conard, N. 56, 57, 67
Connata, E. 184
Connell, J. 105
Connell, M. 109
Connor, G. 97
Constantino, J. 199, 201
Conway, B. 105, 107
Conway, G. 115, 116, 117
Cook, J. 210, 216, 217, 218, 219, 220, 221
Cooper, B. 250

Cooper, P. 149, 151
Corbett, D. 12, 36, 94
Corbett, Jubb 9, 12
Corbett, Jim 104, 105, 106, 107, 108
Corbin, C. 157, 164, 165
Corbin, T. 79
Corboz, M. 206, 207, 209, 212, 213, 214, 215
Corliss, B. 179
Cornwall, Joe 96, 99, 101, 102, 103
Cornwall, T. 93, 94, 95, 96, 97
Corvino, B. 174, 175
Corvino, Sr., T. 68
Costa, B. 206, 207, 209, 212, 213, 214, 215, 216, 217
Cotton, C. 173, 175
Coughlan, M. 146, 147, 148, 149
Coughlin, M. 152, 153, 154, 155, 156, 157, 179, 181, 183, 215, 217, 219, 221, 232
Coughlin, P. 86, 87
Coughtry, B. 102, 103, 104, 105
Cox, C. 61, 107, 109, 228
Cox, P. 68
Crabtree, S. 149
Crandall, M. 162, 167, 168, 169, 170, 171, 172, 173
Croke, D. 179
Croke, D.M. 145
Crosby, B. 153, 154, 155
Crowley-Delman, J. 68
Cuaycong, M. 167, 169
Cummings, M. 221
Cumpton, J. 99, 101
Cunningham, Gordie 101, 102, 103
Cunningham, Granville 115, 116, 117
Cunningham, S. 67, 113

Cunningham, T. 128, 129, 130, 131
Curtis, J. 139
Curtis, P. 149
Curtis, R. 75, 110, 128, 129, 130, 131
Curtis, W. 40
Curtis, Z. 91
Curtiss, T. 93
Cuttic, C. 63
Czaya, A. 235

D

D'Costa, M. 149
Dackerman, R. 127, 128, 129
Daeschler, T. 125, 126, 127
Daglaroglu, R. 171
Danzig, H. 87
Davenport, P. 58
Davich, E. 183, 189, 191
Davis, B. 115, 116, 117
DeAlmeida, R. 215, 216, 217, 218, 219, 220, 221
Dean, J. 93
DeAngelis, C. 194
DeBlecourt, J. 125
Dee, L. 67
DeGraef, P. 132, 133
DeGrande, M. 159, 164, 165, 166, 167, 168, 169, 170, 171, 180, 181, 183, 195, 196, 197, 199, 201, 203, 205, 225, 231, 233
DeGryse, A. 8, 12, 67
DeLaney, F. 125, 126, 127
DeLaney, J. 218, 219, 220, 221
Delfausse, P. 91
Delman, P. 68
Dellmono, P. 120
Delmonaco, N. 98
DeLuca, S. 172
De Niro, R. 250

Dennison, P. 131, 132, 133
DePalma, G. 151
Deren, E. 105, 107
DeRosh, D. 48
Derr, T. 93, 94, 95
Devers, M. 205
Devers, N. 197, 198, 199, 200, 201, 202, 203
Diaz, R. 220, 221
DiBella, J. 132
DiBuono, B. 121, 122, 123
DiChiara, D. 137, 140, 141, 142, 143, 144, 145, 146
DiChiara, J. 149
DiChiara, M. 65, 150, 151, 152, 153
Dickson, M. 189, 191, 193
Dietzel, P. 86
DiLeo, L. 191, 193
DiLeo, M. 195
DiMartino, J. 151
Dimock, G. 12
Dineen, S. 68
Dixon, D. 99
Dolan, J. 101
Donahue, J. 127
Donaldini, R. 235
Donatti, S. 184
Donnantuono, A. 197, 199
Donnelly, A. 157, 161, 164, 165, 166, 167, 197, 199
Donohue, C. 147, 149
Donohue, G. 141, 143
Donohue, J. 155, 156, 157
Donohue, M. 154, 155, 156, 157
Donohue, M. Jr. 25
Donovan, D. 235
Dooley, C. 126, 127, 128, 129
Dormont, P. 119
Dougherty, K. 147, 148, 149
Downs, G. 109

Dressen, R. 9
Drew, C. 27
Dreyer, G. 91
Drysdale, D. 28
duBourg, T. 50, 55, 60, 67, 70
Dudley, R. 97, 99
Dufford, J. 52, 67, 113
Dugan, C.. 221
Duncan, Bill 97, 99, 100, 101
Duncan, Bob 109
Dunlap, D. 149, 150, 151
Dussan, S. 178
Dwyer, B. 96, 97, 98, 99, 227
Dwyer, S. 193, 195, 196, 197, 198, 199
Dziadzio, J. 149, 150, 151, 152, 153
Dziadosz, S. 98
Dzina, D. 12

E

Eagan, J. 86, 87
Eastwood, C. 250
Eboh, K. 213, 214, 215
Eboh, O. 195, 197
Echeverry, G. 235
Echikson, B. 127
Edison, C. 6
Eduardo, 82, 83
Edwards, T. 143, 145
Ehrlich, Amy 133
Ehrlich, Andy 60, 138, 139
Eisenbud, D. 145, 146, 147
Eisenbud, G. 133, 138, 139
Eldon, J. 148, 149, 150, 151
Elkind, D. 203, 205
Elkins, A. 183, 188, 189, 190, 191
Elliot, F. 205, 206, 207, 209, 212, 213, 214, 215
Ellis, G. 52

Ellis, T. 181, 182, 183, 188, 189
Ellis, W. 87
Emmitt, P. 169, 171
Engel, Rick 109
Engel, Rob 109
English, B. 101, 103, 104, 105
English, M. 207, 213
Erickson, G. 95, 97
Erickson, J. 91
Erickson, M. 87
Erickson, R. 95, 96, 97
Errington, J. 107
Eschenlauer, C. 58, 133
Eskaderian, A. 182
Evans, B. 91
Evans, J. 124

F

Faherty, D. 149, 151, 153
Faherty, P. 147, 148, 149, 150, 151
Fahey, D. 66, 159, 176, 177, 178, 179, 180, 181, 195, 196, 197, 199, 201, 203, 205, 208, 209, 215, 217, 219, 220, 221, 229, 232, 236
Fair, D. 145, 146, 147
Faisal, B. 86, 92
Falk, R. 186, 202, 203, 204, 205, 206, 207, 209, 212, 213
Fast, J. 92, 93, 94, 95
Fayen, F. 54, 67, 231
Fechter, B. 191, 192, 193, 194, 195, 196, 197, 207, 213, 215, 231, 240
Fechter, C. 207, 209, 212, 213, 214, 215, 216, 217
Fechter, M. 185, 199, 200, 201, 203, 204, 205, 209
Feigenbaum, J. 145, 146, 147
Feigenbaum, M. 140, 141

Feldman, T. 201, 202, 203, 205
Feldstein, M. 58
Feleppa, D. 12, 16
Ferguson, A. 138, 235
Ferraro, J. 177
Ferry, T. 131, 132, 133
Feuer, J. 177, 179
Fields, J. 123, 125
Fiorillo, J. 92
Fishani, M. 67
Fisher, D. 179
Fisher, G. 97, 99
Fitzgerald, J. 175
Fitzpatrick, B. 105, 107, 108, 109
Fitzpatrick, E. 97
Fitzpatrick, J. 99
Fleming, A. 187
Fleming, D. 99, 100, 101
Flowerman, S. 192, 193, 194, 195
Flugstad-Clarke, H. 207, 209, 213, 214, 215, 216, 217
Flugstad-Clarke, M. 221
Ford, J. 105, 107, 108, 109
Formoso, S. 124
Forte, J. 68
Foster, K. 217, 219
Foster, R. 86, 87
Fraites, J. 115, 116, 117
France, C. 12
Franklin, C. 171, 173, 175
Freedman, A. 195
Freedman, D. 137, 140, 141, 142, 143, 144, 145, 146
Freedman, J. 199, 201
Freeman, B. 101
Freeman, H. 176, 177, 178, 179
Frey, G. 114
Friedland, D. 169

Friedman, Sander 140, 141, 142, 143, 231
Friedman, Seth 129
Fritsche, H. 169
Fuller, R. 143, 145

G

Gadsden, H. 205, 207, 212, 213
Gale, L. 95, 97
Gandolfo, J. 193, 194, 195, 196, 197, 198, 199
Gannon, C. 168
Ganz, F. 93, 94, 95
Garafola, G. 115
Garcia, M. 193, 194, 195, 196, 197, 198, 199, 202
Garcia, T. 67
Gardell, W. 36, 42
Gardiner, T. 157
Gardner, A. 157, 165
Gardner, T. 151, 153
Garrow, A. 145
Gastorek, L. 123
Gatto, J. 119, 121
Geacintov, L. 68
Geddes, J. 71, 90, 91, 92, 93
Gensch, J. 138, 139, 140, 141, 142, 143, 231
Geohegan, J. 120, 122
Geordie 39, 254
George, S. 167
Gernert, D. 65, 118, 119, 120, 121
Gesualdo, C. 67
Ghriskey, B. 90, 91, 92, 93
Gibby, A. 96, 97, 98, 99, 100, 101, 104, 227, 253
Gibby, J. 116, 117, 118, 119
Gibby, T. 146, 147, 148, 149, 150, 151
Gibson, G. 87, 90, 91, 93
Gibson, J. 151, 153

Gilbert, S. 101, 103
Ginden, B. 9
Gino 85
Giorgi, D. 123
Giorgi, G. 114, 115, 116, 117
Gittes, D. 179, 181, 183
Glascock, S. 107, 109
Gleason, D. 95, 96, 97
Goddin, B. 124
Goldstein, J. 155, 156, 157, 161, 164, 165
Gonczy, N. 52
Goodfellow, G. 96, 97, 98, 99
Gormley, T. 169, 171
Gottlieb, A. 156, 157, 164, 165
Gradwohl, J. 128, 129, 130, 131, 132, 133
Graham, J. 12
Grandis, M. 165
Granger, J. 190
Grant, T. 68
Grant, V. 68
Green, Johnny 154
Green, Jacob 213, 215
Green, Z. 219
Greenberg, R. 91
Greene, B. 197, 199
Greer, J. 217, 219
Grey, J. 172
Griepenkel, E. 87
Griesemer, J. 97, 99
Griff, L. 192, 193, 194, 195
Griff, M. 195, 197, 199
Grippo, J. 109
Grover, J. 109, 115
Guijarro, A. 97
Gully, J. 221
Gupta, T. 219
Gustafson, G. 101, 103
Gustafson, T. 107, 108, 109, 114, 115

Guyer, F. 90, 91

H

Hackett, T. 87, 91
Hahn, H. 12, 51
Hale, B. 42, 43
Hall, K. 115, 117
Hall, R. 12
Hall, W. 12
Hallett, L. 121, 122, 123
Haltmaier, B. 215, 217
Hamann, C. 105, 106, 107
Hamilton, C. 36
Hamm, B. 207
Hanger, B. 39, 40, 45
Hanger, W. 103
Hanly, J. 67, 187
Hanson, J. 119, 120, 121
Harbeck, J. 10, 12
Hardin, D. 97, 99
Harris, P. 148
Harrison, J. 235
Harsanyi, Z. 91
Hart, S. 90, 91, 101, 231
Hartstein, J. 153
Haselton, K. 125, 127
Haverstick, S. 179, 181, 182, 183
Hawkins, R. 91
Hazen, B. 59
Heekin, T. 39, 41, 43
Heighway, S. 235
Heins, W. 107
Helfman, M. 215, 217, 218, 219
Hellauer, C. 203, 205
Heller, G. 177
Hennessey, I. 235
Hensten, D. 131, 132, 133
Herberger, S. 102
Herrmann, R. 90, 91, 92, 93
Hesketh, J. 67
Hewson, T. 12

Higgins, B. 121, 122, 123
Hilgendorff, N. 153, 154, 155
Hildebrand, R. 156, 172, 235
Hinton, M. 161, 165, 167
Hirsch, B. 161, 171, 173, 174, 175, 176, 177
Hirsch, D. 191, 193
Hiscano, Doug 125, 126, 127
Hiscano, Duffy 133
Ho, C. 217, 219
Hodge, J. 45, 107
Hoffman, C. 169, 171
Hoitsma, J. 120, 121, 122, 123
Holland, A. 183, 188, 189
Holman, J. 12
Holtzman, M. 123
Homer, B. 121, 122, 123
Homer, C. 115
Homer, S. 107, 109
Homer, W. 207, 213
Hostetter, A. 12
Houston, A. 119
Howard, T. 235
Hoyt, E. 95, 96, 97, 98, 99
Hoyt, H. 9
Huang, A. 169
Hughes, D. 169, 171
Hughes, J. 87
Hugin, J. 213, 215
Hugin, M. 216, 217
Huk, M. 139, 141
Hulke, S. 172
Hulshizer, H. 157
Humphrey, A. 131, 132, 133
Humphrey, M. 145
Hurri, H. 117
Hutchinson, J. 53, 133, 231
Hutchison, C. 125
Hyde, A. 95
Hyde, R. 81, 86, 87
Hymas, E. 68

Hynes, E. 199, 200, 201, 202, 203, 217, 231

I

Ibsen, M. 93
Ike, B. 67
Ike, S. 67
Ikoro, O. 218, 219, 220, 221
III, R. 55
Irenas, J. 12
Ives, T. 206

J

Jackson, T. 25
Jacob Family 211
Jacob, A. 205, 206, 207, 212, 213
Jacobs, R. 135, 150
Jacobsen, B. 58
Jaeckle, F. 104, 105, 107
Jaffee, T. 139, 141
Jarrell, B. 170, 171, 172, 173
Jasper, P. 9, 12
Jencick, M. 108
Jenkins, B. 130, 131, 132, 133, 147, 149, 151, 208, 210, 223, 225, 231, 233
Jenkins, C. 137, 142, 143, 144, 145, 146, 147
Jennings, R. 101, 102, 103
Jensen, B. 99
Jentis, R. 155
Jentis, S. 145
Jesky, J. 89, 235
Jeydel, P. 191
Johannsen, P. 87
Johnson, C. 114, 115, 116, 117
Johnson, D. 95, 97
Johnson, R. 125, 127
Johnson, S. 146, 147, 149, 150, 151
Johnson, T. 53, 67, 146, 225

Johnston, L. 207, 213
Jones, C. 91
Jordan, R. 205, 207
Ju, C. 205
Jurist, S. 197, 199

K

Kaag, M. 180
Kaimer, F. 149, 151
Kaisand, A. 217
Kallop, P. 107
Kaminetzky, A. 214
Kaneko, G. 219, 221
Kapila, V. 148, 149
Kaplus, J. 179, 181
Karet, L. 110
Karp, J. 139, 141
Kassel, H. 89, 235
Kassel, M. 198, 202
Kastl, E. 68
Katz, R. 146, 147, 149
Kaufman, L. 125
Keating, T. 68
Keats, P. 87, 90, 91
Kecici, S. 221
Keel, D. 62
Kehoe, B. 189
Kehoe, T. 178, 179, 180, 181
Keil, N. 197
Kellogg, P. 132
Kelly, B. 220, 221
Keneko, G. 219
Kennedy, K. 93, 94, 95
Kenny, E. 207, 213
Keogh, S. 200, 201, 202, 203, 204, 205, 206, 207
Kertesz, D. 164
Key, D. 205, 206, 207, 212, 213, 214, 215
Khawaja, S. 167, 169
Kietzman, K. 119, 121

Kimber, W. Jr. 9, 11, 12, 56, 211
Kimber, W. III 122, 123, 124, 125, 205, 211, 215, 217, 219, 221, 232
Kimber, W. IV 194, 195, 196, 197, 198, 199, 200, 201, 211, 222
King, J. 142, 144
King, R. 128, 129, 130, 131
Kirdzik, C. 206, 207, 209, 212, 213, 214, 215, 216, 217
Kirk, A. 8
KixMiller, J. 98, 99, 100, 101
Klawitter, E. 217, 219
Kline, G. 133, 138, 139, 140, 141
Knetzger, T. 105, 107
Kogan, R. 116, 117
Korn, K. 167, 168, 169, 170, 171, 172
Korth, P. 221
Koth, D. 36, 67, 70, 230
Koufax, S. 28
Kovacs, B. 189, 190, 191, 192, 193
Kraham, H. 218, 219, 220, 221
Krantz, C. 157, 164, 165
Kreh, B. 9
Kronick, D. 132, 133, 138, 139
Kuchler, T. 164, 165
Kudziela, I. 199
Kunzmann, R. 138, 139, 140, 141
Kurtz, R. 115, 116, 117, 118, 119
Kurz, A. 96, 97, 98, 99, 111, 231, 236
Kurz, R. 111, 114, 115, 116, 117, 118, 119
Kwan, B. 166, 167, 168, 169
Kwan, Jeremy 219
Kwan, Jonathan 219
Kwei, S. 169
Kyle, N. 195

L

Lacey, A. 67
LaCorte, B. 51
LaFontaine, A. 186, 200, 201, 202, 203, 204, 205, 206, 207
Lai, G. 146, 147, 149
Lalley, M. 67
Lan, A. 197, 198, 199, 200, 201, 202
Lan, T. 183, 189, 190, 191
Landis, J. 9
Laporte, J. 92, 93, 94, 95
LaSpada, J. 192, 235
LaValette, N. 68
Lavalley, J. 67
Lavey, S. 65, 72
Lavitt, B. 146, 147, 149
Lawson, A. 117, 118, 119, 120, 121
Layng, E. 199
Leavens, D. 90, 91
Lederman, S. 236
Lee, E. 155
Lee, H. 199
Lee, John 161, 164, 165, 167
Lee, Judy 68
Lee, L. 141, 143
Lee, T. 67
Leedom, G. 12
Leef, J. 68
Legge, A. 168, 169, 170, 171
Leibowitz, A. 193, 195
Leininger, E. 176
Lenci, G. 12, 57
Leonard, T. 191, 193
Lerman, D. 118, 119, 120, 121
Lerman, M. 105, 107
Lesneski, B. 37, 41, 46
Lesneski, V. 7, 12, 36, 39, 67, 84, 113, 254

Leverich, D. 105, 106, 107
Levine, J. 143
Levinson, B. 121, 122, 123
Levy, B. 155, 157
Lewis, A. 156, 157, 159, 164, 165, 166, 167, 168, 169, 233
Lewis, J. 67
Lewis, M. 171, 173, 174, 175
Lewis, R. 91
Lewis, Stephen 159, 177, 178, 179, 180, 181
Lewis, Steve 145
Liberato, F. 167, 169, 171
Lieb, R. 125, 126, 127
Lieberman, A. 205, 207
Lionetti, P. 67
Liotta, S. 143
Lipper, M. 213, 215
Litchard, B. 23
Little, A. 143
Lobo, P. 16, 46
Locke, K. 179, 180, 181, 182, 183, 188, 189
Logan, W. 95, 97
Logio, T. 150, 151, 152, 153, 154, 155
Loikits, S. 155, 157
Londa, P. 157, 164, 165
Long, B. 101
Long, W. 55
Lopes, P. 135
Lord, B. 95, 97, 99
Louria, C. 125, 126, 127, 163
Louria, D. 200, 201, 202, 203, 204, 205
Louria, S. 205, 207, 213
Lovett, P. 129, 130, 131, 224, 259
Lovett, R. 126, 127, 128, 129
Lowish, R. 107, 109
Lubetkin, J. 195, 197

Lucas, J. 169
Lucas, S. 157, 165
Lucciola, C. 217, 218, 219, 220, 221
Luongo, D. 176
Lurie, M. 215, 216, 217, 218, 219, 220, 221

M

Maass, B. 105, 106, 107, 108, 109, 224
Macauley, E. 67
Macfarlane, G. 176
MacLaren, S. 108, 109, 114, 115, 116, 117
MacNeil, D. 87
Macrae, D. 125, 127
Macrae, R. 132, 133, 136, 138, 139, 140, 141, 155, 157, 165, 167, 169, 171, 173, 231
Mading, O. 109, 114, 115
Magadini, J. 68
Magliozzi, D. 104
Magrane, R. 193, 194, 195, 196, 197
Mahr, G. 141, 142, 143, 144, 145, 146
Majkut, R. 106
Makhlin, E. 61
Maldini, P. 162
Malo, B. 172
Malo, J. 165, 166, 167
Mamangakis, S. 129, 131
Mancini, G. 100, 101
Mandelbaum, J. 167, 168, 169, 171
Mangini, M. 213, 214, 215, 216, 217, 218, 219
Manley, D. 72, 92, 93, 94, 95, 108
Manning, T. 90, 91, 92, 93

Marano, F. 115
Marchese, A. 165, 167, 168, 169
Marchese, J. 170, 171
Marciscano, A. 189, 191, 193
Margolis, D. 170, 171, 172, 173
Margolis, M. 178, 179, 180, 181
Markoff, S. 201, 203
Martens, D. 23
Martin, A. 207, 213, 214, 215
Martin, J. 117
Martin, O. 220, 221
Martin, P. 91
Martin, P.S. 203, 205, 206, 207
Marzak, J. 105
Marzoli, C. 161, 173, 174, 175, 176, 177
Matthews, J. 98, 99, 100, 101
Maxwell, D. 68
Maxwell, R. 201
May, E. 87
Mayer, J. 93, 95
Mayhew, T. 67
McCarthy, P. 127, 129, 130, 131
McCarthy, T. 15, 17, 35
McCauley, R. 150
McClelland, C. 12
McClure, L. 100, 101, 102, 103, 108
McCormick, D. 133
McCreery, R. 93
McGinley, G. 9
McGrath, C. 160
McGrath, G. 67
McGregor, G. 219, 221
McInerny, E. 150
McKay, K. 101, 103
McKeown, B. 125, 127
McKeown, G. 209, 231
McKinley, S. 234
McLain, J. 9

McLaughlin, J.F. 128, 129, 130
McLaughlin, J.J. 248, 251
McLendon, J. 123, 125
McNulty, K. 203
Meana, R. 235
Meiring, N. 205, 207
Melin, T. 96, 97
Meola, T. 235
Merrill, A. 153
Merrill, C. 111, 112, 121, 123, 134
Meyer, B. 12
Meyer, C. 125, 126, 127
Meyer, G. 93
Meyer, H. 129, 131
Meyer, P. 95, 97, 98, 99
Meyer, S. 86, 87
Meyercord, J. 156, 157, 164, 165
Michaud, J. 128, 129, 130, 131
Michels, J. 205
Miicke, K. 197, 199
Milano, A. 254
Miller, B. 42, 107
Miller, D. 200, 201, 202, 203
Miller, J. 183
Miller, S. 205, 207
Milutinovic, B. 138, 235
Mindnich, J. 103, 104, 105, 106, 107, 114, 122
Mindnich, M. 116, 117, 118, 119, 120, 121
Mindnich, P. 107, 109, 114, 115, 228
Minter, T. 131, 132, 133
Mitchell, T. 99
Molloy, R. 167, 168, 169, 170, 171
Monaco, C. 177, 178, 179
Monaghan, J. 129
Monahon, G. 91, 93, 94, 95

Monahon, R. 87, 90, 91
Monroe, B. 105, 109
Monroe, C. 119
Monroe, M. 27
Monroe, P. 101, 102, 103
Monroy, C. 103
Montana, J. 247
Monteagudo, L. 215, 216, 217, 218, 219
Moody, E. 51
Mook, T. 87
Moore-Gillon, C. 215, 216, 217, 219
Morgan, Jack 67
Morgan, Jay 109, 114, 115
Morgan, W. 18
Morrell, H. 12
Morrow, S. 130
Moser, H. 93
Moser, R. 125
Mueller, F. 12
Mueller, J. 97, 98, 99
Mullen, J. 133, 138, 139
Mullen, S. 122, 123, 124, 125
Mullett Family 211
Mullett, C. 143, 144, 145, 146, 233
Mullett, G. 219, 221
Mulvihill, C. 153
Munger, W. 190, 191, 192, 193, 194, 195, 196, 197
Murdock, J. 68
Murphy, J. 107
Muvumba, J. 93

N

Naess, K. 76
Nair, R. 217, 219
Naismith, J. 18, 243
Namath, J. 247
Nazario, V. 68

Neary, O. 155, 156, 157
Nebel, Jeff 101, 103
Nebel, John 47
Nedde, B. 23
Neebe, A. 95
Neiswender, J. 56, 67
Nelson, B. 115, 117, 119, 121
Nelson, C. 105, 107, 109
Nelson, E. 124, 125
Nettune, S. 170, 171, 172, 173
Neunert, D. 93
Newhouse, J. 169, 170, 171, 172, 173
Newhouse, P. 81
Newhouse, S. 57, 81
Newman, R. 68
Noe, J. 12
Noonan, T. 84
Norman, M. 131, 133
Norton, J. 91, 92, 93
Nye, B. 19, 20, 21, 25

O

O'Brien, B. 12, 16
O'Brien, J. 12
O'Connell, C. 205, 207
O'Connor, M. 44, 125, 127, 235, 236
O'Connor, R. 116, 117, 118, 119
O'Donnell, Bill 96
O'Donnell, Billy 122
O'Donnell, Brian 111, 130, 131, 132, 133, 137, 138, 139, 143, 145, 153, 167, 208, 210, 231
O'Donnell, C. 205, 207
O'Donnell, F. 96, 122
O'Donnell, J. 98
O'Donnell, S. 67, 75, 111, 118, 119, 120, 121, 122, 123, 124, 225
O'Mara, D. 68
O'Reilly, B. 148

Oh, R. 183, 189, 190, 191, 192, 193
Oplinger, E. 200, 201, 202, 203, 204, 205
Orr, C. 12
Orr, J. 12
Ortner, S. 68
Osmun, T. 143, 144, 145, 146

P

Padula, J. 219, 220, 221
Padulo, D. 149, 151
Page, J. 118, 119
Paglia, A. 129
Palazzolo, S. 205
Palmer, G. 201, 203, 204, 205
Papasikos, J. 191, 193
Pappas, W. 151, 152, 153, 154, 155
Parcells, B. 161
Parisi, B. 156
Parker, G. 109, 114, 115
Parker, K. 146, 147, 148, 149
Parker, P. 121
Parliman, C. 173, 175
Parliman, T. 169, 171
Parreira, C. 138, 234
Parrondo, J. 193
Parsons, C. 177
Pascale, Jerry 73, 233
Pascale, Jon 166, 167, 168, 169, 210, 223, 225
Patrizio, J. 200, 201, 202, 203
Patrizio, M. 215, 217
Paul, A. 102, 103, 104, 105
Pearlman, C. 156, 157, 164, 165, 166, 167
Pearlman, J. 68
Pedrick, W. 97
Pekarsky, J. 179, 180, 181
Pelé 111

Pence, M. 150, 151, 152, 153, 154, 155
Penney, J. 109, 115
Penrose, D. 189, 191
Pepe, C. 126, 127, 128, 129
Perlman, B. 143
Petrie, J. 86, 87
Pfeiffer, V. 58
Pfister, K. 105, 107
Phares, W. 9
Phillips, Dan '59 55, 61, 67, 105, 107, 109, 111, 115, 117, 119, 121, 123, 125, 126, 127, 228, 230
Phillips, Dan '97 173, 175, 176, 177
Pico, M. 116
Pierson, B. 12
Pierson, G. 17, 75
Pike, S. 207, 213
Pinhiero, G. 94, 95
Pingry, Dr. 50, 65, 66, 68
Pinke, W. 203, 205, 206, 207
Pinkin, D. 171, 173
Pizzi, M. 146, 147, 148, 149, 150, 151, 152, 153
Platt, C. 118
Platzman, S. 142, 143, 144, 145, 146
Plum, J. 101, 103
Plum, T. 99
Poli, J. 30
Popper, B. 36
Poppick, D. 116, 117
Porchetta, M. 85
Porges, F. 205, 206, 207, 209
Porges, J. 189, 190, 191, 192, 193
Porter, J. 12
Poster, M. 95
Pratt, D. 175, 177

Prevost, M. 12
Prevost, R. 87
Prideaux, M. 110
Procopio, F. 125
Proudman, D. 154, 155
Puleo, F. 14, 155, 156, 157, 161, 164, 165

Q

Quaas, K. 127, 128, 129
Quieroz, C. 138
Quigley, R. 221
Quinn, P. 133

R

Raabe, C. 129
Raabe, R. 44, 120, 121, 122, 123
Racca, L. 22
Rachlin, J. 138, 139, 141
Rafferty, J. 97
Rakhit, R. 215, 216, 217
Ramirez, C. 199, 201
Ramos, A. 220, 221
Ramos, T. 235
Randall, F. 12
Randolph, F. 17
Range, R. 154, 155, 156, 157
Range, S. 157, 164, 165
Ranzato 193
Rao, A. 217, 218, 219
Rath, D. 98, 99, 100, 101, 104
Reasso, B. 162
Reddy, V. 220, 221
Reid, P. 174, 175, 176, 177
Reiken, R. 143, 145
Reisner, D. 117, 118, 119
Reitman, S. 86, 87
Rentzepis, J. 143, 145
Rentzepis, M. 131, 132, 133
Rettig, J. 97, 98, 99
Rettig, T. 99

Reyna, C. 135, 160, 164
Rhodes, J. 159, 180, 181, 182, 183, 186, 188, 189, 190, 191, 201
Richardson, H. 234
Richardson, M. 67
Richardson, R. 12
Richman, D. 61
Riggi, J. 120
Roberts, M. 66, 159, 174, 175, 176, 177, 178, 179, 180, 181
Robertson, S. 96, 98
Robinson, R. 58, 101, 102, 103
Robson, K. 123, 125
Roder, D. 16
Rodgers, B. 67
Rodgers, C. 93, 94, 95
Rodriguez, N. 235
Rogers, D. 87, 90, 91
Rogers, J. 61
Rohdie, A. 66, 157, 164, 165, 167, 169, 171, 173, 175, 177, 179, 181, 182, 183, 188, 189, 190, 191, 193, 194, 195, 229, 231, 232, 270
Romano, F. 52, 53, 55, 62, 67, 91, 92, 93, 95, 225, 230
Rooke, B. 109
Roos, R. 97, 98, 99, 100, 101
Rosenbauer, P. 153, 155
Rosenberg, J. 91, 93
Rosenberg, B. 98, 99, 100, 101, 102, 103
Rosenthal, P. 155
Ross, Jake 170, 171, 172, 173, 174, 175, 176, 189, 191, 193, 219, 232, 257
Ross, Jere 6, 12
Rothman, H. 165, 166, 167, 168, 169, 170, 171
Rothpletz, P. 219, 221

Rowen, A. 99, 101
Rubin, R. 91
Runnells, C. 167, 168, 169, 170, 171, 172, 173
Ruprecht, C. 140, 141
Rusen, T. 151, 152, 153, 154, 155
Rush, J. 86, 87
Russell, B. 67
Russell, J. 138, 139, 141
Russell, S. 123, 124, 125
Russo, J. 106, 114
Russo, P. 104
Rybak, M. 186, 199, 200, 201, 202, 203, 204, 205

S

Sachs, K. 165
Sacks, D. 109, 115
Sacchi, A. 235
Saetre, S. 199
Salerno, D. 189, 191, 192, 193
Salibello, C. 142, 143, 144, 145, 146
Salibello, P. 149
Samson, B. 143, 231
Samson, S. 133, 139, 141, 143, 231
Santoriello, A. 175
Saraceno, L. 189, 191, 192, 193
Sarkin, R. 103, 104, 105
Sarro-Waite, N. 177, 178, 179, 180, 181, 229
Sartorius, A. 203, 205
Satulsky, L. 99
Savoy, D. 124
Schellscheidt, M. 144, 235
Scher, D. 189, 191
Schlenker, D. 93, 94, 95
Schmid, I. 19, 20, 24

Schmidt, K. 173, 174, 175, 176, 177, 178, 179, 197, 199, 201, 231
Schmidt, R. 109, 114, 115
Schneider, J. 125
Schoen, B. 133, 139
Schoen, K. 139
Schoenbach, E. 204, 205, 206, 207, 212, 213
Schonberg, E. 195, 197
Schonberg, G. 197, 199, 200, 201, 202, 203
Schonberg, R. 248
Schrader, B. 127
Schroeder, F. 12
Schultz, C. 68
Schwartz, M. 121, 122, 123
Schwarz, E. 149
Schwayze, C. 22
Schweitzer, S. 154
Schweizer, S. 135
Scopelianos, G. 189, 191, 192, 193
Scopelianos, S. 195, 197
Scott-Wittenborn, N. 199
Scott, B. 90, 91, 92, 93
Scott, C. 118, 119, 120, 121
Scott, E. 67
Scott, M. 9
Scrudato, Paul 127, 128, 129
Scrudato, Phil 9, 12, 16
Scurci, J. 179
Seabrook, C. 123, 124, 125
Seaman, B. 107, 108, 109
Sellinger, R. 201
Severage, F. 89, 235
Seymor, S. 133
Sharma, H. 165, 166, 167
Sharts, A. 105, 107
Shawcross, E. 67

Shea, G. 16, 73
Shea, O. 16
Sheeleigh, M. 202, 203, 204, 205, 206, 207, 209, 212, 213, 223
Shelby, B. 105, 107, 109
Shelby, J. 118, 119, 120, 121
Sheldon, P. 40
Shepard, B. 221
Shinn, A. 131
Shippee, B. 12
Shrank, I. 107, 108, 109, 114, 115
Shyers, D. 27, 74
Sideris, M. 48
Siegel, A. 123, 125
Siegel, R. 179, 180, 181, 182, 183, 188, 189
Siegel, S. 127, 128, 129
Signorini, G. 162
Silbermann, M. 193, 195
Silhanek, F. 40
Simms, P. 247
Simonson, C. 174, 175, 176, 177
Simpson, J. 209
Simson, P. 103, 104, 105, 106, 107
Sisto, J. 132, 133, 138, 139
Skillman, D. 47
Skinner, H. 213, 215
Slater, A. 169
Slauson, H. 105, 106, 107
Slauson, S. 117, 119
Sloboda, J. 87
Slobodien, D. 109
Sluyter, D. 67
Smart, A. 157, 164, 165
Smith, B. 39
Smith, J. 219, 220, 221
Smith, M. 107
Smith, P. 9

Smith, P.B. 197, 199
Smith, T. 186, 200, 201, 202, 203, 204, 205, 206, 207
Snyder, S. 91
Sokich, J. 123, 125
Solomon, G. 142, 143, 144, 145, 146
Somers, P. 93, 94, 95
Sorenson, J. 219, 221
Southworth, N. 151, 153, 154, 155
Spagnuolo, S. 18
Spalt, A. 90, 91
Spano, K. 189, 190, 191, 192, 193, 194, 195
Sperling, K. 123, 125
Splan, A. 147
Sprague, J. 107
Sprenger, E. 195, 197
Springer, E. Laurence 7, 9, 67
Spurr, S. 120, 121
St. John, D. 9
Staehle, R. 103
Stamatis, J. 190, 191, 192, 193, 194, 195, 196, 197
Stamatis, W. 187, 199, 200, 201, 202, 203, 204, 205, 209
Stanmyre, M. 208
Stanton, D. 133
Starr, C. 201, 202, 203, 204, 205
Stavenick, E. 95
Stawicki, L. 98
Stearns, J. 102, 103
Steel, R. 114
Steinberg, G. 139
Stephens, B. 108, 109, 114, 115
Sterner, J. 96, 97, 98, 99, 108
Sterns, W. 101
Stevens, G. 175, 177
Stickel, D. 93, 94, 95

Stifel, H. 141
Stillitano, C. 122, 123, 124, 125, 126, 127, 138, 162, 163, 182, 210, 225, 234, 235
Stillitano, C. Sr. 85, 162, 163, 166, 231
Stillitano, L. 122, 123, 124, 125, 138, 157, 163, 225, 231
Stone, M. 207
Stowe, T. 86, 87, 90, 91
Strackhouse, T. 193, 196, 197, 198, 199, 213
Stratton, S. 138, 139
Stockhoff, B. 67
Sulcer, G. 73, 84, 87, 90, 91
Sullivan, J. 67
Sullivan, N. 213, 215
Sullivan, P. 48
Susko, M. 183, 186, 188, 189, 190, 191
Swift, R. 156
Szarko, F. 103, 105, 106, 107
Szeles, R. 174, 216, 235

T

Talbot, J. 101
Tant, D. 127
Tatlock, B. 12
Taylor, L. 247
Teague, G. 93
Teixeira, M. 129, 130, 131
Telling, M. 138, 139, 141
Thiam, A. 190, 191, 192, 193
Thiam, C. 183, 188, 189
Thibault, K. 231
Thiele, B. 58
Thomas, C. 165
Thomas, J. 9
Thomas, R. 119, 231
Thomas, T. 12
Thompson, H. 215, 217

Thomson, P. 68
Thurston, B. 10, 12, 34, 71, 259
Tipping, J. 234, 235
Toffey, J. 9
Tomaino, A. 37, 67
Tomaino, B. 37, 45
Tomaino, C. 37
Tomaino, G. 37, 38
Tomaino, M. 37
Tomlinson, B. 125, 127
Tomlinson, N. 9
Tomlinson, W. 60
Topakas, A. 130, 131, 132, 133
Townley, S. 41
Tracy, C. 95, 96, 97
Tramontana, M. 52, 53, 54, 55, 68, 159, 225, 230, 231
Tramontozzi, C. 235
Treveloni, R. 174, 175, 176, 177, 178, 179
Tripicchio, Aldo 82, 83, 184, 249
Tripicchio, Anthony 82, 83, 181, 183, 188, 189, 190, 191, 203, 205, 207, 213, 225, 231
Tripicchio, Gianfranco 66, 82, 159, 176, 177, 178, 179, 180, 181, 182, 183, 188, 225, 231
Tripicchio, Gloria 83
Tripicchio, K. 82
Trynin, T. 112, 128, 129, 130, 131, 163, 223, 229
Trzcinski, E. 22
Tucker, M. 145
Tuller, A. 192, 193, 194, 195
Tuller, D. 197, 199
Tullo, S. 156, 157, 164, 165
Tulloch, A. 217, 219
Tulloch, P. 146, 147, 148, 149
Tweedie, T. 127, 128, 129

U

Ulz, C. 167, 169
Ulz, M. 167, 169
Umbdenstock, T. 175, 176, 177

V

Valente, M. 207
Van Leight, P. 16
Van Wyck, B. 63, 93, 94, 95, 222
Vars, O. 12
Vazquez, G. 68
Vergalito, P. 67
Vieira, K. 190, 191, 192, 193, 194, 195, 196, 197, 198
Villegas, P. 135
Vimond, R. 131, 133
Virzi, M. 68
Vitollo, F. 120
Volgelsinger, H. 112
von der Linde, E. 127, 129
von der Linde, P. 122, 123

W

Wachter, K. 68, 97
Walbridge, J. 109
Walbridge, T. 127, 128, 129
Walder, S. 139
Walsh, B. 182
Walsh, D. 182
Walsh, M. 178, 180
Walter, F. 91
Walters, D. 131, 133
Walters, F. 97, 99, 101, 103, 105, 230
Walters, L. 123, 125
Ward, Ned 12
Ward, Nick 138, 139, 141, 142, 143

Ward, S. 132, 133, 138, 139
Ward, T. 122, 123, 124, 125
Warlick, P. 141, 143
Warren, Carl 36
Warren, Clark 12, 16
Warren, H. 125, 127
Warren, R. 113, 114, 115, 116, 117
Waterbury, D. 147
Waterman, J. 93
Ways, G. 60
Webb, C. 172
Webster, M. 68
Wegryn, K. 129, 131
Weidknecht, F. 165
Weil, M. 189
Weiler, R. 67
Welch, C. 137, 143, 144, 145
Welch, G. 150, 151, 152, 153
Welch, L. 128, 129, 130, 131
Welch, Matt 146, 147, 148, 149
Welch, Miles 138, 139, 140, 141
Welch, S. 155
Weldon, B. 113, 115, 117
Weldon, W. 157, 164, 165
Weller, R. 138, 139, 140, 141
Weltchek, T. 103, 104, 105
Wendell, G. 91
Werner, M. 217, 219
West, D. 86, 87
West, F. 11, 12, 84, 85, 86, 87
Weymar, H. 12
Wheaton, D. 86, 87
White, G. 116
White, L. 148
White, M. 147, 148, 149
Whitehead, G. 116, 117, 118, 119

Whitlock, C. 121
Whitlock, D. 95
Whitlock, J. 71, 86, 87, 92
Whitmarsh, J. 90, 91, 92, 93
Whittemore, J. 58, 67
Whyte, S. 103, 105
Wickenden, T. 93
Wight, J. 90, 91, 92, 93
Wiley, P. 86, 87
Wilkinson, A. 179
Wilkinson, D. 177
Wilkinson, J. 170, 171, 172, 173, 174, 175
Wilkinson, M. 188, 189, 190, 191
Wilkinson, W. 183, 189
Williams, B. 123, 125
Williams, G. 255
Williams, R. 7, 12, 67, 77, 84
Williams, T. 55
Williams, W. 12
Wilmerding, H. 151, 153
Wilson, D. 56, 67
Wilson, D. III 103
Wilson, J. 93
Windylass, W. 22
Witte, J. 99, 100, 101, 102, 103
Wittmann, R. 167, 169
Wixom, C. 147, 148, 149, 150, 151
Wood, B. 86, 87
Wood, J. 142, 143, 144, 145, 146
Wood, P. 87
Wooter, A. 119, 231
Wright, C. 218, 219, 220, 221
Wright, T. 213, 215
Wynn, C. 12, 15, 17, 35

Y

Yeomans, C. 183, 189
Yook, J. 167
Young, A.C. 195, 197
Young, A.Y. 206, 207, 209
Yuckman, P. 91

Z

Zachary, G. 217, 218, 219
Zachary, P. 219, 220, 221
Zahodiakin, P. 115
Zanelli, J. 221
Zashin, M. 44, 121, 122, 123
Zatkowsky, H. 55
Zekiroski, E. 194
Zenker, D. 115, 116, 117
Zhu, C. 219, 221
Ziegenhagen, B. 92, 93, 94, 95, 96, 97, 98, 227
Ziegler, H. 139, 141
Zigmont, M. 167
Zimering, J. 194, 195, 196, 197, 198, 199, 200, 201
Zinsser, N. 226
Ziobro, P. 129, 131
Zoephel, J. 107
Zusi, T. 221

Epilogue

Excerpted from a speech by former coach Adam Rohdie at the celebration of Miller's 700th career victory.

We gather here tonight to honor and pay tribute to a truly amazing individual. If you have been graced with the good fortune to have spent time with this real superstar, you know the impact a single person can have on another.

Elizabeth Bugliari, we honor you tonight as well, because God knows how you have managed to stay married to this kook for 44 years. Actually, Elizabeth and I share a lot in common. I was Coach's assistant for 16 years, and both Elizabeth and I realized after a decade or so that we had to enroll in extensive psychotherapy, because after a few years with Coach you cry out for help. Both Elizabeth and I have paid for every meal out with Coach, because, as most of you know, he has really deep pockets and really short arms. Actually, Elizabeth is the real brains behind the Bugliari operation, and while tonight we pay tribute to the man, we all know that his journey has been taken with Elizabeth next to him the whole way. Every game, every weekend practice, cooking meals for the teams, or just keeping him away from sharp objects after a loss. Elizabeth, we know and appreciate all that you have done for Miller, for your family, for so many students, and for Pingry soccer.

By my calculations I have coached 343 games standing next to Coach B (of course to his left side). I was lucky enough to coach with Miller for his 400th, 500th, and 600th wins. So I feel uniquely qualified to defend him from all wrongful attacks. There have been unfair rumors that Coach has a temper – for example, that I once had to finish coaching a game alone because a referee had banished Coach to a nearby cornfield. Or that another referee did give him a red card during the state playoffs and Miller finished watching that game from a Pingry parent's car in the parking lot – and every five minutes or so would lean on the horn to signal his frustration with a play one of the boys had made. Actually, come to think of it, I had to coach the next two games alone (as the state rule banned Miller from attending), so I want to be the first to congratulate Coach on reaching 698 career victories. We can have another 700th celebration next year! Finally, there are even vicious rumors that Coach is superstitious, is a pack rat when it comes to old artifacts and memorabilia, and can even be a bit eccentric. Once again I say – not true!

Now that I have dispelled these crazy rumors that have existed about Coach, let me tell you what exactly he is. Coach Bugliari is not just Pingry soccer – he is the soul of the Pingry School. It is his phone that rings at 2:00 a.m. with a former student on the other end saying, "Coach, I need your help," "Coach, I have a sick child," "Coach, I am getting divorced," "Coach, I need help getting a job," "Coach, can we have lunch?" It is Miller Bugliari who answers every one of these queries with a simple "Yes, I am here to help."

For 50 years Miller has helped turn children into adults. Imagine how different education was 50 years ago – yet Miller has been the consistent embodiment of a clear set of values which transcend the generations. Players from 1959 to today have been inspired by Miller. They have all learned the importance of sportsmanship, of the value of hard work, and the key characteristic of stick-to-itiveness. It is a tribute to Miller that so many people come back to say thanks for all he has given to them.

Let me close by simply saying I personally feel blessed to have learned at the feet of a master. I feel blessed to call Miller a dear friend. And now, in my job heading the Greenwich Country Day School, not a day goes by where some piece of advice, some pearl of wisdom that Miller gave to me, does not help me move through a vexing situation or a trying problem. Coach, we salute you, and most importantly, we thank you for all you have given to so many of us.